AUTOMOBILES
OF THE WORLD

AUTOMOBILES

Joseph H. Wherry

OF THE WORLD

The story of the development of the
automobile with many rare illustrations
from a score of nations

Galahad Books
New York

With love to my wife, Bettye

Preface

The task of determining who invented the automobile is as difficult as deciding who discovered North America. Both may be impossible.

Incredibly, most otherwise reliable historical sources fail to mention many of the important men in automobile development. The purpose of this volume is not to rewrite history but to bring certain facts to light which are not now generally known or appreciated.

Important names in the history of automobile development that are not known to the reader will crop up, and some will, too, that are better known for other accomplishments. But, to choose one as the inventor of the automobile is beyond good judgment. A machine as complex as the automobile has to be the product of the combined efforts and ideas of many men—it is an evolution rather than an invention.

The author has sought here to tell the story of the pioneering efforts of a number of inventors, and of the historic automobiles of many nations.

It may, for example, come as a surprise to some to know that *Switzerland* has a long and distinguished history of automotive development—a Swiss inventor obtained a pat-

ent on a remarkable self-propelled vehicle which employed an internal combustion engine of novel design in 1806! In *Austria*, the accomplishments of an unsung genius included an amazingly successful automobile. The records of this car were ordered expunged from the history books when Hitler took over that nation—the inventor was of Jewish descent. *Czechoslovakia, Hungary* and *Yugoslavia*, once a part of the empire of the Hapsburgs, made cars of native design. In northern Europe, *Sweden* had a vigorous automobile industry in the early years of this century, and *Denmark* and *Norway* also manufactured automobiles of their own design. Cars were manufactured in *The Netherlands* before the modern American makes were much more than dreams, and *Belgium* had several makes by 1900. On the other side of the world, *Australia* had pioneer automobile makers; so did *Japan* before the first World War. The contributions of *France* to automotive science could fill a separate volume and so could those of *England*, *Germany* and *Spain*. In South America, at least one native design startled the citizens of the capital of *Argentina*.

The doughty highlanders of *Scotland* had

their exclusive cars and there were also distinctive developments in *Ireland*. The author believes these efforts merit attention. Of course, our own country has a rich automotive history as does *Russia*.

That the birth date and birthplace of the automobile are impossible to place with any assurance will be evident to the reader on the sole basis of the more than 500 photographs that come from twenty-one countries. Many of the illustrations are rare; for some, in fact, no negatives exist, and for the use of these the most heartfelt gratitude is due the curators of several important museums.

To relate the entire history of the automobile would be impossible in a single volume. This book, however, highlights the most important developments and considers many that have hitherto been largely unnoticed.

Joseph H. Wherry

Acknowledgments

The author wishes to acknowledge with warm thanks the following organizations and individuals scattered around the world who have so generously helped in the gathering of photographs and data:

Austrian Information Service.
Austrian Trade Delegate in the United States.
Austrian Consulate in San Francisco.
Consulate General of Spain in San Francisco.
The Commercial Office of Spain.
The Vice-Consul of Switzerland, R. Ryser, in San Francisco.
Canadian Consulate General in San Francisco.
Consulate General of Australia in San Francisco.
National Library of Australia and H. L. White, Librarian, Canberra.
Consulate General of France in San Francisco.
French Embassy Press & Information Division.
Italian Embassy.
Italian Information Center & Cultural Institute.
Consulate General of Ireland.
Netherlands Information Service and H. F. von den Broek.
British Consulate General in San Francisco.
German Consulate General in San Francisco.
Argentine Consulate in San Francisco.
Belgian Consulate General in San Francisco.
Institut Belge d'Information et de Documentation.
Embassy of The Soviet Union and Mr. V. Bogachev.
Novosti Press Agency.
Chamber of Commerce of Czechoslovakia.
Rapid Advertising Agency, Prague.
Yugoslav Information Center and Mr. Milos Nikolic.
Embassy of Finland and Mr. Reino Aarva.
Embassy of the Polish People's Republic and Mr. Z. Bidzinski.
Consulate General of Denmark in San Francisco.
Charles W. Walker, Second Secretary, American Embassy in Madrid.
John A. Boyle, Commercial Officer, American Embassy in Rome.
Harry V. Ryder, Jr., Second Secretary, American Embassy, Stockholm.

Harold E. Hall, Commercial Counselor, American Embassy, London.

Howard W. Potter, Assistant Commercial Attaché, American Embassy, Rio de Janeiro.

Frederick Hartley, Press Officer, American Embassy, Mexico, D.F.

California State Automobile Association (AAA) and William C. Ellis.

Austrian Automobile, Motorcycle & Touring Clubs.

Japan Automobile Industrial Association and I. Terazawa.

Automobile Manufacturers Association, U.S.A.

Irish Veteran & Vintage Car Club, Mr. Knollys Stokes and Miss C. Rosborough.

Verband der Automobilindustrie EV, West Germany.

Society of Motor Traders & Manufacturers, England.

Royal Motor Union of Liége, Belgium.

Automovil Club Argentino and José D. C. Rucci.

Automobile Club of Southern California (AAA).

Automobile Club d'Italia and Professor Mario Del Viscovo.

British Automobile Manufacturers Association and William Haworth.

Kongelig Norsk Automobilklub (Royal Norwegian Automobile Club) and Mr. Geir Hvoslef, Oslo.

Dansk Veteranbil Klub and Mr. Bent Mackeprang, Denmark.

Swiss Institute of Transport & Communications and the director, Mr. Alfred Waldis, Lucerne.

Heeresgeschtliches Museum and Dr. J. C. Allmayer-Beck, Vienna.

Technisches Museum and Dr. Josef Nagler, Vienna.

Museo dell Automobile Carlo Biscaretti di Ruffia, Turin.

Archives of the Norges Tekniske Høgskole, Oslo.

Pacific Auto Rentals, Los Angeles.

Dedman's Photo Shop, Skagway.

Canadian Automotive Museum, Oshawa, Ontario.

National Museum van de Automobiel and Mr. G. Riemer, Netherlands.

Tekniska Museet, Mr. Gert Ekström and Mr. Sigvard Strandh, Stockholm.

Haris Testvérek Autó Múzeuma, Budapest.

Danmarks Tekniske Museum and Mr. K. O. B. Jørgensen.

University Museum, University of Alaska.

Gilltraps Auto Museum Pty., Ltd., Coolangata, Queensland, Australia.

Thompson Products Auto Museum, Cleveland.

Harrah's Automobile Collection, Reno.

Henry Ford Museum, Greenfield Village, Dearborn.

The Science Museum, London.

Daimler-Benz A.G., Germany.

SA des Automobiles Peugeot, France.

Daimler Motors Ltd., England.

British Motor Corp., England.

S.A. Panhard & Levassor, France.

Adam Opel A.G, Germany.

AB Scania-Vabis, Sweden.

Auto Union GMBH, Germany.

SA Adolphe Saurer, Switzerland.

Sandoz, Ltd., Switzerland.

Dr.-Ing. h.c.F. Porsche KG, Germany.

S.A. des Usines Renault, France.

Motorwagen Fabrik Berna AG, Switzerland.

AB Volvo, Sweden.

Empresa Nacional de Autocamiones SA, Spain.

F.I.A.T., S.p.A., Italy.

Lancia & C., Italy.

Alfa Romeo Milano, Italy.

Volkswagenwerk A.G., Germany, and Volkswagen of America.

Beyerische Motoren Werke (BMW), Germany.

S.A. André Citroën, France.

Automobiles M. Berliet, France.

Oy Suomen Autoteollisuus (SISU), Finland.

Rootes Motors, Ltd., England.

Standard-Triumph Motors, Ltd., England

Vauxhall Motors, Ltd., England.

The Rover Co., Ltd., England.

Leyland Motors, Ltd., England.

Rolls-Royce, Ltd., England.

A. C. Cars, Ltd., England.

Jaguar Cars, Ltd., England.

Jensen Motors Ltd., England.

Motokov and Messrs. E. Novatna and V. Zadrobileki, Czechoslovakia.

Skoda Automobilov, Czechoslovakia.

Czechoslovak Automobile Works and Zd. Cernocky.

Fabrique Nationale d'Armes de Guerre, Belgium.

General Motors-Holdens Pty. Ltd., Australia.

Steyr-Daimler-Puch AG, Austria.

Willys-Overland Motors, Inc., U.S.A.

American Motors Corp., U.S.A.

Ford Motor Co., U.S.A.

Chrysler Corp., U.S.A.

General Motors Corp., U.S.A.

Mr. V. Bommen, Private Secretary to H.M. the King of Norway.

Mr. G. Riemer, Driebergen, Netherlands.

Mr. George A. Oliver, Glasgow, Scotland.

Mr. W. P. Tuckey, Editor, *Wheels*, Sydney, Australia.

Mr. C. Posthumus, *The Motor*, London.

Mr. Art Ronnie, *Los Angeles Times*.

Mrs. Ethan LeMunyon, Los Angeles.

Sr. Juan Aymerich, Barcelona.

Miss Janet Luoma, Nieman-Marcus Co., Dallas.

Mr. J. R. Davy, Hon. Registrar, *The Standard Register*, Coventry.

Mr. Robert F. Ames, *Car Classics*, U.S.A.

The late Ray Beste.

Mr. L. D. Sutton.

Mr. J. Harvey Newbury.

Mr. David Collins.

Mr. John E. Hallberg.

Mr. Glenn R. Kopp.

Mr. Randolph Brandt.

Mr. Walter J. Speilberger.

Mrs. Anne Carpenter.

Contents

Part I

THE EVOLUTION OF
THE AUTOMOBILE

THE ANCIENTS dreamed of transportation swifter than horses, but it was to be a long time before man was moved across land by any means other than animal power.

Then, in the year 1600 in The Netherlands near The Hague, a military engineer named Symon Stevin tested the zeylwagen, the first land vehicle that did not use muscle as its source of energy.

Stevin had built the zeylwagen (sail wagon) on the orders of Maurice of Nassau, Prince of Orange, a famous strategist who held the dual rank of Marshal of The Netherlands and Admiral of the Ocean Sea. Prince Maurice was leading the Dutch struggle for independence from Spain and it is not unlikely that he conceived of the *zeylwagen* as a land frigate—a gun carrier that could be swiftly deployed in battle. His trusted engineer, Simon Stevin, was the man to build the vehicle.

According to the Dutch poet and Ambassador to Sweden, Hugo de Groot, the zeylwagen was pulled out one day and something like "Eight and twenty persons" climbed in. Among the passengers with the illustrious Prince of Orange and de Groot were diplomatic representatives from Britain, France, Sweden and Denmark plus Admiral Franciscus de Mendoza of Spain who was a prisoner of war.

The coast of The Netherlands is well known for its strong, steady winds, and the day set for the world's first well-witnessed road test was windy as usual. The driver, Stevins, handled the tiller, the rear wheels being the steering wheels.

Across the wave-smoothed sands the zeylwagen whizzed covering 50 miles (about 14 Dutch miles) from a village near The Hague to Petten in just two hours. Any observing beachcombers must have been amazed.

In the year 1600, a speed of 25 miles an hour was remarkable.

Thus, the two-masted land ship dreamed up by Prince Maurice and built of wood and canvas by Stevin, was probably the first wheeled vehicle to travel far and fast without the exertion of muscle by either man or beast.

About three generations later—in 1672—a steam-powered vehicle was built for the Emperor Khang-hi of China. This was possibly the world's first truly self-propelled vehicle. It was the brainchild of a Jesuit missionary priest, Ferdinand Verbiest, a native of the town of Pitthem in Flanders, now a

When the liberator of The Netherlands, Maurice of Nassau and Prince of Orange, returned from the wars, the "Zeylwagen" was built to his order— possibly the first genuinely engineered passenger carrying vehicle not powered by animal muscle. (*Drawing by Beste*)

part of Belgium. Though self-propelled, the practicality of Verbiest's machine is in doubt.

Father Verbiest had gone to China in 1659. Before long, due to his scientific learning, he became a welcome "learned man" in the imperial court. He found favor with the Emperor, established an observatory, built scientific instruments, compiled a world atlas, and authored a score or more scientific works. Clues to Verbiest's inventions are in one of his works, *Astronomia Europaea*, which he wrote in 1681. Though Father Verbiest died in 1688, a copy of *Astronomia Europaea* was brought to Dillingen, Bavaria, by a Jesuit priest, P. Couplet, who had also served in China. The treatise was printed in 1687 in Latin, one year before its author's death in far "Cathay," and described this original vehicle which was

The world's first primitive steam engine is believed to have been the "Aeolusphere" made by Hero of Alexandria about 150 B.C. (*Drawing by L. D. Sutton*)

probably built as a mechanical experiment rather than to carry passengers. Verbiest's book indicates it was hardly more than two feet long although "zwei Fuss" was not necessarily a mere two feet as we reckon dimensions today.

In more recent years, Professor Boeckmann of Karlsruhe, a physicist, researched Verbiest's works and constructed a working model of the vehicle. The steam cart's chassis was a wood platform with four wheels. The axles were solid. On the front axle—this was a front-wheel-drive affair—was fixed a simple gear that meshed with another gear wheel fastened at the bottom end of a vertical shaft. The shaft had a horizontal wheel with radial blades forming a turbine wheel against which steam was directed from a large retort. The retort was bracketed above the cart chassis midway between the driving front and trailing rear wheels. The retort—"Aeolus-Kugel" as Verbiest called it—held water heated by a container holding burning coal. The original contraption must have provided considerable leisure wonderment to the Emperor and his court for Boeckmann's model is said to have worked very well. Unfortunately, Boeckmann's model was destroyed but it was described by its builder in the obscure *Erste Gründe der Mechanik* many years ago.

Father Verbiest's steam cart was able to run about one hour on a single filling of the retort. Curiously, Verbiest did not employ a logical wagon-type steering mechanism. Instead, he used a trailing fifth wheel on an extending lever arm. The steering effect was like that of a boat rudder although the turning force of such a rudder-wheel must have been rather ineffective.

Actually, Verbiest's use of steam propulsion was not new. Ancient Chinese works as far back as the pre-Christian Chow dy-

5

In 1770 in France, Captain Nicolas Cugnot of the Royal Artillery built and tested this monstrous, 3-wheel, steam vehicle. (*French Embassy Press and Information Division*)

nasty refer vaguely to steam vehicles. The power of steam was certainly known in ancient China. (With this in mind, the reader will find the adventure of the "breath cart," a Model T Ford purchased by the Bogdo of Mongolia, to be of interest in Part V.) The ability of steam, escaping through small openings in spherical retorts, to move objects was also well known throughout the civilized world several centuries before Christ. The ancient Greeks were acquainted with the power of steam and it is probable that the knowledge spread from them throughout southern Europe and northern Africa.

At about the same time that Verbiest was inventing his vehicle, Sir Isaac Newton, in 1680, devised a machine which was propelled by the jet action of steam escaping though an orifice from a boiler. Newton was simply applying his own third law of motion—"To every action there is always an equal and opposite reaction."

Ten years later, in 1690, Denis Papin of France invented a simple steam engine having one vertical cylinder inside of which was a piston. The cylinder served as the boiler and was externally heated by a small fire. When the water turned to steam, the piston raised; when the heat was moved away, the pressure of the air in the cylinder above the piston forced it down to its original position. There is no record that Papin's steam engine ever did any useful work.

In 1705, Thomas Newcomen in England developed his "atmospheric engine" which also had one vertical cylinder with a piston. The piston was fitted with a counterweight and a crossarm on a pivot. Low-pressure steam was admitted from the boiler to the bottom of the cylinder, raising the piston to the top. A pressure valve below the piston then opened and a stream of cold water was sprayed into the cylinder condensing the steam and allowing the atmospheric pressure above to force the piston to the bottom. Repetition of this process caused a rod attached to the pivoted crossarm to move up and down. Although slow and inefficient, the Newcomen engine was used widely to pump water out of coal mines. It probably could have been rigged to turn a crank on an axle.

Many mechanics, watchmakers, and tinkerers were inspired by Thomas Newcomen's steam pump. James Watt, a Scotsman and a skilled instrument maker, made several improvements. He built a separate condenser for the spent steam, and introduced the principle of double action which admits steam alternately to each end of the cylinder, thus driving the piston back and forth and increasing power and smoothness. Watt obtained a patent on his improved steam engine in 1769.

Most important to the development of the automobile was Watt's invention of the first known link—or connecting rod—between the piston and a crank revolving a flywheel. This permitted the rapid application of steam power to a driven axle. Watt also developed throttles to control the force of steam against the piston, and thus to vary the speed of the machine.

This brings us to the direct ancestor of the automobile, a military vehicle invented by a French Captain Nicholas Joseph Cugnot of the Military Engineers who seemed determined to unharness horses from heavy field guns. He tried to harness steam to pull the Royal Artillery. Cugnot came close to his goal with an ungainly, somewhat nose-heavy, three-wheeler. Captain Cugnot's monster had two cylinders, each with a piston and a connecting rod linked to a single front wheel. The direct steering must have required the muscles of Hercules with the weight of engine and boiler in front of the vehicle's frame. At any rate, the 1770 Cugnot ran—at about 3 to 4 miles per hour—and on several occasions for as far as several hundred yards.

As is always the case, however, others were working on similar or better ideas, too, and in the same year Richard Trevithick of England is said to have operated a high-pressure, non-condensing stationary steam engine of his own design. This engine probably did not power a vehicle, but it represented an advance in the power department.

A few years later, our old friend James Watt and an associate, William Murdock, put steam power on wheels more successfully than anyone had yet done. Their machine, unlike the Cugnot, was light in weight and large enough to carry two persons. The single front wheel was steered by a tiller and the rear wheels were powered by a small, high-pressure steam engine. Watt and Murdock had invented a horseless carriage—a little steam tricycle that was referred to as the "fiery little devil."

After this association with the already famous Watt, William Murdock struck out on his own and built a model for a steam-powered wagon in 1784. Two years later, William Wymington built a steam carriage and the competition was increasing. In

AUTOMOBILES OF THE WORLD

1790, Nathan Read of Massachusetts obtained a patent for a four-wheeled, steam vehicle; and another American, Oliver Evans, was awarded, in 1789, a patent on a steam carriage, about which little is known.

In 1803, though, Evans built a huge steam-driven, 20-ton self-propelled dredge which he drove one and a half miles through the streets of Philadelphia to the Delaware River where the "Orukter Amphibolus," as

Patent drawing for Trevithick's steam carriage in England in 1801–02 had rear wheels much larger than the coach body. This vehicle was world's first

passenger carrying steamer to utilize high pressure steam. (*The Science Museum, London*)

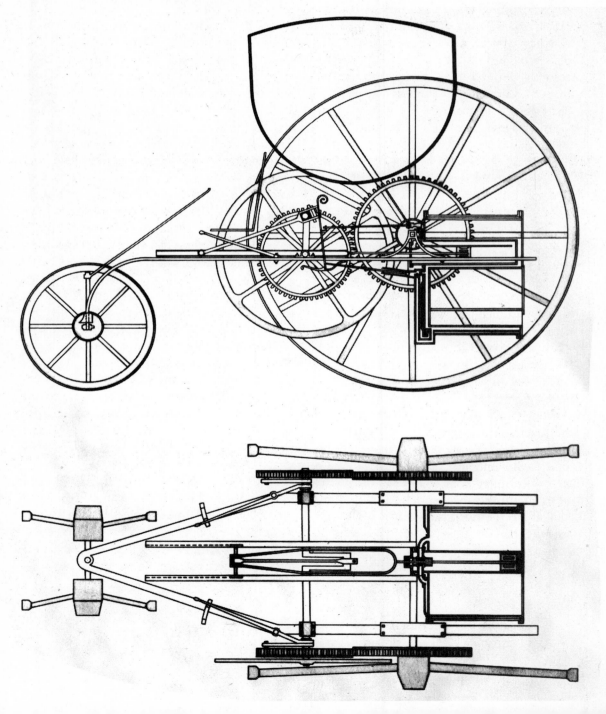

In 1805, Isaac de Rivaz of Switzerland built and drove the original of this remarkable device, the world's first internal combustion powered vehicle.

This is a working model. (*Swiss Museum of Transport and Communications*)

it was christened, dredged space for the docks. Thus, Evans has the honor of being the first American to build and operate a self-propelled vehicle.

During Evans's experiments in the United States, Englishmen had stepped up their inventions, and in 1801, Trevithick built what is generally regarded as the first self-propelled vehicle to carry passengers in addition to the operator. Trevithick demonstrated his strange four-wheel steam car by carrying a number of people, with a combined weight of more than one ton, over a considerable distance. The driver sat in front and steered the two small front wheels which were suspended by the common

horse-coach type of kingbolt. The passengers rode high and comfortably inside a familiar coach-type body. Trevithick built several steamers, and in 1803 carried passengers on the streets of London.

A Mr. S. Goodrich made the following notes in a lengthy memorandum now in the archives of The Science Museum in South Kensington, London:

> "Mr. T. (Trevithick) had prepared an Engine for Driving a Coach. Diam. of Cylinder 5½ (inches) Stroke 2–6 (2 feet 6 inches) 50 Strokes per Minute . . ."

This is believed by authorities to refer to the engine that powered what was probably the world's first steam passenger vehicle. A reproduction of Trevithick's Patent Specification Drawing filed in 1802 is shown here. Trevithick ran his steam vehicle numerous times carrying many passengers during 1802.

A few years later, the development of internal combustion engines threatened to divert attention from steam. An application for a patent, dated 1806, confirms that one Isaac de Rivaz of Saint Gingolph, Switzerland, built the first vehicle in the world propelled by an *internal combustion* engine. The patent ("Brevet d'Invention") was granted in 1807. A biography of de Rivaz by the respected Canon Michelet documents the achievements of this modest Swiss inventor.

The de Rivaz vehicle was a fairly large four-wheeled wagon with a single, vertical cylinder five feet long fixed to a platform extending crosswise between the side rails. The piston operated a connecting rod which was linked to a crossarm beneath the frame. This crossarm, visible in the accompanying photograph of a working model in the Swiss Museum of Transport and Communications in Lucerne, operated a push-pull rod paralleling the cylinder. The rod operated a flywheel by the crank method. The flywheel was grooved to carry a belt which, in turn, revolved an equal-size pulley centered in the driving axle. There was no differential.

A rudimentary electric ignition system was hand-operated as were the inlet and exhaust valves. But the most remarkable feature was the fuel employed—a controlled amount of highly dangerous *hydrogen* carried in a horizontal cylindrical tank over the rear wheels. It seems that de Rivaz was a fairly competent chemist. Despite lack of contact with others interested in automotive development, isolated as he was in the foothills of the Pennine Alps in 1804 when his experiments began, de Rivaz reasoned that a sparking and fuel induction system capable of actuating a controlled explosion inside an open-top cylinder should power an axle more efficiently.

The de Rivaz vehicle ran, although due to a design error the engine stalled frequently. A close examination reveals that the single pushrod on the driving flywheel-pulley would too easily hang up, or down, on dead center. More than likely an alteration in the cross-arm design, or better yet, another cylinder and piston assembly with another pushrod, would have solved de Rivaz's problem. The two pushrods could have been linked to the driving flywheel-pulley on quarters to eliminate stalling out on dead center.

After receiving his patent from the Interior Ministry of France—there were no such facilities at the time in Switzerland—de Rivaz continued his experiments. In 1813, an improved vehicle, illustrated here, made several better runs at a very low speed. The number of strokes per minute—not recorded—must have been small because of hand operation of fuel and air induction into the cylinder, and of the valve on the exhaust. But it ran, though jerkily.

Spurred by the growing acceptance of the first railroads, and occasionally encouraged by a courageous editorial in one of England's many newspapers, the English steam vehicle builders were devising ways to compete with the network of scheduled stagecoach routes. By 1825, several steam coaches were operating in and around London.

Then, an Englishman named Brown patented in 1826 an internal combustion engine that operated without an explosion. A mixture of alcohol and air was drawn into

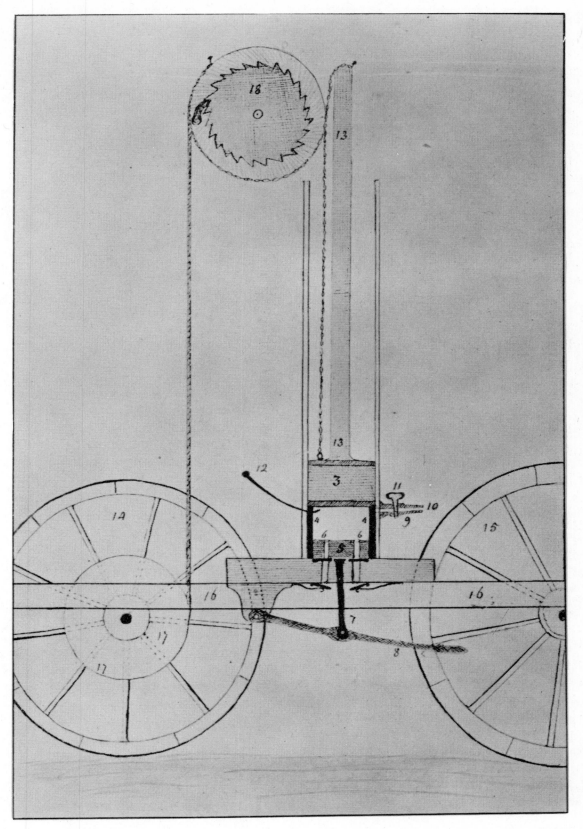

The patent drawing for the remarkable de Rivaz vehicle, 1807. (*The Science Museum, London*)

huge cylinders with a 12-inch bore. When the alcohol was ignited, a fine spray of water was injected, creating a cooling effect that combined with the burned fuel to form a vacuum that opened a valve. This caused the massive piston to move a connecting rod that turned a crankshaft. The piston's stroke was 24 inches and with 3 cylinders the displacement was roughly 2,500 cubic inches. Mounted in a short wagon with five-foot wheels, the engine is said to have run the vehicle quite well. On one occasion Brown's motor carriage drove up a steep London hill, the event being witnessed by J. A. Whitfield of the Bedlington Iron Works who described the event in a book. Brown went no further with vehicular experiments but several of his mammoth engines were produced and used as water pumps.

Soon after, another Englishman, William Barnet, built a double-acting cylinder engine that used either alcohol or coal gas. Whether or not Barnet built a carriage for it is not known.

In America in 1825, Thomas Blanchard of Springfield, Massachusetts, stuffed a steam engine into a wagonlike affair and became the second American to operate a car successfully. Blanchard owned the only car of record in America at the time when they were popping up like mushrooms all over England.

Two years later in England, Goldsworthy Gurney, builder and businessman who knew a good thing, operated a particularly ambitious and efficient steam coach that seated a dozen outside and another six inside. It plied the holiday route between London and Bath. An engraving, reproduced here, originally published by master printer Thomas McCloud of 26 Haymarket Street, London, includes a description of this carriage.

"The Guide or Engineer is seated in front, having a lever rod from the two guide wheels to turn & direct the Carriage & another at his right hand connecting with the main Steam Pipe by which he regulates the motion of the Vehicle—the hind part of the Coach contains the machinery for producing the Steam, on a novel and secure principle, which is conveyed by Pipes to the Cylinders beneath & by its action on the hind wheels sets the Carriage in motion—The Tank which contains about 60 Gallons of water, is placed under the body of the Coach & is its full length & breadth—the Chimneys are fixed on the top of the hind boot & as Coke is mixed for fuel, there will be no smoke while any hot or rarified air produced will be dispelled by the action of the Vehicle—At different stations on a journey the Coach receives fresh supplies of fuel & water—the full length of the Carriage is from 15 to 20 feet & its weight about 2 tons—The rate of travelling is intended to be from 8 to 10 miles per hour—The present Steam Carriage carries 6 inside & 12 outside passengers—the front Boot contains the Luggage—It has been constructed by Mr. Goldsworthy Gurney, the Inventor & Patentee."

The Gurney Steam Coach was novel in many ways, not the least being the steering mechanism. Note that "The Guide or Engineer" controlled two small front wheels by means of a tiller. However, the center-of-weight being well aft, these small front wheels served principally to turn the larger main front wheels by a tongue linking the two axles. Here, then, is an early example of "pilot wheels" which soon became familiar additions to steam railroad locomotives but were shortly eliminated on steam road vehicles. Several of Gurney's coaches operated regularly from February to June, 1831, four times daily from Glouces-

In 1827, Mr. Goldsworthy Gurney built several steam coaches; this one actually carried paying passengers on the roads around London. From an old print. (*The Science Museum, London*)

ter to Cheltenham, a distance of nine miles.

Other skilled technicians and enterprising transportation experts rushed to organize steam carriage firms. All had been inspired to a degree by the earlier success of pioneer Richard Trevithick.

One of their creations with a design far ahead of its time was the "Enterprise" Steam Omnibus of 1832–33 built by Walter Hancock of Stratford to the order of the London and Paddington Steam Carriage Company. The driver sat in a "captain's chair" out front on a spacious platform. A central doorway connected the driver's platform to the salon-like interior which was equipped with shades for the windows. The coke burner, boiler and engine were all placed out of the way beneath; even the "Chimneys" were deleted from this model. By 1838, Hancock had built nine steam carriages, all successful, and had run a Paddington-London service.

Progress with self-propelled steam vehicles was so rapid in England that, in retrospect, one wonders what prevented that nation of entrepreneurs from getting the jump on the entire world where automobiles were concerned.

These idyllic conditions did not last very long. The railroads had a good lobby in

13

THE "ENTERPRISE" STEAM OMNIBUS.
BUILT BY Mr Walter Hancock of Stratford, FOR THE
LONDON AND PADDINGTON STEAM CARRIAGE COMPY

The steam coach, "Enterprise," built by Hancock in England in 1833, enjoyed a brief success carry-ing passengers until the law stepped in. (*The Science Museum, London*)

Parliament and, one must suspect, so did the horses. With happy passengers riding steam coaches, competition was bound to try for some of the receipts.

A Scotsman named Anderson made the try in Aberdeen in 1839 with the first known electrically powered road vehicle. Anderson fashioned a large iron drum which rotated inside a system of iron bars. Existing reports are vague, but according to research by the Henry Ford Museum in Dearborn, Michigan, Anderson built or obtained several recurrent or intermittent primary wet cells to charge the electromagnets causing the iron drum to rotate. The drum was geared to a driving axle but the cells supplied sufficient current for only a few minutes—probably no more than five. Then the unspecified chemicals had to be replenished. Run it did, but as it was no match for the steam coaches, Anderson's electric carriage dropped from sight.

There were few other serious attempts to develop an electric car until much later. One effort, however, deserves attention. About 1870, Sir David Salomons in England devised a battery which, with a small electric motor, he installed in a lightweight carriage. Details are lacking, but this electric car seems to have performed quite well for very short distances. Batteries—the curse of every electric car to date—were too heavy and too limited in capacity. To achieve any range at all, the car had to sacrifice passenger space in order to carry batteries. Not until the waning years of the century were electrics even a possibility.

So horses remained the only alternative to steam on the highways, but with the rising popularity of the steam carriages all over the southern counties, what was to become of the horsedrawn stagecoach? Everybody who was somebody—but who did not own a steam carriage—started writing letters to the editors of the dailies and dignified Members of Parliament were accused of letting the public roads degenerate into a state of anarchy.

Cows along the roadsides were frightened by the steam coaches—and horses bucked and reared and bolted. The thing to do, Parliament was told, was to suppress the steamers.

So restrictive legislation forced the abandonment of a fledgling industry. Steam carriages disappeared from the roads and Englishmen were safe and secure once more. Inventors turned their talents to other devices. England lost the automotive ball.

Although the newfangled steam vehicles were under official condemnation in England, inventors elsewhere had a free hand. Etienne Lenoir in France began experimenting with several fuels to provide combustion inside the cylinder. It is believed Lenoir had heard of the limited success of de Rivaz's experiments during 1806–13. Illuminating gas—a coal derivative—was readily available, and about mid-century Lenoir began developing a means to inject and explode it against the piston. Lenoir's efforts in 1860 were successful and about 1862 he installed his new internal combustion, 2-cycle engine in a high riding carriage. Lenoir's vehicle had a steering wheel—probably the first on any self-propelled rig.

In the U.S.A., most efforts were directed toward the conduct of the Civil War. Yet in New England in 1863 Sylvester H. Roper of Roxbury, Massachusetts, modified a high-wheeled buggy and powered it with a steam engine featuring two separately cast cylinders. Roper's engine and charcoal burner were beneath the seat; nearby on the tonneau was the water tank. The spent steam was exhausted beneath. Roper could have used a condenser. So successful was the Roper that by 1869, he had built and sold ten steamers, becoming the first American to make and market a series of horseless carriages. Roper sold one of his steamers to a travelling showman known as Professor Austin. Austin used to freight his Roper Steamer to his destination, then drive it to the theater and make a grand spectacle much to the amazement of the citizenry. In Grand Rapids, Michigan, the local newspaper, *The Eagle*, trumpeted the Roper Steamer as "The marvel of the age" and boldly predicted that such a "Triumph of inventive skill" would soon "SUPERCEDE THE USE OF HORSES on the ordinary thoroughfare." After making ten cars, Sylvester H. Roper turned to steam-powered two-wheelers and became the inventor of the motorcycle.

The earlier suppression of the automobile in England led to the "Locomotives Act of 1865." According to the *Jubilee Book* of the Royal Automobile Club published in 1947, this Act "very definitely imposed this condition upon the use of the public highway by a self-propelled vehicle, stipulating that the maximum speed should be 4 m.p.h., and that a man with a red flag should walk 60 yards in front of it."

AUTOMOBILES OF THE WORLD

Despite such a restriction, in scores of workshops Englishmen, Scotsmen, Welsh and Irishmen were making steam cars every now and then. Some of them were exceptionally good. A couple of determined men named Catley and Ayres achieved some limited fame with their "Steam Waggonette" in 1868. To test their vehicle properly was as perplexing a problem as mastering the mechanical intricacies. Posing for their pic-

Steering wheel, full-elliptic springs, and advanced chain drive distinguished the car built by E. Lenoir in France in 1862. Internal combustion was by illuminating gas; note the pressure safety pop-off valve on the single cylinder in lower schematic. (*The Science Museum, London*)

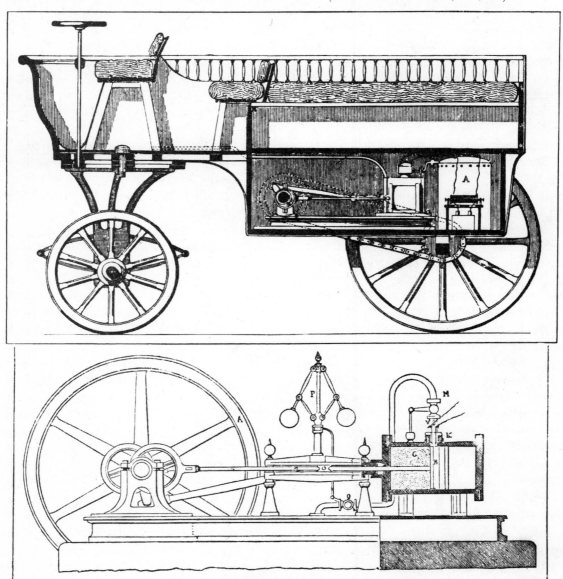

The first organized effort to produce an automobile in series was by Sylvester Roper in Massachusetts; this 1864 model was the first of ten such built and sold. Note stovepipe steam exhaust. (*Henry Ford Museum*)

ture, they appeared ready to start their own political party.

Over in Austria, meanwhile, another inventor, Siegfried Marcus, was having his own troubles with the authorities. His problem—noise made by his 1-cylinder, 2-cycle gasoline engine.

The news from Paris in 1862 told of the successful operation of Lenoir's internal combustion engine. Marcus had achieved a similar piston action two years before Lenoir and had used gasoline as the fuel. Marcus had also invented a means of vaporizing gasoline by jet action and mixing it with air before injection into the cylinder below the piston. Marcus had, in fact, invented the first jet carburetor but had failed to recognize its potential at the time. He had even devised a fairly satisfactory means of supplying a series of electric sparks to the combustion chamber.

News of Lenoir's road trips in the Paris metropolitan area sent Marcus back to his shop where he improved his old engine which he had originally designed in an effort to create light from electricity. Then he mounted the engine vertically on a four-wheel cart. A rod of iron connected the piston with a spiralled spring that powered the rear axle.

According to records in Austria, the Marcus gasoline vehicle made one or two brief, trial—but noisy—runs late in 1864.

To avoid complaints about noise, Marcus

and the police agreed that he should make future tests on a parade ground several miles away near a cemetery at night! For some unexplained reason, Marcus was unable to secure the services of a drayman so the caretaker of the building where Marcus's shop was located was hired to push the gasoline carriage to the parade ground.

So it was that late at night on the 9th of April, 1865—the evening of the day the War between the States ended—Siegfried Marcus directed the caretaker to lift the rear wheels off the ground. As Albert Curjel, a businessman and friend, looked on, Marcus made several adjustments to the carburetor, opened the fuel line, and spun the rear wheels. There was no clutch, no differential—hence the need to lift the rear wheels. Whether it occurred to Marcus that the vehicle might start with a shove is not known. However, after several revolutions of the rear wheels, the single 2-cycle cylinder fired, belched the smoky, burned mixture, then fired regularly and with almost enough noise to arouse the dead in the adjacent graveyard.

As the wheels spun dizzily, Marcus and Curjel climbed aboard, the husky caretaker lowered the contraption and away it went. The world's first gasoline-powered vehicle was a slow-walk success, but it worked. It "conked" out after about one-sixth of a mile.

Despite the vigorous prohibition against self-propelled vehicles in England, Catley and Ayres built and secretly operated this three-wheel steam "Wagonette" in 1868. (*The Science Museum, London*)

In 1873, "L'Obéissante" went into passenger service in Paris. Amédée Bollée built this *Voiture á vapeur* (steam carriage) which was powered by two 20-horsepower engines that gave a speed of about 24 mph. Note the leaf springs mounted outside of the wheels, a feature of railroad locomotives of the day. (*French Embassy Press and Information Service*)

Unfortunately, no newspaper reporters were present. Had there been press coverage, the dispatches the next morning would have caused reverberations in every carriage shop on the continent.

On April 10th, 1865, Herr Curjel made the rounds of potential investors. No one was interested in such a harebrained idea. Vienna was the city of music and entertainment. What could such a Kraftwagen possibly do but fill the air with fumes and noise? Nor was there any interest in the engine itself. What could it do that the per-

fected steam engines were not already doing—silently and without polluting the nostrils? Gasoline was a menace. Who wanted an explosion engine?

Marcus was most discouraged and promptly abandoned the Kraftwagen in a vacant lot next to his shop. He had previously salvaged the magneto-like ignition device he had developed back in 1860 and combined it with a fuse which the Imperial Army purchased on royalties and employed successfully in the war then raging with Denmark. The next year the Austro-

Most probably the first internal combustion powered petrol gas automobile was this "Kraftwagen"
built in Austria by Siegfried Marcus in 1864. (*Austrian Information Service*)

Hungarian Navy adopted the Marcus magneto for marine mines in the Adriatic. The
remuneration for this device, however, was
very slight and Marcus turned to the invention of such things as repeating pistols,
sound amplifiers, a means to project pictures, and carburetors.

But by 1873, Marcus had built another
Kraftwagen. With his vastly improved jet
carburetor and magneto ignition, the new
Marcus-wagen actually looked like an automobile. There was a steering wheel on a py-
lon which steered the front wheels by a
wormgear in front of a bench seat wide
enough for two persons. Over the rear axle
was another seat for two with a backrest.
Underneath was a one-cylinder, 4-cycle
gasoline engine that drove the rear axle
through a band-operated transmission and a

spiral spring clutch that gave some differential action between the two rear driving
wheels. The engine had a rudimentary water cooling system. There was only a single
speed—there were no gears—but this last
Marcus automobile, which the inventor
called the Strassenwagen (street wagon),
made many public appearances at speeds
up to 7 miles an hour in late 1874 and
1875. The power of the vehicle was reputed to be about ¾ H.P.

This time the police gave Marcus full
cooperation. Marcus had in recent years become the official physics tutor to the Crown
Prince, Rudolf von Hapsburg. So, the holder
of the Cross of Merit and friend of the Archduke was allowed to use the streets of Vienna for his road tests.

Still, the 1873–75 Marcus Strassenwagen

Some fortunate Americans had the opportunity to see the 1875 Marcus car from Austria when it was displayed, during the autumn of 1965, in the Nieman-Marcus department store in Dallas, Texas. (*Nieman-Marcus Co., Dallas*)

was considered a useless nuisance. A police report of the time stated that "This remarkable Kraftwagen developed gigantic smoke clouds, smelled badly, and frightened the pedestrians in the greatest proportions."

One run in early 1875 caused a near riot when carriage horses bolted and men and women scrambled out of the monster's path. The general confusion brought spike-helmented mounted police charging into the fray. This event brought Marcus more than a dozen citations summoning him to defend himself against charges ranging from endangering the public security to incitement to violence.

Marcus's solvency was saved only by his personal friendship—a holdover from the days when he was tutor to the Crown Prince

—with Count Hans Wilczek who had once purchased electrical equipment from Marcus for use by the Austro-Hungarian Arctic Expedition. Count Wilczek encouraged Marcus to continue developing his automobile. He even went along as a passenger on several drives to smaller cities around Vienna.

The Count then approached the prominent manufacturer, Prince Salm, who became enthusiastic about the commercial possibilities of the Marcus-wagen, but Marcus was out of the mood and desired to give up automobiles entirely. However, in 1879, when the news of Seldon's application for a patent on his designs for a vehicle powered by gasoline reached him, Prince Salm again begged Marcus to allow him to produce the machine in his iron works. Marcus, needing money, finally relented and in 1885 or thereabout the vehicle was shipped by rail to the iron works in Blansko, even as Karl Benz was readying his first gasoline tricycle. Prince Salm marketed many of Marcus's engines for industrial use and even built two more Marcuswagens, one of which is said to have been exported to the United States and the other to The Netherlands—but the existence or location of neither machine is known today.

Believing his time spent on the automobile had cheated him out of inventing the incandescent bulb, Marcus withdrew into his laboratory. Though he had beaten the German, Nikolaus Otto, by some three years with his 4-cycle gasoline engine, Marcus's name is hard to find in lists of famous inventors.

In the first automobile exposition in Vienna in 1898, the original 1873–75 Marcuswagen was displayed, the only Austrian car of completely Austrian manufacture down to the last nut and bolt. Shortly after, Siegfried Marcus, ill and discouraged, died.

When the Nazis came to Vienna in 1938, they dissolved the Austrian Automobile Club and deleted the name of Siegfried Marcus from reference works. The 1873–75 Marcus-wagen, however, was saved by being secluded in the Technical Museum where it rests today.

While Marcus was testing his first single-cylinder, 2-cycle, gasoline-engined vehicle in Vienna, Nikolaus August Otto and his assistant, Eugene Langen, were preparing a 1-cylinder, 4-cycle, illuminating gas engine in Cologne. In 1866, this engine consistently turned up between 100 and 180 revolutions per minute. When Dr. Otto exhibited his engine—which weighed better than 700 pounds—at the Paris Exposition in 1867, the engineers and scientists of every industrial country were interested. Steam engineers, however, snorted and were generally convinced that such a clumsy, noisy, smoky and smelly affair could never succeed.

But two men, Daimler and Benz, who did not know each other, reckoned that Otto was on the right track; they redoubled their separate efforts.

By 1876, Dr. Otto had greatly improved his engine, and by 1878 had obtained both German and United States patents. The Otto 4-cycle internal combustion engine was simple and effective, and the same intake-compression-explosion-exhaust principle was adopted by a host of engine designers. Today, the "Otto cycle" engine dominates in automobiles of the world.

As news of Otto's achievement spread across the Atlantic, George Seldon of Rochester, New York, saw a golden opportunity and in 1879 filed a patent application for a carriage powered by a gasoline engine, although it is doubtful that Seldon had ever seen anything remotely resembling the components he described.

Dr. Otto had never built a vehicle powered by any of his several engines. Seldon had never built a vehicle or an engine. He had based his claim on an engine known as the Brayton. Seldon was content to submit repeated improvements as amendments to his original 1879 patent application. An attorney, Seldon knew the legal ropes, and he employed every strand to hogtie others who, in the meantime, were forced to pay royalties to him.

Finally in 1895, Seldon's patent was granted and a full-size example of his machine was constructed. Seldon later threatened manufacturers, importers, and even

Karl Benz of Germany set the vehicular world on fire in 1885 with this model, his original "Patent Motorwagen" three-wheel car. (*Daimler-Benz AG*)

customers with suits for patent infringements. When he sued Henry Ford in 1903, Ford fought and, finally, in the Court of Appeals in January, 1911, won his case to the relief of the industry. Seldon's loss was held due to the fact that his patent was valid only when the Brayton-type engine was used and no one was using the Brayton.

Back in Germany in 1876, Gottlieb Daimler was fascinated by Otto's engine but considered it too slow and clumsy. So Daimler devised an improved carburetor and set about to develop a gasoline-powered version of Otto's engine with a few wrinkles of his own. Enlisting the assistance of Wilhelm Maybach, a genius in his own right, Daimler studied the discoveries of other inventors including those of Thomas A. Edison.

In December of 1883, Daimler received a German patent for his "hot tube" ignition system. The "hot tube" was heated electrically and, when regulated, determined the temperature point where ignition occurred. Thus, Daimler was able to increase engine revolutions to as high as 750 RPM. By the 1st of February, 1884, Daimler had had three engines built to his specifications, one of them equipped with a flywheel. All three engines performed successfully on gasoline and soon Daimler had them turning upward of 900 RPM. Otto's illuminating gas engine was achieving some success in various applications but Daimler's gasoline engine eventually doomed them.

The next year, 1885, Daimler installed

23

PATENTSCHRIFT

№ 37435

KLASSE 46: LUFT- UND GASKRAFTMASCHINEN.

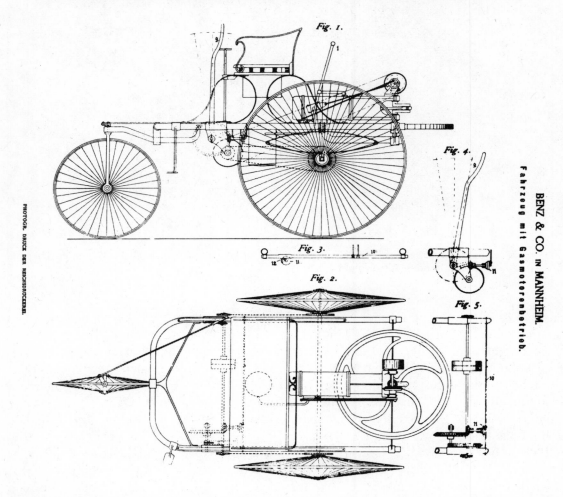

Fig. 1.

Fig. 4.

Fig. 3.

Fig. 2.

Fig. 5.

PHOTOGR. DRUCK DER REICHSDRUCKEREI.

BENZ & CO. IN MANNHEIM.

Fahrzeug mit Gasmotorenbetrieb.

In 1886, Benz received a patent for his three-wheel car; this is the patent drawing. (*Daimler-Benz AG*)

one of his 1-cylinder, 4-cycle gasoline engines on a motorcycle frame and the Daimler Motoren Gesellschaft was on its way in Connstatt, just about 100 kilometres from Mannheim where Karl Benz was also seeking to achieve internal combustion using gasoline as the fuel.

After much trial and error, Benz suc-

Gottlieb Daimler was running neck-and-neck with Benz when he successfully ran his four-wheel "Motorwagen" in 1886. (*Daimler-Benz* AG)

ceeded late in 1879, and his gasoline-fueled, 2-cycle engine became a reality. Benz was the first to employ a direct electrical charge in the combustion chamber.

Benz's next move was to organize Benz & Cie. in October of 1883 and he followed this by obtaining a French patent on his internal combustion, ignition type 2-cycle engine. Benz also completed the "Patent-Motorwagen Benz." Before the year was over this car had proven its dependability and he had, through agents, organized an export outlet in New York City.

With ¾ horsepower, the "Patent-Motor-wagen Benz" delivered the same power attributed to the Austrian Marcus of ten years before. The Benz engine weighed under 200 pounds and wound out a maximum of 450 RPM although Benz actually claimed only about 300 RPM. This three-wheeler employed tiller steering for the front wheel. A convenient lever on the driver's left controlled the engine which, with the gasoline tank, was in the rear above the axle.

In 1886, the German Patent Bureau issued Benz a patent on his Motorwagen and he prepared to produce cars. But there were no buyers. The production of his industrial engines at a respectable ten a month kept the wolf away from his door.

Two years later, in August of 1888, still without orders for the Motorwagen, Frau Benz took it upon herself one day to prove the vehicle's dependability. Loading her two young sons aboard, she spun the crank, and without so much as informing her husband, drove on the public roads to Pforzheim and back again the same day.

And so a lady driver proved her mettle—and the car's—when a lot of men thought motor cars explosively dangerous and only slightly less erratic than those who drove them. With such dependability assured, Karl Benz wound up the Motorwagen and drove 200 miles to Munich where a giant Trade Fair was in progress. He was promptly given a gold medal, congratulated by officials and onlookers alike, and even received a few inquiries from potential buyers.

As 1885 drew to a close, the Seldon Patent fight—already discussed—was brewing in America, Daimler's 4-cycle gasoline engine was a roaring success, and Benz's 2-cycle gasoline engine in the two-three seater, three-wheel Motorwagen was running fine. All that was needed now was customers. Most German States had certain restrictions—not outright taboos—on the use of the public roads by motor vehicles and naturally this discouraged customers. But driving could be done. France seemed to be the country most likely to accept the gasoline car, as were other countries west of the Rhine.

In England, restrictive laws continued to stymie new developments. Any self-propelled vehicle was equated as a "locomotive" without rails. Any testing of steam road vehicles had to be carried out in secrecy. According to the Royal Automobile Club, the last Court Summons for violating what came to be known, collectively, as the "Red Flag Laws" was given to a Mr. Walter C. Bersey of 39 Victoria Street in Westminster on the 20th of October in 1896. Bersey's crime? Here's a part of the summons:

". . . being the owner and having the charge of a locomotive propelled by other than animal power, to wit, a motor car, did unlawfully neglect to have such locomotive whilst in motion preceded by at least 20 yards by a person on foot."

"Emancipation Day" came—some motorists in Britain still use this term—just 25 days after Bersey's arrest. On November 14th, 1896, motorists all over the realm were released from their thralldom to the "Red Flag Laws"; they were set free at last.

The automobile can be said to have been created in recognizable form before the end of the 19th century. With the perfecting of his 4-cycle gasoline engine, Gottlieb Daimler then built the first successful four-wheeled gasoline car.

Called the "Daimler-wagen," this 1886 model was a horseless carriage in the truest sense: the spoked wagon wheels were in two sizes, the largest in the rear; the scuttle of the rear passenger compartment contained the 1.5 H.P. single-cylinder engine which turned 700 RPM. The steering was direct to the front axle by an extension on the king post topped off with a cross-bar, and the remnants of a familiar horse-wagon tongue extended forward a foot or so ahead of the vertical dashboard—just in case an occasional tow became necessary.

The stage was now set for a vigorous three-way competition among successful sources of power for the automobile which was now a reality; and another competition was soon to arise and grow involving makes of cars, the names of which ranged the alphabet.

Part II

THE INFANCY OF
THE AUTOMOBILE

Steamers, Electrics
and Gas Buggies
in a Popularity Contest

B Y THE BEGINNING of 1887, Benz's Patent-Motorwagen and Daimler's equally successful Motorwagen had put the handwriting on the wall—and the word was gasoline. The gasoline engines made by Gottlieb Daimler in Connstatt, Germany, swiftly gained the highest reputation. Although Benz's Patent-Motorwagen, the three-wheeler, had benefited by an initial surge of publicity, he soon found that four wheels were better—more familiar in a horse-wagon age.

Both German pioneers exhibited in the Paris Exposition of 1889; and Benz quickly designed new motor carriages with four wheels. In the same Exposition, Daimler's "Steel Wheel Carriage" powered with a new 2-cylinder, V-type engine cooled by water circulated by a pump was the sensation of the show.

Steam-powered vehicles were becoming popular in France; they were being made by Serpollet, de Dion, Bouton and others in fair variety. Benz gasoline engines were distributed in France by the Emile Roger firm.

Daimler's engines, meanwhile, were gaining favor as power for street railway cars and for motor boats. Daimler's factory had been producing motor boats and, through them, his name was achieving greater and greater fame.

Panhard-Levassor, a respected Paris firm, were already producing Daimler engines under license and Peugeot had been negotiating for the same rights.

Many have long believed that neither Panhard-Levassor nor Peugeot built any vehicles powered by Daimler engines until around 1894. However, the accompanying photographs showing vehicles built by both of these early French manufacturers in 1891 prove otherwise.

In 1893, Benz became the first European to export a car to the United States where he exhibited the "Velo" at the World's Columbian Exposition in Chicago. Daimler exhibited also—six products including engines, but no car. One of the show's hits, the "Velo" by Benz, spurred many Americans to think automobiles, including George Seldon whom we have already discussed. In 1894 the Benz Motor Company of New York was organized to sell cars, followed in about a year by Daimler. The Benz factory, meanwhile, was producing the "Velo" in fair quantity.

By 1894 Panhard-Levassor had built and sold some 400 cars to eager customers and

By 1890, Daimler cars from Connstatt, Germany, were fairly common in London, England, despite the existence of rigid traffic laws. (*Daimler-Benz AG*)

Peugeot soon produced 100 cars of their own design. Both of these manufacturers used Daimler engines. The same year, the Benz "Victoria" was considered the most fashionable of all cars.

Thus the argument as to which presently existing car manufacturer is the oldest requires one—in all fairness—to name three. These are Daimler-Benz in Germany (merged in 1926) and Panhard and Peugeot in France.

In 1893, a British group organized by Frederick Richard Simms, a mechanical engineer of Warwickshire (and a founder of the Royal Automobile Club), purchased rights to build Daimler engines in the United Kingdom and the great Daimler concern in England was born—a relation-

In America, scores of adventurous men were constructing motor vehicles, most of which gained only local and short-lived fame. Such a carriage was the steam car built by Achille Phillion of Akron, Ohio. Phillion, an actor, used this remarkable contraption to go to and from his performances; between cities, Phillion's steamer was shipped by railroad. The Phillion steamer still works; the motion picture, "Magnificent Ambersons," required an archaic steam car and the Phillion filled the bill magnificently. (*Pacific Auto Rentals*)

ship that gave England fine cars the equal of any. By the early 1900s, Daimler of England was building engines of its own design and the tie with Daimler in Connstatt was eliminated before World War One.

By the turn of the century, France had a number of manufacturers turning out cars with their own engines: Renault had a blocky coupe completely enclosed with glass windows in 1895 (one of the world's first closed cars), Delahaye was thriving as were Mors, Panhard-Levassor, and several others.

In America, meanwhile, J. Frank Duryea and his brother, Charles E., built their first

31

Early Serpollet steamers used the simple flash boiler seen here slung between the large rear artillery-type wheels. The half-elliptic rear springs are of interest along with the chain drive. This four-seater three-wheeler has lever steering working off the slightly angled upper post extension of the front wheel fork. Clearly such a steering mechanism reflects early motorcycle influence. Note that the wagon-type brake shoes operate against the iron-tired wheels and that these brakes are actuated by a pull-up spade grip. (*The Science Museum, London*)

The front single wheel suspension of this 1888 Serpollet steamer has dual full-elliptic springs. This French steamer began production in 1887 and lasted until 1907. It was quite popular throughout Europe and some were imported into the United States. (*French Embassy Press & Information Division*)

The Comte de Dion of France began making steam cars in 1883, later turned to petrol power. This 1893 "Tracteur à vapeur" pulling the two-wheel carriage became popular as a taxi. From the uniforms of the crew, it can be assumed that this vehicle was in military service. (*French Embassy Press & Information Division*)

Monsieur Bouton, an associate of the Comte de Dion in France, at the controls of an 1897 steam bus. De Dion vehicles were built until 1948. (*French Embassy Press & Information Division*)

This old Panhard-Levassor petrol car of 1891 is a popular attraction at the French National Conservatory of Arts in Paris. (*French Embassy Press & Information Service*)

car in 1893. In 1894, the second Duryea had 2 cylinders and, like their first one-banger, had spark ignition and the best carburetor to be developed in this country until after 1900. Mounted on the first pneumatic tires in the U.S.A., the 1894 Duryea won the first race in America, a Chicago to Evanston and return affair sponsored by the Chicago *Times-Herald* on Thanksgiving Day in 1895. This was a publicity coup for the Duryeas despite only five opponents—three Benz cars and two electric carriages.

Disputing the claim that the Duryea brothers built America's first successful gasoline car are those who believe that the honor belongs to either Elwood Haynes or

Peugeot had been in business just two years when this 1891 model was built. Note the front-mounted petrol tank for the concealed Daimler engine used at the time by this French marque. (*French Embassy Press & Information Division*)

Stephen M. Balzar. Haynes designed his four-wheeled car around the 1-cylinder, 2-cycle Sintz engine and had his car built in the Kokomo, Indiana, machine shop of Edgar and Elmer Apperson. The Appersons later built cars of their own design including the famous Jackrabbit runabout. The Haynes—now on display in the U. S. National Museum—made its first run on the Fourth of July in 1894 and amazed a holiday crowd with a scorching and noisy 7 MPH.

The other contender for the Duryea "first" claim, the New Yorker, Balzar, built a frame six feet long and used pneumatic-tired, 26-inch wheels in the rear and 17-inch bicycle wheels in front running in bicycle forks linked together for exceptionally good steering in 1894. Balzar's engine was a 3-cylinder, air-cooled rotary running vertically and axially in line with the driving rear axle. There was a 3-speed constant-mesh transmission driving off a stub shaft turning with the rotary's crankcase. Though comparatively dependable, only one Balzar car was made and, like the Haynes, it rests in the National Museum.

Henry Ford built his first car in 1896 as did a G. A. Meyer way out in San Francisco. Without fanfare or notoriety outside

This 1892 Daimler looks at home in this scene in the Black Forest in Germany. (*Daimler-Benz AG*)

of California, Meyer built three gasoline cars in his machine shop; one of them was purchased by a Doctor Jesse of Santa Rosa who used it on his professional rounds for several years. Another Meyer gasoline car owned by a George Colgate of Orland, California, also lasted many years. Only one Meyer remains today, a treasured exhibit in the headquarters of the California State Automobile Association.

The Duryea brothers established the first automobile factory in the U.S.A. in 1896 in Springfield, Massachusetts, undismayed that the *Scientific American* accused them of copying Benz. The same year they pro-

duced 13 virtually identical cars. One 1896 Duryea is preserved today in the private collection of George H. Waterman in East Greenwich, Rhode Island.

The same year also saw the second export of an American-made gasoline car (see Olds steam car). In the first London to Brighton race—an event staged in November of 1896 to commemorate "Emancipation Day"—the Duryea was pitted against Europe's best, but it won. The year before, it seems, Henry Sturmey who founded *The Autocar* magazine, came to the U.S.A. Seeing the Duryea, Sturmey arranged to sell the Massachusetts car in the United Kingdom. However,

A 2¼ horsepower Daimler engine was used in this 1893 Peugeot. (*French Embassy Press & Information Division*)

limited production prevented Sturmey from obtaining cars so he set up shop in Coventry to build the Duryea under license. Finally, in 1904, 10 HP Duryea cars capable of 40 MPH were being produced in the Detroit of England and became the first of a long list of American cars to be built in foreign lands.

Sturmey took his 1896 Duryea to competitions of all sorts. "Those who attended the Irish Trials at Dublin and Castlewellen in 1903 will remember," wrote A. B. F. Young in his book, *The Complete Motorist*, published in 1904, "the successful performance of the 10 HP Duryea which defeated cars of all powers up to 30 HP, and made better time than half of the cars costing over 1,000 pounds."

In 1897, Ransome E. Olds of Lansing, Michigan, built his first gasoline car. Powered by a 1-cylinder, 6-HP, water-cooled engine, this first Olds made 10 MPH with four aboard. One of four built that year by the new Olds Motor Vehicle Company, this car immediately preceded the lovely *curved dash* model now so sought after by collectors. Olds developed the Oldsmobile and Reo cars of later fame.

Then there was the 1897 Clarke three-wheel gasoline car built by Louis S. Clarke,

37

As with other French automobile manufacturers, Peugeot built a wide variety of models to satisfy the design conscious public. This 1892 model "vis-à-vis avec capote" (hood) had a 2-cylinder engine with bore and stroke of 72 and 125 mm; displacement was 1,018 cc. Maximum speed was about 20 mph. (*Automobiles Peugeot*)

1892 Peugeot "Victoria avec capote" four-seater with 2-cylinder, 1,282 cc. engine; speed was about 17–18 mph. (*Automobiles Peugeot*)

The 1892 Peugeot "vis-à-vis avec dais" (canopy) had a 1,645 cc. engine and could seat four to five in comfort. (*Automobiles Peugeot*)

By 1894, the Peugeot "Break avec dais" five seater featured side seats for the passengers and entry from the rear. The 2-cylinder 1,645 cc. engine had a "Boîte 4 vitesses" (4-speed gearbox) with reverse, was cooled by a low-slung core radiator in front, and could reach 18 mph. (*Automobiles Peugeot*)

AUTOMOBILES OF THE WORLD

When Panhard & Levassor began making horseless carriages in 1889, they devised a then-unique separate frame for the chassis and are generally credited with this advancement. This 1891 P.&L. was powered with a Daimler engine. Shown at the tiller is M. Levassor with his wife during an early competition event. (*French Embassy Press & Information Division*)

This fringed "vis-à-vis avec dais" Peugeot, this marque's finest in 1895, had a 2-cylinder opposed-type engine of 1,056 cc. displacement, three forward speeds with reverse, and a bulb horn of shining brass. (*Automobiles Peugeot*)

The same old "Number 5" Panhard-Levassor as it appeared at top speed during the "Paris-Bordeaux run" in which it was awarded first place with a time of 48 hours and 47 minutes in 1895. (*Panhard & Levassor*)

The first Panhard car of 1889–90 had a rear-mounted, vertical, 2-cylinder, 2-horsepower engine; four passengers sat in pairs, back-to-back. (*Panhard & Levassor*)

founder of the Pittsburg Motor Vehicle Company which, in 1899, became the Autocar Company. First of a long line of Autocars, the Clarke Gasoline Tricycle was a success with its single-cylinder engine.

In 1898, the first production model Winton car was built in Cleveland, Ohio, and the French press promptly stated it was copied from the Benz. The Winton had a 1-cylinder gasoline engine mounted horizontally, a make-and-break ignition, and two forward speeds plus reverse. Winton cars became popular and were among the best for many years.

In their own home town, the Duryea brothers had some capable competition: Harry E. Knox. The first Knox had three wheels and an air-cooled, 1-cylinder, horizontal engine that developed 8 HP. Knox went into production in 1899 and continued well into the Twentieth Century.

Another part of the present General Mo-

tors empire also began the manufacture of automobiles in 1897. In Germany Carl and Wilhelm Opel, sons of the founder of Adam Opel A.G., retooled their bicycle shop. In 1898, the first "Opel Patent Motorwagen" appeared and within five years Opel cars were a worldwide success. With its 1-cylinder, 4-HP water-cooled engine, the "System Lutzmann" had two forward speeds plus reverse, a gearshift lever beside the tiller-topped steering column, and a top speed of 20 MPH. It could be purchased with optional pneumatic tires for an additional 300 Reichsmarks—a total of 4300 Marks—at the Rüsselsheim factory.

Benz and Daimler were getting plenty of competition in Germany. One of the smartest of the German cars of the time was the Eisenach. Vertical spindles—similar to king-pins on modern cars—attached to the wheel hubs fitted into receiving sleeves at each front corner of the frame. A transverse semi-

A total of six were built of the 1891 Panhard-Levassor which won the "Paris-Bordeaux run" in 1895. The 2-cylinder engine had three forward speeds and no reverse. (*Panhard & Levassor*)

René Panhard with wife and children aboard an 1892 model equipped with "parasol." (*Panhard & Levassor*)

In 1893, Panhard-Levassor introduced this four-seat "Wagonette" which featured a glass windshield and removable side curtains. The tiller extended inside; engine was mounted high in front, and suspension, as on earlier models, was by full-elliptic springs. (*Panhard & Levassor*)

In the "Paris-Marseille-Paris race" of 1895, three Panhard-Levassor cars ran among the top winners. Here old "Number 5" is speeding along a smooth, tree-lined road. (*Panhard & Levassor*)

By 1898, Panhard-Levassor was featuring steering wheels, rear engines, and front suspension by transverse elliptic springs. This model is from the Lindley Bothwell Collection. (*Photo by Author*)

The Panhard-Levassor "Americaine" model of 1899 epitomized the pioneer French firm's transition to standard design—the engine beneath front hood, full-elliptic springs, and four-seat coachwork fitted with a collapsible touring top. Note the bulb horn fitted to the steering wheel, coach-type carbide lamps and road headlamps. (*Panhard & Levassor*)

The 1899 Panhard-Levassor roadster, with a powerful 16-horsepower engine with radiator in front was an early sports car. Note the ignition controls and valve oiling mechanisms on the dashboard, and the wicker basket on the rear deck. (*Panhard & Levassor*)

The Benz "Victoria" of 1893–94 had a rearmounted, air-cooled, single-cylinder engine developing about 6 horsepower. (*Daimler-Benz AG*)

Inter-urban passengers, eight of them, were comfortably accommodated in the first Benz "Omnibus" of 1895. The one-cylinder, rear engine had a bore and stroke of 150 x 165 mm. and developed between 4 and 6 horsepower. The body was clearly developed from those of the contemporary horse-drawn coaches. (*Daimler-Benz AG*)

elliptical spring gave efficient directional stability to the front wheels, and made this one of the most easily controlled cars of the time. This was one of the earliest independent front wheel suspensions. There were no springs in the rear. A foot brake on the differential and hand brakes operating binders inboard of each rear wheel gave good results. This sharp 2-cylinder, 4-cycle air-cooled gasoline car must have been able to do at least 18 MPH. A dry cell battery and a coil provided jump spark ignition and current for the two carbide headlamps. The 2-speed transmission had sliding gears. The crank-wheel at the driver's right hand provided easy starting. The Fahrzeugfabrik Eisenach still produces cars today in the East German city of the same name.

Automobile development was not con-fined to the larger nations. Skilled engineers and competent mechanics were building cars everywhere. Most of these makes remained obscure. Some virtually unknown cars are shown in this book for the first time.

In The Netherlands, the Spyker brothers founded their firm specifically to build automobiles in 1898. Little is known about the first series of Spyker cars but a production series in 1899–1900 was entirely exported to England where they sold rapidly. The post-1900 Spyker cars and four other makes are illustrated in Part IV. The most famous of all Spyker vehicles was not an automobile but the still-used gilded gift coach of Amsterdamers to Queen Wilhelmina upon the occasion of her wedding in 1901.

In Amersfoort, another Dutch firm

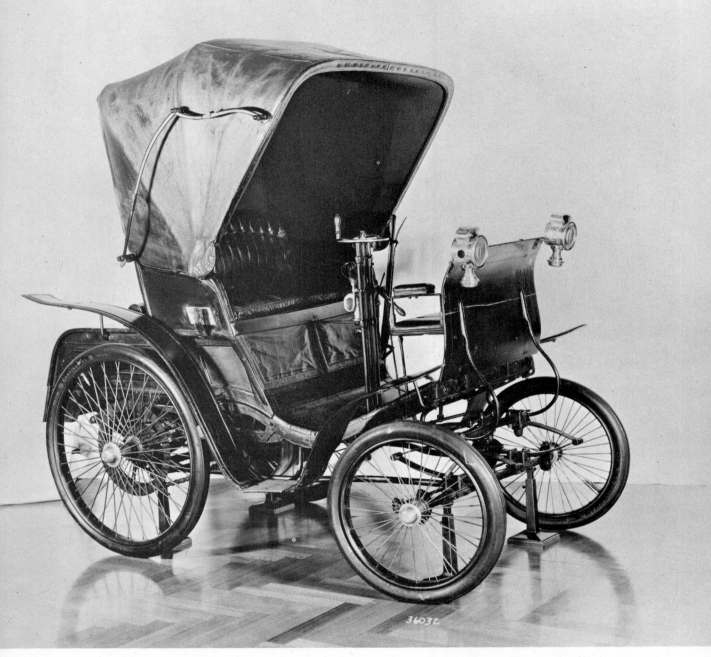

Among cars competing for the Yankee Dollar in 1898 was the Benz "Comfortable" which sold for $1,000. The front wheels were 20½ inches diameter, the rear 31 inches. A 3-horsepower engine drove through two forward speeds; there was no reverse. Hand and foot brakes operated on rear wheels. Side lighting was by candles in the lanterns. (*Henry Ford Museum*)

48

Frederick R. Simms, founder of the Royal Automobile Club, was instrumental in introducing the Daimler gasoline engines to England. In 1898, Simms introduced this tiller-steered, Daimler-powered car. Note the radiator core affixed to the dashboard and the staggered seating. (*The Science Museum, London*)

This 1897 Daimler, built in England, may have been the one demonstrated to the then Prince of Wales, who became King Edward VII, by Simms who organized the firm which produced the British Daimler cars. Simms and the Hon. Evelyn Ellis, later organizers of the R.A.C., are shown with friends in the machine. (*Daimler Motor Co., Coventry*)

When Herbert Austin, later Lord Austin, was employed by the Wolseley Sheep-Shearing Machine Company as an engineer, his thoughts turned to automobiles. The result was this curious, one-off, two-seater, the first Wolseley of 1895. The vehicle has long since dropped from sight but it was powered with an advanced, twin-cylinder, opposed, air-cooled engine and it started its builder on a long and distinguished automotive career. (*British Motor Corp.*)

The first Riley car was this fetching two-seater with steering wheel and full-elliptic springs built by Percy Riley sometime between 1896 and 1898. Though not produced beyond this prototype, the vehicle spawned the marque which still exists today in England. (*British Motor Corp.*)

Frederick W. Lanchester, a brilliant English engineer, formed the Lanchester Engine Company in 1895 and built some of Britain's outstanding cars. This 1897 model had side-mounted, tiller steering and an unusual front suspension: the solid axle was sprung on the tips of half-elliptic springs. A two-cylinder engine produced 8 horsepower. The marque was consistently in the quality car range, later merged with Daimler (of England), then passed from the scene in 1956. (*The Science Museum, London*)

switched from bicycles to cars and, according to information supplied by the Foreign Ministry of The Netherlands, was producing cars upon order prior to 1898. This firm, Eysink Industrieele, switched back to bikes after only a few years. Even small cities in The Netherlands had pioneer automobile builders like the Aarts factory in Dongen which built special cars of high quality.

In neighboring Belgium, a 2-cylinder, air-cooled, belt-driven gasoline carriage with pneumatic-tired wire wheels was in production at the beginning of 1899. Called the Vivinus, this car featured an almost modern depressed steering wheel hub and upward-splayed steering wheel spokes, and a gearshift lever attached to the steering column. Five people rode in style, three up front. The fenders were of steam-curved hardwood. The Vivinus shown here belonged to H. M. King Leopold II and was only recently restored. This was by no means the only Belgian-designed car as we shall see in Part IV.

To the north, mechanically inclined Swedes were turning out one-of-a-kind automobiles by stuffing any suitable engine available into buckboards and town carriages. One engineer, however, Gustaf Eriksson, who lived in a mining district, was hired in 1891 by the Vagnafabriksaktiebolaget Södertälje (Wagon Factory Manufacturing Company in Södertälje) about 24 miles from

AUTOMOBILES OF THE WORLD

Stockholm. Eriksson had apparently built a few experimental gasoline cars before he joined VABIS. Vabis—from the key letters in the firm's name—were manufacturers of railroad rolling stock and knew steam, but they hired Eriksson expressly to develop gasoline cars.

In 1897, Sweden's first factory-built automobile, a carriage seating four people and powered by a 2-cylinder horizontal "Boxer" 4-cycle gasoline engine, rolled out of the factory under its own power—once it was started with a blowpipe. A baggage tonneau sat behind the body. A year or so later, this first Vabis car was slightly restyled by removing the tonneau. But the experimentation went more deeply—Vabis was developing a new 4-cycle, 2-cylinder engine fueled by paraffin. It is not known whether this paraffin engine went into production. The Vabis firm was the basis for a larger manufacturer whose cars became important in Sweden after the century's turn.

In Switzerland, land of Isaac de Rivaz,

Emil Delahaye, a machinery manufacturer, built cars from 1896 to 1952. This restored 1897 model, shown with the Fort Maillot monument in background in Paris, with pioneer motorist Emil Perdreau bundled up in vintage motoring furs, helped celebrate the French Automobile Club's 50th anniversary. The one-cylinder engine developed 4 horsepower; drive was through a belt transmission, and about 20 mph was maximum. (*French Embassy Press & Information Division*)

Another version of the 1897 Delahaye, one of the fine French makes, discloses technical variations from other Delahayes of the same year: transverse rather than longitudinal half-elliptic springs, radi-ator in front beneath mudguard, and folding touring top. (*French Embassy Press & Information Division*)

the foundation was being laid for the truck and bus manufacturing industry that flourishes there today. In 1898, at least a dozen factories were beginning regular series production of gasoline-powered automobiles. In Basel, the Popp Patent Motorwagen used one of the earliest tubular steel frames. A 2-cylinder, in-line rear engine of unlisted power drove the larger rear wheels through a 2-speed transmission by belts and pulleys. A feature still favored by car enthusiasts—rack and pinion steering—must have made this elegant carriage a pleasure to drive. Only two could be seated but the ride was soft on four fully elliptical springs. Only two examples of the 1898 model illustrated

J. A. Meyer built three gasoline vehicles in 1896 and sold two of them. The Meyer cars were excellent; one exists today. (*Courtesy of the California State Automobile Association, copyright owner*)

The 1898 Eisenach built in Wartburg, now in East Germany, displayed unusually clean lines. It featured foot pedals for clutch and brakes, a sliding gear transmission controlled by a lever beside the steering column, and an efficiently simple front suspension system plus wheel starting device on side of seat. (*Henry Ford Museum*)

The first Opel, a famed German marque still active, was a license-built version of the "System Lutzmann" in 1898. Frederick Lutzmann in Dessau began building cars in 1895, discontinued in '99. The 4-HP, 1-cylinder, water-cooled engine had a belt drive to central gearing, then by chain to rear wheels; the two forward speeds (also reverse) allowed a top speed of about 12 mph. Note that the gear change lever is on the steering lever column. (*Adam Opel AG and General Motors Corp.*)

The 1898 "hunting brake" shown in this very old print is an Aarts of circa-1898 built in The Netherlands. A 6-horsepower, Dutch-made engine drove this elegant carriage which carried six to eight persons. (*National Museum van de Automobiel, Driebergen*)

AUTOMOBIELEN-FABRIEK.
ANT. AARTS.
DONGEN (HOLLAND.)

The Vivinus of about 1899 was a popular Belgian make that was exported to other nations including England. Powerplant was a 2-cylinder, air-cooled, 1,420 cc. unit employing belt transmission to rear wheels. This smart four-seater with wicker coachwork was owned by H. M. King Leopold II. (*Institut Belge d'Information et de Documentation*)

were built but more and finer cars were to come from the firm established by Lorenz Popp, professional engineer.

Besides the Popp were the Orion, the Martini, the Saurer, the Dufaux, the cars by Rudolf Egg, the Pic-Pic cars, and others— all built in the land most people think of as making nothing but watches.

Just about 110 miles across Mount Blanc from Geneva and to the southeast in Turin, the largest and longest lived of all car manufacturers in Italy built their first car in 1899. The possibility exists that the first Fiat incorporated many parts also used in several German, French, Belgian, Swedish and Swiss cars, indicating a common source of supply. Though lacking any sensational innovations, the '99 Fiat had immediate sales acceptance not only in its native Italy but also in the world market. Dependably rugged, this first of a long line of high-quality cars covering all price ranges had a 2-cylinder, water-cooled gasoline engine, and 3-speed transmission, and seated four in relative comfort. The radiator core was mounted unusually low considering the roads of the time, but the four fully-elliptical springs made it one of the better riding cars. Perhaps its makers determined that sound engineering was the key to attracting and

The first Vabis car was built in 1897 by designer Gustav Erikson. Powered by a 2-cylinder, 2-cycle engine, this model was prototype for all Vabis cars. (AB *Scania-Vabis*)

keeping customers. If such is the case, they were right as nearly seven successful decades in the Italian industry testify.

Automotive pioneers were at work even in far-distant Australia. There on the 6th of July, 1888, a strange looking car appeared in Melbourne—a steam car built by Herbert Thompson with the assistance of his cousin, Edward Holmes. According to Mr. John Goode, writing in a 1959 issue of *The Bulletin of the Business Archives Council of Australia*, the Thompson Steam Car ran well and when pitted against an imported Benz in early 1889 trounced the German gasoline car.

The Thompson Steamer weighed about 1,900 pounds with burner fuel (2 gallons of kerosene) and 20 gallons of water ready to run. The steam engine was a 2-cylinder, vertical compound mounted immediately behind the front axle. The drive was transmitted to the transmission shaft by a leather belt. Only one gear was fitted at first but, before the race with the Benz, another ratio was added. The power was delivered to the rear axle by a chain and sprockets. By 1900, this first-documented Australian car engendered so many purchase orders that the Thompson Motor Works was formed in Victoria.

Lorenz Popp, a talented Swiss engineer, built this 2-cylinder, two-seater in 1898 in Basel. Beautifully finished, its engine was in the rear; the 2-speed transmission used belts and steering was by rack and pinion. The '98 Popp still exists. (*Swiss Museum of Transport & Communications*)

Swiss Saurer cars are no longer made, but their trucks and buses are known throughout the world. This first Saurer model of 1898 had a single-cylinder motor with two opposing pistons; displacement was 3,140 cc.; it developed 5 horsepower at 600 rpm. (*Société Anonyme Adolphe Saurer*)

The second version of the 1897 Vabis was powered with a 2-cylinder, paraffin-fueled engine experimentally; other changes were in driving controls, elimination of dashboard and in the rear of body. Suspension was by half-elliptic springs. (*Tekniska Museet, Stockholm*)

In 1901, the prototype had the future King George V as a passenger on his state visit to New South Wales and the production version, as a consequence, was named "The Royal." Production ceased in 1902 and was limited to ten steamers. Customers included the New South Wales government. Now only the prototype remains. Herbert Thompson, a steam engineer by profession, made no more cars but he became an importer for various European makes. He is the inventor of the clip-on type fuel tank cap, the patent rights for which he sold to an American manufacturer.

As is true elsewhere, Australian car enthusiasts debate whether or not the Thompson Steamer was actually their country's first native car. Some hold that the J. & D. Shearer Company in Mannum, South Australia, began to construct a car in their shops prior to anyone else. Shearer manufactured agricultural equipment, had the facilities and the engineering knowledge. The story goes that the Shearer car was begun in 1885. By all evidence available, originality in most respects distinguished the imposing vehicle.

A much modified, husky "outback" ranch wagon appears to have been the platform for a very large boiler container over the rear axle. Inside the container were "three drums, the upper holding the steam and the two lower (drums) the water, while a nest of

The Fiat built in 1899 was the first of a long line of cars that have made Italy famous among enthusiasts. In line with period competitors, this model had a one-cylinder, 3.5 horsepower engine. (*Henry Ford Museum*)

water tubes on either side connect the three (drums) together, the steam drum forming the top of the triangle while the water is held in the tubes and lower drums, which have the fire grate between them. The boiler is tested to 500 lbs. per square inch, and works with a pressure of 220 pounds. The boiler is very strong and should stand a bursting strain of 1,500 lbs. The motor is a pair of engines, worked with a linked motion, and reversible at pleasure, and by a system of superheating all steam and water from the exhaust is dried, so that no emission of steam can be seen, and all oils are burnt up by the same means, so that there is nothing to frighten horses from the use of steam, nor any nuisance from oils which are burnt up after leaving the cylinder."

The above quotation is from the September 1, 1899, issue of *The Australasian Ironmonger*, a prominent machinists' and engineers' trade journal of the time.

The performance of the Shearer Steamer is variously documented at from 10 to 15 MPH. Grades of 10 percent were· said to have been ascended without loss of speed. The roughest going, the steepest hills, and 100-mile-long trips were taken in stride due, partially at least, to an efficient differential worked out several years previously. Iron-tired wagon wheels were used but: "Of course, with pneumatic or rubber (solid) tires, a much higher speed could be obtained," said the *Ironmonger's* correspondent.

From the old photograph kindly supplied by the National Library of Australia in Canberra—probably the only one in existence—the Shearer must have accommodated at least six people plus considerable luggage. A grand safari machine the Shearer would have been for a pre-gasoline journey to the vast Australian interior.

A New South Wales man, W. M. McIntosh, is said to have built and run a wood-burning "steam engine on wheels" about 1893. In the same year, an H. Knight Eaton is supposed to have built some sort of gasoline car in Queensland. There was a successful gasoline 3-wheeler in Sydney, and in Allansford, Victoria, a Johann Ziegler built a motor car. G. W. Wood of Leitchhardt, New South Wales, built a "four wheel motorcycle" and two other motor cars.

The Australian Horseless Carriage Syndicate, organized by an Austin, a Ridge, and a Copeland in 1897 in Melbourne, appears to have been a well financed project to produce for the public. A Grayson kerosene-burning internal combustion engine, also made in Melbourne, supplied power through a chain drive to a high, well sprung, locally built carriage complete with carbide lamps and push-me-pull-you seats for six persons. A public demonstration in early February of

'97 was a feature of a Cycle Show and Lord Brassey, the Governor of the then Victoria Territory, went along for the ride. The makers, claiming it to be Australia's first, christened the motor rig "Pioneer."

As the century drew to a close, *The Autocar*, probably the world's oldest living automotive magazine, published reports of two cars, also called Autocar, built in Melbourne by an engineer named Henry Sutton. The *Bulletin of the Business Archives Council* attributes "a certain elegance" to Sutton's cars and goes on to say, "Using numerous cylinders for his engine, he recorded all details of its performance. The suspension design was well considered and with a weight of 9 cwt. the designer claimed the car to have a maximum speed of 18 m.p.h. on good asphalt roads with an economy permitting four persons to be carried a distance of 16 miles at a cost of 2d per passenger."

The name of Tarrant at the time meant cars "made in Australia and available on order." This firm stayed in business for an entire decade.

Back in London, the Electric Cab Company in 1889 obtained a permit to operate a fleet of about four dozen electric omnibuses despite the continuing prohibition on gasoline and steam cars. Just what strings were pulled to manage this is one of the mysteries of the time. Over in Paris, electric taxicabs were the rage so somebody in authority must have felt that what Paris had London deserved. The electric cabs on London streets were good public relations for an automobile—any kind—particularly with automobiles beginning to be really appreciated in most places outside of England.

Happily, there were fewer outright restrictions in the U.S.A.—just prejudices. Electric carriage exponents argued that the voltage burners were cleaner than either gas

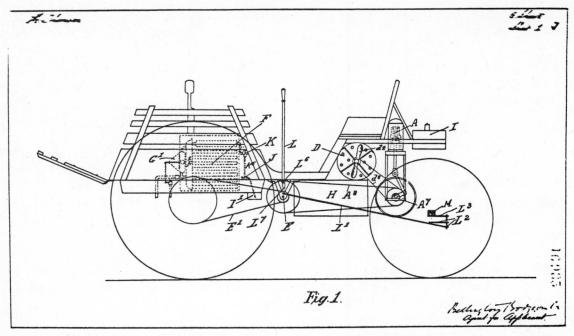

Fig.1.

One of Australia's earliest motor vehicles was the Thompson steam car; above is the original patent drawing of 1888. (*Bulletin of the Business Archives Council of Australia*)

The first Australian automobile that can be documented was the Shearer steamer built about 1885. (*National Library of Australia*)

Mr. Tom Myers, engineer of Melbourne, Australia, shown in his workshop where he built a replica of a four-wheel, light motor vehicle of the cyclecar type. It is believed that this represents a cyclecar built about 1890 by G. W. Woods. (*Wheels Magazine, Australia*)

buggies or steamers—or horses for that matter. Benz and Daimler had set up sales and service shops in New York City and about the only effective competition on the home front were the products of Duryea, R. E. Olds, Winton and a very few others. Electric trolleys were coming along fine, and the few imported French steam cars could be brushed aside with some good home-grown electrics. Electrics were polite and inoffensive which was more than could be said for their competition. The situation was favorable for electrics.

So when Fred Kimball up in Boston started "tooling" about in the electric he had built in 1888, others quickly followed suit. (Kimball built and sold a few and continued his experiments until about 1912.)

First of record to get off the mark was William Morrison of Des Moines, Iowa; by 1891 he had built at least two and had sold at least one. The buyer was well selected —none other than J. B. McDonald who was President of the American Battery Company in Chicago. McDonald made himself as conspicuous as possible in Chi-

In 1897, The Australian Horseless Carriage Syndicate was formed to produce the successful "Pioneer" motor vehicle; the internal combustion engine burned kerosene and was tested widely in Melbourne and vicinity. (*Wheels Magazine, Australia*)

cago. Why not? He made and sold batteries and what was good for the A.B.C. was good for the country's pedestrians. The press covered McDonald and his Morrison Electric with the result that people got charged up with a yen to own one.

In 1898, the Electric Vehicle Company was organized in Hartford, Connecticut, as a subsidiary of the Pope Manufacturing Company, makers of the very popular Columbia bicycles. The assignment: build and sell electric cars. Colonel Albert A. Pope was a farsighted industrialist who kept his hand in automobiles for many years—later his firm made the Pope-Hartford, a truly excellent gasoline car. Hiram Percy Maxim, the son of the famed Sir Hiram S. Maxim who invented the machine gun, was hired by Pope as chief engineer.

Young Maxim's efforts were soon successful, and in 1899 he drove a Columbia Electric carriage 60 miles, without a battery recharge, from Atlantic City to Philadelphia. This was good range but the speed, for '99, was impossibly slow for customers who wanted a bit of dash.

This 1899 Mobile Steamer, built in Tarrytown, New York, was a close copy of the better known Stanley Steamer. This beautifully restored example, owned by E. H. Taliaferro of San Diego, is attractively occupied by Lynne Stewart during a gathering of steam-car enthusiasts in 1959, exactly sixty years after the Mobile was built. (*Author's archives*)

But, electric cars bloomed for a time after 1900.

The steamers were already doing better. Even an actor, Achille Philion, of Akron, Ohio, had built one in 1892; it looked strange but it was good. In 1893, Ransom E. Olds built a three-wheel steam car in Lansing, Michigan. This was four years before Olds established his factory for series production of cars. Though not generally known, Olds rebuilt the steamer as a four-wheel car and shipped it to Bombay, India, in 1893 on the order of a customer. This corrects the general impression that an 1896 Duryea was the first American car to be exported.

A number of Serpollet and DeDion-Bouton steamers had been imported into the United States. In many public demonstrations they topped gasoline cars. Besides, they were more reliable.

The popularity of the rapidly expanding network of railroads, familiarity with imported steam cars, a supply of steam mechanics and designers, all set the stage for production of American steam cars.

When the Stanley twins sold out their interests, this 1899 Locomobile Steamer replaced the Stanley; about the only change was the name. Priced at $1,200, this vehicle was built in Newton, Massachusetts. (*Henry Ford Museum*)

One day around 1895, a DeDion *Voiture à vapeur* from France was being demonstrated publicly in Massachusetts. Sales representatives extolled the virtues of the steamer and rides were given to spectators who looked as if they might be cajoled into buying one. In the crowd were a couple of bearded gentlemen, twin brothers named Francis E. and Freeling O. Stanley, who had a prosperous business making photographic dry plates. They also appreciated the finer things in life and, in their factory, also made quality violins. They thought the DeDion steamer put on a pretty fair show, but also reckoned they could make a whale of a lot better steam car if they put their minds to the task.

They decided to do it.

After hiring a good steam mechanic to build a test engine, they prepared a portion of their plant for their plunge into the automobile industry. Neither of them had ever

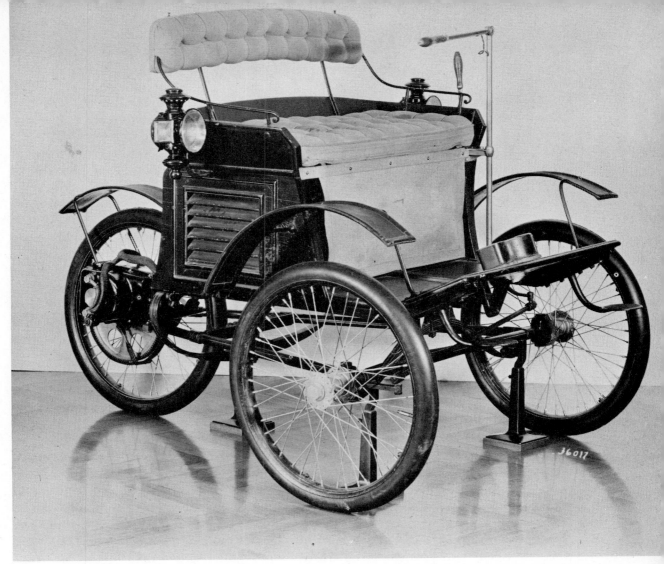

As the steam cars gained ground, electrics were quickly introduced. This 1898 Riker electric three-wheeler was the first of its specific type in the United States. (*Henry Ford Museum*)

owned a car but that was of no consequence.

In 1896—less than a year after they had watched the DeDion-Bouton steam car do its stuff—the first Stanley Steamer automobile took to the road. The first test runs were exceptionally satisfying and the Stanley fame as automobile manufacturers spread faster than the twins could stock materials for regular production. At every opportunity, they challenged gasoline car owners to a contest. The Stanley was seldom the loser in either impromptu races or in the speed trials and reliability runs which were becoming regular occurrences in eastern metropolitan areas. When the Mobile Steamer came out in '98, the brothers entered races. The long black beards of the Stanley brothers must have added to the entertainment value. The gasoline cars were consistently beaten.

Orders began to come in so fast that

the Stanleys sold their photographic plate business to Eastman Kodak and concentrated on building cars. They tooled up for mass production, and sold a few more than 200 steam cars in the first months of '99 —a direct result of the publicity gained when F. E. Stanley drove the steamer to the top of 6,288-foot Mount Washington, the highest mountain in New England. This was a 'sensational accomplishment. The road to the top was rutty and steep, and several highly touted gasoline cars had failed miserably in recent months.

Any car in 1899 that could negotiate Mt. Washington had to be a good car.

Then a funny thing happened.

The Stanley twins sold out, lock, stock, and patents to J. B. Walker, publisher of *Cosmopolitan* magazine, for around a quarter-million dollars.

Walker and several associates immediately formed the Locomobile Company of America, moved into the Stanleys' Newton plant, and immediately began to produce the Locomobile, nee Stanley, Steamer, the 1899 model. Only minor details were changed. By the middle of 1900 there were well over 1,000 Stanley and virtually identical Locomobile steamers in use. In the same year, Walker drove a steamer to the top of Pikes Peak and sales increased rapidly as news of the feat reached the public.

Steam cars caught the public's fancy— there were, besides the Stanleys, the new Locomobiles, Genevas, Grouts, Mobiles, Whites and others, all resembling the Stanley in varying degrees.

The Stanley twins took a rest and looked around. The Locomobile people soon had a falling out among themselves; the Stanleys picked up the pieces and the golden age of steam cars in America really began.

Lack of speed was working against the quiet electric cars in America, but in Europe speed and the gas engine were dominant factors in automotive development.

Then a remarkable non-gas car, the Jenatzy, designed by an engineer named Jeantaud, established the official world speed record of more than 100 kilometres per hour (65.23 MPH) late in 1899! With a metal body, this speedster looked like a passenger-carrying submarine torpedo with a one-man cockpit. The chassis was advanced and rugged but this was a development vehicle—there would be few takers for such a machine despite rapid acceleration, silence, and generally good performance. Batteries supplied the energy and the radius of operation was, therefore, severely limited. The Jenatzy is one of the cars, however, that profoundly affected the career of the automotive genius, Ferdinand Porsche, as we shall see.

Around 1895, several well-established engineering firms in Austria-Hungary had begun to experiment with automobiles. Benz and Daimler engines were imported and used in prototype cars by several companies, the most important of which for many years was Austro-Daimler A.G. in Vienna.

Cars of Austrian design were built as early as 1895 by Lohner, Nesselsdorfer, and Gräf & Stift. The latter firm's first car in 1897 deserves fame as one of the very first—possibly the first—to have front-wheel drive, a system virtually like that on the few cars using front-wheel drive today. A later Gräf & Stift car was to play a tragic role with dramatic effects on world history.

The first Nesselsdorfer cars of 1897 used a Boxer engine of German origin—the same power plant used in Sweden's first Vabis car of the same year.

Ludwig Lohner of Vienna was coach builder to the Emperor. In 1896, Lohner

Looking for all the world like a torpedo on wheels, this Belgian Janetzy electric speedster established a world speed record in 1899 of 106 kilometers per hour. (*French Embassy Press & Information Division*)

obtained patent rights from the Frenchman, Jeantaud, builder of the later speed record holding Jenatzy. Convinced that the noise, need for cranking, and offensive odors of the gasoline engine would prevent popularity of gas-powered cars, Lohner's works turned to electric cars in 1897. The first models were generally unsatisfactory, and just as he was about to forsake automobiles, Lohner met young Porsche who was only 23 years of age. Porsche was working as a designer of motors in an electrical firm. He had already come under the spell of one of the first Gräf & Stift cars—the front-wheel drive impressing him particularly.

Perceiving that Porsche was a young man of rare ability, Lohner hired him as chief engineer of his motor car enterprise as a sort of last resort. This chance association was to have important consequences among the automotively inclined, particularly in the U.S.A.

Porsche has generally been considered primarily an engine man, but with his training and few years of electric motor design experience behind him—plus Lohner's preoccupation with electricity—Porsche at once devoted himself to the problems associated with power transmission to the driving wheels. The Lohner electric was of acceptable style, and it was well built; it merely needed the master touch of a competent

The young Ferdinand Porsche designed this "Chaise" in 1899 for Jacob Lohner, a Vienna coachbuilder turned automobile manufacturer.

Known as the Porsche-Lohner Chaise, this was a gasoline-electric car employing wheel hub motors in both front wheels. (*Porsche Werkfoto*)

electrical engineer. This ingredient Porsche had in abundance, and quickly he evolved a driving system that is used increasingly even now—nearly seven decades later—on heavy industrial vehicles and off-the-road equipment all around the world.

The Porsche innovation combined front-wheel drive, which he admired, and his wheel-hub-mounted electric motor. Thus, he did away with the power-consuming chain drives and belts, eliminated the troublesome differential, and doubled the basic motor power by using a motor in each front wheel hub. Porsche had already patented his hub motors in 1897, a world first. In all probability, this innovation increased fourfold the power delivered to the wheels. Called the

"Lohner-Porsche Chaise," the car was the sensation of the 1900 Paris World Exposition. It won young Porsche the grand award and gold medal—a supreme achievement, in a massive display of more than one thousand cars, for one so young who had been in the rough-and-tumble automotive game only a few months. The Lohner-Porsche Chaise was the world's first electric car able to travel 50 miles on one charge and do this at 9 MPH steady speed.

As the century closed, Porsche was hailed in Europe as the foremost automotive engineer of the day and the Lohner Company leaped from obscurity into the sunlight of sweet success. Moreover, electrical engineers everywhere, particularly in the U.S.A.,

70

The Porsche-Lohner combine produced this "Re-kordauto" around 1900, a four-wheel-drive racing version of the front-wheel-drive Chaise. Porsche is seldom remembered as the designer of outstanding electric-powered machines. (*Porsche Werkfoto*)

breathed deeply once more and decided to charge boldly forward and give steamers and gas buggies a run for the money.

Motive power was derived from a variety of fuels—gasoline, steam, electricity, kerosene, paraffin, naphtha. In New Zealand, the first DeDion-Bouton to be imported was tuned for naphtha because there was no gasoline available.

In France, 300-mile automobile trips became commonplace. In Sweden, the automobile proved to be dependable near the Arctic circle, and before 1901 arrived a big game hunter named Stephenson used a steam car professionally in India.

Automobiles were carrying the Royal Mail in Ceylon. Deeper in the Orient, engineers of Nippon were studying Europe's best while preparing to build their own cars.

Although pioneer "automobilists" were a hardy lot, many sought protection from the elements. All sorts of face masks, electrically heated driving suits, and other gadgetry were offered for sale but the idea persisted that there was a more practical solution. The comfort formula came from France where

The Leesdorfer Automobilfabrik manufactured a little known marque of the same name utilizing some features of the French De Dietrich vehicles from about 1897 for several years. The 1898 Grand Duke "Tourenwagen" illustrated featured full-elliptic leaf springs all around, wheel steering, front engine with two cylinders developing 9 horsepower, and core radiator mounted high in front. Four passengers were accommodated. (*Austrian Automobile, Motorcycle & Touring Clubs; photo by Author*)

Louis Renault tinkered in a tiny workshop on his wealthy father's estate in Billancourt, a Paris suburb. In 1898, Louis, just 21, bought a ¾-HP DeDion three-wheeler and rebuilt it into a four-wheel vehicle. Soon Louis Renault was amazing his father, and his father's more progressively minded friends with the prototype Renault car which efficiently climbed hills, where other cars stalled, and sped along reliably at 30 MPH without clanking chains or flapping belts. The lad who had baffled his father, school teachers and the truant officer was a born engineer.

This first Renault had its engine in the front, a lesson probably learned from the Panhard & Levassor. Power was transmitted through a cone clutch and a 3-speed plus reverse gearbox. Top gear was a direct drive to the rear axle via a propeller shaft—a Re-

72

As English motorists approached the 20th Century, the Daimlers built in Britain were perhaps the dominant marque; they had achieved the stamp of Royal approval. Six passengers were carried in this leather-topped model, the four in the rear entering by a tailgate and seated laterally. (*Daimler Motor Co., Coventry*)

nault first—which terminated in a differential with bevel gears. At a Christmas party in 1898, an old friend of his father bought Louis's little car and other friends ordered a total of a dozen. Suddenly, Louis Renault was in business and his older brothers, Marcel and Fernand, joined him in founding Renault Frères with capital of 60,000 gold francs in February, 1899. Louis's remarkable inventions were patented immediately. They set the pattern for other well-established marques. Before the summer was over, some sixty open Renaults were sold, all DeDion-powered. Except for the engine, Renaults were like no other cars.

The Renault received no gold medal in the 1900 Paris World Exposition but the brothers did show the world's first, glass-enclosed, two-passenger coupé. A curious little affair as high as it was long—to ac-

73

One of the first creations of Louis Renault was this 1898 model powered by a 1-cylinder, 3–4 horsepower De Dion-Bouton engine. The entire weight of the unladen car was a mere 800 pounds. (*Renault, Inc.*)

The 1900 Renault closed coupé, the world's first completely glass-enclosed gasoline-powered automobile. (*Renault, Inc.*)

Maurice Chevalier and a motion picture starlet in one of the first 1898 Renaults during a celebration on the Champs Elysees several years ago. (*Renault, Inc.*)

The 1900 fully-enclosed Renault coupé was made for the comfort of the high-hatted elite. In con-trast is the modern "4-CV," dwarfed beside its ancestor. (*Renault, Inc.*)

commodate top hats—the Renault coupé was the solution to comfortable driving in bad weather, and the automotive world took note and followed the lead. The all-weather car had arrived—and from one of the youngest manufacturers.

Part III

THE STEAMERS FLASH TO A GOLDEN AGE

As the Electrics Flicker Brightly, and Then Grow Dim

THE LOCOMOBILE PEOPLE had moved from Newton, Massachusetts, to Bridgeport, Connecticut, very early in 1900 where they increased production of their 1899–1900 model. The Stanley twins soon wished they had not sold out. Their photographic plate business was gone and automobiles were by now so thoroughly in their blood that even their violin making sideline could not assuage the anguish they felt when steam cars started selling like hotcakes.

Their original steamer, now a Locomobile, was being copied left and right, and most of them ran like sewing machines. In fact, word drifted to their ears that out in Cleveland, Ohio, the White Sewing Machine Company was going to bring out a steam car shortly. The Stanleys had only a brief wait.

In 1901, the White Steamer was on the market—and the resemblance to the brisk selling '98 and '99 Stanley models was startling. What's more—Grout, Henrietta, Houghton, Keene, Kraft, New England, Milwaukee, Mobile, Squire and other makes —were so much like the Locomobile that it was more than the twins could bear. So they hired some help, and late in 1901 were back in business in Newton turning out Stanley Steamers faster than before.

At about this time, the White Steamer was using an improved flash boiler invented by Rollin White late in 1899. The White was able to get up steam in about half the 15 to 20 minutes required by the Stanley; but the Stanleys, never ones to fiddle around, made several improvements and, relying on their established reputation, proceeded to outsell the White within a year after re-entering the game.

Naturally, the Locomobile management hauled the Stanleys into court to face a new kind of music for the twins—infringing on their original patents which Locomobile had purchased. But the twins were sharp—they got out of trouble quite easily. Rather than fighting in court, they switched. In the original Stanley—and in the proliferating copies —the engines were under the seat and drove the rear axle by chain and sprockets. The Stanleys moved the engine back and geared it directly to the rear axle.

The changed location of the engine eliminated some power loss, brought the noise level even lower, and made a better steamer

The 1899 Locomobile Steamer was produced in 1900–01 without change and was virtually identical to the Stanley Steamer. Three levers operated the vehicle: throttle lever admitted steam into the two cylinders, the degree of speed depending upon how far lever was moved; second lever reversed direction of motor; third lever controlled the water supply to the boiler. The car weighed approximately 660 pounds and cost $1,200. Bothwell Collection. (*Photo by Author*)

than they'd had before—better than the several dozen makes with which their new 1901 Stanley was competing.

It would seem that everybody with any sort of shop simultaneously decided to build a steam car. Out in Ann Arbor, even a student at the University of Michigan, Howard Coffin, made his own steam carriage, and it was as good as most of the "store-bought" ones—looked about like them, too.

In all fairness, some of the competing steamers had different features. The Geneva, for example, was powered by a small marine-type, 2-cylinder engine and developed 6 HP. The throttle and reverse levers were combined and were located, along with the steering post, in the center allowing either passenger to drive. The Stanley and most others had the operating controls at the right side of the seat. The Locomobile had a hinged lever on top of the far right steering column. Mobile, the White "Stanhope" and a few others employed a centrally mounted steering tiller which allowed either occupant to steer, but the boiler burner and the other controls were at the right for the driver only.

While the Locomobile people in Bridgeport were indulging in a management fight, most of the other steam car makers indulged themselves by quietly adopting the patented Locomobile chain drive system. Most of Locomobile's competitors modified the chain drive in slight details in order to have a potential defense should Locomobile send a summons.

As things developed, the troubles at Locomobile became so critical that promotion of the product became secondary to the game of management musical chairs. Locomobiles

The Mobile Steamer was another copy of the Stanley. The owner of this well preserved model is E. H. Taliaferro of San Diego; here the Mobile emits a cloud of spent steam. (*Photo by John E. Hallberg*)

An open sprocket on the differential supplied the final drive of the Mobile Steamer; note the yoke on rear axle which took the place of the later differential cages with shaft drive. Variations of the same system were used on most of the other domestic steam cars like the Geneva and Locomobile. (*Photo by John E. Hallberg*)

weren't selling well because the Stanleys and others were beating them to the customers, and this made the corporate struggle all the worse.

By 1903, the Stanley was the best selling steamer in the U.S.A., and the brothers, shrewd as always, offered financial assistance to Locomobile in the form of an offer to buy back all their original patents for a dime on the dollar. Locomobile management fi-

nally agreed on something and accepted the Stanleys' offer.

In 1904, the Locomobile Steamer vanished from the market, a casualty of bad judgement by management more than of any other single factor. Locomobile switched to gasoline rather than fight the other steamers.

This was a notable year for another reason —a few engineers were building experi-

82

1901 White "Stanhope" cost $1,000 and had 10-horsepower, 2-cylinder engine. Boiler was heated by gasoline from 8-gallon tank under footboard. Hand-pumped air pressure forced gas through vaporizer to burner. Advertised as "The Incomparable White," car was stiff competition for Stanley. (*Henry Ford Museum*)

mental automobiles in Japan and one of the first cars there was a steamer. A Mr. Torao Yamaba built the car shown in the very rare photograph reproduced here, a chain-drive machine with a 2-cylinder, 25-HP, condensing-type steam engine. The Yamaba family was large so this automobile was 15 feet long, 4½ feet wide, and could seat ten people. Yamaba equipped this extremely early Japanese car with wire wheels and solid rubber tires. Little, unfortunately, is known about the Yamaba Steamer's performance or whether more were built.

In 1906, Grout stopped production after selling about 3,000 fairly good steamers. So the Stanleys had things pretty much their own way until 1906, even exporting a number of cars to Canada and England. Then

White ran advertisements in the papers and began to cut a larger piece of the sales pie. Rollin White had hit the market with a condenser that gave his cars four times the range of the Stanley and the lesser competitors. The White condenser, adopted from the French-built Serpolet, saved the exhausted steam and routed the water back to the boiler so it was used over and over again rather than wasted. White relocated the engine beneath the hood and, with the condenser looking like a radiator, the White looked like a gasoline car. By this time, gasoline cars were becoming more refined and less offensive; they looked better and were selling well.

Instead of installing condensers—as they finally did in 1914—the Stanley brothers re-

1902–03 Stanley Steamer had 8-horsepower, double-acting, 2-cylinder engine. Without the folding top, price was $725, a fine value in its day. By this date, Stanley engines were in unit with rear axle which eliminated chain drive, improved performance, decreased maintenance. (*Henry Ford Museum*)

One of the first Japanese automobiles—possibly the very first—was this large 10-passenger steam car built by Torao Yamaba. The 2-cylinder engine developed 25 horsepower. The entire Yamaba family turned out for this photograph. (*Japan Automobile Industrial Association*)

sorted to a familiar course of action: they made some sensational news! They stuffed a 2-cylinder engine with a bore of 4½ inches and a stroke of 6½ inches, making a displacement of 263.25 cubic inches (roughly five times that of their standard engine), into a specially built Stanley racer.

The brothers Stanley then hired Fred Marriott, a famous driver, and headed for Daytona Beach. On January 26, 1906, Marriott flashed the Stanley's boiler up and sizzled across the smooth Daytona sand at a timed 127.659 MPH to set a new world's record!

There wasn't an airplane or any other man-carrying object that could come close to that mark.

The speed record helped, but not enough and by 1907 the White was giving the Stanley a bad time where it counted—in the salesrooms. People liked steam cars, but they also liked gasoline cars—they looked better for one thing. Moreover, any gas car, and the White Steamer, could pass up several filling stations. The Stanley always seemed too thirsty. Other than White or Stanley models, there weren't many available steamers anymore, either.

The Stanley solution to the continuing sales problem in 1907? Rap out another

The 1907 White Model G steam tourer had a two-stage, compound, double-acting engine mounted beneath floor boards between chassis side rails. The gasoline tank was in the rear. On a wheelbase of 116 inches, this steamer originally belonged to a Mrs. Domouriez of Paris; cost new was $3,700. (*Henry Ford Museum*)

The final changes in the White steam cars were made on this 1909 Model "00" which had a now-compact overall length of 149½ inches. The price new for this car which had the lines of a gasoline engined car was $2,000, comparatively reasonable but not low enough to stave off failure. (*Thompson Auto Museum*)

The coffin-nosed Stanley Steamer of 1910 cost $850 as a two-seat runabout; the tonneau seat shown cost extra. Painted red with black and gold pin striping, it had undeniable advantages over some of the gasoline cars of the time: it was quiet, had smooth torque and good acceleration, vibration was almost non-existent because there were no gears or clutch, and it emitted no obnoxious odors. (*Henry Ford Museum*)

record—and they did. Along with driver Marriott, the twins hustled back to Daytona and Marriott put his foot through the Special's floor. He drove that Stanley Special 197 miles per hour!

Still gaining speed, Marriott would have passed the 200 MPH mark easily if the steamer had stayed on the ground. It became air-borne because of speed and the flat bottom, took off, flipped, and was totally destroyed. Marriott recovered but not until after a long stay in a hospital.

The records disclose that the 197 MPH Stanley was carrying boiler pressure of 1,200 pounds per square inch. Though rated a mere 30 HP that steamer had covered the ground at a rate beyond the capability of all but a few specials even today.

White brought out a more popularly priced model, the "00," in 1909. This excellent type was the last of the line and future White cars were gasoline-powered. The White Steamer could, in all probability, have outlasted the Stanley for by this date the White had a two-stage, double-acting compound engine of excellent design.

Compound steam engines, later brought to a high point of efficiency by Doble, have a double set of cylinders, one set with a smaller bore than the other. Initial admission of steam is into the larger cylinder but the exhausted steam, instead of returning to the condenser immediately, is then admitted to the smaller cylinder where, even at reduced temperature, it exerts nearly as much thrust as it did in the big bore because of acting on a smaller piston area. The stroke is the same in each set of bores.

Thus, while Stanley stuck to the relatively simple but considerably less efficient two cylinders, the rest of the steam field nearly ran away with the ball, and Stanley, though

87

remaining the only important steam car maker, quickly started to lose ground to gasoline cars which were taking the country by storm after a bad first decade.

Stanley had had the coffin-nose styling for several years and, despite decreased sales, was not going to change it. The high mark for their cut of the market was 1910. Their entry that year was a 4–5 seater with a runabout body, boiler beneath the hood, no condenser, and engine still bolted to the rear axle. The Stanleys held the runabout's price to a very competitive $850.

A glance at the accompanying roster of steam cars shows that all the significant competition had fallen by the wayside. The Stanleys now had the steam car field to themselves, nor would any effective competitor challenge them. Only a handful of these steam cars achieved success, and that was fleeting. The exceptions were Stanley, Lane, and White in that order.

ROSTER OF AMERICAN STEAM CARS *

Coats 1921–22	Johnson 1905–08	Puritan 1902 only
Coffin 1901 (Exp.)	Keene 1900–01	Randall 1905 only
Cunningham 1900–07	Kellogg 1903 only	Reading 1900–02
Delling 1924–27	Kensington 1899–1903	Remal-Vincent 1923 (only)
Detrick 1957 (Exp.)	Keystone 1909 only	Riley & Cowley 1902 only
Detroit 1922	Kraft 1901 only	Rochester 1901 only
Doble 1921–32	Lane 1899–1910	Rogers 1899 only
Dodge 1913–24	Larchmont 1900 only	Roper 1864–70
Eclipse 1901–02	Locomobile 1899–1904	Ross 1905–09
Electronomic 1901 only	Lozier 1901–02	Scott-Newcomb 1901 only
Elite 1901 only	Lutz 1917 only	Skene 1900 only
Endurance 1922–23	MacDonald 1923 only	Spencer 1901 only
Essex 1906–08	Malden 1914 only	Squire 1899–?
Federal 1905–?	Marlboro 1900–02	Stammobile 1905 only
Foster 1898–1904-or–05	Mason 1898–?	Standard 1900 only
Gaeth 1902–06	McKay 1900–02	Stanley 1896–1925
Gearless 1920 only	Meteor 1902–08	Steamobile 1901–02
Geneva 1901–09	Milwaukee 1900–02	Stearns 1898 only
Grout 1899–1906	Mobile 1899–1902	Stringer 1901 only
Hartley 1898–?	New England 1899–1900	Taunton 1901–04
Henrietta 1901 only	Olds 1886 †	Toledo 1900–03
Hess 1902–03	Ormond 1904–05	Trinity 1900 only
Hoffman 1902 only	Overman 1899–1900	Victor 1900–02
Houghton 1900 only	Pawtucker 1901–02	White 1900–09
House 1901–10	Philion 1892 (Exp.)	Whitney 1899–?
Hudson 1901 only	Porter 1899–1900	
Jaxon 1903 only	Prescott 1900–05	

Doubtless, there were other steam cars, which makers intended, or tried, to market commercially. However, those listed have more substantial records. Some of the lesser known makes were very few in number.

† One only, a 3-wheeler; rebuilt in 1893 as 4-wheeler and exported on order to Bombay, India. First exported American automobile.

The 1923–24 Stanley Steamer had the appearance of a gasoline car until the hood was raised. The massive boiler with its feed valves and burner took more space than a gasoline engine. This model was the last true Stanley. (*Photo by John E. Hallberg*)

The Lane, built in Poughkeepsie, New York, got off to a slow start in 1899 and lasted one year more than White. A quality car priced at a basic $1,500 for the final 1910 model, the Lane used a relatively simple 2-cylinder, double-acting engine as did the Stanley. The Lane, however, employed a condenser mounted in front like a radiator. Styling was comparable to the gasoline cars of the period including full-length running boards, attractive tool chests, and well-fitted interiors, although not as lavish as the much more expensive White. Another victim of the steamers' slow warm-up time, Lane was marketed in rather limited quantities primarily in the East.

Finally, by 1914, the Stanleys realized that a condenser was the obvious solution to public reaction against the too frequent stops for water. The additional steam and water lines leaked badly at first, but worse, the modified boilers leaked due to engine lubricating oil leaking into the tube joints. This oil solidified in the tubes and caused formations of carbon to accumulate that seriously affected heating efficiency. The Stanleys never licked this problem although they tried many types of filters. Gradually they were losing out but the Massachusetts brothers refused to give up as dozens of steam car makers had been forced to do.

The Stanleys eventually turned out some better styled models as the First World War came along. Getting rid of the famed coffin nose by 1918, the Stanley car had taken on the appearance of its gasoline powered competitors. By 1923, the twins finally realized they were in serious trouble and built their last steamer, the Model 740. Then a new name came into a short-lived existence, the Delling Company, and the Stanley twins again sold out. Delling, without any changes, produced the 1924 Stanley steamer and then closed out the line in 1925 with the "750" and "252" models. These still took up to 20 minutes to get up operating steam.

Delling unsuccessfully tried to market a much improved car under their own name until 1927, but despite excellent styling and a 3-cylinder, double-acting engine, it was too little and too late. The Delling could, however, develop 62 HP and travel some 250 miles non-stop due to the large 22-gallon fuel tank and an equally large water tank. The Delling also had 4-wheel Lockheed hydraulic brakes ('25) and, for a large comfortable car with a 132-inch wheelbase, was a comparatively good buy at prices from $2,500 to $3,200. The boiler had no welded seams and was guaranteed not to explode—something Stanleys were unfairly blamed for.

The Delling had styling equal to that of its gasoline contemporaries and the interiors were almost elegant. The boiler and engine were hidden beneath a long hood nosed off by an attractive shell around the condenser. An improved flash boiler allowed operation one minute after turning up the burner, and a small pilot flame prevented freezing in winter. This final 1927 Delling had the then new Ross cam and lever steering, a heater, a choice of disc or spoke wheels, and custom-built aluminum bodies.

Dellings were so rare that photographs of them are virtually non-existent. One of the very best, the Delling failed primarily because of lack of financial resources. Also the times dictated a jump-in-and-go time of considerably less than the '27 Delling's.

The finest of all the steamers, and a classic in its own right, was the magnificent Doble. Built to the most exacting standards of the time, this $10,000-and-up beauty was for the person of means who could afford the best and knew it when he saw it. Emeryville, California, an enclave in Oakland, was Doble's home base. In his fastidiously run plant, Adam Doble turned out just forty cars between 1921 and 1932. Doble's engine had 4 cylinders cast in pairs and was of the compound type with two high-pressure and two low-pressure bores of 4.5 and 2.67 inches respectively. The stroke was 5.00 inches. The engine was integral with the rear axle and the crankshaft geared directly to it. The huge boiler had 575.75 feet of cold-drawn seamless steel tubing that, when coiled and installed, had a diameter of 22 inches and a height of 13 inches. Doble tested his boilers to 7,000 psi. Beneath the toe boards on the right side was the auxiliary unit which incorporated the water and oil pumps, vacuum pump, the Bosch electric generator, the air pump for the fuel pressure, and the speedometer drive.

The Doble's condenser was a standard type radiator through which cool air was drawn by a 24-inch-diameter fan that turned 3,200 rpm at 60 miles an hour. At this speed the mighty car was merely loafing. The chassis alone weighed a bit over 3,000 pounds and, when the custom coachwork was added, the road weight was upwards of 4,000 pounds. Some fine Doble limousines are said to have weighed as much as 5,000 pounds dry. At 750 pounds steam pressure and a temperature of 750 degrees F., the Doble cruised effortlessly at 75 MPH. Maximum speeds exceeded 100 MPH by a comfortable margin and getting under way after a cold start usually took less than 30 seconds. Frank Thomas, a well-known steam car engineer in the '30s, recalls

Queen of the steamers was the Doble; this 1923 phaeton weighed more than 5,000 pounds but achieved 100 miles per hour with ease. (*Henry Ford Museum*)

Massive frontal design distinguished the great Doble Steamer. This is the 1930–31 model which often appears at steam gatherings. (*Photo by Author*)

The engines of the Doble Steamers occupied the space between the longitudinal frame members beneath the floor of the rear passenger compart-ment. The floor was flat in front and rear; there was no propeller shaft for the engine was built integrally with the rear axle. (*Photo by Author*)

driving Dobles that could get under way in as little as 15 seconds from cold.

Doble, a perfectionist, insisted on excellent roadability and good braking. He made the brake drums of 50-point carbon steel. They were 16 inches in diameter and 5 inches wide, and were externally reinforced by fins which also aided cooling. The shoes were aluminum for lightness and to dissipate heat; the highest priced lining material available was ground to a precise fit with the drum after assembly of the shoes. Chrome vanadium steel was used for the rear axle shafts. The steering was worm and wheel and, despite a standard wheelbase of 142 inches and a tread of 57, this huge car turned in a circle of just 42 feet diameter.

The steering wheel, like the car's other finely executed details, had a cast and polished German silver spider with a rim of hand-rubbed African ebony.

If there was ever a near perfect steam car, the Doble was that car. Doble's warranty was for 100,000 miles.

The crash of '29 pulled down many of this country's fine cars and Doble was forced in 1932 to cease production of one of the finest of any type. Doble, however, licensed the Henschel Acktiengesellschaft in Germany during the early '30s. Henschel, later to become great in World War II as an aircraft and engine producer, adapted the Doble engines, in varying horsepowers of 120 to 200, to a new line of heavy-duty

Although of massive dimension, Doble Steamers had excellent lines. This is the 1930–31 phaeton; each car was custom built to order. (*Photo by Author*)

trucks and busses. These Doble-powered vehicles were produced in the early years of the war and did yeoman service. The Sentinel Steam Vehicle Company of Great Britain also used some of the Doble's features in trucks that made a great reputation for themselves in such difficult places as the jungles of Burma.

So many references to the various types of generators, or boilers, for steam cars requires an explanation of the characteristics of the three principal boiler types.

Flash boiler (Doble): very rapid heat exchange was possible by exposing to heat small amounts of water distributed over a large area. Doble had 575.75 feet of tubing. An extremely long steel tube was coiled so that flame played over the entire tube. The Doble could move off from a cold start in 15 seconds and after 80 seconds could maintain a continuous 60 MPH. Pressures exceeded 500 psi.

Water tube boiler (Stanley, Mobile, Locomobile): separate, short lengths of tubes were connected at the feed water end and at the opposite end by the header tank. The water capacity was greater because the tubes were of considerably greater diameter. The disadvantage was that flame played over only the lower tubes (if horizontal) and/or lower ends of a vertical boiler. Thus, it took much longer to get up steam. Even the last Stanleys (1924) took upward of 12 minutes to get up sufficient steam pressure to cope with traffic. Pressures were generally 250 to 400 psi.

93

A set of top quality tools was standard equipment with every Doble; they were concealed in a panel on the left front door. (*Photo by Author*)

Water level boiler (mostly used by home built types and specials): a simple tank was used as the boiler with flame at the bottom. The only advantage was a greater water capacity. The disadvantage: upward of 50 minutes to get up steam for adequate speeds. The pressure was usually 250 psi.

The end, though, is not yet, for the fans across the country will keep their steamers going for many years. In Newton, Massachusetts, the home of the Stanley Steamers, the American Steam Automobile Company is reportedly still able to supply some parts from the factory which, as late as 1942, was

William J. Besler (left), owner of the magnificent 1930–31 Doble, and Bernard Becker, steam car authority, with their favorite marque. (*Photo by Author*)

able to accept orders for complete steam cars before wartime restrictions prevented it. The last engine development from this firm was a single-acting V-4 engine which was used in a number of wartime civilian conversions, the engine being mounted under the hood with the fuel oil or coal-fired boilers in the trunk.

Bernard Becker studies the full facia of instruments in the 1930–31 Doble. In addition to the usual performance gauges, steam cars had pressure, water temperature, water level, fuel level, and other gauges. (*Photo by Author*)

The old Doble factory in Emeryville, California, is now called The Bessler Company and they're supposed to be tinkering with some ultra-modern steam car ideas not yet ready for airing.

The late Forrest R. Detrick, an attorney, long-time steam car expert William Mehrling, and steam engineer Lee Gaeke were preparing some years ago to market, on order, engines and parts for enthusiasts. The unfortunate death of Detrick apparently ended this project.

The electric cars as opposed to the steamers were never spectacular. Suitable for short ranges only, they were popular with some professional people and with the ladies. They lacked the rough-and-tumble excitement of the gas or steam cars. They were made-to-order for the city-bred when the automobile was, to some, a frightening contraption.

The history of American electric cars requires a brief mention of Seldon, for he began licensing car manufacturers in 1903

Warranty

NUMBER OF CHASSIS

NAME OF OWNER

DATE OF DELIVERY

TO THE OWNER ABOVE NAMED:

This is to certify that we, Doble Steam Motors, warrant the steam generator unit of the above chassis, including tubing and firebox, for 100,000 miles, and the balance of said chassis, with the exception of standard equipment manufactured by others, for three years from the above delivery date.

Under the terms of this warranty, we will replace or repair, as we deem advisable, without charge to you, any portion of the steam generator unit which develops any fault during the first 100,000 miles of service, unless the cause thereof is due to accident or to change by you, without our consent, of the automatic pressure and temperature regulators.

Likewise, we will replace or repair, as we deem advisable, without charge to you, any other part of the above chassis which, within three years, develops any fault other than by dirt, misuse, neglect or accident.

This warranty shall not be binding upon us,

1.   Unless immediately upon the discovery of any fault, you shall forthwith communicate the facts to us at Emeryville, California, or at any factory branch or agency from which the car was purchased, giving the above chassis number.

2.   Unless the chassis shall be delivered to us at our factory or at any factory branch or agency or the defective part shipped, charges prepaid, to the factory at Emeryville, California.

3.   If the automatic pressure or temperature regulator adjustments are altered by you without our written consent, or if the chassis is driven when the power gauge indicates a continuous operating pressure in excess of 900 pounds or continuous operating temperature in excess of 900 degrees Fahrenheit.

4.   If the chassis is equipped with any special body which shall make the total weight of body and chassis in excess of 5,000 pounds.

5.   If the chassis or any portion thereof has been altered by any person outside our employ, in any way so as, in our judgment, to affect its stability, or reliability.

This warranty runs only to the owner above named as long as the above chassis has been continuously and is still owned by said owner and is expressly in lieu of all other warranties, express or implied, and of all other obligations and liabilities on our part, and we neither assume nor authorize any other person to assume for us, any other liability in connection with the sale of our chassis.

If there shall be a difference of opinion between you and us as to whether the fault is covered by the terms of this warranty, the difference shall be referred to arbitration.

This warranty does not apply to bodies, electrical equipment, tires or equipment not manufactured by us.

Dated this   day of   , 192

DOBLE STEAM MOTORS.

By

Doble cars were covered with a warranty rivalled only by the Rolls-Royce; the steam generator was guaranteed for 100,000 miles while the rest of the chassis was covered for three years. Dobles were made in Emeryville, California. (*Photo by Author*)

The two-seater Baker electric car of 1902 had a wheelbase of just 63 inches and, unusual for its time regardless of motive power, featured a shaft drive. Bakers were built in Cleveland. (*Henry Ford Museum*)

when he formed the Association of Licensed Automobile Manufacturers. One of the first outfits to sign up with Seldon was the Electric Vehicle Company of Hartford, Connecticut, which had been manufacturing the Columbia Electric cars since 1898. Columbia cars were among the first of the electrics to use a driveshaft instead of a chain drive.

Some automobile pioneers hold that the early success of electric cars was largely due to the advantages of the driveshaft and the smoother ride that resulted. Clanking chain drives on almost all of the gas and steam cars alienated many people, especially those in cities.

The traction railroads which had spread like wildfire by 1900 gave tremendous impetus to electric motors, whereas the gasoline engine was still somewhat primitive by comparison. Electrical repair shops were everywhere. There was, therefore, a fairly widespread network of "service stations" where owners of the new electric cars could have repairs made. Parts either were readily available for electric motors of all types or were made in these numerous shops. Wet batteries were fairly well understood by many people, and as a consequence the market for electric cars was already there at the turn of the century. Columbia celebrated the new century by tossing the tiller overboard in 1901 and adopting the steering wheel, the first electric to do so.

The Riker Motor Vehicle Company of Elizabethport, New Jersey, introduced a three-wheeler in 1898. The motor powered

Waverly electric cars were among the finest. Built in Indianapolis from 1898 to 1916, they were quality vehicles. This tiller-steered, 1904, family-size model had two motors, a wheelbase of 77 inches, and electric brakes which required only a light touch. (*Henry Ford Museum*)

the single rear wheel. Riker also went into the commercial vehicle business the same year with trucks and vans and in 1900 began building large hansom cabs that seated four persons in closed coach-style bodies. The windows could be opened. Driver and footman sat high aft where they drove by tiller and levers. Tubular frames were used in the early Rikers—and other electrics too—as were various combinations of transverse and longitudinal semi-elliptic and elliptic springs. The Electric Vehicle Company supplied many of the other builders with motors and Wagner Electric Company of St. Louis, Missouri, marketed motor generators used by repair shops, and many private owners, to recharge the batteries of electric cars. Weston, still in business, manufactured circuit breakers, ammeters, voltmeters, rheostats, switches, and other parts.

Completely closed electrics preceded closed gas cars in the U.S.A. by at least four years, another factor enabling the latter to gain early acceptance.

The early Columbias were very light in weight giving them longer range than most others. The motors were geared to the axles with ratios often as favorable as 10 to 1.

Three persons, one sitting with his back to the windshield, were accommodated in plush luxury in the 1906 Waverly Brougham, one of the most comfortable of all the electric cars. (*Photo by Author*)

Detroit Electric cars were built from 1907 to 1923 by the Anderson Electric Company; parts and service continued to be available until about 1938 The 1910 Model "D" shown was owned by Mrs. Vanderbilt. Note the wrap-around windshield and the generous headroom and road clearance. (*Automobile Manufacturers Association*)

One 2-seat runabout built in 1903 was used until 1931 in daily service by a physician in Washington, D. C. Displayed in the National Museum, this car had a frame of oak sills reinforced by angle irons. The roller bearing rear axle was chain-driven by a single 6-pole motor made by General Electric (probably a replacement) rated at 30 amperes at 40 volts. The motor was mounted inside the body beneath the seat—increasing motor life—instead of on the rear axle or in front of it as was the case with many Columbias and other makes. This car's styling was similar to the '02 Baker illustrated here.

The encouraging prospects of electric cars prompted General Electric to look into the matter. G. E. imported a DeDion gasoline engine from France and experimented with it as a generator to supply power to electric

Another finely hand-built luxury electric car was the 1910 Baker. The body was entirely of wood, framing, sheathing and all, and was highly finished. Note the monogram on the door. Upholstery was usually red velvet unless customer specified otherwise. Luggage was placed beneath the front deck, tools were carried in the rear. Note the shaft drive and the low-hanging steering rod. Price new was $2,600. Bakers were built from 1899 to 1916. (*Henry Ford Museum*)

In 1927, Fiat of Italy experimented extensively with an electric car of conventional appearance in which the current was generated by a small-displacement, gasoline engine beneath the front hood. The batteries were housed low behind the rear axle and beneath the rear deck, the electric engine between the frame rails below the front compartment floorboards. The speed control, a rheostat, was on the right hand door adjacent to the steering wheel. The Fiat is reported to have been a good performing car but limited by the usual battery current life to short range trips. (*British Crown Copyright, Science Museum, London*)

motors driving rear wheels. Had G. E. pursued the project, electric cars might have survived their adolescence. By 1906, however, G. E. had shelved the idea—this was four years after Porsche's Lohner Mixt car in Austria had proven a great success.

The early electrics changed over to left-hand controls before the gas or steam cars did. Columbia's light vehicles, for example, often had the control handle moving forward and back in a rack with two slots with an offset connecting the slots. The forward slot gave from three to five or more forward speeds and the rear slot anywhere from one to three reverse speeds. The first speed was obtained from the two sets of batteries arranged in parallel and connecting them in series, through a resistor, with the motor. For second speed, the two sets of batteries were used without the current going through the resistor while third speed was derived from the two battery sets acting directly in series. Changing the polarity of the motor, or motors, provided direction reverse. A mass of cables emanated from the bottom end of the controller, sometimes as many as eight or nine separate cables being used.

Though most electric cars were built elsewhere, the Detroit Electric Company's lovely, silent cars were favored by many women by 1910. This firm continued to offer electrics into the early '30s.

A home-made, 2-cylinder, double-acting steam engine based upon the Stanley designs. The dog in front of the gear (center right) disengages the gear to allow the final drive to free-wheel, thus allowing a car so powered to be coasted or towed if need be. This would have been an advantage in the old Stanley engines which allowed neither emergency measure. (*Photo by John E. Hallberg*)

Kerosene, carbide or electric lights operating off the car's batteries were commonplace by 1901–02. Urban dwellers preferred electric lights while those in isolated areas generally preferred the non-electric lamps for the sake of battery life.

The Buffalo, made in Buffalo, N. Y., was one of the earliest to offer foot control of the motor, an "exclusive" no other electric had as late as 1913. Buffalo advertising described it as follows:

"The action of walking is so natural you never give a thought to how it is done, although, to start, you raise one foot—to stop, you place both feet on the ground. Just as simply and unconsciously the owner of a Buffalo Electric controls the starting, stopping and speed of his car—all by the foot

This modern V-4 steam engine is now under development on the West Coast. (*Photo by John E. Hallberg*)

control—an exclusive Buffalo Electric feature."

The Buffalo Electric driver would start out by raising or releasing the foot pedal which automatically released the expanding shoe brakes and the car then started forward, the speed being determined by the amount the driver released the pedal or allowed it to rise. This system was even simpler than that employed on two modern experimental electric cars in 1959. The Buffalo had a single pedal that did everything. The '59 Stinson and Nic-L-Silver electrics had both a foot speed-controlling pedal, or accelerator, and a brake pedal like modern gasoline cars.

The claims of the Buffalo are open to question though, because the Argo, made in Saginaw, Michigan, in 1912, also had a foot control that applied the brakes when depressed. When raised, the pedal activated any of six forward speeds. The Argo advertised a second foot pedal, however, which operated brakes "on the axle and not the motor." The designers gave their product another enticing feature—the front end looked like that of the popular air-cooled Franklin gasoline cars. Slung lower than most gaso-

line cars, Argo also had a longer wheelbase, 110 inches, said to give it "a long look."

Advertised as "luxurious" because "dollars do not count—under these conditions," the Broc offered five-passenger broughams with a choice of either wheel or lever steering and either "pedestal or stationary front seats" because this was a "rear-drive model."

And then there was the rare Borland made in Chicago on Michigan Avenue. Borland buyers were assured such economical and trouble-free driving that "men as well as women, in ever increasing numbers, are making it their choice." A 1913 Borland

Four steamers during a gathering of enthusiasts. Left to right: a home-built model, 1914 Stanley, 1912 Stanley, and a 1900 Mobile. (*Photo by John E. Hallberg*)

roadster or a luxury brougham cost $2,550, while the "Outside Drive Limousine, The Electric De Luxe" cost $5,500. The bodies were aluminum, front seats were of the "revolving" type, and the Exide 40-cell batteries gave enough current to attain 22 MPH top speed. Standard equipment included skid chains, hydrometer, odometer, toilet cases and a flower vase. Borland would also supply a color-matched umbrella to go with the upholstery. A fine car in its day, a rare car today.

The ultimate in electric car elegance was the 1914 Rauch and Lang six-passenger Town Car. Large and with a splendidly finished closed passenger saloon interior, this car had a driver's compartment beneath the forward extension of the roof that lacked both windshield and windows, one of the last such to be produced.

The most neglected of car enthusiasts are those devoted to electrics, for there are few battery cars displayed in museums in comparison to steamers or gas cars. Probably the largest number of restored electric cars still in running condition are in the Henry Ford Museum at Dearborn, Michigan. Even the U. S. National Museum has only a handful.

The 1916 Wood Dual Power was another outstanding car. For $2,650 the owner bought two engines, one burning gasoline, the other electricity, either capable of sustaining respectable speeds.

By the end of World War One, electrics were declining in popularity. By 1925, they were rarely seen. Never did they outnumber steamers or threaten the gasoline cars.

Part IV

THE TWENTIETH CENTURY OVERSEAS
The Finest Cars of Twenty-One Nations from 1900 to 1940

BY THE TIME the automobile had huffed and puffed, clanked, whined and clattered its unsteady way through infancy and had established itself as a vehicle to be taken seriously, factories were producing them commercially—although often in very small numbers—in a score of countries.

The historic cars of the major nations are generally well known; invariably they have received the lion's share of attention. This is particularly so in the United States where popular enthusiasm for *antique, veteran, vintage* and *classic* cars (the differentiation often is confusing and rather academic) has been directed toward the automobiles of England, France, Germany and Italy when interest strays outside of our own borders.

It is the purpose of Part IV to give long overdue consideration to the historic automobiles of other nations, too, where automotive history has been colorful and important. Not a few automotive pioneers contended against overwhelming odds in geographical areas isolated from the mainstream of industrial development. To be sure, the finest old cars of the major car-producing nations are present and accounted for. However, the text covering them is deliberately subordinated to permit inclusion of large selections of photographs in each case; text covering these cars is in abundance elsewhere.

Not a few of the cars illustrated herewith —nation by nation—are receiving their first exposure to American enthusiasts in Part IV. Many of the photographs are exceptionally rare; in fact, a number are reproductions of archive photos for which no negatives exist. In several countries, destruction of archives during two world wars spread havoc among the records of early automotive activities. Yugoslavia is one where destruction was so extensive as to make impossible the inclusion of photographs of that country's two marques, the Rosa and the Friese, which were manufactured in relatively small though noteworthy numbers in the years between the two wars. Poland, too, is not represented for similar reasons.

The intent here is to place on view many of the automobiles of the world that have contributed to putting the modern world on wheels. There are omissions, of course. To cover every marque ever built would require a shelf of volumes and these would be incomplete. Nevertheless, it may be that all readers who love cars will meet some new friends in these pages. Some will strain the eyesight; others will strain belief. Yet all are part and parcel of the fascinating evolution of the automobile.

Argentina

As EARLY AS 1907, there were a few small plants in and near Buenos Aires where European cars—mostly French—were assembled. The automobile, however, had achieved comparatively little acceptance because of economic and social conditions. Although industry was beginning to assert itself, there was no effort to produce an Argentine car.

However, in 1911, a young engineer, Horacio Anasagasti, set up a workshop to produce automobiles. Only the vaguest details of the Anasagasti cars—as they were registered—remain to this day. That the frames, semi-elliptic spring suspension systems and coachwork were in line with the current practice in Europe is evident from a handful of ancient newspaper pictures. The entire automobile was built in engineer Anasagasti's works with the exception of the engine and the ignition equipment. The engine was a 4-cylinder Ballot unit, imported from France, which developed approximately 15 HP.

Introduced to the public in 1912, the first Anasagasti cut quite a sight on the streets of Buenos Aires and its inventor was convinced that his car was at least as good as those which were being imported. Thus encouraged, Anasagasti laid down a small series based upon his prototype which was successfully entered in several local races. Within a few months, at least three cars were built. From the sketchy records at hand, two of these were artillery-wheeled, four-passenger tourers like the one illustrated here; the other was a 2-seater roadster with flat-topped fenders, wire wheels and a single spare tire mounted on the running board. The frame of the roadster was a bit longer —at least the dumb irons extended farther to the front.

At any rate, Anasagasti apparently took three of his cars to Europe in 1912 where he proceeded to enter several sporting events for touring cars. The most difficult event was the Tour de France which was over a tough course of about 3,400 miles, much of it in mountainous terrain. The equipo Anasagasti included three 15-HP cars and a trio of drivers—an engineer named Brown, the Marquis D'Avaray and one Repousseau. Finishing well up among the leaders and "without loss of points," the Anasagastis were next entered in a race at San Sebastian, Spain, where they again turned in good performances. The available records, however, fail to state how the trio of Argentine cars were placed at the end of the tussle.

A plaque in Buenos Aires honors pioneer automobilists. Shown is the portion memorializing Horacio Anasagasti who built the first Argentine automobiles. (*Automovil Club Argentino*)

With his cars proven in the heat of competition on the roads of Europe, Sr. Anasagasti returned to Argentina where he built a total of about fifty cars which were priced from 10,000 to 12,000 pesos. There is a possibility that a few of the engines were of Argentine design and manufacture. More likely, however, the Anasagasti works assembled imported engines but there is no certainty on this matter. Unfortunately, Argentina was supplied with more than enough European and American cars to satisfy the limited needs of the country, and most of the Anasagasti cars became taxicabs. Thus, Argentina's first national marque went out of production in 1914 at about the time when proper financial backing could have meant survival and success due to decreased importations from Europe because of war.

Many years passed before the next Argen-

One of the successful Anasagasti tourers of 1912– 14, Argentina's first car. (*David Collins*)

tine marque made a faltering effort to stem the flood of imports. In 1936, the Hafdasa was introduced only to wither quickly after a few found buyers. In 1940, Carlos Ballester Molina, an engineer, succeeded in organizing a new firm, Hispano-Argentina, from which a prototype or two emerged only to meet with apathy on the part of a public conditioned to purchase cars of foreign design.

Only a large plaque set in marble in Buenos Aires, a recent installation, honors Argentina's first native automobile designer and manufacturer, Ing. Horacio Anasagasti.

Australia

THE GENESIS of the automobile in Australia occurred a decade or more before the turn of the century and is covered in Part II. When the twentieth century arrived, the most vigorous Australian car builder was the Tarrant Automobile & Engineering Company in Victoria, New South Wales.

Organized in 1897 by Captain (later Colonel) Harley Tarrant and Howard Lewis (who was a bicycle dealer in Melbourne), the firm also imported and sold European and American marques. The first Tarrant car was chain-driven by a 2-cylinder horizontal engine mounted in the rear and is generally credited with being the first Australian-built gasoline car. During this first Tarrant's test run in 1898 or '99 according to contradictory accounts, it proved difficult to handle and crashed through a brick wall. Whether Tarrant or Lewis was driving is not known, but the car's remains were ignored and the builders returned to begin another car.

The second Tarrant, a lightweight four-seater, was powered by a 2-cylinder Argyle engine imported from Scotland. So as to avoid any public disclaimers, Tarrant and Lewis, like Marcus in Vienna, waited until eleven o'clock one night in 1901 before trying out their second car. The test run proceeded as planned until they started down a long hill where the builders suddenly became aware that something vital was lacking. In their enthusiasm, they had forgotten to equip their mechanical creation with brakes. Details of this 1901 Tarrant gearbox are lacking, but disaster was averted when Tarrant cut off the engine and Lewis hopped off to exert his own strength against gravity. Vehicle and designers, happily, survived the grueling experience without damage. After some necessary changes, this second Tarrant was sold to a hardware store owner in Melbourne, a Mr. Chandler, for the equivalent of around $1,200 and was used for a number of years.

In 1903, a young Australian engineer named William S. Ross returned from England with a 2-cylinder Argyle and joined Tarrant and Lewis. The firm also obtained importing rights for several cars including the Argyle. While in the United Kingdom, Ross had studied many cars and the third Tarrant was vastly improved with a larger Tarrant-made 2-cylinder engine and shaft drive in place of the former sprocket chain. One of these 2-cylinder cars was entered in the cross-country Dunlop Reliability Trial in

W. S. Ross, engineer and automobile pioneer in Australia as he appeared in 1955 at the wheel of a 1905 Tarrant which was built for the police chief of Victoria, New South Wales. (*Wheels Magazine*)

The "double-seated" Grayson of circa-1907 carried at least five persons. Little is known of this early Australian gasoline car (*National Library of Australia*)

1905 where it was pitted against a field of European machines. The Tarrant acquitted itself well by covering 1,276 miles from Melbourne to Sydney, over the Blue Mountains and back again to Melbourne without loss of points.

Late in 1905, a series of 4-cylinder Tarrants was begun. The gearbox had three speeds and the L-head engines were of Tarrant design. Some of the 4-cylinder Tarrants had dual ignition, according to William S. Ross, because "electrical failure was so common." In the 1906 Dunlop 1,000-Mile Victorian Trial, a 4-cylinder Tarrant driven by Sir Russell Grimwade won the large-car class. In appearance, the Tarrant was in conformity with moderately priced cars of the time—not unlike the Ford Model T—as is indicated in the accompanying old photograph taken in the final assembly department in the works. The only surviving Tarrant is known to have covered more than 150,000 miles by 1927 with just two minor engine overhauls.

Manufacturing costs were high in Australia in the early years because many small engine accessory parts, generators and the like had to be imported. Hand-made with a basic hardwood frame, the Tarrant finally went out of production sometime in 1910. Nevertheless, the Tarrant firm continued in the motor car business as distributors of

The final assembly shop of the Tarrant automobile works about 1910 in Australia. (*Automotive News Service and Wheels Magazine*)

DeDion cars and other marques. Tarrant also organized the Ruskin Motor Body Works and was very successful in that endeavor. In 1917, a government decree required that two-thirds of all cars imported must be brought in without bodies. Hence several coachworks sprang up including Holden's Motor Body Builders in Adelaide. Holden's thrived and in 1931 merged with the Australian branch of General Motors; this eventually led to the 1948 introduction of the Holden, an Australian-designed car tailored to the rugged topography of the continent.

More than two dozen home-built marques struggled for recognition in Australia up to 1940. Many were one-offs or prototypes, of course. One of the most likely candidates for success was the attractive Australian Six manufactured from 1918 to 1924 in Sydney by the F. H. Gordon Co. Ltd. Around 700 in all were sold. On a wheelbase of 122 inches, the Australian Six had an interesting double-acting brake system: conventional internal expanding brake shoes were supplemented by external brake shoes which acted upon the outer circumference of the 15-inch drums. Semi-elliptical leaf springs

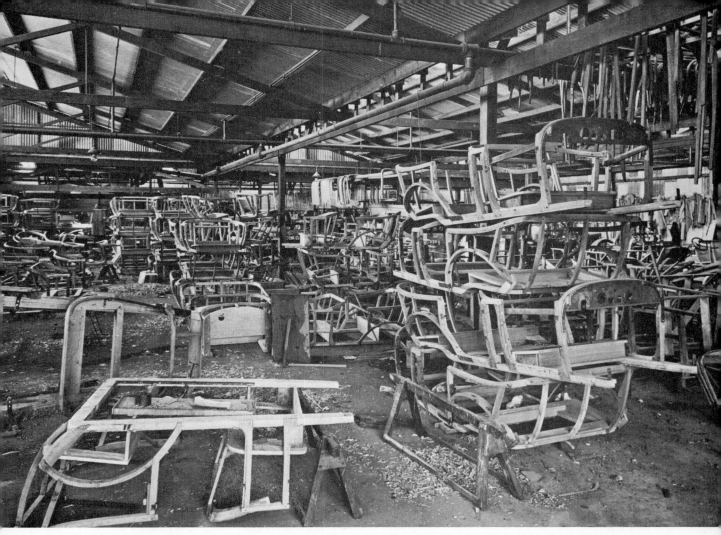

Hardwood frames for automobile bodies in the Holden coachworks in 1918. (*Wheels Magazine*)

were used front and rear. The 6-cylinder, L-head engine had a 3.125-inch bore and a full 5-inch stroke making the displacement 230 cubic inches (3.6 litres). Low-speed torque must have been excellent but durability with just three main bearings sounds questionable. A three-speed gearbox was standard and output of 45 BHP at 2,400 rpm provided fairly good performance. Touring equipment included an engine-driven tire pump and, around 1920, the Australian Six was one of the best sellers in the country.

When Ford, General Motors and a host of English manufacturers established assembly plants in Australia after the 1914–18 war, the outlook for local builders became even more precarious than it was before, when marques like the Grayson, the Campbell in Tasmania in 1901, the 1904 Scarsdale, the 1901–03 Sutton in Victoria, the 1901 Lewis in South Australia, the 1901 Trackson in Queensland and a dozen others were introduced only to disappear quickly for lack of sales. One of the most intriguing was the Haines & Grut of 1904 of which five were built in Victoria. The H. & G. had a 2-cylinder, 10/12-HP, horizontally opposed engine but the means of delivering power

117

The final assembly line of the Holden coachworks in Adelaide, South Australia, in 1920. (*General Motors-Holden's Pty., Ltd. and Wheels Magazine*)

from the 2-speed transmission left something to be desired. The rear axle was divided—not for the usual differential—but because each half axle was fitted with a belt-driven pulley. Depending upon which gear ratio was selected, just one wheel received the power; there was no differential. In 1910, Caldwell Vale trucks achieved some success and an attempt was made to market an advanced four-wheel drive car without success.

Between the wars there was no dearth of popular demand for a home-built car, but there was too little money and only scanty

supporting industry. From 1919 to '25, a fairly fine car was the Lincoln made in New South Wales. Not related to the American marque of the same name, the Lincoln's radiator shell had a Packard look while the engine was a 6-cylinder Continental imported from the U.S.A. The Roo thrived spasmodically from 1921 to 1925 and the Chic from 1925 to 1930 in South Australia.

Two courageous efforts were launched in the '30s. In 1931, Marks Motor Construction Ltd. of Sydney made a valiant attempt to market a truly advanced car. After two years of development, the Southern Cross

From 1918 to 1924, the Australian Six was in regular series production in Sydney. (*Gilltrap's Auto Museum Pty. Ltd.*)

was christened in July, 1933, by Lady Kingsford-Smith, the wife of the famed aviator, Sir Charles. The latter was a member of the firm and success seemed assured. An integrated or "chassis-less" car as it was advertised, the body of the Southern Cross was fabricated by laminating and bonding ten ⅛-inch sheets of alternating pine and walnut. Casein glue was used and the entire lamination was then molded into a one-piece body, after shaping the body contours, by an 80-ton press. Even the bottom of the body was in unit with the sides and top. The resulting body, with walls approximately 1½ inches thick, was immensely strong, and the bottom was perfectly flat and smooth. The *Australian Motorist* of August 1, 1933, stated that the tensile strength was 16 times that of a conventional steel body. Two cross members, made by the same process, formed the firewall and a bulkhead between the front and rear seats and provided additional strength. Suspension units, the engine and transmission were bolted directly to the bottom of the frame-body. The Southern Cross was subjected to the tortures of a 2,000-mile test over the worst trails of New South Wales. At the conclu-

119

sion of the tests, no rattles, cracks or other damages were evident. A 6-cylinder engine not made by the builders was used and during the tests fuel consumption averaged nearly 33 miles per Imperial gallon. Unfortunately, imported cars were so dominant that the Southern Cross never progressed beyond the prototype stage despite good design and widespread publicity.

Other attempts to market an Australian-built car in the '30s included the Hamard and Olympia in 1930 and '31 respectively and the Egan Six. The latter contended against impossible odds for financial support from 1935 to 1940 when the war precluded further efforts. All three were launched in Victoria which offered a comparatively favorable atmosphere for industrial development. Even naming a car for the folk-hero bandit of the "outback," Kelly, could not turn the trick and the Australian automotive industry, which had earlier shown great promise, gave up in the face of European and American manufacturers.

Austria

THE FIRST AUSTRIAN CAR to go into production was the Gräf & Stift. About 1895, the brothers Carl, Heinrich and Franz Gräf allied themselves with Josef Hans Stift to produce automobiles. The four combined engineering, coachbuilding and merchandising talents and introduced their first car in 1897. It is not surprising that the young Ferdinand Porsche was inspired by this first Gräf & Stift, a two-seater bristling with innovations. The nucleus was a single-cylinder, 3.25-HP DeDion engine imported from France, but the outstanding feature was the gearbox fabricated by Heinrich Gräf, the engineer, in unit with the differential which drove the front wheels. A steel frame with half-elliptic springs completed the chassis. Wheel steering with the gear change lever on the column, three foot pedals and rear-wheel brakes were used. One of these early front-wheel-drive cars is preserved in the Technical Museum in Vienna. Hans Ledwinka who later became famous as the designer of the Tatra (see Czechoslovakia), had a hand in the design of this first Gräf & Stift car.

By 1905, Gräf & Stift was well established in a new factory in Weinbergstrasse in Vienna where 18/22-HP, five-passenger open and closed cars were in series production. The "double-phaeton" illustrated was typical. It was powered by a 2.2-litre, 4-cylinder engine with cylinders cast in pairs and the rear wheels were driven by shaft. Progress was rapid and the marque found favor with the royal family; in fact the Archduke Franz Ferdinand was riding in the large 1914 phaeton shown when he was assassinated by the Serbian nationalist, Princip, in Sarajevo on the 28th of June, 1914. This car is preserved in Vienna's Museum of War History.

After the 1914–18 war, small Citroëns were built under license but the upper classes were catered to with several series of luxury cars such as the straight-8-cylinder SP-6 of 1928. Production of large cars ceased in the early '30s and by 1935 Gräf & Stift closed down its assembly lines.

Several other Austrian cars had much shorter lives. The Simmeringer was named for the hill near Vienna and was manufactured in Vienna from 1903 to 1905 by Michael A. Wyner who was inspired by the 1902 Peugeot. The "Wyner Populaire" model was the most noteworthy product of the Simmeringer Waggon-Fabrik. Shaft drive was used with a 3-speed transmission

The Gräf & Stift 3.25-HP voiturette of 1897 had front-wheel-drive. This innovation so impressed the young Ferdinand Porsche that it inspired him to experiment with f.w.d. (*Austrian Automobile, Motorcycle & Touring Clubs*)

The 1905 Gräf & Stift 18/22 HP tourer had a 4-cylinder, 2.2-litre, T-head engine and conventional rear-wheel-drive. (*Austrian Automobile, Motorcycle & Touring Clubs*)

In 1910, the finest Gräf & Stift was the 40/45 HP torpedo. (*Austrian Information Service*)

connected to a 1-cylinder, 9/10-HP DeDion engine by a cone clutch. Weighing a scant 1,100 pounds, closed and open two-seaters had fairly sparkling performance with a maximum speed of a shade over 30 MPH.

Less successful was the 6-HP Celeritas, another Viennese car. Better known than its French counterpart, the Crouan, the Celeritas suffered from technical problems stemming from a complicated 5-speed gearbox. A more powerful version employed a compressed air device which actuated the transmission and this made matters worse. The Perl achieved some success from 1907 onward but is rarely heard of. Production of the Perl was limited during its active years which continued until 1939, while the Avis, an outgrowth of an aircraft firm was produced in small numbers only during the '20s.

The coachbuilder to the royal family, Jacob Lohner, had the greatest potential of all the early car makers in Austria. Lohner's big opportunity came when he hired Ferdinand Porsche, the young electrical wizard. Porsche glowed with ideas and believed that front-wheel drive—as used on the 1897 Gräf & Stift—deserved development. Lohner gave Porsche a free hand to experiment and, as was discussed in Part II, the Lohner-Porsche car with an electric motor in each front wheel hub won the top award for engineering excellence at the Paris Exposition in 1900.

Despite an astronomical price, the electric chaise and open models sold well.

The 1914 Gräf & Stift in which the Archduke Franz Ferdinand von Hapsburg was riding when he was assassinated in Sarajevo, Serbia, on June 28, 1914. (*Museum of War History and Austrian Information Service*)

The large, luxurious Gräf & Stift limousine Type SP-6 of 1928. (*Austrian Information Service*)

The 1904 Simmeringer "Wyner-Populaire" had a 1-cylinder, 9/10-HP De Dion engine, 3-speed gearbox and shaft drive. Weighing only 950 pounds, the speed was about 31 mph. (*Austrian Automobile, Motorcycle & Touring Clubs*)

The 1900 Lohner-Porsche "Elektromobil" was the production version of the record breaking prototype; 80-volt electric motors in each front wheel hub provided 5 HP and more than 20 mph. (*Austrian Automobile, Motorcycle & Touring Clubs*)

Ferdinand Porsche at the wheel of one of his Lohner-Porsche "Mixt" cars during his military service in 1902. Beside Porsche is his colonel, the Archduke Franz Ferdinand. (*Volkswagen of America, Inc.*)

Porsche won the Semmering Hill Climb on one but he was not satisfied with the performance, 37 MPH in a stripped racing model, and an operating range of 50 miles when the batteries had to be recharged. Moreover, the batteries alone weighed approximately 900 pounds. The two electric hub motors together weighed nearly 500 pounds. It was obvious that means had to be devised to reduce the dead weight that severely handicapped electric cars. (This same problem faces electric car designers today.)

Porsche's solution was to toss out the heavy batteries and to replace them with a small gasoline engine coupled to a gener-

Porsche driving one of his Lohner-Porsche "Mixt" cars to first place in the 1903 Exelberg race. *(Volkswagen of America, Inc.)*

The 1901 Austro-Daimler 30/35 HP tourer was a duplicate of the Connstatt-Daimler Type I-35. The 4-cylinder, 5.9-litre engine peaked at 1,000 RPM. *(Austrian Automobile, Motorcycle & Touring Clubs)*

For the carriage trade: the 1911 Austro-Daimler 60-HP limousine. Note stone shields on lights. *(Austrian Automobile, Motorcycle & Touring Clubs)*

The 27/60-HP Austro-Daimler tourer of 1911–12. *(Austrian Information Service)*

Most popular sports car of the period was the 80-HP Austro-Daimler "Prince Heinrich" of 1910. Porsche-designed, this 5.6-litre, 4-cylinder car had an overhead camshaft and a top speed of about 85 mph. The "tulip" body shape influenced a score of manufacturers. (*Austrian Automobile, Motorcycle & Touring Clubs*)

A 1913 Austro-Daimler "Prince Heinrich" with special coachwork by Healey of New York City.

(*Robert E. Burke Studio courtesy of Thompson Auto Museum*)

Open valve gear, separately cast cylinders, and magnificent workmanship—the engine of the Austro-Daimler "Prince Heinrich" sports car. (*Joseph H. Wherry*)

ator. The electric motors in the front wheel hubs remained and the new car was called the "Mixt" for rather evident reasons. In both roadster and racing runabout form, the Lohner-Porsche "Mixt" was an immediate sensation with astounding performance and an operating range limited only to the need to stop for gasoline. When he was called up for summer military maneuvers with his regiment, Porsche took along one of his "Mixt" roadsters and was assigned to drive his Colonel who was none other than the Archduke Franz Ferdinand. The "Mixt" sold well and the works garnered good publicity by entering every race at hand. Porsche was an excellent driver and loved to race. Speeds exceeding 50 MPH were achieved by the "Mixt" models and they inspired imitation by Mercedes, Austro-Daimler and others. Porsche next reckoned that if a front-wheel-drive "Mixt" was good (and it was), a four-wheel-drive model

130

Monocle windscreen for driver and "cloverleaf"
seating—the Healey-bodied Austro-Daimler
"Prince Heinrich." (*Joseph H. Wherry*)

The Porsche-designed Austro-Daimler "Sasche"
racer was the sensation of the 1922 Targa Florio
in Sicily. The 4-cylinder, 1,099-cc. engine developed 45 HP. (*Porsche Werkfoto*)

The 1924–28 Austro-Daimler luxury cabriolet Type ADM. An overhead-camshaft, 3-litre, 6-cylinder, aluminum-alloy engine was rated at 110/ 115 HP. On a 109-inch-wheelbase chassis, speed approached 100 mph. (*Austrian Information Service*)

The 6-cylinder, overhead-camshaft, 120-HP Austro-Daimler "Bergmeister" of 1932–33 was another Porsche design. A tubular, backbone type frame with independent rear suspension was used. (*Austrian Information Service*)

The 1932 Austro-Daimler Type ADR was an 8-cylinder, 100-HP, high performance sports and grand turismo. (*Austrian Information Service*)

would be better. So with electric motors in each wheel hub, the new Lohner-Porsches bowled along at 70 MPH and in 1903 Porsche drove such a machine to an overall victory in the important Exelberg Race against some of the best gasoline-powered cars of the day. Having proven himself as a courageous innovator, Porsche was hired away from Lohner in 1906 by the manufacturers of the Austro-Daimler.

During the First World War, Lohner produced highly successful naval fighter planes. From 1919 to about 1938, the Lohner works built electric cars in limited numbers but they never matched the success of the marque's early years when Porsche headed the engineering department.

When Austro-Daimler was established just before 1900 in a suburb of Vienna by German and Austrian interests, the aim was to produce duplicates of the designs of Gottlieb Daimler's firm in Connstatt, Germany. This mission was fulfilled under the direction of Gottlieb's son, Paul, until 1906 when Ferdinand Porsche took over engi-

neering responsibilities. Gradually the Austro-Daimler took on an individual character. Porsche's first all-gasoline car was the 30-HP "Maja." (It is interesting that the "Maja" and the German "Mercedes" were named for the daughters of the Austro-Hungarian financier, Jellinek. Also that Josip Broz Tito was a test driver at Austro-Daimler.) In 1909, the first version of the most famous model of this marque was introduced, the 4-cylinder "Prinz Heinrich Wagen" or Prince Henry. Rated at 50 BHP, the 1909 model utilized chain final drive and weighed slightly more than 2,000 pounds. It served as the basis for an improved version which the works was bent upon entering in the famous Prinz Heinrich Trials named for the brother of Kaiser Wilhelm of Germany. Initially, the 1910 production Prince Henry, designated as the 27/80 model, developed 86 BHP at 1,400 rpm and showed a top speed of about 85 MPH. The increased power was due to a new Porsche-designed, 5.6-litre engine with the four 105 x 165 mm. cylinders cast in-

133

The 1905 Puch "Doktorwagen" cabriolet gave mobility to many a country physician. Engine was a V-2 of 8/9 HP. (*Austrian Automobile, Motorcycle & Touring Clubs*)

dividually and steel cylinder liners. An enclosed overhead-camshaft operated valves, inclined at 45 degrees, through open valve gear. The combustion chambers closely approached the hemispherical shape. Ignition was by dual magnetos, and an up-to-date shaft drive replaced the clanking chains. On a relatively short, 109-inch-wheelbase chassis, elegant coachwork was crafted which was called "Tulpenform"—tulip form—because of the outward splay of the body side panels.

A team of three production Prince Henry models were entered in the June, 1910, Trials of the same name, several hundred miles around Germany in which more than 100 cars were entered. The Austro-Daimlers won the top three places with Porsche himself driving the first-place machine. Later, Porsche squeezed nearly 100 BHP out of the Prince Henry engine by modifying the camshaft for increased efficiency. With its sharply pointed radiator shell topping off either works bodies or custom coachwork, the Prince Henry model promptly became one of the most emulated of sports

The 9/10 HP Puch "Sport Voiturette" of 1908 had a 900 cc., 2-cylinder, water-cooled engine. A similar touring car was fitted with a 10/12-HP, 4-cylinder engine. (*Austrian Automobile, Motorcycle & Touring Clubs*)

cars and was exported throughout Europe. In 1910, the Mercedes-Knight's body design was almost identical in style. A number were imported into the United States. One of the most unique Prince Henrys with a three-seat body by Healey of New York City has been displayed widely and is owned by the Thompson Auto Museum; though striking, this version's style is a far cry from Porsche's originals.

After the war, Porsche designed a small sports racer, the 4-cylinder, 1.1-litre Type-ADS IIR "Sascha" which was named for Count Sascha Kolowrat. Small and light—some had short engine bonnets, and others had long bonnets like the example illustrated—a team of three was entered in the 1922 Targa Florio in Sicily where they captured first, second and sixth places in their class. Good as it was, the "Sascha" failed commercially, causing the works to con-

centrate on large 4- and 6-cylinder cars. Porsche left Austro-Daimler in 1923 and went to Daimler in Germany as director of engineering. From 1924 to '28 the Type-ADM was popular in the luxury field and was exported as far as England where the 3-litre, 109 and 137-inch wheelbase models sold complete for $6,000 and up. A 2.6-litre version of the ADM cost considerably less.

Austro-Daimler's next important car was the Type-ADR "Bergmeister"—Mountain Master—a large, 4-litre, overhead-camshaft, 120-brake-horsepower car that bore the stamp of Porsche's long technical leadership. Aluminum alloy was extensively used in the cylinder block and crankcase. A tubular backbone-type frame was one of the Bergmeister's outstanding features along with independent rear suspension with transverse leaf springs and swing axles. On

135

The 1914–20 Puch "Alpenwagen" Type 8 was straightforward and typical of the time. (*Austrian Information Service*)

a short, 109-inch wheelbase, the type had considerable success in trials, races and hill climb competitions. At the same time, Austro-Daimler went all out in 1932 for the top of the market with a huge, 8-cylinder, Type-ADR-8 that developed 100 BHP and was promoted as the ultimate mount for touring in the "grande" manner. The ADR-8 was produced through 1933 but both luxury types were too big and too costly at a time of economic change. Sales dropped alarmingly and Austro-Daimler management sought shelter by merging with Steyr in 1934.

Motorcycles occupied the production facilities of Johann Puch's factory in Graz from the time it was established in 1899 until 1901. In that year Puch decided to build motorcars. The first Puch to be produced in series was the cabriolet "Doktorwagen" of 1905; an open two-seater was also made. Both were powered by 8-HP, 2-cylinder, Vee-type engines using 3-speed

gearboxes and shaft final drive. The Puch sold well and would go about 35 MPH flat out. Though not marketed to any extent outside of Austria, the Puch developed into an attractive sports runabout powered by a 900 cc., water-cooled, 2-cylinder engine in 1908. The next year, 3-litre, 12-HP, 4-cylinder engines were used leading to the 1913 Type-VIII "Alpenwagen" which gained fame in the Alpine Trials. Known as the 14/38-HP model, the "Alpenwagen" was produced all through the war for military use and remained the principal issue of the Puch works through 1923. Type-XII was a smaller 6/20-HP version of the same model current during 1919–20. After 1924, the works reverted to building motorcycles until 1928 when Puch joined Austro-Daimler in a merger.

With the merger of Puch and Austro-Daimler, one large independent manufacturer remained, the Steyr Werke AG of Styria. Established in 1853 by Josef Werndl,

Dependable, sturdy and conventional, the 6-cylinder, 3.3-litre Steyr Type V of 1925–29 sat on a wheelbase of 139 inches, developed 24 HP, and cost upward of $3,500. (*Austrian Information Service*)

the firm became famous for their rifles and other small arms. By World War One, the Steyr factories included the production facilities for a wide range of products. In the midst of the war in 1917, automobile production commenced. With Hans Ledwinka in charge, the 6-cylinder, 12/40-HP, Type-II Steyr was placed in full production along with the 4-cylinder, 7/23-HP Type-IV and the 6-cylinder Type-VI. The Type-VI "Klausen" was a 19/145-HP, 4-litre, passenger tourer while the "Sport" was a smaller 15/90-HP model. All of these types remained in production through 1924, some 6,000 in all being built. Ledwinka left Steyr in 1921 but his influence remained when he returned to Czechoslovakia and Tatra.

In 1925, the Type-V became the leading model after long and careful development. Type-V was a large, sturdy car with a wheelbase of 137 inches and an 80 x 110 mm., 3.3-litre, 24-HP, 6-cylinder engine which sold in England for approximately $3,000. When brakes were added to the front wheels, Type-V was redesignated Type-VII and was produced through 1929. Development continued through the Type-XX of 1928 which was powered by a 4,014 cc., 6-cylinder, overhead-valve engine. Steyr, by this time, was Austria's largest car maker, outproducing even Austro-Daimler.

Designed by Porsche, the 1929 Steyr "Austria" had a 5.3-litre, 8-cylinder, 100-HP engine with dual ignition and was a sensation at the Paris Salon. (*Porsche Werkfoto*)

For the middle class, the 6-cylinder, 1937–40 Steyr 220-S. (*Austrian Information Service*)

In January, 1929, Porsche joined the firm as head of engineering and promptly set to work designing the Steyr "Austria." The finest Steyr of all and one of Porsche's most ambitious projects, the "Austria" had a 5.3-litre, straight-8 engine featuring dual ignition, pushrod-operated overhead-valves and dual carburetion; the output was 100 BHP. Advanced four-wheel, hydraulic brakes, independent rear suspension with swing axles and a backbone type frame were other features of the luxury car designed to dominate that market in Austria. Selecting a five-passenger cabriolet, Porsche personally drove his "Austria" the 700-odd miles non-stop to Paris where it was the hit of the autumn Motor Show. Only a handful were built, however, because financial manipulators in Vienna had brought about a change in the firm's management and a decision was made to build no luxury cars. Porsche left Steyr forthwith and moved to Stuttgart, Germany, where he organized his own engineering and design bureau early in 1931.

Steyr continued to build cars of original design including taxicabs and commercial vehicles. The Type-100 was a popular, 32-HP, 4-cylinder family car of moderate price in 1934–36 but the Type-220, a 55-HP, 6-cylinder sedan of 1937–41 was even more popular. In the mid-'30s, the Steyr Werke merged with the Austro-Daimler-Puch combine but the marque retained its identity. There is a possibility that had Ferdinand Porsche remained with Steyr, his Volkswagen might today be an Austrian product. In 1936, the Type-50/55 went on sale and became the most numerous of all pre-war Steyr models. Porsche designed the little four-passenger sedan which was a style variant of the VW prototypes covered in the section devoted to German cars. An air-cooled, 4-cylinder, opposed-type engine displacing 1-litre developed 22 BHP. More than 13,000 units of the Steyr "VW" were built before all production was diverted to war materials in 1940.

Since the war, the Steyr-Daimler-Puch organization has been instrumental in revitalizing the auto industry in Austria.

Belgium

BETWEEN SIXTY AND SEVENTY distinct marques were produced in Belgium, most of them appearing and disappearing before World War One. The "Mixt" electric and gas, a racing version of the Jenatzy which made a name for Belgium in 1899 by setting a world speed record (see Part II), was out of the picture by 1904. Quite popular after the turn of the century was the Vivinus, also mentioned earlier, which was raced in 2.8-litre, 4-cylinder versions in 1905. The Vivinus was also built under license as the New Orleans in England. Alexis Vivinus did not revive his make after the war but he became associated with Minerva.

By 1906, Charles Fondu's reputation as an engineer was so high that he was retained by Russian interests, as already mentioned; during the same year he launched his own Fondu cars. Mostly large 4-cylinder limousines and town cars, Fondus displayed some of the finest coachwork of the time, mahogany bodies trimmed with ebony and other exotic woods. In 1912, the Fondu passed from the scene. The little known Aquila began in 1900, the Alberta in 1906, Baudouin in 1903, Bastin in 1908, Belgica and Bovy about 1902, Cockerill in 1904, Daneels in 1902, Elga in 1912, Frenay in 1911, Koppel in 1900, LaLocomotrice and Latafie about 1902 and so on for several dozen marques, most of them lasting only a few years.

Of the pre-1915 cars that failed to survive after hostilities, the Pipe was one of the most advanced. Introduced in 1900, it was immediately entered in competition at Spa and in the international cross-country races to Berlin and Madrid which started at Paris. In the 1904 Gordon Bennett Race, a Pipe placed sixth and in 1907 won second place in the Kaiserpreis race. Chain drive gave way to shaft drive on the Pipe about 1909. When ex-manufacturer Camille Jenatzy won first place in a Mercedes in the Boulogne race in 1912, his son placed a close second on a big, 4-cylinder Pipe with six valves per cylinder, 175-brake-horsepower and 125 MPH top speed. Racing Pipes all had dual camshafts in the cylinder block driving overhead-valves by push-rods.

The first Germain cars, founded in 1897, used Daimler and later Panhard engines until 1903 when the firm began making en-

The 1899–1900 Vivinus 6-HP model (2 cylinders, 1,420 cc.) was popular in western Europe. (*Institut Belge d'Information et de Documentation*)

The 2.8-litre, 4-cylinder Vivinus 15/18 HP of 1905. (*Royal Motor Union of Liége courtesy of Fabrique Nationale*)

A 1905 chain-driven Pipe somewhere in Algiers at a desert camp. (*Royal Motor Union of Liége courtesy of Fabrique Nationale*)

gines of their own designs. At the end of the first decade, Germains were large cars with 4-cylinder, 3.6-litre engines. Many of them were equipped with electrically operated gear changing mechanisms. Germains survived as quality cars until 1930.

Metallurgique was another high-quality car. The first models appeared about 1903. This make may have originated the pointed radiator in 1908, a feature copied far and wide for its rakish appearance. In 1907, a shaft-drive Metallurgique placed second to a Mercedes in the Herkomer Trials, an endurance event, out of a field of some 170 entrants. In 1909, the Metallurgique entry in the Prinz Heinrich Trials was an unusual

Luxurious mahogany coachwork and a widely admired 4-cylinder engine distinguished the 1906 Fondu limousine. (*Institut Belge d'Information et de Documentation*)

machine with dual camshafts and five valves in each cylinder—one huge inlet valve in each cylinder head and a pair of small exhaust valves on each side. This powerful, 100-BHP engine propelled the large, 138-inch-wheelbase car at more than 80 MPH. For 1910 competitions, aluminum was used extensively in an overhead-valve engine—even the connecting rods were aluminum—developing 90 BHP. The war prevented production of a V-8 engine, and a fuel system eliminating valves was dropped. After the war, competition and passenger cars were built, a 2-litre model with four 80 x 130 mm. cylinders being quite popular and enjoying some export success in England where the price was around $5,000. The marque finally merged with Imperia and lasted until 1928. Of particular interest, Metallurgique's chief engineer, Paul Bastien, came to the U.S.A. in the

The first Nagant 3-HP car of 1900. Front seat passengers faced to the rear. (*Royal Motor Union of Liége courtesy of Fabrique Nationale*)

The 1911 Nagant 16-HP car had a 4-cylinder, L-head engine. (*Royal Motor Union of Liége courtesy of Fabrique Nationale*)

Excelsior was called the "royal car." This 1921 "Adex" chassis had a 6-cylinder, 4.7-litre engine. *(Royal Motor Union of Liége courtesy of Fabrique Nationale)*

The 1929 Impéria 6-cylinder cabriolet. *(Royal Motor Union of Liége courtesy of Fabrique Nationale)*

1913 Minerva 26-HP, seven-passenger, dual-cowled touring car. The 4-cylinder engine had sleeve valves, bore and stroke were 100 x 140 mm. Wheelbase was 138 inches, overall length a reasonable 195 inches. (*Henry Ford Museum*)

'20s and joined Stutz. After World War Two, Bastien was associated with Kaiser-Fraser.

Another little known Belgian car, the S.A.V.A. built in Anvers from about 1908 to 1927, was an active racing competitor from 1910 onward. The 4-cylinder, 3-litre engine was an F-head with an unusual twist: the exhaust valves were overhead with the inlet valves on the side instead of the other way around. Shaft drives and 4-speed gearboxes were used on all models. In 1919, a 3.4-litre model was produced along with a 2-litre; both had four cylinders. In 1927, this fine car faded from sight after an earlier merger with Minerva.

In 1900, Leon and Maurice Nagant, manufacturers of armaments in Liége, decided to make cars. Initially the Nagant engines were opposed piston types built under license in cooperation with the Gobron-Brillié firm in France. In the first Nagant illustrated, the vertical engine was beneath the driver's seat and mounted transversely; the gear change lever was on the steering column. By 1907, Nagant was building L-head, 4-cylinder engines of original design in 12-, 16-, 24-, and 40-HP models, all fitted with 4-speed gearboxes and chain drive. Shaft drives were standardized in 1911. When the Automobile Club of France sponsored a Grand Prix race at Lyons on the eve of World War One, a 4.5-litre, overhead-valve, 4-cylinder Nagant that developed 130 BHP was well placed in a particularly rigorous race that saw many cars eliminated because of engine failures and collisions. Limited production resumed after the war with 4- and 6-cylinder passenger cars. In 1925, a Nagant racer won the Grand Prix of Belgium. Finally, the marque was merged with Impéria and then disappeared in 1931.

Belgium's finest car is considered to have

A 1925–26 Minerva 16-HP, Type AG, 4-cylinder chassis. (*Institut Belge d'Information et de Documentation*)

been the Excelsior. Introduced in 1898 by Arthur de Coninck as a 2-cylinder carriage, the marque progressed to a fine 85 x 130 mm., 6-cylinder car in 1911 which had the engine and 4-speed transmission in one unit. The output was 66 BHP at 1,800 rpm. A 4-cylinder sports car also was raced successfully well into 1914 as was a racing version of the "six" which weighed less than one ton. After the war, de Coninck placed four-wheel brakes of his own design on his cars and also developed a stabilizer bar which was almost universally adopted for high-performance cars. The finest of

all Excelsiors was the "Albert I" model of the mid-'20s, a 5.3-litre machine developing 115 BHP in standard touring and limousine trim and 130 BHP in the triple carburetor sports models which did 90 MPH with ease. The engine of the Albert I was an advanced, single-overhead-camshaft unit with aluminum pistons, tubular connecting rods, and a seven main bearing crankshaft. De Coninck's braking system linked diagonal front and rear wheels and was called the "Adex" system. Highly successful, the 5.3-litre Excelsiors won first and second place in the 24-hour Grand Prix of Bel-

147

An unrestored 1932 Minerva with 4-door cabriolet
Van den Plas coachwork resting in storage. (*Institut Belge d'Information et de Documentation*)

1930 Minerva Type AE with coupé coachwork by
Verhaest of Deinze. (*Institut Belge d'Information
et de Documentation*)

1929 Minerva landaulet. (*Joseph H. Wherry*)

A steering wheel on a vertical column and a 2-cylinder engine mark the 1902 FN. (*Fabrique Nationale*)

1907 FN Type 2,000 "Super de Luxe" double phaeton used a 4-cylinder engine and shaft drive. An automatic carburetor dispensed with the hand pump, still quite common, and the cooling system had a pump. (*Fabrique Nationale*)

gium at Spa in 1928 and garnered widespread publicity, but the overly expensive marque was merged with Impéria during the same year and was discontinued in 1932.

Impéria itself was merged with Minerva in 1934. The origin of Impéria is variously reported as having been in 1906, 1911, or sometime between these years. In any event, the first Impérias had side-valve, 16/20-HP, 4-cylinder engines with 3-speed gearboxes and shaft drive. Soon a 4-speed, 24/30-HP model was produced as was a big 50/60-HP model which regressed to chain drive. In 1913, a Spanish enthusiast named Abadal joined the Liége-based firm and helped to design a model named for him. The "Abadal" engine had four cylinders with 80 mm. bore and an exceptionally long 180 mm. stroke.

In 1920, the firm became Automobiles Impéria-Abadal and the Abadal was often listed as a marque in its own right although it was usually referred to as the Impéria-Abadal, a single-overhead-camshaft, straight-8, high-performance sports car with 80 x 140 mm. cylinders and dual carburetors. Though comparatively small on its 108-inch wheelbase, the Impéria-Abadal was a frequent racing contender. It went out of production

150

This 4-cylinder 1907 FN Type 2,000 limousine resides in a warehouse for veteran cars. (*Institut Belge d'Information et de Documentation*)

about 1924 because it was too expensive. Impéria next turned to 1.1-litre, 4-cylinder and 1.6-litre, 6-cylinder models on 106.5 and 114-inch wheelbases which were moderately priced from about $1,800 upward. Passenger cars of far above average quality,

The 1908 FN Type RS tourer. (*Fabrique Nationale*)

these were powered with double-sleeve-valve engines. The "four" was called the 11/24-HP model. It established a Belgian class record of more than 80 MPH. The "six" was the 17/50-HP model. By a licensing arrangement with Adler (see Germany), Impéria produced that firm's front-wheel-drive, 4-cylinder models in 1935 after the merger with Minerva. In 1936, the Impéria-Minerva combine scored a first with their 3.6-litre, V-8, transversely-mounted engine and an Impéria-designed automatic transmission. The V-8 was a sensation with its

100 MPH top speed. It was the last prewar car named Impéria.

Most famous of all Belgian cars was the Minerva which began with a one-cylinder, 5-HP two-seater in 1904. Outgrowth of Sylvain de Jong's successful bicycle and motorcycle works in an Antwerp suburb, the marque made an immediate impression by winning the Paris to Bordeaux race in its first year of production. In 1907, the new Minerva 8-litre, 4-cylinder, 40-HP "Kaiserpreis" model took the first three places in a well-attended race on the Ardennes cir-

152

1909 FN Type 2,100 with 14 CV engine. Note magneto box on running board. (*Fabrique Nationale*)

The FN Type 15 landaulet of 1909–10 had a specially reinforced frame; was an outstanding attraction at the Paris Motor Show. (*Fabrique Nationale*)

1913 FN Type 2,700 RA two-seater roadster. What appears to be a second door on the near side is an access to luggage hatch. Chains on rear wheels facilitated going in the rough. (*Fabrique Nationale*)

cuit. With success apparently assured, de Jong obtained license rights in 1908 to produce the double-sleeve-valve system originated by the American, Charles Y. Knight. In fact, de Jong never built another Minerva with poppet valves. The clouds of blue smoke that issued upon rapid acceleration were bearable in those days before "smog" became a word because the sleeve-valved Minerva engines were quiet, powerful and reliable. These virtues enabled Minervas—named for the helmeted Roman goddess who was patroness of craftsmen—to become favorites with millionaires, aristocrats and royalty before World War I. The new 1909 4-cylinder Minerva engines were rated at 15, 28 and 38 HP; these were fitted to a full range of bodies from sporting two-seaters to town cars on wheelbases up to 125 inches. In 1911, '12 and '13, Minervas won the Swedish Winter Trials, the 1911 Russian Grand Prix against more than four dozen other entrants including a gaggle of Russo-Baltiques, the 1912 Reliability Cup in the Grand Prix of Spain, and two Coupes des Alps . . . all before the 1914–18 war during which some of the first Allied armored cars were built on Minerva chassis. After the war, passenger cars outnumbered the sporting models as the factory withdrew official support from racing.

From 1920 until 1930, Minerva models

The FN Type 1,250 of 1914 was a stylish roadster powered by a 4-cylinder 60 x 110 mm. engine with an aluminum block. Full pressure lubrication, magneto ignition and a Zenith carburetor were employed. Tires were mounted on detachable rims. (*Fabrique Nationale*)

ranged in wheelbase size from 118 inches to 149.5 inches. Four-cylinder engines were of two principal sizes: 75 x 112 mm., 2-litre and 80 x 112 mm., 2.25-litre units rated at 15 and 16 HP by the factory. Six-cylinder engines were in greater variety and were developed from the 4-cylinder engines by adding two cylinders. Initially, to achieve high torque, the basic six had a long, 140-mm. stroke in relation to a bore of 90 mm.; this was the 5.3-litre, 30-HP engine. As fuels and carburetion improved, a 3-litre, 20-HP, 6-cylinder engine was introduced in 1922 followed by a 3.4-litre, 20/24-HP unit in 1924.

To compete with increasing numbers of "light six" models rapidly becoming popular, Minerva brought out the Type-AH with a 68 x 92 mm., 12/14-HP, 2-litre engine in a 118-inch-wheelbase chassis in 1927; the price of the bare chassis was around $2,000 with complete cars running upwards from about $2,400. Exports were booming to England and France where locally owned firms were assembling complete cars. To top off the range, a magnificent, 5.9-litre six, the Type-AK, was introduced in 1928 with a 32/34-HP rating. On the long 149.5-inch wheelbase, the AK chassis cost $4,000 up; complete cars with works bodies brought $6,000 and more. Quality coachworks like Van den Plas and Hibbard

155

The FN two-passenger sports roadster, Type 1,250A of 1920, had an interesting seating arrangement with luggage hatch behind driver's seat on near side. (*Fabrique Nationale*)

Dual-cowled FN Type 1,300 Sport four-seater of 1924 with boat-tailed Weymann fabric-covered coachwork. A frequent sports racer, Lieutenant LaMarche drove one of these cars over a flying kilometer at 116.47 km per hour in October, 1924. The 1.3-litre, 4-cylinder engine used a horizontal Solex carburetor. In 1925, this type placed well in the International Monaco Rally. (*Fabrique Nationale*)

The 1930 FN 1,800 Sport roadster had four 68 x 75 mm. cylinders. Taxable rating was 11 CV and maximum speed was 65–70 mph. (*Fabrique Nationale*)

& Darrin in Paris crafted bodies bringing double the works price for well-heeled customers around the world.

The death of de Jong, the Minerva founder, coincided with the onset of the worldwide economic crisis. To counter rapidly declining sales, the works sponsored several high-speed cross-country runs to introduce a new 4-litre straight 8-cylinder model. On a short wheelbase and designated as the 28-HP model, it developed 80 BHP at 3,000 rpm with a single carburetor and 130 BHP at 4,000 rpm with a three-carburetor modification. With four persons aboard, the top speed of this luxurious grand turismo type was 85–90 MPH at full throttle. Roadability was excellent with cantilever semi-elliptic rear suspension, adjustable hydraulic shock absorbers, centralized chassis lubrication and servo-assisted brakes.

In December of 1930, André Pisart hurtled a 130-HP, 8-cylinder model over the 1,500-mile Ostend-Marseilles-Ostend route in 32½ hours. The next year Pisart eclipsed this publicity feat in a Type-AK six by blasting his mount over 10,250 miles of Europe's worst roads in the Pyrenees, the Alps, and the Balkans in six days at an incredible average of 48 MPH. Sales continued to decline, however, and even G. L. Baker's success on the Brooklands circuit—including a lap at more than 96 MPH—with a Type-AK 32/34-HP six modified for racing did not prevent a merger with Impéria in 1934. As already observed, each firm continued to market selected models until production of passenger cars was discontinued late in 1938. Minerva revived after the war and today assembles other European cars in the Brussels area.

The distinction of producing the widest range of Belgian cars over the longest period of time belongs to the Fabrique Nationale d'Armes de Guerre. Popularly priced cars in series were continued until

157

In 1933 the FN Type 42 "Prince Baudouin" was a 4-cylinder, 2-litre, four-passenger touring sedan in "de l'ancien classique" tradition. (*Fabrique Nationale*)

the outbreak of war late in 1939. This arms and heavy industrial firm, based in Liége, brought out the first FN car in 1900, a 2-cylinder carriage with trembler coil ignition, chain drive and a steering wheel. Within two years FN progressed to shaft drive and by 1904 the firm was producing 4-cylinder engines, with cylinders cast in pairs, developing up to 40 BHP. From 1907 through 1909, magneto ignition was standardized and coach-built bodies were fitted to the 2-litre Types 2,000 and 2,100 which were better known as 14CV models, a reference to the taxable horsepower formula.

The 1913 Type-2,700 RA and 1914 Type-1,250 were distinctly sporting. They had four cylinders, full-pressure lubrication, detachable rim wheels which helped make them favored for trials events, and optional electric starting.

When production resumed in 1919, the new Type-1,250 was introduced in two versions: the "N" and "T" passenger car variants and the sporting "A." The 1,250-A bore unmistakable styling resemblance to the pre-war Prinz Heinrich trials cars of other manufacturers, and led to the outstanding Type-1,300 sports cars of 1924–26. Bodies ranged from lightweight two-seaters to elegant boat-tail, Weyman-type, fabric-covered custom coachwork seating four persons. Five series in all were built on the 15-HP, 1.3-litre, Type-1,300 chassis. The four 68 x 100 mm. cylinders were cast en bloc and had pushrod-operated overhead-valves. Four-wheel brakes were also used. The final series, the Type-1,300 Sp—the competition model—had a 4-speed gearbox with close ratios and maximum speed in excess of 70 MPH. One of them placed third in its class in the Monte Carlo Rally in January, 1925. A more impressive performance was exhibited by a 1,300 Sp team in the 1926 Grand Prix of Belgium at Spa

158

One of the last FN series production models was the 1934 "Prince Albert." The "Suprofille" streamlined coachwork was on a wheelbase of 110.2 inches. An L-head engine had four 85 x 100 mm. cylinders. (*Fabrique Nationale*)

where they placed one-two in the overall classification; and in the Luxembourg G.P., a 1,300 Sp placed first in its class. The same year, Lieutenant Lamarche placed first in the 3-litre class in the Tour de France in a new 16-CV, 2.2-litre, Type-2,200 G. What the FNs lacked in numbers, they consistently compensated for when capably driven, as in 1931 when a trio of Type-1,625 FNs captured a team first place in their class in the Alpine Trials, winning a coveted Coupe des Alpes.

The 1930 Type-1,800 (1.8-litres) and the 1933 "Prince Baudouin" 2-litre sedans were noteworthy 4-cylinder models advertised as being in "the ancient classic tradition" by the works. These sold better than the larger 3.3-litre straight-8 introduced in the upper middle class in 1931 which, in special sporting trim, won first place overall in the 1933 Liége-Rome-Liége Rally.

During the mid-'30s the management of Fabrique Nationale obtained control of the British branch of Minerva. Whether or not this involvement, plus the poor sales of the big straight-8, sped the decline of the FN is not known. At any rate the 2.2-litre, L-head, 4-cylinder "Prince Albert" model introduced in 1934 with rather pretty, streamlined coachwork proved to be the last all-new type FN passenger car. With a 4-speed gearbox and a wheelbase of 110.2 inches, the "Suprofille" was a sturdy, fine-quality, four-five passenger, family sedan with a better than average performance. Gradually sales declined although the FN was produced and sold right up to the outbreak of war in 1939. Since 1945, the Fabrique Nationale has reverted to heavy industry and military products for Belgium and the NATO countries.

159

Canada

The INDUSTRIAL HUB of Canada is centered in Ontario—in the triangular region formed by Hamilton, Kitchener and Toronto with the latter city dominating the whole. Since World War I, Windsor, Ontario, has come to the fore as an automotive production center. Proximity to Detroit and economic domination by the U. S. have served to subvert efforts to produce an all-Canadian marque.

In the early days, however, there were numerous attempts to develop and market distinctly Canadian cars. In 1893, the Dixon electric car was marketed in To-

The Queen was built in 1901–02 in Toronto. Owner of this rare example is Wesley Wallace of Embro, Ontario. (*Joseph H. Wherry*)

The McLaughlin was a distinctively Canadian version of the Buick. (*Canadian Automotive Museum*)

ronto, and George Foss introduced the now obscure Fossmobile gasoline car in Sherbrooke, Quebec, in 1896. Both efforts were admirable but short-lived. From the first years of this century, manufacturers in the United States began establishing subsidiaries in Canada where cars were assembled. Some parts were made in Canada.

Unfortunately, scarcely more than the names of a few dozen Canadian marques have survived and little technical information has been unearthed. Nevertheless, the accompanying roster of cars which appear—from the meager details available—to be of definite Canadian design will serve to verify the efforts of Canadian automotive pioneers.

Except where noted, the following marques were manufactured in the Toronto area.

1893	Dixon (electric)	1898	Redpath
1896	Fossmobile (Sherbrooke, Quebec)	1898	Leroy
1897	Neff (steamer)	1901	Leader (front drive)
1897–01	Still (electric)	1901–02	Queen
1898	CMS	1903	Conner (steamer)

Canadian-built Overland of about 1919 had a reliable 35-HP, 4-cylinder engine. (*Canadian Automotive Museum*)

1924 Canadian-built Chevrolet. (*Canadian Automotive Museum*)

1925 Canadian-built Star built in Leaside, Ontario. (*Canadian Automotive Museum*)

1927 Canadian-built Model T Ford owned by Ron Fawcett of Whitby, Ontario. (*Canadian Automotive Museum*)

1903	Ivanhoe (electric)	1910	Sager
1903	Menard (Windsor, Ontario)	1910	Walker
1904	Austin	1911	Dominion
1906–08	Chatham	1911–13	Galt
1907	Bourasse (Montreal, Quebec)	1912	Canadian
1907–09	Comet (Montreal, Quebec)	1912	Tate
1909–17	Russell (sleeve valves)	1913	McKinnon
1910+	Brooks (steamer)	1913	Nova Scotia (Kentville, N. S.)
1910	Clinton	1913	Oxford (Montreal, Quebec)
1910	Gereau (Montreal, Quebec)	1913–14	Tudhope
1910	Kennedy	1914	Bartlett
1910	McKay (Kentville, Nova Scotia)	1914	Canada Baby Car (Montreal, Que.)
1910	Royal Windsor	1914	Dart

Many lesser known cars like the Case built by the J. I. Case farm equipment firm of Racine, Wisconsin, were assembled in Canada, the Case in Lethbridge, Alberta. This 1916 Racine-built tourer owned by William P. Robinson of Lockport, N. Y. took part in the 1958 Glidden Tour. (*Joseph H. Wherry*)

1915	Acme
1915	Maritine (St. Johns, N. Bruns.)
1920–23	Forster (Montreal, Quebec)
1920	Standwell (Amherstburg, N. S.)
1921	Fulton
1921	Le Marne
1921	Mercury (Lachine, Quebec)
1921	Roberts (Lachine, Quebec)
1922	Birmingham
1922	Glenn (3-cyl.)

1922	London
1923	LaVoie (Montreal, Quebec)
1923	Parker (Montreal, Quebec)
1924	Derby (Saskatoon, Sask.)
1924	Davis
1927	Crosley (Montreal, Quebec)
1931	Frontenac

Czechoslovakia

MOST OF THE industrial muscles of the old Austro-Hungarian Empire were located in Bohemia and Moravia, provinces which became the nucleus of the Republic of Czechoslovakia at the end of the First World War. Before then, however, Czech industrialists had built up a viable automotive industry.

Nesselsdorf, now Kopřivnice in Moravia, was the site of the wagon factory established about 1850 by Ignaz Schustala who later built railroad cars. In 1897, the Nesselsdorfer Wagenbau Fabriks Gesellschaft was a large enterprise, and the proximity of raw materials and steel mills facilitated production of motor vehicles. The first Nesselsdorf, now a treasured possession of the National Technical Museum in Prague, was largely the work of Edmund Rumpler whose aircraft became famous during the 1914–18 war. Much like many other contemporary automobile designs, the "Präsident" used hard-tired wagon wheels and chain drive, and was powered by a 2-cylinder, water-cooled Benz engine with square bore and stroke of 120 mm. A system of belts and pulleys of different diameters transmitted power from the under-seat engine to the countershaft carrying the sprockets for the final chain drive. At 600 rpm the output was 5 HP, sufficient to propel the "Präsident" at about 18 mph. Late in 1897, Hans Ledwinka, born near Vienna and barely 20 years old, came to work for Nesselsdorfer after helping to design the successful front-wheel-drive Gräf & Stift car (see Austria).

Ledwinka next helped design a new model in 1898 which had pneumatic tires and an improved frame composed of steel tubes. Six of these were built and named "Metrans," "Bergsteiger," "Wien" and the like. The "Wien" was entered in numerous cross-country races by the Baron Freiherr von Liebig and won many awards including first place in a 210-mile race from Nesselsdorf to Vienna and return.

These initial racing successes prompted Ledwinka's next assignment to build two racing cars. Improved carburetion, a large front-mounted radiator and a manually adjusted Bosch ignition and other modifications increased the output of the 2,755 cc. Benz engine to 12 HP at 1,300 rpm. This was mounted in a heavy steel-reinforced, wood frame on full-elliptic springs. The driver sat in the open between the radiator and the rear engine. Beneath him was a 4-

The first automobile built in what is now Czechoslovakia, the 1897 Nesselsdorf "President" had a 5-HP, 2-cylinder, four-cycle, 2,750 cc. Benz engine mounted beneath the rear seat. Steering was by handlebars on column. Top speed was about 18 mph. (*Motokov*)

speed gearbox. Topping off the whole affair was the vertical exhaust pipe which looked like a smokestack and must have belched forth great amounts of exhaust gases at the top speed of around 60 mph. Early in June, 1900, von Liebig drove the racing monster to second place behind a 24-HP German Daimler in the 201-mile Salzburg-Linz-Vienna race in 8 hours and 16 minutes. Racing dominated the activities of the Nesselsdorfer works for several years. The lessons learned were incorporated into the 4-cylinder, 5.9-litre, Type-D family tourer of 1902 and a steady succession of passenger cars. In 1906, Ledwinka designed the 4-cylinder Type-S, a tourer with shaft drive, which remained in production with progressive styling changes through 1912. The 6-cylinder Type-U was introduced in 1910; in its final 20/65 HP S-6 form it was produced well into 1915 despite the war.

Like his contemporary, Porsche, Ledwinka frequently became embroiled with management over technical matters and, after one such blowup, resigned, went back home to Vienna and joined the Steyr firm as technical director. In 1921, Ledwinka returned to the Nesselsdorfer works—renamed Tatra for the nearby mountains—in the newly independent Czechoslovakia.

Given freedom to innovate, Ledwinka developed a design concept that was to make him famous. When the Prague Automobile Show opened in May, 1923, Ledwin-

Hans Ledwinka helped design the improved 1898–99 Nesselsdorf. Named "Metrans," six identical vehicles were built, first of marque with pneumatic tires. (*Motokov*)

The 1912 Nesselsdorf S-6 was a large 6-cylinder prestige car. (*Austrian Information Service*)

The Type D Nesselsdorf of 1902 was powered by a 4-cylinder 5,878 cc., 24-HP engine mounted — transversely. Speed was about 30 mph. (*Motokov*)

One of two identical Nesselsdorf racing cars built in 1899. A steering wheel was used as were pneumatic tires. A huge front radiator served the 2.7-litre, 12-HP Benz engine. Maximum speed was 60–62 mph, and one racer won the 1902 Paris-Vienna race. (*Motokov*)

Tatra Type 11 of 1923–26 had backbone-tubular frame and independent suspension on all four wheels. The 1-litre, air-cooled, 2-cylinder engine developed 12 HP at 2,000 RPM and drove light four-seater 40–44 mph. (*Motokov*)

The Type 12 Tatra closed car was the mechanical duplicate of the open Type 11. Note the sloped nose. (*Motokov*)

The revolutionary Tatra 77 type, introduced in 1933, had a 3.4-litre, V-8, 70-HP air-cooled engine. Streamlined body was mounted on backbone frame with 124.5-inch wheelbase. Maximum speed exceeded 90 mph. (*Motokov*)

ka's new Tatra Type-11 was the outstanding design in an exhibition filled with the best cars from all of Europe. Instead of the conventional chassis frame, a longitudinal steel tube carried the propeller shaft. Independent suspension with transverse leaf springs was used at front and rear, the latter incorporating swinging axle half shafts outboard of the differential cage which was integral with the central tubular backbone. Wheelbase was approximately 105 inches. The engine was of the air-cooled, 2-cylinder opposed, flat type displacing 1,056 cc. with the shrouded finned flywheel acting as an air impeller. Compression ratio was 4.9 to 1 and the output at 2,000 rpm was 12 HP although the engine would safely wind up to 2,800 rpm. With the crankcase and 4-speed gearbox bolted to the backbone, the engine unit actually carried part of the chassis load. The entire chassis weighed a mere 1,105 pounds. Cross members secured to the central tube carried the lightweight open or closed bodies. Type-11 had rear-

Type 97 Tatra of 1936–37 was powered with an air-cooled, 1.8-litre, 4-cylinder engine developing 40 HP. Top speed approached 80 mph. (*Motokov*)

wheel brakes and was produced through 1926 when four-wheel brakes and a few minor changes were incorporated on the same basic design with a numerical change to Type-12. Exceptionally easy to handle and very roadable, the Types-11 and -12 carried four persons, were economical, sturdy, and had a maximum speed of 40–45 MPH which could be sustained for hours on end because of the engine's low speed. Large numbers were built of the nearly identical Types with Type-12 being discontinued in 1934, eleven years after introduction of the basic

design. The sloped nose resembled Renault lines.

There was continuous development of the concept of 1923 through Type-14, the 4-cylinder sports Type-30 and the Type-43. A larger Type-17 of 1926 was powered by an in-line, water-cooled, 6-cylinder engine of 1,950 cc. rated at 40 HP. Next came the Type-70 of 1930 with a 60-HP engine. Public demand, however, was for economical "people's cars" so Ledwinka went back to the small Type 11/12 and shortened the tubular backbone chassis to a wheelbase of

More conservative customers were catered to with the Type 57 Tatra of 1938–40. Engine was a 1.25-litre, opposed, flat, 4-cylinder unit developing 25 HP. Wheelbase was approximately 100 inches. (*Motokov*)

approximately 99.5 inches. Powered by a spunky 25-HP, air-cooled, flat, 4-cylinder engine of 1,250 cc. displacement, the Type-57b was born in 1938. Weighing just 2,056 pounds complete, top speed was 55 MPH. So successful was this model that it was produced until 1940 and again after the war until 1947.

In 1930, Ledwinka introduced a very large luxury car, the T-80, on a tubular chassis and suspension system that was virtually an enlarged version of those on the smaller Tatras, except that quarter-elliptic springs were employed at the rear. With a 6-litre overhead-camshaft, V-12-cylinder engine, the big Type-80 had a maximum speed of 90–95 MPH. Very expensive, the T-80 was produced only in limited numbers during the '30s.

In 1933, the Tatra Type-77 went into production. Again the proven backbone chassis was used but lengthened to a 124-inch wheelbase. An entirely new, air-cooled, 3.4-litre, V-8 engine with a single overhead-camshaft on each cylinder bank and 6.0 to 1 compression ratio powered the new

173

The 1907 Laurin & Klement "Doktorwagen" Type BS had a 4-cylinder engine and was especially designed "to meet the needs of country doctors." (*Motokov*)

model. The bore and stroke were 80 and 84 mm. respectively—nearly square—and the output was 70 BHP at a lazy 3,100 rpm. Mounted in the rear of the chassis with the 4-speed gearbox integral with the differential, this engine was cooled by two large airscoops, and there was a discrete fin on the sloping rear deck of the aerodynamic body which was of monocoque construction. Sedans with fixed or sliding roof panels were built. The remarkably spacious interior accommodated six adults most comfortably.

The V-8 powered Type-77 was supplemented in 1936 by a slightly smaller, 5-passenger Type-97. An in-line, 4-cylinder, overhead-valve engine developed 40 BHP at around 3,000 rpm. This engine's bore was

75 mm., stroke was 99 mm. and the compression ratio was 5.8 to 1. Quite naturally, the speed was decreased to about 66 MPH flat-out. At a distance, only the side location of the airscoops above the skirted rear wheels distinguished the Type-97 from the more powerful Type-77. Both streamlined Tatras were discontinued in 1937 when production was concentrated on the 1.25-litre Type-57b. In all fairness, it must be mentioned that the tubular backbone chassis was not originated by Hans Ledwinka; the 1904 Rover (see England) introduced the first known example of this construction. Ledwinka, however, brought this concept to its highest state of development, applied the idea most consistently with his own innovations, and inspired other designers in Ger-

174

In 1907, Laurin & Klement produced this 40-HP, 8-cylinder engine. (*Motokov*)

Laurin & Klement racing cars participated in many events throughout Europe. This is the 100-HP Type FCR of 1908 on the Brooklands circuit in England. (*Motokov*)

Many Laurin & Klement cars were exported to the Far East. Here two Japanese ladies are apparently driving a 1910 Type F limousine on a country estate. (*Motokov*)

The 1911 Laurin & Klement KB with 32-HP, 4-cylinder engine. (*Motokov*)

The 1912 Laurin & Klement 10/12-HP Type SV had 4-cylinder engine. (*Austrian Automobile, Motorcycle & Touring Clubs*)

many and elsewhere. In truth, Hans Ledwinka was the guiding spirit of the Czechoslovakian automobile industry and his designs are much admired throughout Europe to this day.

When Václav Laurin, an engineer, and Václav Klement, a distributor of books, joined in 1894 to build bicycles in Mladá Boleslav in Bohemia, there was little to indicate that they would produce the world's first V-twin and 4-cylinder motorcycles in 1903 and 1905 respectively. Before 1900, the partners had devised their own magneto, when suitable ones were unobtainable, as well as carburetors. Expanding rapidly with their motorcycles selling briskly in many countries, their venture into the automobile

business was a foregone conclusion. The first Laurin & Klement cars produced in series were the 1905 2- and 4-seater, lightweight voiturettes powered with 7- and 9-HP, water-cooled, 2-cylinder, V-type engines and shaft final drive. The marque achieved quick success when a team of the two-seaters won first, second and fourth place awards in the classic Semmering Hill Climb. This event, held near Vienna, attracted enthusiasts and cars from all over Central Europe.

Larger cars with 4-cylinder engines followed quickly. The Type-BS, originally conceived as a "doctor's car," was widely used and a large order for 1,000 similar cars was filled during 1909–10; these became Vien-

The 1921 Laurin & Klement touring Type 210. (*Motokov*)

na's taxi fleet with many of them still in service as late as 1928. Type-E was a large touring car with a maximum speed of about 45 MPH. L & K roadsters, tourers and limousines were popular in England where they were sometimes marketed as the Hewetson before the 1914–18 war. A limited number of 8-cylinder cars were built after 1907; two 4-cylinder cast iron blocks on a common aluminum alloy crankcase developed 40 BHP. According to the successors of Laurin & Klement in Czechoslovakia to-

In 1925, the final assembly department of the Laurin & Klement works looked like this. (*Motokov*)

The 1924 Laurin & Klement dickey-seated sports roadster Type 150. (*Motokov*)

day, this was "the first eight-cylinder car engine built in Europe." The marque gained fame throughout Central Europe as a reliable trials vehicle and as a suitable racer for the chassis-busting roads of the time by winning the St. Petersburg-Moscow-St. Petersburg endurance run, a grand prix race at Château-Thierry, and other grueling events in 1908.

In 1908, the "first L & K sports car" appeared. As the accompanying illustration shows, this Type-FCR 2-seater looked al-

The 1924 Laurin & Klement limousine Type 450, a luxurious 6-cylinder vehicle. (*Motokov*)

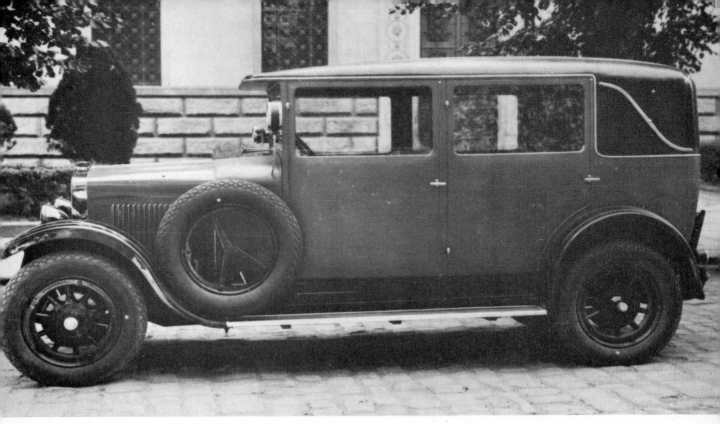

The 1924 Skoda Type 120 with fabric-covered coachwork. (*Motokov*)

most as high as it was long. Those were the days of ultra-long stroke engines in order to obtain high torque and acceleration. The FCR put out 100 HP and demonstrated speeds around 70–75 MPH on the Brooklands course in England with the factory designer, Hieronymus, at the wheel. Hieronymus designed the Hiero aircraft engines used in World War I. By 1910, the L & K works in Mlada Boleslav ranked among the top dozen European manufacturers in output, and exports were being made to England, Germany, Australia, Japan which sent a special purchasing delegation to Europe, China, Mexico and other nations. Reportedly 35 percent of the output went to Russia where L & K passenger cars, trucks and buses were used as far afield as Turkestan in Central Asia where roads were mere tracks. By the time the war started, Laurin & Klement cars had bagged

57 first places, 25 second and 11 third places in competitions including a whole shelf of awards in the Alpine Trials of 1910 through 1914.

After the war, L & K produced a variety of 4-cylinder cars. The Type-210 with an 80 x 120 mm., 4-cylinder, 9/25-HP engine on a wheelbase of 120 inches was the most popular from 1921 through 1924. Production of passenger cars took second place to commercial vehicles during the early '20s when the plant's total floor space was approximately 60,000 square metres, making it one of Europe's largest. In 1924, the rakish Type-150 roadster emphasized the marque's sporting tradition while the Type-450, a large luxury limousine with a 6-cylinder engine behind a dashingly pointed radiator, was marketed in an attempt to reestablish the prestige enjoyed before the war. Expansion capital, however, was lack-

180

The luxurious Skoda 6-cylinder phaeton, Type 6R, of 1928. (*Motokov*)

The 1929 Skoda landau sedan, Type 860, had an 80-HP, straight-8 engine. (*Motokov*)

Skoda 6-cylinder Type 645 cabriolet of 1929. (*Motokov*)

The Type 633 Skoda of 1931 for the middle class, 6-cylinder market. (*Motokov*)

The experimental Skoda Type 932 of 1934 had its 4-cylinder engine in the rear. Note the spare wheel and tire in the luggage boot in front. (*Motokov*)

ing and a merger was effected in 1924 with the giant Skoda Werke industrial complex headquartered in Pilsen.

Prior to the acquisition of Laurin & Klement, Skoda had produced Hispano-Suizas under license. After the merger, production continued in the L & K factory but many components were manufactured in the Skoda works in Pilsen. The designs were based upon L & K models but the marque was renamed Skoda. Late in 1924, the Types-110 and -120 appeared, powered by 4-cylinder, overhead-valve, in-line, 75 x 110 mm. engines. Chassis were conventional with semi-elliptic springs, 4-speed gearboxes and four-wheel brakes.

In 1928, a decision was made to broaden the range with overhead-valve, 6-cylinder models in the middle and luxury markets.

Conventional in design, the large Type-6R appeared in 1928 in open phaeton and closed models, and the multi-carburetor Type-645 of 1929 was a high-performance variant of the basic model. The medium size Type-633 entered series production in 1931. Despite the worldwide recession, the large Type-860, first introduced in 1929, continued in limited production although the market was slim for this 80-HP, 8-cylinder car. The luxury line lingered on until the war with the magnificent "Superb" of 1938.

Demand for dependable, low-priced, family cars led to the 1933 Type-420, a sensible car with an overhead-valve, 995 cc., 4-cylinder engine which developed 20 HP. With independent rear suspension by swing axles the 420 was an excellent car and sold well. The revolutionary Tatras designed by

Rear-mounted engine of the Skoda Type 932. (*Motokov*)

Slide-back roof on 1937–39 Skoda "Popular" had headliner for winter warmth. (*Motokov*)

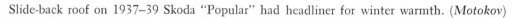

The 1937–39 Skoda "Popular" sports car. The 4-cylinder, overhead-valve engine displaced 995 cc., developed 22 HP. (*Motokov*)

1938–39 Skoda "Popular" sedans were built in two- and four-door models. (*Motokov*)

The 8-cylinder "Superb" limousine of 1938 was Skoda's finest car. (*Motokov*)

Hans Ledwinka and the rumors of Porsche's "people's car" experiments had their effect on the Skoda engineering department at this time and prototypes of the air-cooled, rear-engined Type-932 were tested in 1933. Four-wheel, independent suspension beneath a unitized frame-body structure and a 1-litre opposed-flat, 4-cylinder engine were successful features but Type-932 never entered series production. Instead, the 995 cc. "Popular" of 1934 proved to have been well named. In 1937, new 1.1-litre, 4-cylinder engines with overhead-valves were introduced and the "Popular" was produced in roadster, two- and four-door sedan and convertible versions through 1939. With a single carburetor, the output was 22 BHP but with modifications and dual carburetion, it was raised to 30 BHP which gave sprightly performance with the curb weight scarcely 2,000 pounds. Though low-priced, the "Popular" was of high quality; even the convertible models had woolen headliners making the

drop-heads as warm in winter as the steel-roofed models.

To the enthusiast, the most interesting pre-war Skoda was the "Rapid" which appeared in 1937 in a streamlined sports model named the "Monte Carlo." Customers familiar with the sporting heritage of the parent Laurin & Klement cars were delighted with this high-performing 1.5-litre model. Relatively few were built although the same overhead-valve, 4-cylinder engine became the nucleus of the "Rapid" sedan which was something of a medium priced grand turismo model for the one-car family man who wanted to be able to scoot along at 90 mph. Post-war Skodas were based upon the "Popular" and "Rapid" models.

Of the lesser Czech cars, the Praga was one of the better known. Although trucks were the main automotive output of the Czecho-Moravian Machine Works in Prague, prototypes of passenger cars were

The Skoda Rapid "Monte Carlo" of 1937 had a 1.5-litre, overhead-valve, 4-cylinder engine. (*Motokov*)

first tested in 1907. Renault influence was evidenced on the Praga touring cars of 1908; large and expensive, their 4-cylinder, L-head engines were in front of the radiator which was immediately forward of the firewall and dashboard in the Renault manner. In 1911, the 1,850-cc. "Mignon" was quite popular although the large "Grand" of 1912 was the most numerous of pre-1914 Pragas. Achieving some export success in eastern Europe, the reorganized Prague Motor Works set up a subsidiary plant in Poland after World War I. During the '30s, passenger cars eventually were phased out in favor of trucks.

About 1928, the Aero Aircraft Works of Prague marketed a tiny roadster. This first Aero car was minimum transportation with a two-stroke, single-cylinder engine of 10 HP. Next came a 2-cylinder, two-stroke model of 18 HP. In 1934, the Aero Type-30 "people's car" achieved considerable fame with its opposed, 2-cylinder engine of

1-litre displacement and front-wheel drive with four-wheel independent suspension. The last pre-war Aero was Type-50 with a two-stroke, 4-cylinder, 50-HP engine.

The first Brno car was not a great success when marketed in the early '20s because of an inefficient friction drive although its 4-cylinder, two-stroke engine was satisfactory. Built by the Brno Small Arms Works in Moravia, the Brno Z-18 of 1926 was better. A family car powered by a 1-litre, 2-cylinder, two-stroke engine, the Z-18 was a small vehicle just 12 feet long in sedan and roadster versions. The Z-4 appeared in 1933 as a front-wheel-drive car powered by an opposed, 2-cylinder, air-cooled, two-stroke engine. During the '30s, the Z-4 was a frequent competitor in light car races and once placed first in the annual Czech 1,000 mile reliability run.

The Walter cars, like so many European marques, were the outgrowth of motorcycle manufacturing. Josef Walter founded his

The 1.5-litre fastback Skoda Rapid two-door sedan was the production grand turismo version of the high performance "Monte Carlo" model. (*Motokov*)

firm in 1910 in Prague. Before and during the 1914–18 war, Walter made the "Trimobil," a 1-cylinder, three-wheel vehicle, and aircraft engines. After 1919, the small 18-HP Types-WZ and -WIZ were built, and during the '30s the 1-litre, 4-cylinder, 24-BHP "Junior" was fairly popular. Passenger cars were discontinued in 1939 in favor of trucks and aircraft powerplants. One Walter of the '20s had a unique 2-cylinder engine with the bottom of each cylinder bathed in oil and the cylinder heads cooled by a blower.

In 1927, the Wichterle & Kovarik Werke in Prostejov brought out the first Wikov, a 4-cylinder, overhead-camshaft car that lasted only a few years. The engine was used in a line of trucks after cars were discontinued in the early '30s.

Equally obscure is the Enka produced in Prague in 1928 by the Enka Automobilwerke. Little is known of this marque other than that it was a three-wheel mini-car with a water-cooled, 1-cylinder, two-stroke engine. The Enka must have been well designed, however, for it was capable of nearly 50

MPH. Another mini-car was the 40-MPH Favorit which was marketed briefly in 1931–32. Just over 9 feet long, the Favorit had an air-cooled, single-cylinder, two-stroke engine. A dozen other Czech cars failed to make the grade like their counterparts in other countries. The Isis of 1923–25 was a small, two-place sports car with a 2-cylinder, two-stroke engine that was water-cooled. Kan cars made their first appearance in a 1912 reliability run staged over a 285-mile course by the Vienna Automobile Club in which it won a class first place. This success spurred the builders in Prague to series-produce a range of 20- and 30-HP, 4-cylinder cars which lasted until 1915. In 1934, another of the myriad attempts to build a successful "people's car" appeared—the Myron of uncertain origin. An interesting specification included a rear-mounted, air-cooled, two-stroke engine developing around 18 BHP but under-financing soon forced it off the market.

One of the most likely designs failed—as so often happened—when the Special was shown with much fanfare in the 1925

188

Praga cars were built in Bohemia from 1908 on-ward. This is the "Grand" of 1912, a quality 4-cylinder model. (*Motokov*)

International Motor Exposition in Prague. A 1.5-litre engine lurked beneath a bonnet that was all grille. Very streamlined and un-usually low, the Special weighed under 1,-800 pounds. It soon disappeared despite fine performance and the initial surge of pub-licity. Lasting longer, from about 1922 to the early '30s, was the Start built by the Königgrätzer Automobilfabrik in Kralove, Bohemia. Small, water-cooled, 80 x 110 mm., 2-cylinder engines powered the Type-B, the first small 2-seaters. In the late '20s, the Type-C appeared with a 4-speed transmission, a 4-cylinder engine of un-known specifications, and 4-passenger bod-ies. The final Start was a 2-cylinder, air-cooled model with a flywheel-operated ig-nition system. There were others, too. The Vaja mini-cars with air-cooled, 2-cylinder, ¾-litre engines developing 12 HP weighed only about 750 pounds and could dash along at nearly 40 MPH. And there was the Asta of 1922–23, and the Fross-Büssing. There was even a car named the Z made in Brno between 1931 and 1937. As in other countries, the majority of distinct makes came and disappeared with little notice and with even less in the way of details re-maining.

Denmark

DENMARK ENTERED the automobile age when the proprietors of a cycle factory were stimulated to try their hands at doing what others were doing in other countries. The resulting Hammelvogn still operates, a car that in 1954 participated in the London to Brighton veteran car run completing the 56 miles in 12½ hours. The venerable 68-year-old vehicle "flashed" across the finish line after averaging a little less than 5 mph over the route.

Built in 1886 by A. F. Hammel and H. U. Johansen, it is the only one of its kind. The Hammelvogn's 2½-litre, 2-cylinder, horizontal engine has a bore and stroke of 104.5 and 160 mm. Mounted in the rear, the water-cooled powerplant has a hot tube ignition and develops 3.5 HP. The radiator is so small that it must be refilled every few miles. Candles in front of polished reflectors provide flickering light. The wagon body seats four persons riding back-to-back in pairs. One of the oldest operating cars in the world, the Hammelvogn is on display in the Danish Technical Museum in Helsingør, the town made famous by Shakespeare in "Hamlet." The elaborate front springs contrast sharply with the semi-elliptic leaf springs used in the rear.

In all, Denmark has produced nearly a score of marques. The Brems of 1900 was a 1-cylinder, air-cooled carriage that resembled the Eisenach of Germany; the maker, A. L. Brems, built a total of eight cars. More long-lived was the Dansk Automobil & Cycle Fabrik founded by H. C. Christiansen in Copenhagen. A success, the 1899 Christiansen had a 1-cylinder engine, friction drive off the flywheel and chain final drive. This car also is preserved in Denmark's Technical Museum. The later cars built by this firm were named Dansk. Limited production of elaborate, tiller-steered cars continued until 1906 when Denmark's parliament legislated against driving at night. This suppression caused a scheduled automobile service, started by Christiansen and a partner, to be discontinued.

During the first decade of this century the Brunn, D.K., Ellimobil, Flak, Fridensken, Jorgensen, Nordisk and several other experimental and limited editions sought the limelight in and near Copenhagen only to succumb because of under-financing, the pressures of a limited market and the weight of successful foreign makes.

One industrialist, Jan Hagemeister, very nearly succeeded in establishing a long-last-

HAMMELVOGNEN

One of the oldest cars in the world still operable is Denmark's first motor vehicle, the Hammel-vognen of 1886. Note the elegant front springs, and warning bell on the steering lever. (*Danmarks Tekniske Museum*)

ing, Danish, automotive manufacturing enterprise. Hagemeister had invented a gas turbine in 1913 and his marque, the Jan, was produced in series with bull-nosed sedans, open tourers and large, sporting two-seaters. Most Jans had L-head, 4-cylinder, 62 x 110 mm. engines but about 1916 the firm introduced a 6-cylinder engine that was considerably ahead of its time. With inclined valves in hemispherical combustion chambers, the Jan Six was a meritorious development, but wartime restrictions on raw materials held up production and necessitated a merger with Thrige & Company.

Thrige cars were built in Odense on the island of Fyn in 1909. An engineer of note and an industrialist of considerable financial ability, Thomas Thrige built in 1910 large touring cars and sedans that were quite popular. They frequently had full-elliptic springs in the rear and semi-elliptics in front. L-head, 4-cylinder engines were used. Thriges offered such touring niceties as luggage trunks shaped to fit the coachwork.

Early in the First World War, in which Denmark was neutral, Thrige organized De Forende Automobilfabriker—The United Automobile Factories—around his own

191

H. C. Christiansen built his first car in 1899.
The chassis is of tubular construction. (*Danmarks
Tekniske Museum*)

Thrige cars were series-built in Odense. This is the 1912 tourer. (*Danmarks Tekniske Museum*)

Jan cars included closed and open models like this
sporting roadster, a 4-cylinder type of circa-1914.
(*Danmarks Tekniske Museum*)

This 1928 Triangel was one of the last passenger
cars built by the United Automobile Factories in
Odense. (*Danmarks Tekniske Museum*)

plant, the aforementioned Jan and the curiously all-Danish Anglo-Dansk. The latter had been quite successful until the austerities imposed on motoring in 1914 forced manufacturer H. C. Frederiksen to seek a larger corporate alliance. By 1915, the Thrige, Jan and Anglo-Dansk marques had lost their separate identities and, by virtue of the three-way merger, had become the new Triangel, which emerged only to play second fiddle to a line of trucks until the late 'thirties. For some Triangel models, engines were imported, including Continentals from the United States, while the factory in Odense built 4-cylinder units. Some of the latter had aluminum alloy pistons and developed around 50 BHP. As had been the case with Danish cars before the 1914–18 war, this one remaining Danish marque retained its sporting background. In the 1927 Rome to Copenhagen Race, a large Triangel six-passenger tourer placed second. By 1928, however, car production was tapering off. The accompanying illustration shows one of the last passenger cars made by Triangel, the last Danish automobile to enjoy series production. Foreign competition was just too much for the resources of the small nation.

England

BECAUSE THE CARS of England are better known in America than those of other European nations, consideration of many marques will be brief. The pre-1900 English Daimler cars are shown in Part II. Initially marketed under license from the German firm, Daimler eventually emerged as an all-English car as will be seen.

Despite restrictions and prejudice against automobiles in England, several English inventors had been making internal combustion engines for many years—for pumping water, powering small boats, and for other industrial purposes. One of them, John Henry Knight, who had built several steam vehicles, built a single-cylinder, 1-HP, belt-driven, three-wheel gasoline carriage during 1894–95, and made a few secret runs. An interesting vehicle, the one and only Knight car, was rebuilt in either 1895 or 1896 into a four-wheeler with independent front suspension by means of separately sprung front wheels in bicycle type forks. Though it ran successfully at a steady 7–8 MPH, Knight did not develop his car further; but he did write in 1896 one of the first automobile books, *Notes on Motor Carriages*. Knight claimed to have been the first Englishman to build a gasoline car and to operate it on a public highway in England.

The other claimant to the honor is the Lanchester which, if it wasn't the first all-English gasoline car to run on public roads, was almost certainly the first produced for sale. The marque was created in 1895 when Frederick W. Lanchester, a gasoline engine designer in Birmingham, assisted by his brothers Frank and George, built a 5-HP, 1-cylinder, air-cooled car. In 1897, Lanchester began the development of a 12-HP car powered by a horizontally opposed, 2-cylinder, air-cooled engine. A unique single valve in each cylinder handled both inlet and exhaust and was very efficient. Forced lubrication by a pump assured long life for the bearings. Mounted alongside the driver, who steered by a tiller, this engine was one of the most durable of the period and drove the rear wheels through a 3-speed epicyclic gearbox and a worm gear final drive. The marque retained the latter feature for many years. Placed in production, after four years—an unusually long testing period for those times—this model continued with few changes, other than conversion to water cooling, until

195

The 21-HP Lanchester, introduced in 1924, was a popular base for luxury coachwork for several years. Chassis cost around 1,000 Pounds Sterling. 129 and 133-inch wheelbases; 78.7 x 114 mm., 6-cylinder, 3.3-litre engine of superb quality. The 1925 three-quarters landaulet. (*Daimler Motors Ltd.*)

From 1919 on, the 40-HP, 6.2-litre Lanchester on wheelbases from 126 to 152 inches was a leading luxury car; coachwork ran the gamut of the times. Six 101.6 x 127 mm. cylinders. Radiator header tank had "see through" glass window to facilitate checking water level. Chassis alone cost around 1,900 Pounds. The seven-passenger tourer of about 1924. (*Daimler Motors Ltd.*)

Limousine coachwork on a Lanchester "40" chassis of about 1925. Note handgrip near rear door latch. The Royal Family owned several Lanchesters. (*Daimler Motors Ltd.*)

From a rare old print, the 1928–30 Lanchester "Straight Eight" sports saloon. Usually on long 142.5-inch wheelbase, this expensive car was very fast with 5-litre engine rated 82 BHP at 2,800 rpm. (*Daimler Motors Ltd.*)

H.M. King Edward VII owned this luxuriously fitted 1902 Daimler. Note curved windows, curtains. (*Society of Motor Traders & Manufacturers*)

1905. Lanchester's own amazingly efficient wick-type carburetor, though simple, continued for the next ten years. Using no jets, the petrol was vaporized by being drawn through cloth. This car had a long, roomy wheelbase—from around 126 to 138 inches by 1909—that was continued until the war. So, also, was a new line of 20-HP 4- and 28-HP, 6-cylinder, overhead-valve engines. Luxury cars all, there was a wide range of coachwork. Some of these excellent cars even had disc brakes of Lanchester's own design.

Jet type carburetors were adopted after the 1914–18 war; and Lanchester's patented "Harmonic Balancer" was itself adopted on several other cars including the Willys-Knight in the U.S.A. This "Balancer" was a system of gear-driven weights beneath the crankshaft; virtually vibrationless running resulted. The excellent 40-HP model appeared in 1919 with a 6,178 cc., 6-cylinder engine in the conventional front position, but with the usual worm drive on rugged, smooth riding chassis of 141- and 150-inch wheelbases. The block for the 101.6 x 127 mm. cylinders was cast in pairs of three cylinders each. There were also open touring models able to top around 80 MPH despite weighing nearly 4,000 pounds. Brake horsepower was 90 at 2,500 rpm. In 1925, four-wheel brakes were fitted; in '26 hydraulic operation

One of the early double-sleeve-valve, 4-cylinder Daimler tourers of 1910. Finned radiator header tank, for better cooling, became an identifying hallmark of this fine car. (*Daimler Motors Ltd.*)

was standardized. With few other changes, the "Forty" remained in production through 1929.

The 3.3-litre, 70-mph, 21-HP model was produced from early 1924 through 1931 and was the first Lanchester to have a conventional, 4-speed gearbox. In 1928, the rare 5-litre, 30-HP overhead-valve Lanchester "Straight Eight" entered production. Bore and stroke were 78.7 x 114 mm. respectively, the same as that of the "Twenty-One"; the output was 82 BHP at 2,800 rpm. With a 4-speed gearbox, the Straight Eight had a quite sporting performance—some models were capable of 80 MPH—but it was short-lived due to financial difficulties which

caused Lanchester's absorption by Birmingham Small Arms, the firm which was associated with Daimler at that time. After 1931, the Lanchester struggled on, most models being distinctive smaller variants on the Daimler theme, until eventual disappearance in 1956—a sad end for the oldest of English-designed, production cars and one of the finest.

When Frederick R. Simms, an engineer, met Gottlieb Daimler during a business trip to the continent, he struck up a friendship that culminated in the organization in 1893 of the Daimler Motor Syndicate in London. Initially, the aim was to act as sales agents in the United Kingdom for Daimler gaso-

Royalty on all continents used Daimler cars. H.I.M., the Emperor of Japan, owned this 1913 limousine. Note long air horn and the speaking tube. (*Japan Automotive Industrial Association*)

Pointed windshield and heavy all-steel roof graced this 45-HP, 8-litre Daimler six of about 1910 which often had long, 150-inch wheelbase. (*Daimler Motors Ltd.*)

The 3.6-litre Daimler 24-HP six of 1938–39. With standard saloon works body, price was 795 Pounds. (*Daimler Motors Ltd.*)

line engines for marine and other industrial applications. Despite the restrictions on motor cars, Simms imported his first Daimler in 1895 and in 1896 introduced the Royal Family to motoring by giving the future King Edward VII his first ride. The same year H. J. Lawson, a speculator, entered the picture. Forming the British Motor Syndicate, Ltd. along with associates Ernest Hooley and Martin Rucker, Lawson tried to buy every available automotive patent in anticipation of monopolizing the new industry in England. After paying Simms 35,000 pounds for his Cannstatt-Daimler rights, Lawson organized the Daimler Motor Co., Ltd. in Coventry. Until about 1900, the supposedly English Daimler cars were essentially imported German models, but production began in Coventry and Edward VII purchased one of the first English-built models thus beginning a long period of royal patronage.

Until 1904, a vast range of 2- and 4-cylinder models appeared with displacements of 1 to 4.5 litres. Then Lawson's bubble burst

and the firm was reorganized with a more progressive directorate. Connections with the Daimler works in Germany were dissolved, Simms became a consulting engineer with the experienced J. S. Critchley as works manager, and original English designs were placed in production. At this point it is well to note that the Daimler was never a mass-produced car; all models were built to order for customers who could afford the best. Extreme care was taken in all aspects of fabrication and the slightest imperfect component was discarded even to complete chassis assemblies failing to meet the rigid standards of inspection.

Daimler produced a wide range of high-quality, 4-cylinder models in 6-, 8-, 12- and up to 22-HP versions, all with chain drive until 1909. Numerous awards were won in trials and competitive tours. The finned radiator became world famous. In 1909, the works switched from conventional poppet valves to the double sleeve-valves of the Knight type. Sleeve-valves were not abandoned until 1936 when a range of "Straight

201

The 3.4-litre Daimler straight-8, two-plus-two roadster of 1936–39 was frequent contender in long distance rallies. Model shown has coachbuilt body by Charlesworth. (*Daimler Motors Ltd.*)

Eight" cars was introduced in a wide selection of piston displacements. Immediately after World War I, 4-cylinder engines were discontinued with the exception of brief production of a 20-HP four on a 132-inch wheelbase in 1922. Sixes up to 8.5-litres on wheelbases to 162 inches were built in an expensive range. In 1926, the superb "Double-Six," an enormous V-12 engine was introduced in a limited, super luxury range that, on the 163-inch-wheelbase model, cost upward of 2,800 pounds complete with lavish coachwork by the most carefully selected body builders. Most of the Double-Sixes displaced from 3.8 to 7.2-litres and the 6-cylinder models of the same period varied from a modest 1.8 to 6 litres.

During the late '30s the Daimler 3.6-litre six and the high-performance 3.4-litre "Straight Eight" were the most numerous while the big, rare "Double-Six" topped the Daimler range from about 1932 until World War II. In 1930, Daimler pioneered the fluid flywheel in combination with the Wilson "pre-selector" gearbox (one selected the next gear ratio in advance of need, then simply depressed and released the clutch pedal to accomplish the gear change). Always conservative, Daimler gingerly approached independent front-wheel suspension in 1938.

Why have the magnificent Daimlers escaped the attention of classic car enthusiasts? The answer probably lies in an amazing

202

Belt drive from front engine and a countershaft which transmitted power to rear wheels by sprock-ets and chain. The 1901 Wolseley. (*British Motor Corp.*)

The 1904–05 Wolseley roadster had a 6-HP, single 114.2 x 127 mm. cylinder engine. An iden-tical car was made for Vickers as the Wolseley-Siddeley. (*British Motor Corp.*)

The Wolseley "Stellite" of 1913–20 had four 62 x 89 mm. cylinders with a tax rating of 9.5 HP. Wheelbase was 99 inches. This sturdy model eventually acquired a single overhead camshaft and evolved into the Wolseley Ten. (*British Motor Corp.*)

variety of models and the small numbers produced in each. Certainly Daimlers were unexcelled in quality; they were favored by the aristocracy and royalty and their durability and comfort excelled. The Daimler deserves attention as one of the oldest English production marques. Daimler was acquired—lock, stock and factories—by Jaguar in 1960. Daimler never built low-priced cars although long associated with Birmingham Small Arms which built popular cars during 1907–40. B.S.A. 2-, 4- and 6-cylinder models are scarcely remembered with the exception of the front-wheel drive "Scout," a small sports car of 1935–40 that achieved some popularity on the home market.

Second in seniority among the popular, early, English-designed cars is the Wolseley, which began in 1895 as a 2-cylinder tri-car with the third wheel in the rear. It was designed by Herbert (later Lord) Austin who worked for Wolseley Sheep-Shearing Machine Company, first in Australia and later in Birmingham. Able to interest his employers only after building a second machine, Austin finally built in 1900 a four-wheeler of the type shown here. With his 1900–01 car, Austin won a class first in the One Thousand Miles Trial in 1900 and so impressed Sir Hiram Maxim of Vickers Ltd. that the latter firm bought out the Wolseley works. In 1902, after several broken crank-

The late Sir Winston Churchill (at wheel) and Stanley Baldwin leaving 10 Downing Street in a large Wolseley 3.9-litre six in the late twenties. (*British Motor Corp.*)

shafts in the Paris-to-Vienna Race, Austin devised a forced lubrication system and the next year he entered a team of three 4-cylinder, 30-HP cars in the disastrous Paris-Madrid Race. All three Wolseleys, one driven by Austin, either broke down or crashed. In 1905, Austin left Wolseley and founded his own firm, but his co-worker J. D. Siddeley remained and continued to produce the 6-HP, single-cylinder model which was marketed as a Wolseley and as the Wolseley-Siddeley.

A variety of 2- and 4-cylinder cars up to 50 HP were produced thereafter and late in 1913 the "Stellite" was introduced. An excellent car with a 9.5-HP tax rating, the "Stellite" came back after the 1914–18 war.

Soon bore and stroke were increased to 65 x 95 mm. and the new "Ten" appeared with a fine 1,267 cc. single overhead-camshaft engine and was produced through 1928; one version, the "Moth" sports model, could top 70 MPH easily. Two years earlier, the Wolseley firm had failed financially despite successful fours and sixes of up to 3.9-litre displacements. Thus it was that W. R. Morris, later Lord Nuffield, bought the marque around 1926. Until 1940, the most noteworthy Wolseley models were the 6-cylinder, 75-MPH "Hornet" sports cars, an 8-cylinder, 2.7-litre model and a 4,021 cc. passenger car known popularly as the 32/80 (taxable and brake horsepower respectively).

The eights were current in 1927–28 and

The 1,271 cc., single-overhead-camshaft, 6-cylinder Wolseley "Hornet" sports roadster of 1930–34 with coachwork by Swallow. (*British Motor Corp.*)

The 1904 Riley "Tricar" was obviously a bit behind the times although the single 4.5-HP cylinder did provide economy at scarcely more cost than a motorcycle. (*British Motor Corp.*)

The 1910 Riley 10-HP two-seater had a pair of square 96 x 96 mm. cylinders, 102-inch wheelbase and a round radiator. (*British Motor Corp.*)

The first production Humber was this 1-cylinder, 5-HP car of 1900. (*Rootes Motors Ltd.*)

The 2-cylinder Humber roadster of 1909 delivered for 290 Pounds complete with "Side and Tail Lamps, Horn, Tools and Hood." The "Hood" is the folding top in the Queen's English. (*Rootes Motors, Ltd.*)

some of the engines were used in Morris's unsuccessful effort to resuscitate the failing Léon Bollée cars (see France). The Wolseley 8-cylinder cars were large (up to 141-inch wheelbase), expensive (bare chassis costing well over 1,000 £), and were ordinarily fitted with luxury coachwork. Thoroughly integrated into the Morris empire, the sporting "Hornet" in the hands of private owners raced with considerable success, even winning a class first in the Donington Twelve Hour Race in 1937. The more sedate pre-war sedans, with 6-cylinder engines, were much favored by police departments all over the United Kingdom for their sturdy dependability; these vehicles are prominent in many old English movies on the late, late TV shows. Incidentally, new late shows of English origin now give exposure to post-war Wolseleys.

Another early English car eventually to come under the Morris wing in 1938 (later the Nuffield Organisation and now the British Motor Corp.) is the Riley, founded by William Riley near Coventry in 1898. Three-wheelers and V-twin, four-wheel machines priced from 200 to around 400 pounds, some large enough to require 120-inch wheelbases, had earned a good reputation by the time Britain went to war in 1914. From 1919 until 1926 a single 1.5-litre, 4-cylinder (65.8 x 110 mm.) engine rated at 11 HP was produced on 108-inch wheelbases. A sporting variant appeared in 1924, the "Redwing" on a wheelbase of 114 inches but Riley really blossomed late in 1926 when the "Nine" sports car appeared with a spunky 1,075 cc., 4-cylinder (60 x 95 mm.) engine. This engine (increased to 1,089 cc. in 1928) had dual cam-

208

The Humber 8/18-HP "Chummy" of 1923 had four 56 x 100 mm. cylinders, a 94.5-inch wheel-base and cost about 275 Pounds. Refined economy. (*Rootes Motors Ltd.*)

shafts placed high in the cylinder block, driving valves, inclined at 45 degrees by pushrods, and hemispherical combustion chambers. The sporting chassis with big 13-inch brakes had a 106-inch wheelbase and, ready to race, weighed barely over a half-ton.

Reid Railton took the "Nine" in hand, squeezed 50 BHP at 5,000 rpm out of it, and the resulting "Brooklands Nine" established a world 6-hour record by averaging a hair over 85 MPH in 1928. In 1930, the new "Nine" won the Irish Grand Prix outright. The thrilling succession of Riley developments were many and varied, 4- and 6-cylinder sedans like the "Monaco," "Merlin" and the amazing 1,100 cc. closed "Kestrel." There were a few V-8 Rileys and the blown and unblown "Grebe," "MPH," and "Imp." Independent front suspension was introduced about 1935. In 1936, the 1.5-litre "Sprites" (the name originated with Riley) won the top four places in the Grand Prix of France. After the 1939–45 war, the Riley declined and lost its individuality.

As it was with so many others, Humber cars were the outgrowth of a bicycle factory. Thomas Humber's works was founded in Coventry in 1867; twenty years later Humber bicycles were popular in America and a score of other countries. Entry into the automotive industry came via the efforts of Lawson who sold rights to Humber to build the Léon Bollée motor tricycles. Lawson's operation, being what it was, did not satisfy the firm so in 1899 Humber introduced its own first experimental four-wheel car powered with a DeDion engine. This led to Humber's first production model, the 5-HP 1900 car illustrated. Known also as the "Humberette," it abounded with unusual

Captain Molyneaux of London and Paris designed the body of the 12-HP Humber "Vogue" close-coupled saloon of 1934. Note the pillarless "hardtop" styling. (*Rootes Motors Ltd.*)

The 1938 Humber sports saloon with 4.1-litre, 6-cylinder engine. Similar open models were Army staff cars two years later. (*Rootes Motors Ltd.*)

First of the famous Sunbeam cars was this high-riding 1899 model built by John Marston. The 1-cylinder engine was vertical when those of most other English cars were horizontal. (*Rootes Motors Ltd.*)

features like a radiator that swung aside to allow access to the engine and a single spoke steering wheel. Improvements were rapid. A 4-cylinder car was built in 1905 on a 96-inch wheelbase, and in 1908 the firm experimented with four-wheel brakes. It is not clear whether any production cars were so equipped, but if they were, this feature could be a Humber first. The 1912 model, a 4-cylinder, 12-HP car designed by Louis Coatalen, is said to have been the first sizeable English car to retail at 300 pounds or less. This model was produced until late 1914.

After the war, two series of 4-cylinder models with monoblock engines proved popular: a 65 x 120 mm., 10-HP car on a 105.5-inch wheelbase and a refined car costing around 600 £ with a 75 x 140 mm. engine rated at 14 HP. The latter was on a 113-inch wheelbase which was enlarged in 1920 to 123.5 inches. From about this time, F-head engines (with overhead inlet and side exhaust valves) were widely used by Humber. The "Chummy" of 1923 and the larger 116-inch-wheelbase, 2-litre 14/14 models of 1923 and 1928 followed. Next came a 6-cylinder, 3-litre quality car, the 20/55, on 126- and 132-inch chassis, which cost from around 900 £. Depression economy brought the need for outside finances and Humber became a part of the burgeoning Rootes Group, a move followed by improved fours and the 2-litre 14/40 selling for well under 500 £. During the '30s the most important Humbers were the fine 4.1-litre, 6-cylinder "Snipe" and the luxurious larger "Pullman" limousines that put

211

Wheels seemed to be everywhere—except where one would expect them—on the first production model Sunbeam, the curious Sunbeam-Mabley of 1901. One 74 x 76 mm. cylinder; tufted seats inside. Driver sat in the aft cubicle and steered, somehow, by a tiller. (*Rootes Motors Ltd.*)

the Rootes Group into the carriage trade with Royal "Appointments." For the enthusiast, however, *the* Humber of the era was the very sporting, close-coupled "Vogue" shown, a briskly performing, 1.8-litre, two-plus-two with "hardtop" type styling that was several years ahead of its time. Humber converted to war work in 1939–40 that included large orders for open touring "Snipes" adapted to rigorous military staff car purposes; one of these became famous throughout North Africa as Field Marshal Montgomery's personal machine, "Old Faithful." Humber resumed passenger car production after 1945 as the quality car branch of the Rootes Group.

After a tinware plant was founded by John Marston in 1887 near Coventry, the works expanded to Wolverhampton, made bicycles, and produced its first Sunbeam in 1899, a design by Thomas Curreton. Eventually to be acquired by the Rootes Group in 1935, Sunbeam had about thirty-six years of glory spiced with corporate involvement with Clement, Clement-Talbot and Darracq as already mentioned in the section on French cars. The second Sunbeam, the bewildering 1901 Mabley affair illustrated here, had wheels at each side and dead-center at the front and rear extremities. Oddly enough, the curious Sunbeam-Mabley was produced in some numbers, an anachronistic, motorized loveseat that must have looked out of place among the cars of most other manufacturers which were ultra-modern in comparison. Nevertheless, the en-

The penned words on an old negative tell the tale: Mills and Swift drove this big 6-cylinder Sunbeam to victory in the "Heavy" class in the 1907 Tourist Trophy Race. (*Rootes Motors Ltd.*)

gineering department gathered its wits and came up with the excellent big sixes, one of which won first place in the "Heavy" car class in the important Tourist Trophy Race in 1907.

Louis Coatalen, the Frenchman who found fame in England, joined Humber in 1909, brought his already established reputation along, and introduced the 16/20-HP model in 1911 with such immediate success that the factory had to be enlarged to meet the demand. In the 1912 Coupé de L'Auto race at Dieppe, France, a team of 16/20s captured the first three places against Europe's best cars and went on to the French Grand Prix where they took fourth, fifth and sixth places. At Brooklands in 1913, a 30-HP Sunbeam racer nailed down all the

international records from 50 to 1,000 miles and 1 to 12 hours in a series of runs with Dario Resta, K. Lee Guiness (of K.L.G. sparkplugs) and J. Chassagne driving. Sunbeam had arrived! To prove the point, Guiness won the Tourist Trophy after a 600-mile race in 10 hours, 38 minutes with a 12/16-HP passenger car in 1914; this model had dual overhead-camshafts and four valves for each 81.5 x 156 mm. cylinder.

The marque Talbot (an English car made in London from 1903 and later involved in a combine with French interests as mentioned) entered the scene in 1913 by producing a 25.6-HP, 4-cylinder car that became the world's first to travel more than 100 miles in an hour. Percy Lambert drove one 103 miles in 60 minutes and then pro-

213

The 1924 supercharged Sunbeam 2-litre machine in the pits at the Spanish Grand Prix at San Sebastian. (*Rootes Motors Ltd.*)

The very attractive 1936 Sunbeam-Talbot 3.5-litre sports saloon offered the Wilson pre-selector gearbox; available also in open models. (*Rootes Motors Ltd.*)

The first production Singer was the 1904 roadster which came complete with spare tire, lamps, and "all-weather equipment." (*Rootes Motors Ltd.*)

ceeded to cover a flying half-mile at 113.28 mph. Sunbeam and Talbot merged in 1920. Though their technical and financial resources were combined, the two marques retained some distinction in the British Isles with Talbot producing a range of high-quality cars—and often expensive at around 1,000 £—with 4- and 6-cylinder engines. During 1925–34 Georges Roesch was chief engineer and his Talbot type 105, a 3-litre six of the early '30s, is considered one of the best examples of the period in the sports-touring category.

Sunbeam placed fourth at Indianapolis with a 4.9-litre six in 1916. After the war, came the years of record breaking. In 1922, fifty-one world time and distance records fell to the marque and in 1923 a team of 2-litre (new formula) cars driven by Segrave, Divio and Lee Guiness took first, second and fourth places respectively in the French Grand Prix. Divio also won the G.P. of Spain the same year in a Sunbeam, and

Segrave repeated by winning the same event in 1924. The marque's string of sensational victories swelled with Segrave taking the world's speed record at Pendine in Wales with 150.87 MPH in 1925. Sir Henry Segrave used a streamlined, 1,000-horsepower Sunbeam special in 1927 to set a new world speed record of 203.79 MPH on Daytona Beach, the first time 200 MPH had ever been exceeded on land. Sunbeam, until World War II, was a threat in motor racing of all types.

The marque more than held its own outside of record breaking with notable cars like the race-bred 6-cylinder (75 x 110 mm.), dual overhead-camshaft, "3-Litre," open touring and sports models of the mid-'20s and the related "Speed" model closed sports saloons of the early '30s. After acquisition by Rootes in 1935, the Sunbeam 3.5-litre, 6-cylinder series offered pre-selector gearboxes optionally and were the top of the line. The last prewar Sunbeam was the

215

A race meeting on the Marne in 1912. Singer racing specials with dagger tails had 1,097 cc., 4-cylinder engines; gearboxes in unit with rear axle. Top speed of over 65 mph kept them winning races through 1914. (*Rootes Motors Ltd.*)

The 1928–29 Singer "Junior" had four 56 x 86 mm. cylinders (capacity 848 cc.) and single-overhead-camshaft and a variety of sturdy bodies on 92-inch wheelbase sporting chassis priced about 150 Pounds up. This saloon is engaged in the Monte Carlo Rally. (*Rootes Motors Ltd.*)

The famed 972 cc. overhead-cam Singer "Le Mans" 1934 sports car during the Lawrence Cup Trial the same year. A. T. K. Debenham driving. (*Rootes Motors Ltd.*)

"Ten," a thinly disguised Hillman with a peppier version of that car's 1.1-litre, 4-cylinder engine. Rather pretty open Tens with cut-down door sills combined the feel of a sports car with the space requirements of small families. For a few years after the war, the Sunbeam-Talbot 90 sports sedan was quite popular in America.

The Singer is another car based in Coventry where the first of the marque was built in 1900 as a three-wheel experiment by George Singer who had made bicycles since 1876. There was no connection with the Singer firm in America. With the first production model a success in 1904, the firm was producing four models by 1909 ranging from a 7.9-HP, 2-cylinder to a large 24.8-HP, 4-cylinder. Sometime during 1911, the young William Rootes was employed as an apprentice. About the same time a Singer raced an Avions Hanriot, a French airplane, at Brooklands. The best the monoplane could do was about 40; the Singer won at 78 mph! When the Singer "Ten," a 4-cylinder, 1,097 cc. car appeared in 1912, it had its 3-speed gearbox in unit with the rear axle and it lapped the Brooklands course at 65 mph. Stripped racing versions, some with streamlined aluminum bodies with stiletto tails, campaigned as far afield as France in light car races.

William Rootes was so impressed with the type "Ten" that he opened a dealership and contracted for an entire year's production. This event set the course of the man who became Sir William and who later formed the Rootes Group beginning with Hillman, in partnership with his brother Reginald. The "Ten" was a winner and was kept in production for the army after war began. Perhaps the finest early Singer, though, was the 1.7-litre, 14-HP model of 1913–14 which had all four cylinders cast en bloc and inclined valves operated by a single overhead-camshaft. The "Ten" was built in 1923 into a full four-passenger

217

A 1904–06 Napier fast tourer with powerful 45-HP, 4-cylinder (102 x 107 mm.) engine cost 1,000 Pounds in chassis form. (*Society of Motor Traders & Manufacturers*)

model, and in 1927 the 8 HP "Junior" was introduced, a very competitive model that remained in production until the early '30s. With its lusty overhead-camshaft, 848 cc. engine, the "Eight" could be coaxed to around 65 MPH and more with special tuning. The tuned sporting Eights were called the "Porlock" after a well-known grade where the car enjoyed many hill climbing achievements.

The "Eight" led to the "Nine," a 972 cc. overhead-cam four in 1932, which promptly won a Glaciers Cup in the Alpine Trials. Despite a long 96-mm. stroke, in contrast to a 60-mm. bore, and a two-bearing crankshaft, this engine could safely rev to 6,000 rpm. In competition, 2-seater, sports car trim, the "Nine" became popular as the

"Le Mans" model and qualified at 50 MPH for the 1933 Le Mans event. Though it failed to place well at Le Mans, the "Le Mans" did win many races. Four-door sedan versions were extremely popular and kept the "Nine" range in production through the '30s.

Independent front suspension and an optional fluid clutch were introduced in 1934 on a new line of 1.5-litre, 11-HP models that included an "Airstream" four-door saloon model priced at 300 £. Though of moderate cost, the quality Singers were the world's only cars with a guarantee "against cylinder bore wear." After the Second World War, the S.M. 1,500, open 4-seater was highly favored in sports car racing in America for several years where it competed di-

218

Reid Railton built splendid, high performance cars of high quality in Surrey (1934–49) and powered them with tuned Hudson engines. The limited production, 8-cylinder, 4-litre Railton "Cobham" saloon of 1937–39. (*The Motor*)

rectly against the M. G. TC on very favorable terms with its excellent 1.5-litre overhead-camshaft engine. Since 1956, Singer has been a part of the Rootes Group—the marque was the first love of the Rootes brothers.

The first Vauxhall, 1903. Air-cooled, 5-HP, single-cylinder car with pointed nose, tiller steering and coil spring suspension at front and rear. (*Vauxhall Motors Ltd.*)

The 1908–14 Vauxhall 12/16-HP model designed by Lawrence Pomeroy, Sr., the marque's first sporting car. Cylinder dimensions were 92 x 95 mm., later became 85 x 102 mm. In the 2,000 Mile Trial of 1908, this tourer won its class and became world's first car of any make to complete such a distance without any involuntary stop. (*Vauxhall Motors Ltd.*)

Napier, barely remembered now, was one of England's finest cars. Montague Napier was impressed by a Panhard in 1896 but thought he could improve it with an engine of his own design. He did and added wheel steering. Soon he was in business. In 1900, he began building cars of his own design under the aegis of the family business, D. Napier & Sons Ltd. in London. During his first year in the new industry, young Napier's first car, a 2-cylinder machine, won second place in the 1,000 Miles Trial of 1900. In the same year, Napier and C. S. Rolls (later of Rolls-Royce fame) drove a 4-cylinder Napier (tax rated at 16 HP) in the Paris-Toulouse race in France. Though the car retired with mechanical problems, it was the first English-designed car to race on foreign soil and the first Napier with four cylinders.

After a series of trials and errors, Napier built a 30-HP, 4-cylinder racer with shaft drive in 1902 and, with S. F. Edge and a cousin, set out for Paris to enter the Gordon Bennett Trophy Race. Lesser men would have despaired because en route and during the race they replaced a broken cylinder head, repaired gears, and virtually rebuilt the car. Their efforts paid off, for the big Napier was the only entry to finish the race to Innsbruck, Austria, and Napier won the G. B. Trophy. Hearing of the mighty Napier, the American paint manufacturer, Charles Glidden, bought a 24-HP, touring, 4-cylinder model and used it on a 2-year, 46,-000-mile world tour from temperate zones into the Arctic and return during which the car suffered only one minor illness which a half-hour roadside treatment remedied. Mrs. Glidden went along on this epic journey which prompted Glidden to sponsor the

The "first car in the world with an engine of 20 HP R.A.C. rating to reach a speed of 100 mph" was this razor sharp Vauxhall special which set its record in October, 1910; the mark stood for two years. (*Vauxhall Motors Ltd.*)

famous Glidden Tours which have been revived in recent years as working outings for antique cars.

In 1903, Napier introduced the world's first production car with six cylinders—a tribute to the pioneering Spyker of The Netherlands. Rated at 18 HP, a Napier six entered the 1903 Gordon Bennett Race in Ireland wearing Napier's distinctive green paint, a tribute to the host country—British "racing green" was born. A Napier six was also used by S. F. Edge in 1907 on his incredible, 24-hour endurance run on the then new Brooklands track when he averaged an astonishing 66 MPH without a relief driver. Though a test of man and machine, such feats were expected of Napiers by that time for two years previously a driver named MacDonald had set a new world speed record of 104.64 MPH at Daytona with a 159 x 127 mm. six with a hood-length radiator around a pointed nose.

Of very high calibre and costing as much as 2,100 pounds during the '20s for the complete chassis before calling in a coachbuilder, the Napier was in a class with Maybach, Bugatti, Locomobile and a small handful of cars built with one aim—perfection. In addition to sixes, a 2.7-litre, 15-HP four was produced during 1912–14. During 1914–18, Napier made aircraft engines and other implements of war. After 1919, the long 137- to 144-inch-wheelbase chassis, with servo-assisted, four-wheel brakes and powered with a single line of hand-machined, 6.1-litre, 6-cylinder (101.6 x 127 mm.) engines, were favored mounts for the finest creations of the best coachbuilders.

When the lean years came, there were few buyers for this fine car and in 1927 the

221

Lasting fame for Vauxhall and engineer Pomeroy with introduction of "Prince Henry" model. Current 1909–14, car had four 90 x 120 mm. cylinders, 115-inch wheelbase. Pomeroy's magic eventually extracted 60 BHP at 2,800 rpm in 1910, enabling it to win trials and races all over Europe. (*Vauxhall Motors Ltd.*)

last Napier was built. The firm survived and is still a dominant factor in British industry. Napier did supply racing engines to such drivers as John Cobb who used a Napier-Railton at Brooklands in 1935 when he set the 143.44 MPH record for that track.

Reid Railton, incidentally, had high regard for some American engines. Railton cars used the Hudson 4-litre, 8-cylinder chrome steel engines in firm, sportive chassis. A specialist works, Railton's factory produced quality cars during 1934–39 and 1945–49. The 1937–39 "Cobham" is illustrated.

There would be no Vauxhall if King Harold had not lost the Battle of Hastings. For his services to William of Normandy, one Fulke le Bréant was awarded an estate in Bedfordshire which he named Fulke's Hall. Centuries later an ironworks was established on the estate's remains and the place was called Vauxhall. In any event, the first successful Vauxhall car was built in 1903 by F. W. Hodges who worked for the Vauxhall Ironworks. He had already built a 5-cylinder radial engine and tried it without success in a primitive car about 1893. The 1903 car had an air-cooled, single-cylinder (101.6 x 119.6 mm.), 5-HP motor with chain drive and coil spring suspension, but the 1904 model had a more powerful, water-cooled, 3-cylinder engine. This was put into full production. During 1905–06, Vauxhall produced Hansom cabs driven from an exposed pulpit high above the body at the extreme rear. Cabs and other models of 1904–06 had flat-topped pointed bonnets suggesting a possible alliance with the makers of the New Orleans, an English license-built duplicate of the Belgian marque Vivinus.

When Laurence Pomeroy, Sr. joined Vauxhall in 1905, he designed a shaft-driven

The lesser known Vauxhall type B12 chassis of 1912–16 usually carried formal coachwork; this example was supplied to the Czar of Russia in 1916. (*Vauxhall Motors Ltd.*)

The legendary 30/98 Vauxhall type "OE" of 1922–28 with 4-cylinder (98 x 140 mm.), overhead-valve, 4.25-litre engine and 118-inch wheelbase and fluted bonnet. Car could lap Brooklands at 100 mph in touring trim; was developed from 1913 30/98 type "E" which had L-head 98 x 150 mm. engine and 115-inch wheelbase. (*Vauxhall Motors Ltd.*)

The 6-cylinder (73 x 110 mm.), 2.8-litre Vauxhall 20/60-HP model of 1927–29; wheelbase 123 inches. The head above that of the chauffeur is that of H.R.H. the Prince of Wales (later Edward VIII) during a visit to University College at Cardiff. (*Vauxhall Motors Ltd.*)

12/16-HP (12 taxable), 4-cylinder model on a 102-inch wheelbase which, along with the 115-inch 20-HP (90 x 120 mm. four) sporting tourer of 1908, was produced until war broke out. Our photo shows the 1908–14 version of Pomeroy's 12/16-HP model. The 20-HP engine developed 39 BHP. Pomeroy modified one (by attention to lubrication, pistons, camshafts and the like), extracted 52 BHP at about 2,400 rpm, and installed it in the needle-tailed racer shown which proceeded to crack the flying half-mile record at Brooklands with 88.6 mph. The same car became the world's first 20-HP (tax rating for 3,054 cc.) automobile to "reach a speed of 100 mph" in 1910.

For the Prince Henry Trials in Germany, Pomeroy produced his most famous car, the Prince Henry Vauxhall which he began to work on in 1909. Soon put into production, it was a beautiful four-seat sports car with semi-elliptic springs fore and aft and was equally at home in a race or on the road. Producing 38 BHP originally, the engine was refined to give out 60 BHP at 2,800 rpm in 1910.

Some of the Prince Henry's greatest successes came in races in Russia where the abominable roads seemed a natural for this car which knew few peers. By increasing both bore and stroke to 95 x 140 mm. in 1913, the 3,969 cc., 30/98 type "E" was created. In turn, the "OE" was produced after the war during 1922–28 with a 98 x 140 mm. overhead-valve engine. Between 1920 and '23, these sporting Vauxhalls of both pre- and post-war years won 75 first places, 52 seconds and 35 third places in competitions plus countless other awards. The 4-litre models topped 70 MPH with ease; the OHV, 4.25-litre versions, well over 80.

224

The 1935 Ford "Ten" with L-head 1,172 cc., 4-cylinder engine looked like a miniature American Ford V-8 of 1934. (*Society of Motor Traders & Manufacturers*)

In 1926, Vauxhall came under the General Motors banner and during the '30s solid but uninteresting family sedans were produced. The famous fluted engine bonnet remained as a hallmark until this decade but, now, that too is gone and Vauxhall has become another motoring sacrifice upon the altar of quantity production.

After successfully exporting to the British Isles for several years, Ford established a factory in Manchester in 1911 where the models "T" and "A" were assembled from Canadian and American manufactured parts. Also, there was a long 131-inch wheelbase model "AA." The 4-cylinder model "B" and the 60- and 80-HP V-eights were similarly turned out from late 1931.

Finally in 1932, a distinctly English type, the 933 cc., L-head, 4-cylinder, four-passenger model "Y" appeared. Designed in Detroit, the small two-door economy car looked like a scaled-down American "B"; in the English scheme of horsepower rating for tax determination, it was the Ford "Eight" and was the first Ford tailored for England. Interiors were of leather and all fittings, etc., were in English style. Slightly larger and looking like a big Ford V-8, of the same year, the 1,172 cc. "Ten" came out in 1935. Open tourers had notched doors, looked very sporting and the 63.5 x 92.5 mm. engine, though still having side-valves, was receptive to modifications and went into hundreds of home-built specials that battled for glory in that most English of motor sports, the "mud-plugging" trials—or ordeals. Eminently successful, the little Ford "Eight" and the nearly-as-small "Ten" were face-lifted and renamed "Anglia" and "Prefect" in late 1938, but the engines retained their L-heads. After the war the engines were eventually upgraded with overhead

225

The first Standard car was this 6-HP, shaft-driven, 1.4-litre, single-cylinder (127 x 76.2 mm.) wicker-trimmed carriage of 1903. (*Leyland Motors Ltd.*)

valves and powered the basic models of such famous new marques as the Lotus which is indicative of Colin Chapman's regard for the little Ford engines.

The Standard Motor Co. Ltd. which was founded in Coventry by R. W. Maudslay turned out the first Standard car in 1903, the handsome vehicle in the accompanying photo. The single-cylinder engine was strange with 127 mm. bore and 76.2 mm. stroke. (The Maudslay car of 1902–26, also made in Coventry, is virtually without record, but was a 1.7-litre, 6-cylinder car costing around 800 £ in the marque's final years. Known to have been a high-quality machine built in limited numbers for the carriage trade, the Maudslay was an early user of overhead camshafts. The manufacturer was a distant relative of R. W. M. of Standard but there was no known relationship between the two makes.) The Standard was so named because R. W. Maudslay, a well-known industrial engineer, intended to mass-produce only a few models but to the highest "standards" and at a low initial price.

The extremely short stroke in relationship to the bore produced a relatively quiet engine able to idle at low rpm's without undue vibration considering the early stage of the automotive arts. Standard's second model, the 2-cylinder, 12/15-HP car of 1904 continued this policy—the bore was extremely oversquare, nearly twice the stroke —and would idle at around 250 rpm and accelerate without a quiver to some 2,000 rpm. Ahead of its time, this engine was an L-head (valves on one side) when most others were T-heads. It also had an accelerator jet in the carburetor, a 4-speed gearbox when most cars had three ratios, shaft rather than chain drive, and other features.

Like others, Maudslay admired the pioneering Spyker six and he joined the race to be first in England with such an engine. As we have seen, Napier won the race and Sunbeam copped second place, but in 1906 the new 5.2-litre 24/30-HP Standard became England's third production car with a 6-cylinder engine. The car shown here is the 1907 model. Maudslay also produced a larger 9-litre, 50-HP Standard six. The radiator shells of the early Standard sixes were distinctive, and from the front the sharply dropped center of the I-beam front axle added to its attractiveness. The works rarely indulged in fielding competition teams but the marque immediately gained a devout following and, because of its dependability, King George V used one during a side trip into mountainous Nepal in 1910.

The most famous prewar Standard was the 1.1-litre, 4-cylinder "Rhyl" of 1913, the make's first "light car" (under 1.5 litres displacement). During 1914–18, the Standard factory built airframes and engines for the air arm. When peace returned, 4-cylinder cars of 1.1 to 2-litres were produced on straightforward, no-nonsense chassis with wheelbases ranging from 90 to 116 inches. During 1927 to '32, there was also a 2.3-litre six on a 122-inch wheelbase. Outstanding were the 1.6-litre models of 1920, mostly open tourers, and the discreetly elegant 9-HP "Fulham" saloon of 1928–29;

the Weymann type fabric-covered coachwork was quiet and distinctive on this popular low-priced (190 £ up) family car.

By 1935 Standard was suffering from the universal business recession which necessitated reorganization by John Black, a merchandising genius. Late in 1935, the "Flying" Standards appeared and a promotion campaign was waged to remind the public of the marque's wartime experience in the aeronautical field. This ploy with the evidence presented by the advanced range of modern 4-cylinder, 9- to 16-HP models, plus the introduction of the little 1,009 cc. "Eight" late in 1938, brought Standard back into a strong position which enabled the firm to play an important role in war production. After 1945, the little Eight (and larger models) was produced again and a number of them found their way into the U.S.A.; occasionally one turns up unexpectedly for they do not wear out easily.

The year 1903 was also the birth year of the once famed "Leaf"—the Lea-Francis— another Coventry car. Built in relatively small numbers, until 1922 as a sideline to the motorcycle manufacturing business of Lea & Francis Ltd., the only noteworthy early production car was the curious 1903 model which had a 3-cylinder, two-stroke engine with connecting rods nearly 24 inches long. Little data remains of that car which was marketed for several years. In 1922, the 12-HP, 4-cylinder (69 x 130 mm.) Meadows engine was adapted for a rapid little sports car. There was also a 75 x 130 mm., 14-HP model; both had overhead valves and quickly established enviable reputations in trials and sports car races.

During the late '20s and early '30s, sporting closed cars—some with fabric bodies— were produced. These had radiator shells looking remarkably like M.G.s of a few years later. The most famous "Leaf" of all was the 1.5-litre, 4-cylinder (69 x 100 mm.) "Hyper" of the late '20s. When a Cozette supercharger was made optional in 1927, the "Hyper Leaf" was England's first production car to offer a blower. In 1928, a blown "Hyper" won the Tourist Trophy Race in Ulster by a comfortable margin over a very fast front drive Alvis, a marque yet to be discussed. In the same year a "Hyper" finished in overall 8th place at Le Mans against formidable opposition and added insult to injury again in 1930 by nabbing 6th place. The same year the firm suffered financial woes but began production again in 1933 with an excellent 2-litre, 6-cylinder, 2-seater that had few equals in roadability and handling. Early in 1938, a new pair of dual overhead-camshaft, 4-cylinder sports cars appeared, an improved 1.5-litre model and a more potent 72 x 100 mm., 1.6-litre car. Hugh Rose, formerly with Riley, was the designer. Pre-selector gearboxes were optional. The brakes were among the best on any car at any price. Both of these 1938 cars were produced after the war with enlarged 1.8- and 2.5-litre engines and restyled bodies. The smaller of the two powerplants was modified later for use in the Connaught Grand Prix racers—a sidelight indicative of progressive Lea-Francis engineering. Finally in 1953, the "Leaf" was no more; its builders were some of the last of the rugged individualists who were submerged in a world where there was little room for the small, quality manufacturer.

Mention of the Meadows engine in connection with the Lea-Francis prompts brief reference to several limited production cars that used this unit, one of the better known proprietary powerplants of the vintage years. Built in small quantities in Isleworth, Middlesex, from 1924 until the late '50s, the

Frazer-Nash was the creation of Captain Archie Frazer-Nash and H. R. Godfrey who had cut their manufacturing teeth on the G.N. cycle car. The latter was a V-twin, air-cooled sports car of tiny proportions and the barest minimum of frame and body driven by a system of belts. For about 225–250 £, the buyer got an ultra-lightweight 2-seater which could be tuned to produce more than 70 MPH in the later models. The G.N. won hundreds of light car events, a tribute to the builders' philosophy that anything unnecessary, if left off, could not impede performance.

The natural outgrowth of the success of such a small sports car was a demand for something larger and faster and so the Frazer-Nash began with Powerplus and 20 BHP Anzani engines. By about 1929, the 1.5-litre Meadows engine (similar to the Leaf's) was fitted into 99- and 105-inch-wheelbase chassis. An unusually short propeller shaft drove a cross-shaft by bevel gears; the cross-shaft transmitted power by means of four pinion gears to four sprockets on the solid rear axle. There was no differential. Dog clutches and chains controlled the system resulting in an amazingly smooth power transmission and excellent acceleration. Continually developed, the Frazer-Nash was by no means inexpensive and in the '30s won awards and honors out of all proportion to its specifications. The last of the chain-driven cars, the Frazer-Nash of 1936 could reach 60 MPH in around 15 seconds and had plenty of power left. A brief postwar resurrection with BMC engines brought new fame and a third place at Le Mans.

The Meadows 2.5-litre, 6-cylinder engine also powered many of the Invicta cars. Built in Cobham from 1925, fewer than 100 of these high-priced, sports-tourers were built

The 24/30 HP Standard of 1907 with 6-cylinder (102 x 108 mm.) engine; displacement 5,250 cc. Note the odd V-shaped front axle. This particular car is believed to be the oldest survivor of the marque. (*Leyland Motors Ltd.*)

to the most fastidious standards. After 1928, the 4.5-litre Meadows engine with dual ignition was available. With 95 BHP at 4,000 rpm on tap, the 126-inch-wheelbase car could top 85 MPH easily. Heavy with expensive coachwork, Invictas usually weighed well over 3,000 pounds. Honors were many. Two sisters named Cordery once drove their 4.5 model 70,000 miles in 70,000 minutes in a fantastic endurance feat. Another won the Alpine Rally in 1931 driven by Donald Healey (the designer of the postwar Austin-Healey and other cars). Another 4.5 with coachbuilt body established records in the Prescott Hill Climb which stood for many years. When the firm failed in the mid-'30s, Reid Railton bought the assets and the marque struggled along only to fade away when war came. There were other Meadows-engined cars; chief among them were the

229

Royal carriage for the late King George V during the Delhi Durbar in 1910. Here the King stands beside his car somewhere in Nepal. The car: a 6-cylinder (89 x 108 mm.) 20-HP Standard. Cylinders were cast in pairs; wheelbase was 116 inches. (*Leyland Motors Ltd.*)

Aston-Martin and Lagonda, both covered in due course.

Bicycles were the mainstay product of the Rover Cycle Company founded in Coventry by John Starley and William Sutton in 1877. Eleven years later Starley built an electric car but the project lapsed in favor of tricycles and two-wheel pedal vehicles. In 1902, motorcycles were added to the product list. The first Rover car was introduced in 1904. Designed by Edmund Lewis, the car's central backbone chassis frame was a revolutionary development that was later adopted on the Continent. Rover's own "Patent Automatic Carburetor" and shaft drive were used. Shown in complete and chassis form in the accompanying old photographs, the new 8-HP Rover (there was

230

The 4-cylinder (62 x 90 mm.), 9.5-HP "Rhyl" of 1913 was the first light car out of Standard. This 1.1-litre model had worm gear final drive, 90-inch wheelbase, and was continued in production after the war. (*Leyland Motors Ltd.*)

The 4-cylinder (60 x 102 mm.), 9-HP Standard "Fulham" with fabric-covered body. This 1928 car's displacement was 1,155 cc.; 92-inch wheelbase. (*Leyland Motors Ltd.*)

The "Flying" Standard 20-HP model of 1936 represented the best of the pre-war range which included 9, 10, 12 and 16-HP models. (*Leyland Motors Ltd.*)

also a 6-HP version) won its first race over a field of other English and European cars at the Easter races at Bexhill. Hill climb victories quickly followed and the 8-HP Rover found a ready market.

Single-cylinder models rapidly gave way

The first Rover, 1904, a diminutive, two-seat runabout with 8-HP, 1-cylinder (114 x 130 mm.), 1,250 cc. engine on a 78-inch wheelbase. (*Leyland Motors Ltd.*)

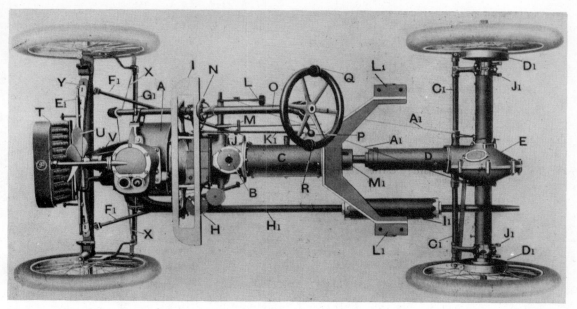

The revolutionary box girder and central backbone chassis frame of the first Rover in 1904 was the first known example of this type structure. Note six-spoke steering wheel with handgrips. (*Leyland Motors Ltd.*)

to a successful range of 4-cylinder models, the most illustrious being the 1906–07 tourers with 20-HP engines. One of these numbered "22" won the 1907 Tourist Trophy Race in the Isle of Man, an important annual event. Rover concentrated on refinement rather than on extensive gadgetry. By 1913, only 4-cylinder cars were being built with a 12-HP model pre-eminent. Cars were quickly replacing motorcycles and bicycles. By 1913, Rover cars were priced from around 100 to 600 £.

New facilities were needed due to wartime expansion, and in 1919 the most famous early Rover, the air-cooled 8-HP "Twin" was introduced; the model shown was produced during 1920–25. More than 17,000 were sold—a big figure in England in those days. Next came the 14/45 model of 1925–28 with a 4-cylinder (75 x 120 mm.) engine displacing 2.1 litres. Open and closed tourers were on a 120-inch wheelbase costing around 500 £ and up, but there were lower priced 1.1-litre fours as well. In 1925, the 14/45 model won the Dewar Trophy presented by the Royal Automobile Club for outstanding performance in RAC-observed trials in an industry-wide competition.

Rover's first 6-cylinder car, a 118-inch wheelbase, 2,023 cc. model, was introduced for the 1928 season. Quite sporting coachwork of low profile was offered on this chassis plus other more conventional bodies. One of these, a "Light Six Sportsman's Saloon" with racy lines, was used in the first successful effort to beat the fast and famous Blue Train from St. Raphael across France to Calais. The Rover triumphed in this enterprise in which other better known makes had failed in previous years and arrived in Calais ahead of the express train. Rovers came to be regarded as "the poor man's Rolls-Royce" and, as such, it was a favorite with professional men of moderate means.

In 1934, Rover came its closest to producing a sports car when the "Twelve Sports Tourer" was introduced to round out a range of 4- and 6-cylinder cars in the 10, 14, 16 and

233

The 1907 Rover 20-HP, 4-cylinder (97 x 110 mm.) model's hallmark was its distinctive shield-shaped radiator. Cost of this 114-inch-wheelbase tourer was 400 Pounds. A similar car won the 1907 Tour-ist Trophy Race. This particular car used to be a familiar sight at old car meets in America; was recently purchased back by Rover. (*Leyland Motors Ltd.*)

20 HP classes. The "Sports Tourer" featured very sporting, open, 4-seat coachwork on a firm, superb handling chassis containing a 4-cylinder (69 x 100 mm.) 1.5-litre engine. A close ratio 4-speed gearbox, folding windshield and cut-down doors helped to popularize the car but production was limited in favor of closed sedans and stylish cabriolet coupes. One of the most successful of the old line independent firms, Rover's factories in Coventry were destroyed in the war, but new works in Solihull were opened after the war and Rover built the world's first successful gas turbine-powered car in 1950. More recently, Rover has joined the Leyland group of companies along with other automobile producers but the cars retain their distinctive identity with such famous vehicles as the Land Rover and excellent passenger cars.

When Frederick Henry Royce, an electrical engineer of Manchester, bought a

234

Decauville in 1903 (a French car of 1898–1910), he was so disappointed with its lack of refinement that he set about to build a car for himself according to his own standards of perfection. The initial success of the first Royce 2-cylinder car in 1904 so impressed the wealthy Charles Stuart Rolls that a partnership was formed and Rolls-Royce Ltd. was organized the same year.

From the first 2-cylinder model, all Rolls-Royce cars have had overhead inlet and side exhaust valve (F-head) engines until recently. Built with the greatest care, hand-machined and polished to perfection, Rolls-Royce has always shunned innovation for the sake of innovation preferring to refine the best possible materials to the point where improvement is all but impossible. Ettore Bugatti—also a perfectionist but of a different sort—is once supposed to have observed that "the Rolls-Royce is an example of craftsmanship over engineering." At the same time, when management discovered a part made by a competitor to be of equal perfection, they rarely hesitated to buy in the item. Consequently, in later years wheel hubs made by Hispano-Suiza were used, and the like.

The distinctive, often copied, radiator shell began to become famous in 1905. Satisfied with the first 2-cylinder car, Royce made a 4-cylinder model and entered it in the first running of the Tourist Trophy Race. The new four performed well but managed only a close second to an Arrol-Johnston. Undaunted, Royce was back in 1906 and won the same event outright. Late in 1906, the most famous Rolls-Royce was introduced, the incomparable "Silver Ghost" with its 7-litre, 6-cylinder engine (square at 114 x 114 mm. but later increased to 114 x 121 mm. and 7.4 litres). Wheelbases were 134 and 142 inches. Cast in two blocks of three cylinders each, the engine had a drilled crankshaft with massive journals and pressure lubrication supplied by a pump made by Royce who also designed the jet-type carburetor and ignition components. A 4-speed gearbox—third gear was in direct drive and fourth was overdrive for fuel economy and speed—was controlled by a cone-type wet clutch.

Although Rolls was inclined toward flamboyant promotions—he was a pioneer aviator and loved to race cars—and held the purse strings, Royce preferred a subtle sales approach, a characteristic infused into his cars which have always been quiet, dignified and efficient. Claude Johnson, the works manager with the advent of the "Silver Ghost," sided with Royce and even recommended that experiments with 3-, 4- and 8-cylinder engines be discarded in favor of the Ghost. Thus the "Legalimit" V-8, silent, looking like an electric car and governed to 20 MPH, was dropped. Rolls was convinced and the "Silver Ghost" remained in production through 1926 with only minor changes. The conservative engineering approach is exemplified by the transmission brake system. The marque's position was secure when Rolls died in an aircraft crash in 1910.

During 1914–18, Rolls-Royce built aircraft engines and produced armored cars by fitting armor plate to modified car chassis. Recently the works received an R-R armored car built in 1914 that fought through both world wars and racked up more than a half-million miles. It is still fit and ready for another round with its "Silver Ghost" engine in fine fettle after service all over Europe, the Middle East and North Africa. Such a lifetime of service surpasses, of course, the achievement of the 1907 reliability run of 15,000 miles during which a

235

The immensely popular 2-cylinder (85 x 88 mm.), air-cooled Rover of 1922; wheelbase 88 inches. (*Leyland Motors Ltd.*)

The rare 1934 Rover "Twelve," a 1.5-litre sports tourer; 4 cylinders (69 x 100 mm.), overhead valves and open four-seated coachwork. Cost, 288 Pounds. (*Leyland Motors Ltd.*)

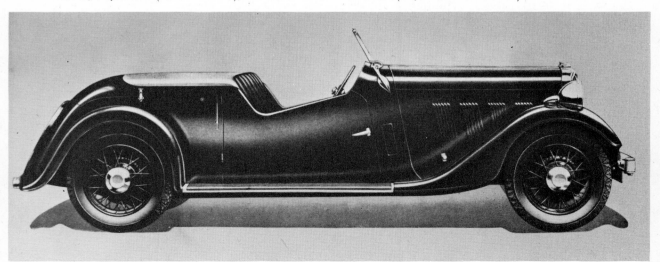

The 1930 Rover 6-cylinder "Light Six Sportsman's Saloon" was just 66 inches high, had Weymann fabric body, cycle fenders, and was fast enough to race and beat the Continental Express's famed Blue Train from St. Raphael to Calais, a distance of 750 miles. (*Leyland Motors Ltd.*)

During 1937–39, the Rover range included 1.4-litre, 10-HP; 1.5-litre, 12-HP; 1.6-litre, 14-HP and 2.1 litre, 16-HP models. A two-plus-two drophead coupe of 1939. (*Leyland Motors Ltd.*)

The 1905 Rolls-Royce 10-HP, 2-cylinder model, instantly a success due to unexcelled craftsmanship. Royce pioneered full pressure lubrication in England. In 1906, a 4-cylinder model won the Tourist Trophy Race on the Isle of Man. (*Rolls-Royce Ltd.*)

$10 parts replacement was the only impediment to an otherwise perfect run. One of the rare competitions entered was the 1914 Alpine Trial. The single Rolls-Royce entry was the only car out of a starting field of 6 dozen to finish the route; many of the cars were larger and more powerful. The winner was the "Alpine Eagle" tourer.

One rarely needs to change gears in a Rolls-Royce regardless of vintage; they will crawl along at 5 MPH in fourth gear on level ground and accelerate smoothly despite total weights of 4,000 pounds and sometimes more. Royce disliked noise, so in 1909 the gear ratios were altered to eliminate the slightly noisy overdrive. In 1912, the rear suspension was changed to the cantilever type for a smoother ride. From about the same time, the works refused to release HP figures. To prolong engine life and keep fuel consumption down, rpm were kept within limits; good design, faultless machining and careful selection of gear and axle ratios provided sufficient power transmission to enable many a stripped Ghost to attain around 100 MPH in tests.

In 1919, the new "Silver Ghost" reflected modifications made to the "Alpine Eagle" model of 1914. An improved ignition system, huge mechanical drum brakes on the rear wheels, and a cautious increase of the compression ratio to 3.8 to 1 allowed the engine to peak at 2,200 rpm when the road speed of a full-bodied tourer or saloon was 70–75 MPH.

From 1925 to 1929 the 40/50 "Phantom I" was produced with the displacement increased to 7,695 cc. on wheelbases almost always of 144 inches. The chassis alone cost a minimum of 1,850 £ and, in general, the finest of coachwork by such houses as Figoni & Falaschi, Barker, Hooper, Charles-

The original Rolls-Royce "Silver Ghost," a 40/50-HP, 6-cylinder car that performed faultlessly in a 15,000-mile endurance run conducted by the Royal Automobile Club. Still surviving, this car has run a half-million miles. Platform rear suspension, 48 BHP at 1,900-2,000 rpm. (*Rolls-Royce Ltd.*)

The 1914 Rolls-Royce "Alpine Eagle" tourer. (*Rolls-Royce Ltd.*)

Mrs. C. F. Coburn in her elegant 20/25-HP Rolls-Royce duck-tailed sports roadster with beautiful mahogany coachwork. (*Joseph H. Wherry*)

The sporting 20/25 Rolls-Royce 3.1-litre roadster owned by the Coburns. Wheelbase 122 inches. (*Joseph H. Wherry*)

The Rolls-Royce "Phantom I" was current during 1925–29. Six-cylinder 7,695-cc. engine in 144-inch-wheelbase chassis. A formal town car. (*Rolls-Royce Ltd.*)

A recently restored Rolls-Royce "Phantom I" shooting break of circa-1927 owned by Nick Reynolds of the Kingston Trio. (*Joseph H. Wherry*)

A rakish Rolls-Royce "Phantom II" leather-hooded sports coupe of about 1930 on 150-inch wheelbase. (*Henry Ford Museum*)

worth, Gurney Nutting, and others was fitted.

A smaller Rolls-Royce, the 20-HP model with a 3,103 cc. engine in a 129-inch-wheelbase chassis was also available during 1925–30. It enjoyed the same care in its construction as the large cars. Sporting bodies were often fitted to this model.

The "Phantom II" of 1929–36 had a longer 150-inch wheelbase with four-wheel hydraulic brakes, 5.25 to 1 compression ratio, and semi-elliptic springs front and rear. Though often weighing around 5,000 pounds and considerably more with the lavish coachwork available to nobility and the wealthy, a P-II can attain 80 MPH while aluminum bodies permit around 90 MPH—always in silence except for the wind ripple. During the decade, the various models were license-built in Springfield, Massachusetts, but the "Springfield Rolls" never fetch as much when changing owners. When Royce died in 1933, the background enamel in the medallion was changed from red to black.

Most powerful prewar model was the "Phantom III" made from 1936 until the outbreak of war. A V-12 engine with 82.5 x 114.3 mm. cylinders (7,340 cc.) and—of all things—independent front suspension with upper and lower members and coil springs were the principal changes. Like its splendid forerunners, the P-III was fitted with every imaginable type of coachwork, but always in the best of taste. The last of the classic Rolls-Royces, a 7.4-litre Phantom III, can effortlessly extend itself to around 100 MPH. Speed, however, was never the purpose of this fine marque. The present successors of the founders remain as dedicated to the best possible quality in their cars.

The Lagonda is another car having a connection with the shearing of sheep. In a nutshell, Wilbur Gunn was born in Ohio near Lagonda Creek by Lake Erie where his family ran a firm that made sheepshearing machinery. The firm's name, Singer, did not pertain to sewing machines or the English car. Trained as an engineer to enter the business, young Wilbur chose to emi-

242

Rolls-Royce "Phantom III" Sedanca de Ville with coachwork by Franay. Current during 1936–38, "Phantom III" had 7,340-cc., V-12 engines and were first of marque to have independent front suspension. (*Harrah's Automobile Collection*)

grate to England to pursue his ambition to become an opera singer. Instead, he started making motorcycles and powered tricycles around 1898.

By 1905, he had won a reputation for quality vehicles and several races, had established a small factory near Staines Bridge, had hired an engineer named Cranmer, and had begun production of a 4-cylinder, 20-HP and a 6-cylinder, 30-HP car. The cylinders were cast in pairs. Like Royce, Gunn was a perfectionist; he was also sentimental and named his cars Lagonda which means "smooth running waters" in an Ohio Indian tongue. Until 1913, all but a handful of Lagondas were exported to Russia, the rea-

son there seem to be no surviving pre-1913 models.

The pre-1915 Lagondas had some interesting features like the four longitudinal rods —two above, two below—which positioned the rear axle much like modern trailing links. Leaf springs, front and rear, were employed. Gunn made several trips to Russia where he participated in trials and races, winning most of them including a long distance reliability trial in 1910. In 1913, a handsome 1.1-litre, 4-cylinder (67 x 77.8 mm.) F-head Lagonda went on sale in England priced at about 140 £ with touring, closed or cabriolet bodies welded into a solid unit with the frame. On a 93-inch wheelbase, this car had

243

The 2,931 cc., 6-cylinder (72 x 120 mm.) Lagonda 16/80 sports two-seater of 1933 owned by G. Vaughn. The 6-cylinder engines were made by Crossley. Wheelbase 129 inches. Four-seaters were also made as well as longer 138-inch wheelbase closed cars. (*Joseph H. Wherry*)

The 1937–39 Lagonda V-12, designed by W. O. Bentley, was fast enough to place third at Le Mans in 1939. England's first closed cars to achieve 100 mph, stripped models lapped Brooklands at more than 125 mph. This Tickford-bodied 1939 drophead is owned by Tony Luther. (*Joseph H. Wherry*)

Excellent lines of the 1939 Lagonda V-12 are evident. Closed salons were built also. Marque was acquired by the David Brown Group in 1947. (*Joseph H. Wherry*)

ultra-quick, direct steering and good performance, probably the best value in the light car field during 1913–15 but war broke out in little more than a year after introduction. From this model on, all cylinder blocks were single castings.

Gunn died in 1920 just as the 1.1-litre model resumed production. Produced at the same time was a 108-inch-wheelbase version with the same engine. This remained current until 1926 when two larger fours were introduced, a 1.4-litre and a 2-litre on 108- and 120-inch chassis respectively. In the following year, one of the 1.1-litre cars broke the one-hour class record at Brooklands by averaging 80 MPH. Dual chain-driven camshafts located high in the block drove inclined valves. A 4-seat sports car was added to the range the next year on the 2-litre chassis as the "Speed Model." Smooth running but heavy due to sturdy construction, these were guaranteed for 80 MPH. They cost 675 £ up. Simultaneously, the first 6-cylinder (69 x 120 mm.) model since about 1910 was produced, a 2.7-litre known as the 16/65 on a 129-inch-wheelbase chassis; prices started close to 750 £. These were high-calibre cars, among the finest in their class and price range. In 1929, a larger 2,931 cc., 20-HP model on a 138-inch wheelbase at near 1,000 £ ready to roll was introduced.

In 1932, the firm began buying engines on the outside. A 2-litre Crossley six engine in the 16/80 produced a very sporting tourer. Choicest of the Lagondas of the '30s was the dual overhead-camshaft, 1.1-litre "Rapier." With 60 BHP at 5,000 rpm on tap and dashing coachwork with firm suspensions and good brakes, the "Rapier" could have been a gold mine had the cast iron engine not been so heavy. The complete 2-seater weighed nearly a ton. Nevertheless, the flexibility afforded by the preselector gearbox and superior roadability enabled a "Rapier" to qualify for the Rudge-Whitworth Trophy—sponsored by the equip-

245

The 1909 single-cylinder, 7-HP Austin, one of the marque's first production models and the original "Baby Austin Seven." Side curtains were extra. (*British Motor Corp. Ltd.*)

ment firm—in the 1934 Le Mans. Optional superchargers put this model into the 125 MPH class. The 4.5-litre Meadows engine was used in the very potent "Rapide" sports car and one of these was the overall winner at Le Mans in 1935. A rash of models included the 3-litre "Speed" models, some of which were fitted with an unusual 8-speed pre-selector gearbox made by Maybach in Germany.

This confusion of models ended when W. O. Bentley—footloose since his firm had been bought out by Rolls-Royce—joined Lagonda as chief engineer late in 1934. Taking the 4.5-litre "Rapide" in hand, Bentley made a luxury sports car out of it. He refined the chassis and reduced the wheelbase to 123 inches; standardized a four-speed fully manual gearbox; increased the capacity from 4,429 to 4,453 cc.; upped the compression ratio to 7.0 to 1; brought the weight down to around 3,750 pounds; gave a written guarantee for 100 MPH; placed them on sale at 1,000 pounds; and sold them as fast as they could be made. Road manners were greatly improved with independent front suspension. With 150 BHP at 3,800 rpm and built with Bentley's traditional care, the resulting "Rapide M-45" was a car for the connoisseur. There were also 4.5 Meadows-engined passenger models on wheelbases up to 135 inches that carried coach-built bodies.

The ultimate prewar Lagonda, and probably the finest design of Bentley's career, was the V-12 introduced in late 1937. Each bank of 6 cylinders (75 x 84 mm.) had one overhead-camshaft and one Solex carburetor; in its highest stage of tune the compression ratio was 8.8 to 1 and output was 225 BHP.

The popular Austin "Town Carriage" of 1911, technically a landaulet. Driver sat over the engine. (*British Motor Corp. Ltd.*)

Coachwork was by the best builders, the one illustrated having an aluminum two-plus-two cabriolet body by Tickford. After the war the marque resumed production. H.R.H. Prince Philip was a Lagonda enthusiast.

As already observed, when Herbert Austin left the Wolseley works, he set up his own firm in Birmingham where he began production of the first Austin in 1906. A large 25/30-HP tourer, it was soon joined in 1909 by a low-priced 1-cylinder roadster rated at 7 HP, the forerunner of a later "Seven." Both cars sold well and a formal car, the "Town Carriage," was introduced in 1911. Two years later the 4-cylinder 20/30-HP Lancaster went on sale, a quality car with luxurious interiors. The Vitesse of 1913–15 was a powerful 20-HP, 4-cylinder (95 x 127 mm., 3.6-litre) on a long 129-inch wheelbase which, like the other Austins, was immediately popular. Austin cars now covered the market from the lowest priced range through the medium and into the fringe of the luxury market. During the 1914–18 war, Austin's works expanded rapidly. Staff cars, aircraft engines and even complete airframes were built in quantity.

When peace returned the "20" resumed production in a variety of body styles, the cheapest costing nearly 500 £, and in 1922 a medium sized 12-HP, 112-inch-wheelbase car, the "Heavy Twelve" with four 79 x 102 mm. cylinders (1,661 cc.) with a basic price of 450 £ was marketed. In the meantime, rising prices had forced the "20" into the high-priced 695–1,145 £ range. The old 1-cylinder, 7-HP model was hopelessly out of date.

To cover the low-priced mass field, Austin

247

Austin design had progressed with the 1913 "Lancaster" landaulet. The 20/30-HP engine had four cylinders. (*British Motor Corp. Ltd.*)

introduced the famous Baby Austin, the immortal "Seven" with its remarkable little 4-cylinder, 749 cc. engine in a 75-inch-wheelbase chassis. Weighing less than a half-ton, the little "Seven" was sensational and remained in production with improvements naturally, through 1939. Leaf springs, transverse in front and quarter-elliptics in the rear, beneath a light frame, and four-wheel brakes—the latter most rare on a light car costing but 165 £—translated into big-car features in a small package.

As the public bought the Baby Austin at a glance, the future Lord Austin had motoring England in his pocket. Although the tiny crankshaft had but two main bearings, it was tough—Austin always used the finest materials obtainable—and the 10 HP, trans-

mitted through a 3-speed gearbox, pushed the Baby along at 50–52 MPH flat out. Scanty, 2-seat bodies were offered alongside the tiny, 2-door sedans. Although not intended initially as a sportster, so many owners raced the 2-seater in club events that a supercharged version appeared in 1928 and in 1930 the remarkable marks posted in the Tourist Trophy Race in Ulster prompted the blown "Seven" to be named for that race. Fuel consumption of the standard 4-seat model was minimal, around 45 miles per 5-quart British gallon. "Seven" chassis were popular mounts for Swallow coachwork in both open and closed versions. During the '30s the "Seven" appeared as the "Nippy" with the same little L-head engine tuned to give around 70 MPH.

The 129-inch-wheelbase, 20-HP Austin "Vitesse" heavy tourer of 1914; many were employed by the army as staff cars. (*British Motor Corp. Ltd.*)

The 1922 Austin "Heavy Twelve" tourer; four 72 x 102 mm. cylinders, 112-inch wheelbase. (*British Motor Corp. Ltd.*)

The 4-cylinder (56 x 76 mm., 749 cc. displacement) Austin "Seven" of 1923 brought motoring within the means of the masses; continued with few internal changes until 1940. Wheelbase 75 inches. (*Society of Motor Traders & Manufacturers*)

Austin built large vehicles during this period, too, fours and big 6-cylinder cars in the medium-priced range and 4-litre limousines. As the second round with Germany approached, the long, dignified 18-HP "York" topped the Austin range. Since the war, Austin associated with the Nuffield (ex-Morris) Organisation to form the British Motor Corporation.

A year after the future Lord Austin founded his own firm, William Hillman and Louis Coatalen established themselves, with the latter as designer. Coatalen stayed long enough to marry Hillman's daughter and to launch the first Hillman in 1907, the large 2.3-litre model illustrated. The four cylinders were cast singly in this conventional shaft-driven car that was the marque's mainstay for several years. In 1909, square bore and stroke were becoming the vogue in some quarters and new 4- and 6-cylinder Hillmans with 127 x 127 mm. cylinder dimensions were introduced as the 25- and 40-HP models. Until 1914, all Hillmans had 3-speed gearboxes and cost upward of 150 £.

The 1914–18 war turned the Hillman works into a large enterprise as it did so many others. During 1915–17, the 1.5-litre, 11-HP model, the marque's first with all four cylinders cast in a single block, was produced in limited numbers on a 102-inch wheelbase. After hostilities this model cost around 370 £, evolved into a varied range and remained current through 1925. Coachbuilt bodies were fitted frequently to the chassis which, by 1922, had risen in cost to 415 £.

In 1928, the Rootes brothers, William and Reginald, acquired control of Hillman

Developed from the famous "Seven," the 1923 Austin racing sportster weighed about 950 pounds, topped 50 mph with ease; was available with supercharger after 1928 as the "Ulster" model which topped 70 mph. (*British Motor Corp. Ltd.*)

Motor Car Co. Ltd. when the top Hillman was a 2.6-litre, straight-8 on a 120-inch wheelbase. The Rootes brothers stamped their mark on the Coventry firm by concentrating on low-cost fours. The 1.2-litre "Minx" appeared in 1931 and progressed

The Austin "Seven" plus Swallow coachwork became the Austin-Swallow economy custom car during 1928–31. (*British Motor Corp. Ltd.*)

Dignified coachwork on the big 18-HP Austin "York" of 1938–39. (*British Motor Corp. Ltd.*)

The first Hillman, 1907, with designer Louis Coatalen at the wheel. Four 89 x 96 mm., separately cast cylinders (2.3-litres); half-elliptic front and three-quarter elliptic rear suspension. (*Rootes Motors Ltd.*)

The 1912 Hillman drophead coupe with half elliptic suspension front and rear. (*Rootes Motors Ltd.*)

The 1915–17 Hillman 11-HP model had four 65 x 120 mm. cylinders cast en-bloc. Basic price was 370 Pounds. (*Rootes Motors Ltd.*)

The famed Hillman "Minx" was introduced in 1931 with four 63 x 95 mm. cylinders (1,185 cc.), an R.A.C. rating of 10 HP, and a wide choice of open and closed bodies. This is the 1933–36 "Aero Minx" in closed form, a development of the sports "Husky" of 1928. The late Lord William Rootes personally tested first "Minx" throughout Europe, Middle East and Africa. (*Rootes Motors Ltd.*)

into a popular range including the streamlined "Aero" model of 1933, a quite sporting open car.

The 1939 "Minx," still using the dependable L-head four displacing 1,185 cc. with a 4-speed gearbox, introduced a fully integrated unit-type body and frame structure. By this time, the Rootes Group of companies

The 1939 Hillman "Minx" had an integral or "unit" type chassis-body structure. (*Rootes Motors Ltd.*)

had materialized with the control of Humber and Sunbeam, and the Hillman division had solidified its position as a leader in light cars for the mass market. In the early '30s, Sir William (later Lord Rootes) participated personally in testing new models. It is said that he refused to introduce the original "Minx" until he had assured himself that the car would withstand the rigors of Europe's worst roads and the scorching heat of the Sahara.

When the prosperous owner of a chain of meat shops named Portwine and engineer John Weller joined forces about 1900 to pro-

duce the Weller car, the future of the motorcar industry in England was not yet secure. The Weller car lasted only a few years and little is known of it today.

Reorganizing their enterprise, the partners founded Autocarriers Ltd. in Thames Ditton in Surrey, the forerunner of A. C. Cars Ltd. in the same location today. The first motor vehicles were a series of three-wheelers powered by a vertical, 1-cylinder, 5-HP motorcycle engine driving the rear wheel. The pair of central pivoting front wheels supported a large parcel box. One can imagine that Portwine put the first batch

The well-curtained, 3-wheel "Sociable" of 1910, the first A.C. passenger car; one 5-HP cylinder (90 x 100 mm.). Minimal but efficient transportation. Price, 87 Pounds. (A. C. Cars Ltd.)

The 5-HP motorcycle engine and drive mechanism of the 1905 A. C. "Mighty Atom," the commercial forerunner of the first A. C. passenger carriage of 1910. The horizontal rod by wheel is the gear box control lever. Note asbestos-wrapped exhaust pipe. Owner, Lindley Bothwell. (*Joseph H. Wherry*)

of rigs in service to supply his butcher shops. The "Mighty Atom" caught on, became popular with all sorts of service firms (the 1905 model illustrated was used by a tobacconist as a delivery vehicle), and by 1909 had evolved into a sprightly little 2-seater car called the "Sociable" for obvious reasons. This was the first A. C. car. It sold well through 1914 when war interrupted Weller's plan to market his first 4-wheel design, a 10-HP model, which reached dealers in 1919. The 106-inch-wheelbase chassis was conventional. At first, 4-cylinder (59 x 100 mm.) engines of French manufacture were used. In 1920, a switch was made to English-made, 4-cylinder (69 x 100 mm.) Anzani engines of 12 HP. These were used in this

basic A. C. car until 1926. Seven years earlier, Weller had designed one of the finest 6-cylinder (65 x 100 mm., 1,991 cc.) engines ever to come out of England. The block was aluminum alloy with wet steel cylinder liners, there was a single overhead-camshaft, and the initial output was 40 BHP although the tax rating was just 15.7 HP. Constant development of this tough 2-litre unit eventually increased the BHP to well over 100 and it was used in a range of excellently engineered cars. Constant improvements with triple carburetion, hotter camshafts, and the like, kept this engine in production around 40 years. A 56 BHP, 2-litre roadster broke the world record for 24 hours—with one man driving—on the

An ultra lightweight A. C. hill climb and trials two-seater of 1923. Little is known of this rare machine; engine is believed to have been a 69 x 100 mm. Anzami four. (*A. C. Cars Ltd.*)

Montlhery circuit with an 82-plus MPH average in 1925. Another 2-litre A. C. coupe was, in 1925, the first British car ever to enter the grueling Monte Carlo Rally. The next year, with a light aluminum body, the A. C. won the same event.

In 1933, the Earl of March (later the Duke of Richmond and Gordon) came to

The 1924 A. C. tourer was available with a 4-cylinder (69 x 100 mm.), 1,496 cc. or the fine Weller-designed 16-HP, 1,991 cc. 6-cylinder single-overhead-camshaft, aluminum-alloy engine. The latter engine was produced for nearly 40 years with only detail changes. (*A. C. Cars Ltd.*)

A. C. as a designer and consultant; the Earl had been a successful competition driver for some years. During the '30s, 4-speed synchromesh gearboxes, multiple carburetors and a variety of tuning options made A. C. 2-seat sportscars (and the only slightly slower 4-seat tourers) favorites for hill climbs and all-out racing. In the mid-'30s, the "March Tourer," one of the hairiest and most popular models with its 4-speed, non-synchromesh, crash gearbox, added to a long list of class wins.

A. C. adopted the Italian scheme of stressing all body openings to provide strength at such normally weak places; consequently this make's bodies were stronger than many others. Polished aluminum hoods were popular on A. C.s and in 1937 an A. C. two-seater, at certain angles, looked strangely like the S.S. 100 Jaguar—or vice versa. A few A. C. "Flea" models, a short variant on the 2-litre theme, were imported into the U.S.A. shortly before the war. In the late '40s, A. C. became one of the most eagerly sought English marques in this country, a noteworthy achievement for a relatively small, independent builder. Happily, the A. C. survives.

Less fortunate was the Jowett. From their first prototypes of 1906, the brothers William and Benjamin Jowett experimented and tested for four long years before introducing the first Jowett car to the public at their Bradford factory in 1910. The two horizontally opposed cylinders (72 x 101.5 mm.) were air-cooled, drove the rear wheels by a shaft and bevel gears, and were set in a sturdy 72-inch-wheelbase chassis. Curiously, tiller steering was still used, possibly the last car so fitted. A 3-speed gearbox, shaft drive and leaf spring suspension filled out the brief specifications of the immediately popular though small 2-seaters which

cost just 137 £. The production models, by the way, had steering wheels.

Production resumed in 1919 with few technical changes except extension of the wheelbase to 84 inches, a size that remained popular until 1929 when another 6 inches were added. During 1924, longer 96- and 102-inch-chassis appeared beneath 4-seaters with open and saloon bodies. When the "Javelin" appeared in 1936 with a new, flat, 4-cylinder (72.5 x 90 mm.) engine, Jowett joined the swelling ranks of popularly priced 1.5-litre cars. There were two carburetors, one for each pair of the horizontally opposed cylinders, and a 4-speed gearbox which made these firmly sprung open models suitable for sporting events although the marque was never intended to be a sports car. After the war, the Jowett enjoyed a following in America until 1954 when the small firm found it impossible to obtain certain component parts and another venerable marque faded away.

Retaining much of its classic styling to this day, the Morgan loses nothing by its stubborn refusal to envelop itself in the characterless sheet metal which makes many modern marques virtually indistinguishable from others at first glance. When the Reverend Mr. Morgan's son, H. F. S. Morgan, decided upon an engineering career rather than the ministry, the automotive world gained a rugged individualist of the old school. Perhaps this explains the underlying appeal of the first Morgan, the 1910, three-wheel, 2-seater which was still in limited production more than forty years later after surviving the technical changes brought about by two world wars. Legend has it that Morgans are still enameled by hand by the same man who painted the first production models; the story is engaging but fanciful.

Incredibly, the last "Moggie" was finally built in 1951, a world record for a single model—and a three-wheeler at that—which began with an 85 x 85 mm., V-twin located in an exposed position in front of a mere hint of a body. What was a hood—or bonnet —on other cars covered the legs of the passenger and driver. For a time, only the rear wheel had a brake but the widespread use of the Moggie in hill climbs and voiturette races required front-wheel brakes within a few years. Just two forward speeds transferred power to the single rear wheel by shaft and chain. In the mid-'20s, a reverse gear was added. Until 1928, the wheelbase was 72 inches; in that year an 86-inch model was produced for a time. The overhead valve

J.A.P. engine powered most Moggies, usually the 980 cc. version, although in the late '20s the 1,078 cc. Anzani engines were fitted. Many also employed a 1,096 cc. J.A.P. unit.

The Morgan is also notable as a pioneer of independent front suspension from the first production models in 1910. Sliding pillars with coil springs proved their strength and roadability. (Lancia of Italy has used a similar sliding-pillar front end since 1922.) This excellent front, and a new firm semielliptic rear suspension, were used when Morgan brought out his first four-wheel model in 1936, the "4/4"—four wheels, four cylinders—powered by the 63 x 90 mm., 1.1-litre, Coventry Climax, F-head engine driving through a tough 4-speed box. Type 4/4

From the first in 1910, the Morgan was a high-performance, three-wheel machine with independent sliding-pillar front suspension powered by a V-type, 2-cylinder, air-cooled, 1-litre J.A.P. engine until 1936 when the "Moggie" was supplemented by a four-wheel sports car. (*Joseph H. Wherry courtesy of Car Classics*)

Owned by J. A. Prestwich, this 1931 Morgan has a 72-inch wheelbase, a stark cockpit for two, and a slot for a bit of luggage. Prices began at around 100 Pounds. (*Joseph H. Wherry*)

had a maximum speed of more than 75 MPH, was economical to buy and run, was slung low and firmly for flat cornering and racked up victories in club events to match the hundreds its three-wheel predecessor had garnered.

As for awards, a "Moggie" with H. F. S. Morgan at the wheel broke the one-hour record for cars of less than 1,100 cc. in 1913 with approximately 60 miles. Later in the Grand Prix for voiturettes at Amiens, a "Moggie" won a clear-cut victory over a field of four-wheel cars. A list of all of the Morgan racing awards—for either the three-wheeler or the 4/4—would number well over 400 for the years between 1910 and 1940. Morgan is still situated in Malvern Links where Sir John Black, later of Standard, once worked as a draftsman. As popular now as during the vintage years, the Morgan's lasting success is proof of a market for a modest car of quality that does not suffer style changes with every whim but relies upon proven engineering features.

The Morgan was the most famous car to employ the Coventry Climax engine during the late prewar period. However, a score or more marques—now forgotten—used the engine that later was adapted as a water pump for wartime service. This famous engine's origin goes back to when the young H. Pelham Lee returned from the Boer War with the Hussars. After completing his engineering education, Lee worked for Daimler until he set up his own business with a Mr. Stroyer. Together they built a vertical, 2-cylinder engine and installed it in their own Lee-Stroyer cars during 1903–04. Details of this car are obscure; probably very few were made. When Lee determined to manufacture engines rather than complete cars, the partnership broke up and Lee formed Coventry Simplex Ltd., which be-

came a supplier of engines for a variety of applications.

In 1910, the firm of Grice, Wood & Keiller introduced the G.W.K., a 91-inch-wheelbase car with the Simplex, 2-cylinder (86 x 92 mm., 1.3-litre) driving the rear wheels through a friction transmission that provided an infinite number of ratios. After 1919, G.W.K. cars used 4-cylinder (66 x 100 mm.), 1,368 cc., Coventry engines on wheelbases of 109 inches and longer until the end of the marque in 1931.

In 1914, the Coventry Simplex vertical-twins were selected to power the snow tractors used by Sir Ernest Shackleton's Trans-Antarctic Expedition. The low, 120-pound weight of Lee's engines made them extremely popular. At about this time one of the Simplex, 1,368 cc., L-head fours was used as the powerplant in Lionel Martin's prototype of the Aston-Martin; some production models of this marque, covered later, also used Coventry Climax engines. The Invicta prototype also used a Climax. Lee's engines powered military searchlight generators during the First World War during which Lee changed his firm's name to Coventry Climax.

Between the big wars, Lee built engines of four and six cylinders with side, F-head and overhead valves to fit the requirements of many customers. Makes of the cars that used Coventry Simplex and Climax engines are forgotten vehicles, although they contributed to the growth of the industry in England: the Seymour-Turner (1906–31), the Crouch (1912–28), the Foy-Steele.

There were also the Coventry-powered Horstman (1914–29) which used 1,247 and 1,296 cc. Simplex and Climax engines in quite attractive cars, some with pointed radiators, in up to 116-inch chassis; the Eric Campbell designed by Noel Macklin

A 3-wheel Morgan will always attract a crowd at a concours d'elegance. Note that each of the cylinders on the V-twin engine has its own throaty tailpipe. (*Joseph H. Wherry*)

(1919–26), attractive sporting machines on 87- to 102-inch wheelbases, one running well in the 1919 Targa Florio in Sicily; the Swift passenger cars of 1920–31, a marque that emerged from a bicycle plant in 1899 with little fanfare and were often fitted with Swallow coachwork; the Waverly (1920–31); the Wigan-Barlow (1922–23); the Clyno that rivalled Morris for a time (1922–29); the Bayliss-Thomas (1922–29), some with stylish boat-tails; the Albatross (1923–24), some costing as little as 160 £; the Marendaz; the A.J.S. (built 1930–35 by the A. J. Stevens motorcycle firm) the Vale Special, an extremely well-designed, 1933–36, 1.1-litre, sports two-seater based on Triumph components but with distinctive body; and others too numerous to list.

For a time, the Crossley was very popular. This marque began in 1904 in Manchester and was possibly the first English car to fit four-wheel brakes. Crossley made many of its own engines and some were large, 3.2-litre sixes on wheelbases up to 137 inches. After 1932, however, the Crossley made wide use of Coventry Climax F-head and full overhead-valve engines of 1.1 to 2.7 litres displacement in open and closed models of excellent design. A difficult marketing situation hastened this marque's demise in 1936.

Four- and 6-cylinder Coventry Climax units were also used in many Triumph cars from that marque's origin in 1923 in Coventry, among them the 1.2-litre, F-head "Gloria" sports saloon of 1933–34 and the better known 1936, overhead-valve "Vitesse"

Ancestor of the M. G. and the first production Morris was the 1913 "Oxford," a 90-inch-wheelbase, 10-HP, 4-cylinder (60 x 90 mm.), 1,018 cc. car that was the basis of B.M.C. (*Society of Motor Traders & Manufacturers*)

The 1,550 cc., 4-cylinder (69.5 x 102 mm.), 12-HP Morris "Oxford" of 1928, a refined quality car on 106.5-inch wheelbase priced moderately at 205 Pounds up. (*Society of Motor Traders & Manufacturers*)

The 1929 Morris "Minor" had a 4-cylinder (57 x 83 mm.), 847-cc. engine with a single-overhead camshaft, yet it was an economy car available at just 100 Pounds. Wheelbase 78 inches. The "Minor" inspired several M. G. models. (*Society of Motor Traders & Manufacturers*)

and "Monte Carlo" models which achieved success in the Monte Carlo and Alpine rallies. This marque's wide use of Coventry Climax engines has not been generally realized. More than any other specialty engine manufacturer, Coventry Climax became a major supplier to the automotive industry in the 1920–40 period when these high-quality engines were usually disguised with the symbols of the automobile maker concerned. After 1945, Grand Prix car builders eagerly turned to Coventry Climax for engines, and many of these units were used in a succession of world championship cars. In 1963, Jaguar acquired this famous engine manufacturing enterprise.

The late Lord Nuffield built the first Morris car in 1912. William R. Morris had been an apprenticed worker in a cycle factory; later he made bikes and still later established Morris Garages in Oxford where he sold and serviced a wide range of English and American cars. The Morris Garages were the incubator of the Nuffield Organisation which took shape in the '20s with the acquisition of three other well-known marques as we have already observed. Late in 1912, the Morris "Oxford" went into production. Morris relied on the reputation of the 4-cylinder, side-valve, 1,018 cc., White & Poppe engines, on S.U. carburetors and other components which he used in the 50-MPH, 3-speed, bullnosed "Oxford," and it was an immediate success in the low-priced light-car field at 175 £. Continental engines, imported from the U.S.A., were

264

The 2,468-cc. Morris "Six" of 1933, a refined 6-cylinder (69 x 110 mm.) family car on a 118-inch wheelbase. Priced at about 350 Pounds up, the "Six" was introduced in 1928 in open as well as closed models. (*British Motors Corp. Ltd.*)

also used, but in the '20s Morris began manufacturing his own engines.

When production for peacetime resumed in 1919, the "Cowley" was introduced as a low-priced model. In 1921, Morris chopped all his prices by 100 £. Both "Cowley" and "Oxford" had 1,548 cc., 12-HP engines in 102-inch-wheelbase chassis of conventional design. The bodies, designed by Morris, were above average in durability for the price. By 1924, the "Oxford" had a 1.8-litre (75 x 102 mm.) engine and in 1927 the power was increased with an 80 x 125 mm., 2.5-litre engine in a 115-inch chassis; the smaller engines were still available. In 1928, Morris introduced the "Six" (later called the "Isis") powered by a 17.7-HP, overhead-camshaft, 6-cylinder (69 x 110 mm.), 2,468 cc. engine. All of these engines figured in the development of the early M.G. sports cars.

It was the Morris "Minor" of late 1928, though, that caused the greatest sensation. The remarkably tough, long-stroke, 847 cc. engine had an overhead camshaft and, on a tiny, 78-inch wheelbase, brought Morris's version of economy motoring to the average man for just 135 £. Directly competitive to the Austin "Seven," the "Minor" chassis could be purchased bare for just 100 pounds and hundreds of them were the basis for homebuilt trials cars. The "Minor" also inspired several of the M.G. sports cars which derived their marque from Morris Garages, which were still under W R. Morris ownership even after he established his factories in Cowley and Coventry. From the humble garages and showrooms, the Nuffield Organisation had become one of the industry's giants by the start of the Second World War.

Little known today is England's first production car with a V-8 engine, the Guy, introduced in 1919 with a 72 x 125 mm. engine in a 130-inch wheelbase. An expensive quality car, the initial price for a complete car with a works body was 1,395 £; eventually the price decreased to a more

265

Drophead sports coupe coachwork on 1929 Bentley 3-litre. Mrs. Ronald Sullivan, owner, with her concours-winning car. (*Joseph H. Wherry, courtesy of Car Classics*)

reasonable 495 £ in 1924. Built by Guy Motors Ltd. of Wolverhampton, old established truck manufacturers, the Guy had inclined valves operated by camshafts located high in the V-block, detachable cylinder heads, and unusually long semi-elliptic springs. The 4-speed gearboxes were integral with the engines, and there was automatic chassis lubrication. Guy also produced a range of 4-cylinder, 2-litre cars and in 1923 four-wheel brakes were fitted. Open touring bodies were works-built (some were of polished aluminum) while closed bodies were made by various coachworks.

Guy cars disappeared in 1926. In the same year, the firm absorbed the Star Engineering Company which had built the obscure Star cars since 1898, 2- and 4-cylinder

models of medium size until 1915 and larger fours and sixes on up to 135-inch wheelbases with 3.2-litre engines in 1926. Good but conventional cars, Stars were priced up to nearly 1,000 £. Some of the saloons had Weymann fabric bodies and were quite elegant with wire wheels and luxurious interiors. In 1935, the Star, too, faded from the scene but Guy Motors remained as a leading truck and bus manufacturer and was absorbed by Jaguar in 1961.

Bentley Motors Ltd. of Derby enjoyed eleven exciting years as an independent from 1920 to 1931 when the firm closed down; eventually Rolls-Royce took over in 1933. Walter O. Bentley was an exceptional man and an engineer-craftsman with few peers. He didn't believe cars should be sub-

266

jected to punishment in races like Le Mans, but built superb cars that won that and many other similar ordeals of performance and endurance.

He had been an engineer in a steam locomotive factory, and a dealer of French cars with his brother, H. M. as partner. While in the Royal Navy, he designed the famous Bentley rotary aircraft engines during the 1914–18 war.

At the war's end, Bentley began designing his own car and in 1919 the first Bentley, a 3-litre, 4-cylinder vehicle of generous size appeared—the prototype of the marque that Ettore Bugatti once called "the fastest lorry in the world." These wonderful lorries won Le Mans in 1927, 1928, 1929 and 1930.

Production finally began in 1921 with the 4-cylinder (80 x 149 mm.), 3-litre open tourers and two-seaters which were hand-built right through 1927 at a bare chassis price of 1,050 £ for the early years and for 895 £ in its final years. The 3-litre chassis was, incidentally, available until 1930. The 2,966 cc. engine had double valves (four per cylinder), cast iron block and head, aluminum alloy pistons, one overhead-camshaft, and an oil sump located below the crankcase. Touring versions had one carburetor and delivered approximately 65 BHP at 3,500 rpm. The 3-litre "Speed" models of around 1926–27 had dual S.U. carburetors and were tuned for a minimum of 86 BHP and slightly more than 90 in the case of cars prepared for long-distance racing. Most of the 3-litre "Blue Label" Bentleys until 1924 had 117.5-inch wheelbases. The "Speed" model of 1924 wore the famous "Red Label" (background enamel on the winged-B emblem) and sat on a 108-inch wheelbase.

Very rare, only fifteen "Speed" models were built. Until 1923, only rear wheel brakes were fitted; in that year, brakes were on all four wheels. Suspension was by semi-elliptic springs with friction shock absorbers all around and, before the coachwork was added, the chassis weighed a bit over 2,700 pounds. The gearbox had 4 speeds and the propeller shaft was open. There was also a "100 MPH" version and these were the seldom seen "Green Label" Bentleys. From about 1926, the oil was contained in the crankcase except on a few racing specials.

The 6.5-litre "Blue Label" Bentley was current from 1926 to 1931. This was Bentley's first 6-cylinder model. Bore and stroke were 100 x 140 mm. (6,597 cc.) and the engine structure and materials were as in the first production model. Compression ratio was 4.4 to 1, and there were eight main bearings. These were larger, heavier cars weighing as much as 5,500 pounds complete and had either 132- or 144-inch wheelbases. The 6.5-litre "Speed Six," generally marked with a "Green Label," had higher 5.5 to 1 compression ratio, a special camshaft, large dual S.U. carburetors and ignition changes to assure a catalogued output of 180 BHP at 3,500 rpm. The "Speed Six" was capable of a bit over 85 MPH.

Production of a new 4-cylinder (100 x 140 mm., 4,398 cc.) model on a 130-inch-wheelbase chassis began in 1927. Known as the 4.5-litre Bentley and wearing a "Black Label," most were supercharged. The blower was located between the dumb irons and cowled over as on the leather-bodied tourer illustrated. Weighing more than two tons with touring bodies and famous for their thundering performance, a 4.5 blower Bentley driven by Birkin placed second in the Grand Prix of France in 1930.

Near the end of his tenure, W. O. Bent-

Weymann leather-covered coachwork on a 4.5-litre Bentley of 1930 in a period scene during a show in the Henry Ford Museum. (*Joseph H. Wherry*)

ley brought out the 8-litre model. Just one hundred were built. Also marked with a "Blue Label," this heavy car (upwards of 5,500 pounds depending upon the coachwork) had two chassis lengths, 144 and 156 inches. The bore was 110 mm.; the stroke was the same as the 6.5 model. With a displacement of 7,983 cc., the output of 220 BHP at 3,500 rpm was sufficient to assure 100 MPH without strain. Despite their generous size and heftiness, Bentleys were superbly roadable cars with mechanical brakes, fitted with a mechanical servo assist from 1928 on, that did what brakes are supposed to do. A Bentley's steering rarely brought cheers from the ladies. A Bentley was a man's car and a splendid one at that. After late 1933, the 3.5 and 4.5-litre Bentleys

made by Rolls-Royce had hydraulic brakes, F-head, 6-cylinder engines and such refinements as overdrive but the classic models were those of the 1920–31 period.

Alvis cars were created by T. G. John, a marine architect who had once worked for Siddeley-Deasy, and G. P. H. de Freville who was a minister's son. Together they organized as T. G. John Ltd. in Coventry in 1919. Marked with a point-down red triangle, this car was introduced in 1920 and soon earned a "never wears out" reputation. The first 10/30-HP Alvis was a somewhat ordinary looking car on a 110-inch wheelbase, but the price put it in the quality bracket. To justify this Capt. G. T. Smith-Clark, the designer, fitted 4-speed gearboxes with well selected ratios to L-head engines

The potent 4.5-litre Bentley engine in one of the last cars made by W. O. Bentley prior to acquisition of the marque by Rolls-Royce. (*Joseph H. Wherry*)

and with 30 BHP the top speed was 60 MPH, enough more than other 1.5-litre cars to impress the public. In 1922, the bore was enlarged to 68 mm. (stroke remained 110 mm.), increasing the piston displacement to 1,645 cc., resulting in the 11/40-HP model. The next year the 12/50-HP "Super Sports" appeared with a vastly improved overhead-valve engine in a slightly shorter 108.5-inch chassis. When Major C. M. Harvey took a competition 12/50 to the 1923 Brooklands 200 Mile Race, he astonished his opponents by winning a clear-cut victory.

Alvis had earned its place as a marque of distinction and a new overhead-valve model appeared in the 12/50 HP range which, by 1926, included cars for every pur-

pose. The next year, Alvis returned to Brooklands and established a new 12-hour class record with more than 86 MPH. Even more impressive was winning the top three places in its class in the Essex 6-Hour Race by a works team led by the well-known Sammy Davis.

The most famous Alvis sports competition models, though, were the front-wheel-drive cars. The 1,496 cc., pushrod, overhead-valve engine was supercharged to develop approximately 100 BHP, and reversed to allow location of the differential at the front of the aluminum alloy frame. An adaptation of the De Dion swing axles drove the front wheels which were equipped with inboard brakes. Quarter-elliptic springs were used front and rear. Ready to race, the

weight of the 1925 model was under 1,100 pounds and Brooklands was lapped at 104.4 MPH.

The next development was the front-drive, 8-cylinder (55 x 78.75 mm.), supercharged Grand Prix models in 1926. With dual magnetos, light alloy pistons and connecting rods, and horizontal valves actuated by a high camshaft on each side of the block, the output was on the order of 110 BHP without the usual flywheel. Maximum speed exceeded 110 MPH. The low streamlined bodies were aluminum with belly pans over a pressed steel frame; weight was about half again that of the 4-cylinder cars of 1925. Major Harvey might well have won the 1926 Brooklands 200 Mile Race for 1.5-litre cars in one of these machines but for a crash caused by a slower car. It is said the front-drive Alvises, though not as fast as the opposing, dual overhead-camshaft, supercharged Talbot-Darracqs, were quicker in the corners.

For 1927, a similar pair of Alvises was readied but with new, dual overhead-camshafts which increased the output to 125 BHP. Again misfortune dogged the Alvis team; clearly faster than the principal opposition in the Brooklands 200-miler (the Bugatti team), both cars retired with mechanical trouble. With the 1.5-litre G.P. formula, a thing of the past, the front-drive, 4-cylinder engine was redesigned as a 1,482 cc. sports car powerplant with a single overhead-camshaft. Output with supercharger was 75 BHP and, without blower, was 50 BHP. Popularly, they were the FWD 12/75 and 12/50 types. Two-seat bodies of fabric or aluminum were available on 102-inch chassis in the "FA" and "FD" models for 1928 and '29 respectively, while full four-place touring sports models on 120-inch wheelbases were designated "FB" and "FE" for the same years. Blown or unblown, the top speed was 85 MPH, the blown model having the better acceleration. Prices ranged from 597 to 750 £ for the supercharged sports saloon which was usually referred to as the 12/75 "Alvista."

The dual, overhead-camshaft straight-8, modified with roller bearings and steel connecting rods which decreased the stroke and altered the displacement to 1,491 cc. were also available on the 120-inch-wheelbase chassis. These cost 975 £ with either closed saloon or open 4-seat coachwork. The FWD fours and eights were the world's first mass-produced front-wheel-drive cars. The 4-cylinder model was an especially brisk seller. Vindication of this pioneering effort came in 1928 when a team of the unblown production 2-seater FWD cars placed first and second in their class at Le Mans.

Alvis also built conventional rear-wheel-drive cars during the '30s. The "Speed 20" introduced in 1932, an overhead-valve, 2.5-litre six with triple carburetion, would do 90 mph with sports saloon body. Another world first was scored in 1933 with all four gear ratios fully synchronized. The final pre-war rear drive Alvis car was the "Speed 25," a luxurious, 4.3-litre sports-tourer. Introduced in 1937, this model had independent front-wheel suspension. One of the fastest English-built cars of the period, it had a maximum speed of 105 MPH. The "Speed 25" illustrated is a familiar sight at Concours d'Elegance.

Leyland Motors Ltd. of Lancashire had a chief engineer named J. G. Parry Thomas. His assistant was Reid Railton. Parry Thomas became a legend in the few short

A supercharger lurks beneath the shroud between the dumb irons of this 4.5-litre Bentley; note the friction snubbers. (*Joseph H. Wherry*)

Only one hundred 6-cylinder, 8-litre Bentleys were built in 1930–31. Bore and stroke of this magnificent car were 110 x 140 mm. respectively. Double valves, single-overhead camshaft and wheelbases of 144 and 156 inches were available on this rare classic. A 1931 model with drophead coupe coachwork by Windovers. (*Harrah's Automobile Collection*)

A 3.5-litre Bentley sports tourer of 1934 owned by A. B. Mullaly. Built by Rolls-Royce, a 20/25 R-R engine was employed. (*Joseph H. Wherry*)

4.25-litre, 6-cylinder (89 x 114 mm.) Bentley of 1937 with aluminum coachwork by Gurney Nutting. Note the filled seams between body and fenders, an unusual original feature. Owners, Mr. and Mrs. A. B. Mullaly. (*Joseph H. Wherry*)

Rare streamlining on the Gurney Nutting 4.25 litre Bentley of 1937. (*Joseph H. Wherry*)

4.25-litre Bentley, 1938, with saloon coachwork by Van Vourman. The owner is G. W. Caulkett. (*Joseph H. Wherry*)

First production Alvis, the 1920 model 10/30 (4 cylinders, 65 x 110 mm., 1,460 cc.) was comparatively advanced with full pressure lubrication. 30 BHP drove the 112-inch-wheelbase car 60 mph. Refinement at 720 Pounds delivered. (*Leyland Motors Ltd.*)

The Twentieth Century Overseas

years before he died in a crash in 1927. Hardly less famous were the eighteen Leyland-Thomas cars built between 1920 and '24. Thomas began designing his car in 1917 while Leyland was producing aircraft engines. He had carte blanche to produce the best possible car regardless of cost, and the Leyland was introduced in 1920 at the London Show. The chassis price was 2,500 £.

The only suitable adjective for the Leyland is magnificent. The 8-cylinder (89 x 140 mm.), 6,967 cc. block was cast integrally with the top of the crankcase. One overhead-camshaft was driven by eccentrics and actuated the valves which were inclined at 90 degrees in hemispheric combustion chambers. Patented valve springs eliminated bounce at high speed. Connecting rods were tubular, the crankshaft had six main bearings lubricated by full pressure. This was the

first English touring car with an in-line, 8-cylinder engine. In standard tune with one Zenith carburetor (sometimes more than one were used), the output was 145 BHP at 2,800 rpm. After the first few engines, the capacity was increased to 7,266 cc. by lengthening the stroke to 146 mm. The torque was terrific with such a long stroke and high crankshaft speeds were not necessary.

Chassis details are no less intriguing. Semi-elliptic springs of immense length controlled the solid front axle. The rear combined torsion bars and quarter-elliptic springs. Brakes were mechanical with a vacuum servo with drums nearly as large as the disc wheels. Box section steel members comprised the frame which was finished in the finest classic tradition. Buyers had the option of three wheelbases: 126, 141 or 150

When this overhead-valve, 4-cylinder (68 x 103 mm., 1,496 cc.), competition version of the 12/50 won the Brooklands 200-Mile Race, it achieved lasting fame and assured the Alvis's future. The average speed was over 93 mph. Wheelbase 108.5 inches. Price 535 Pounds. (*Leyland Motors Ltd.*)

First production sports car with front-wheel drive, the 1928 Alvis 12/75 (75 BHP with supercharger) competition sports car. Single overhead camshaft, 4-cylinder (68 x 102 mm., 1,482 cc.) and four-wheel independent suspension. Speed 85 mph supercharged and unblown. Supercharging aided acceleration. Wheelbase 102 inches. Le Mans models had fabric body, those for the Tourist Trophy had all-metal. Prices started at 597 Pounds. (*Leyland Motors Ltd.*)

On a longer wheelbase, the front-wheel drive 12/75 Alvis four-seat closed sports saloon, the "Alvista" of 1928–29, with racing type 4-speed gearbox and full independent suspension. (*Leyland Motors Ltd.*)

The 1937–39 Alvis "Speed 25" had a 4.3-litre engine driving the rear wheels, and topped 105 mph; a full four-seater sports tourer with impeccable roadability. Owner of this 1939 version, T. Mudd. (*Joseph H. Wherry*)

The incomparable Leyland Eight designed by J. G. Parry Thomas. Introduced in 1920, the 6,967 cc., straight-8 engine had a single overhead camshaft operating inclined valves in hemispherical combustion chambers. The suspension system combined leaf springs with torsion bars. The designer is at wheel. (*Leyland Motors Ltd.*)

The 1922 Leyland Eight saloon with Vanden Plas coachwork had 7,266-cc. engine. Leyland wheelbases varied from 126 to 150 inches. Price of bare chassis was from 1,875 to 2,700 Pounds Sterling. (*Leyland Motors Ltd.*)

inches. With few takers for chassis costing more than those for the Rolls-Royce, the Leyland Eight went out of production in 1923 and was no longer listed.

In its heyday with Parry Thomas driving, however, a boat-tailed 2-seater on the short chassis broke the lap record at Brooklands with 129.4 MPH. About this time, Thomas left his position with Leyland, took his racing model along, and moved into a house at Brooklands. In 1922, Thomas and his racing Leyland captured four first, seven second and three third places in races on the famous track. The next year the pair were on tap with a new crankshaft, a new induction manifold with four carburetors and 7.5 to 1 compression ratio. Now the output was 200 BHP at 2,800 rpm. In 1923, Thomas's Leyland took eight firsts, four sec-

onds and one third, the 7.3-litre car even thrashing a huge 21.7-litre, prewar Fiat in a match race. During the 1924–26 racing seasons at Brooklands, the Leyland captured fifteen more first places while in 1922 through 1926 the mighty car shattered around sixty records for up to 100 miles. After becoming the major racing attraction at Brooklands, Thomas established a world land speed record of 171.09 MPH in 1926 in another one of his specials powered by a 27-litre, Liberty aircraft engine at Pendine. When he tried to better his mark in 1927 on the Welsh seashore, he was fatally injured in a crash and England lost one of her most talented engineers.

Eyeing the lower priced market, Leyland Motors produced another car, the curious Trojan. The first model came out in 1923,

The last Leyland Eight was built sometime after 1927. Coachwork by Thomson & Taylor. (*Leyland Motors Ltd.*)

The 1.5-litre Aston-Martin "Le Mans" of 1932 had a 4-cylinder, single overhead-camshaft engine. One of these set a class speed record of 75.5 mph at Le Mans in 1935; the mark stood fifteen years. Owned by Christopher Coburn. (*Joseph H. Wherry*)

The 2-litre 1936 Aston-Martin "Ulster" model was guaranteed for 100 mph despite a weight in excess of 2,200 pounds at the curb. (*Henry Ford Museum*)

Created by Cecil Kimber in 1923, this first of all M.G. cars was based upon the Morris "Oxford." In 1925, M.G. "Number One" driven by Kimber won a Gold Medal in the London to Lands End Trial, and M.G. was off and running. (*British Motor Corp. Ltd.*)

the same year the Leyland was discontinued. Something of a case of going from the sublime to the near ridiculous, the Trojan had solid rubber tires on most models and a 1.5-litre, 2-cycle, horizontal, 4-cylinder engine. A 2-speed gearbox drove the solid rear axle by a chain. Instead of electric starting, an interior mechanism was operated by hand. Wheelbases varied from a short 81 to around 110 inches, the latter having saloon coachwork. Though minimal in specification, Trojans were durable, rode smoothly because of soft springs, and were roomy inside. Costing 125 to about 200 £, a tiny fraction of the cost of the Leyland Eight, this strange car was popular but it expired in 1936. Leyland built commercial vehicles before, during and after the two passenger marques. In this decade, the Leyland Group has expanded tremendously into a world-wide enterprise with the purchase of Standard-Triumph and the Rover-Alvis

companies; the latter two merged just before joining Leyland.

The Aston-Martin has had more than its share of ups and downs since Lionel Martin's 1914 prototype which was a special based upon an Isotta-Fraschini chassis and a Coventry Simplex engine as already mentioned. Martin tacked a part of the location name of a famous hill climb in front of his own in christening his car. In 1920, Robert Bamford and Martin formed a firm in Kensington to build fine light sports cars and produced a few the same year, exquisite little two-seaters powered with 1.5-litre, 4-cylinder (66.5 x 107 mm.) Coventry Simplex engines. Tax rated at 12 HP, the engines were L-head types developing 35 BHP at 4,000 rpm. Only the craftsmanship could justify a price of around 850 £.

Times were difficult but the enthusiastic Count Zborowski invested in the firm, enabling development of a dual overhead-cam-

Fabric-covered coachwork on a 2.5-litre overhead-camshaft, 6-cylinder type 18/80 Mark I M.G. Wheelbase 114 inches; 3-speed gearbox; high performance. Expensive at 520 Pounds Sterling. (*British Motor Corp. Ltd.*)

shaft modification of the Coventry engine. Four-wheel brakes were fitted in 1923. Known also as the Bamford & Martin Aston, 4-speed gearboxes were standard on the 126-inch-wheelbase chassis from the first. Wheelbase grew to 131 inches in 1924, but one must remember that overhang was unheard of in those days, and the seemingly long wheelbase facilitated fitting of light streamlined competition or more commodious touring coachwork. L-head models topped 70 MPH and technical refinement enabled one overhead-cam model to capture some two dozen class awards at Brooklands in 1922.

About sixty cars had been built by late 1926 when bankruptcy threatened and Messrs. W. S. Renwick and A. C. Bertelli bought the name and assets. The Aston-Martins for 1928–30 were very few in number and had sleeve valve 6-cylinder engines of 3 and 3.5 litres in 135- and 147-inch wheelbases. Bertelli, an engineer, desired to perpetuate the marque's competition tradition and he designed a new, single, overhead-camshaft 1.5-litre engine. Lubrication was by dry sump, and the coachwork was aluminum over hardwood frames. The new model achieved success in the Tourist Trophy races at Le Mans and elsewhere and

The rare 1930–31 M.G. 18/100 Mark III "Tigress," a 2.5-litre, 6-cylinder, 95–100 BHP racer on a 114-inch wheelbase. Only five were built; catalogued price was 895 Pounds. The vented covering between dumb irons shielded a dry sump. (*British Motor Corp. Ltd.*)

was called the "International" but when one set a new 75.5 MPH 1.5-litre class record at Le Mans, the name of that course stuck. Though expensive, the "Le Mans" models have often been referred to as English equivalents of the Bugatti. By 1933, the firm had changed hands again. R. C. Sutherland, the new owner, introduced the 2-litre "Ulster" model in 1935 with a highly developed engine featuring a hollow crankshaft. Light and low, weighing under a ton, the 100-BHP model won scores of races. In 1947, the firm came under the control of the David Brown Group which also acquired Lagonda.

Cecil Kimber, manager of the Morris Garages in Oxford, had customers who wanted something just a little peppier than the Morris "Oxford" and "Cowley" models he sold and serviced. A motor sports enthusiast, too, Kimber stuffed an overhead-valve Hotchkiss engine into a modified "Oxford" chassis in 1923, staggered a pair of bucket seats to reduce width, and bolted on a narrow aluminum body shell behind the Morris bullnose radiator. He added scanty mudguards and a single road light, and tightened the suspension. He named his car for the Morris Garages, and the first M.G. was born.

Two years later, Kimber drove "Number One" in the 1925 London to Lands End Trial and won a gold medal. In a sometimes confused succession of M.G. variants, the 1.8-litre, 4-cylinder Mark IV followed as did the overhead-camshaft Mark I which did 75+ MPH, the Mark II and the 6-cylinder, 2.5-litre Mark III.

Most dashing of the large M.G. types was the Mark III "Tigress," an out-and-out racer of which five were built; one or two still exist as does "Old Number One." In its first race, the Junior Car Club's Double

12-Hour Race at Brooklands in 1930, the Mark III was blasting around the track at speeds upwards of 85 MPH when the butterfly valve in one of the S.U. carburetors let loose, and was swallowed in the valve gear. The car retired, never to race again.

In 1929, Kimber had fielded a team of new types "M," the first of the famed Midgets. Based upon Morris components again, type-M had a 4-cylinder, 847-cc. overhead-camshaft engine. There were just two main bearings on the crankshafts and the tiny rigs had the scantiest of fabric-covered bodies. Unlikely as it seems, the M-Midgets ran off with top awards in a field of big machinery in the Junior Car Club's High Speed Trials at Brooklands. The Austin "Seven" was the new Midgets' natural opponent and they went down in a series of duels with Kimber's creations. M.G. Midgets sold as fast as they could be built.

The M.G. builders became the M.G. Car Company Ltd. in Abingdon, a self-contained division of the Nuffield Organisation, as matters developed. All of the Midgets had overhead-camshaft engines until the "TA" of 1926 when the overhead valves were pushrod-operated for the first time. The "TB" was a slightly changed model just prior to the war and, afterwards, was closely duplicated in the "TC" which had more to do with the rise of interest in sports cars in the U.S.A. than any other marque before or since.

There were M.G. family sedans, open 4-seat tourers, supercharged fours and sixes (various models on the K-type "Magnette" theme, some of which exceeded 75 MPH comfortably) and record cars like the 750-cc. EX127 "Magic Midget" that astonished the motor world during 1931–36 by smashing records. Drivers of the calibre of Cap-

The view enjoyed by opponents of the 1931–33 M.G. Type C Montlhery Midget. Four 57 x 73 mm. cylinders (746 cc.) with overhead camshaft developed 44 BHP unblown and 52.5 BHP at 6,500 with supercharger. Wheelbase 81 inches. For 295 Pounds Sterling the buyer had a road car or racer capable of 80 mph without blower; another 180 PS gained the supercharged version and full race performance. (*Joseph H. Wherry*)

tain George Eyston proved that just three fourths of one litre can be tuned to propel a car at 120 MPH. Brakes and road holding were an obsession with the manufacturers and their "Safety Fast" motto has become a motoring byword around the world. By 1939, the M.G. record books were fat with awards won on courses from Ulster to Le Mans, Liechtenstein and the Mille Miglia while its roster of competition drivers listed names like Count Johnny Lurani, Prince Bira of Siam, Tim Birkin, and a host of others.

Production of motorcycles and leg-powered two-wheelers occupied the manufacturers of Triumph cars in Coventry until 1923 when, reorganizing as Triumph Motor Co. Ltd., they brought out their first car, a 1,393-

During 1931–36, the EX127 "Magic Midget," a tiny 750 cc. supercharged machine, set dozens of class records in the hands of Captain George Eyston and other drivers. Here, Eyston gets a start for his 120-mph run at Montlhery in 1932. (*British Motor Corp. Ltd.*)

cc., 4-cylinder (63.5 x 110 mm.) open tourer on a conventional frame with a 102-inch wheelbase. The "Ten" model was well accepted. From the first, the gearboxes had four ratios and quality had been a good cut above the average. Prices of the "Ten" began at around 425 pounds in 1923 and not until the advent of the type "K" in 1928 (an 832-cc., 81-inch wheelbase small car) did prices come below the 150 £ line and place the firm in the mass market. Called the "Super Seven," this was one of the very few English cars with hydraulic brakes at this date; final drive was by worm gear. As already observed, Coventry Climax engines were used in many Triumphs throughout the '20s and '30s.

Largest Triumph in the '20s was the 2,169 cc. "TPC" of 1926–28. A 4-cylinder car, this was the first M.G. to forsake the cone clutch for a dry plate type. The price for this 112-inch car was from 395 £ for the open tourer. Closed models were also available. In 1930, the 1.2-liter "Scorpion" appeared. Slightly sporting in character, this was the firm's first 6-cylinder car but it lasted only through 1931. Donald Healey came to Triumph at this time and designed the 2-litre (Coventry Climax F-head engine), "Southern Cross" sports car. There was also a 1.2-litre version. Smart, open two-seaters and closed models, the "Southern Cross" placed high in the Monte Carlo rallies and in numerous British trials, hill climbs, and the like. Production lasted well into 1927.

285

The single overhead-camshaft J2 "Midget" M.G. had 4-cylinder, 847-cc., 36-BHP engine; was light, fast, and roadable on its 86-inch wheelbase. Owner-restorer is Jarl de Boer. (*Joseph H. Wherry*)

The rare 1934 supercharged Type K3 Magnette, a six-cylinder M.G. racer, could reach speeds in excess of 120 miles per hour. (*British Motor Corp. Ltd.*)

The 1936 M.G. TA set the style for the post-war invasion of America with the TC. Four 63.5 x 102 mm. cylinders, 1,292-cc. displacement, 50 BHP at 4,500 RPM; wheelbase 94 inches. This was the first "Midget" with pushrod-operated overhead-valves. (*British Motor Corp. Ltd.*)

Finest pre-war M.G. was the elegant Type WA 2.6-litre Six on a 123-inch wheelbase. (*British Motor Corp.*)

The 1938–39 Triumph "Dolomite" was powered by a 4-cylinder, 1,767-cc., 60-BHP engine or a 2-litre, 72-BHP six; both had overhead valves. Open and closed models were produced. (*B. C. Wherry*)

The Triumph "Gloria" and "Vitesse" of 1933 and '36 respectively, also had Coventry Climax engines and became famous in the Monte Carlo and Alpine rallies. "Gloria," a styling coupe with near classic lines, had the F-head four (1,232 cc., 42 BHP at 43–4500 rpm) engine and introduced free wheeling to this marque. Later, a dual-carburetor, 1.5-litre engine became optionally available. With the "Vitesse," the firm began building its own engines. With overhead-valves, the 1.8-litre, 4-cylinder unit put out 62 BHP and was adaptable to power tuning with multiple carburetors and higher compression ratios than the customary 6.0 to 1 of the mid-'30s.

The future of the excellent "Dolomite" was shortened by the war. Introduced in 1937 in open and closed 2- and 4-seat versions with excellent aluminum coachwork, the "Dolomite" 2-litre, dual overhead-camshaft, 8-cylinder engine brought the firm legal problems when Alfa Romeo brought suit after spotting a prototype in 1935 in the Monte Carlo Rally with Donald Healey at the wheel. The Italian firm had a point for the engine was a virtual carbon copy of an Alfa engine. As a result, only six eights were made. "Dolomites" were produced up until the war with the 1.8-litre four and with the 6-cylinder, 2-litre engine with dual S.U. carburetors and a compression ratio of 6.8 to 1. Dolomites were luxury cars in a small package. After 1945, Triumph merged with Standard and the combined marques have recently joined the Leyland Group.

When William Lyons entered into a part-

Bodies of the Triumph "Dolomite" were coach-built, sheathed with aluminum, and fitted with luxurious interiors; limousines in miniature. (*Joseph H. Wherry*)

nership with William Walmesly in 1922 in his hometown of Blackpool, their first products were sidecars for motorcycles. From this modest start with borrowed capital, they prospered, were well established by the end of the '20s as the Swallow Coach-building Company Ltd. and were building wood-framed, aluminum-sheathed, open sporting and closed bodies on chassis supplied by Swift, Fiat, Standard, Wolseley and Austin. Bodies for the Austin "Seven" were the most numerous but the larger Standard chassis were evidently the most interesting and by early 1932 Lyons—now on his own —began series production of the S.S. I, a long, sleek, Continental looking two-plus-two closed coupe powered by side valve 2, 2.5 and 2.6-litre Standard engines with six cylinders. Wheelbases were 112 and 119 inches. Carefully built and beautifully finished, the new S.S. marque was popularly thought to mean Standard-Swallow but this seems not to have been so; more likely the initials stood for Swallow Sports but this cannot be confirmed. These were the finest cars available on the British market for less than 400 £. Obviously, they would have sold at twice the price and the motoring press asked "How does Lyons do it?" With the streamlined "Airline" body, the 2.5-litre S.S. I could reach 80 MPH.

Also current during 1932–35 were similarly styled models on 89.5 to 104-inch wheelbases powered by 1-, 1.3- and 1.6-litre, Standard, 4-cylinder, L-head engines; these were designated as the S.S. II range. Eventually a full selection of body types was available in both lines. Frames were box-

289

Basis of the future Jaguar cars was the Swallow coachworks. This 1929–30 photo shows wood-framed saloon bodies for the Austin "Seven" under construction; on the right are roadster bodies. (*Jaguar Cars Ltd.*)

sectioned and semi-elliptic suspensions were employed, well snubbed by friction shock absorbers, and there were massive, four-wheel, mechanical brakes.

Because the S.S. I and II models looked faster than they were, Lyons—now relocated in Coventry—introduced the S.S. 90. The "90" was supposed to indicate the speed of the very low, open, 2-seater sports car which sat on a 104-inch chassis adopted from the S.S. II tourers. However, the 2,663.7 cc. Standard six engine devel-oped only 90 BHP at around 4,000 rpm even when fitted with two RAG carbure-tors, and only about fifty were built. Thus it was that the famous S.S. 100 appeared in the Motor Show late in 1936 on much the same chassis but offering a choice of either the 2.5-litre engine or a new 3,485.5 cc. unit. Each 6-cylinder engine now had overhead valves and a pair of S.U. carbure-tors. Output was a more impressive 102 BHP at 4,600 rpm and 125 BHP at 4,250 rpm for the 2.5- and 3.5-litre units, respec-

In near original condition, this 1934 SS-I will be restored by owner, attorney Ronald Sullivan. Current during 1932–35, the 6-cylinder engines ranged from 2,054 cc. to 2,552 cc. All were L-heads. (*Joseph H. Wherry*)

The limited production SS-I "Airline" model of 1934 topped 80 mph. (*Jaguar Cars Ltd.*)

Radio and television personality Jim Dunbar owns this 2.5-litre, overhead-valve, 6-cylinder SS-100 Jaguar. (*Joseph H. Wherry*)

The upward sweep of the frame over front axle can be seen in this photo of Dave Garroway's SS-100 Jaguar displayed in the 1953 International Motor Sports Show in New York City. (*Joseph H. Wherry*)

The pre-war, all-steel-bodied saloons, circa 1938–40, included "2½-" and "3½-Litre" models. (*Jaguar Cars Ltd.*)

tively. As the curb weight of either model was approximately 2,575 pounds, each gave a fair turn of speed, the 3.5 model topping 100 MPH in perfect tune. The S.S. 100 was a sensation and somewhere around 300 were built by August, 1939.

Simultaneously, a line of exceptional family sports saloons and drophead coupes was introduced on 120-inch wheelbases. There were two series using engines identical to the S.S. 100 sports roadsters and they were the first cars to carry the marque Jaguar. During 1937, several dozen of the "2.5-Litre" and "3.5-Litre" S.S. Jaguars, as they were officially designated, were exported to the United States. After 1945, the so-called Mark IV, nearly identical to the 1937–39 saloons, became exceptionally popular in this country where its superb handling and 80 MPH speed presented a sharp contrast to domestic cars.

Between 1934 and 1939, various privately entered S.S. and S.S. Jaguar models engaged in class racing and in the Alpine Trials and Monte Carlo Rallies where they won their fair share of honors. In 1945, Lyons renamed his firm Jaguar Cars Ltd. Within a few years he was knighted, and as Sir William had the supreme joy of seeing the C- and D-type Jaguars trounce all opposition three times and win the Le Mans 24-Hour Endurance Race.

When a trio of experienced competition drivers got together under the name Halford, Robins & Godfrey Engineering Co. Ltd., they were determined to build a sports car that was not an undressed, hopped-up touring car. To put it another way, H. R. Godfrey, who had built the G.N. cars already discussed, believed that sports cars had become a bit soft; his partners agreed. Their deliberations in their Surrey workshops promptly resulted in a sports car, the H.R.G., that remained in production until 1956 with few changes.

Introduced in 1936, the new marque was in the best classic tradition. The 4-cylinder, 1.5-litre, Meadows 4ED engine, beefed

293

"Grace, Space, Pace" was a promotion appeal. The 1938–40 Jaguar 2.5- and 3.5-litre cabriolet and saloon models were duplicated after the war.

Wheelbases, 120 inches with mechanical brakes; engines, 6 cylinders and pushrod overhead valves. (*Joseph H. Wherry*)

up with a heavier crankshaft, delivered 58 BHP at 4,500 rpm with dual carburetion. Installed in front of a 4-speed crash gearbox and between the longerons of a simple, rigid frame, the center of gravity was low and total weight was held to 1,600 pounds. Semi-elliptic springs were on the stiff side and, just to make sure that creampuffs wouldn't badger owners for a second ride, the friction shock absorbers were also tied down tightly. Tubular front axle and big drum mechanical brakes on all four wheels plus ultra-fast direct steering finished off the specification—in condensed form.

Open, 2-seat coachwork came down low and over the frame rails between the wheels; wheelbase, front to rear, measured 103.2 inches and the tread was 48 inches. Wheels,

naturally, were wire knock-offs by Rudge-Whitworth. Mudguards were cycle-type. With an interior as deliciously spartan as the exterior—leather over thinly-padded bucket seats and round dial instruments carefully calibrated for accuracy—this was a car made to order for tough trials, mud-plugging or flat-out racing. Top speed of the prototype checked out at a bit over 90 MPH with the windscreen folded flat over the bonnet.

At Le Mans one year later, the H.R.G. was second in the 1.5-litre category and a satisfying thirteenth overall with not a few 2-litre types trailing. In 1938, the H.R.G. placed first among all British entries of all classes. Until the war, H.R.G.s won awards in all types of events throughout the Brit-

The classic formula of the desirable H.R.G., from the first model in 1936 to the last some years later, was four highly tuned cylinders in a light but rigid frame. Road-hugging performance of a high order took proper precedence over comfort with this sports car. David M. Daniel is the owner-restorer of this superb example. (*Joseph H. Wherry*)

ish Isles. Identical chassis were available with 1,100 or 1,180 cc. engines. Similar bodies with pointed tails or as coupes were also built and in 1939 synchromesh gearboxes were optional, as was a Godfrey-modified, 1.5-litre Singer engine with an overhead-camshaft which provided approximately 60 BHP. The extra power meant nearly 100 MPH. Post-1945 H.R.G.s were produced at the frustrating rate of about one per week, cost around $2,600 at the factory, and were enthusiastically distributed in the U.S.A.

Streamlining was intriguing designers in England as on the Continent between the wars and some curious automobiles resulted. Take the North-Lucas for instance: the 5-cylinder (70 x 76 mm.), radial, air-cooled engine was fastened to the front of a body that looked like a stubby cabin aircraft fuselage. Independent suspension was employed, the windshield of the cabin was V-shaped, and there was a roof vent like those on old-fashioned railroad cars. Then there was the Burney whose designer, Sir Dennis Burney, had made his name with dirigibles. The aerodynamic model shown is one of several built during 1929–31. Neither of these streamliners caught the public's fancy.

All told, more than 700 distinct makes of cars were manufactured in Britain to the south of the Scottish border. The vast majority of them are long since forgotten. The same holds in every car-producing nation. A few deserve brief notice:

295

The very rare streamlined Burney was a 1929–31 attempt to popularize air-flow designs. Public wasn't any more ready in England than in U.S.A. (*The Motor*)

The 1922 North-Lucas had a 5-cylinder, radial, air-cooled engine in the rear. A very rare prototype. (*The Motor*)

There was the Weigel, made by D. M. Weigel Motors, Ltd. in London (1907–10), a car with a 15-litre, straight-8 engine. A pair of them were the only British entries in the 1907 French Grand Prix.

Between directing the affairs of other firms, Frederick R. Simms was involved intimately in building the obscure Simms-Welbeck car intermittently during 1900–07. A few of these cars may have been the world's first to use bumpers in 1905—hard rubber bumpers.

Then there was the Hutton of 1900–08; its destiny was involved with that of the early Napier. Built in Surrey, the Hutton tried with scant success to popularize two-wheel hydraulic brakes.

For the first decade of this century Messrs. Horsfall and Bickham of Manchester built the Horbick in limited numbers. One- and 2-cylinder cars, they had propeller shafts by 1904–05. About the same time, this marque had a 3-cylinder engine made by White & Poppe and the radiator looked like that of the Rolls-Royce (also imitated in America by the Roamer). Later Horsfall and Bickham made their own 6-cylinder engines, and they built some taxis.

The Dennis, made in Surrey during 1901–15 by Dennis Brothers Ltd., tried water-cooled brakes and later sold quite well. The firm still makes fire engines and other utility vehicles.

For a time, the Bean (1920–29) built substantial cars which were in direct competition to the Morris Oxfords and Cowleys, reliable 1.8- and 2.3-litre fours and finally 2.3-litre sixes on wheelbases up to 122 inches.

Gwynne Cars Ltd. in Chiswick made the Gwynne from 1923 to '29. Quite stylish fours with 1- and 2-litre engines, this marque's styling was along European lines.

Easily mistaken, if approached from the front, for a vintage Bugatti, the H.E. was made in Reading by Herbert Engineering Ltd. during 1920–29. It had a radiator shell design much like that of the famed French car. The emblem was oval and placed at the top of the inverted horseshoe as on Bugattis. Mostly 4-cylinder, 2-litre cars, a few 2.3-litre supercharged and unblown sixes were built during the last two years of the marque. The most expensive H.E. cost nearly 900 £ and had a sporting 126-inch-wheelbase chassis with four-wheel brakes which were standard from 1925 until the end.

Also inspired by the Continent were Sidney Straker and R. L. Squire who made the expensive Straker-Squire from 1908 to 1926. Elegant sports cars and luxury tourers in small numbers came out of this partnership which built to an ideal, not to a price. With fours and sixes of up to 4 litres capacity in long and expensive chassis fitted with racing or touring coachwork, this marque once lapped Brooklands at 103 MPH, no mean feat in the early '20s.

Unrelated to the foregoing marque, the Squire was made in Oxford by Adrian Squire in 1934–36. Hand-built, the Squire was one of several expensively exclusive cars built to match the best supercharged 1.5-litre cars of the continent. Anzani engines of 1,496 cc. with chain-driven, dual, overhead-camshafts were supercharged and secured low in deep frames. The latter were very rigid with eleven beam and tubular cross members. Hydraulic shock absorbers and wide semi-elliptic springs were used as were hydraulic brakes with alloy drums approximately 16 inches in diameter. Buyers received a guarantee for 100 MPH and the car would do it. Road holding was exceptional with either the 102- or the 123-inch

An early Jensen special, Number Three of late 1928, probably based upon a Standard chassis. The customizing partnership of the two brothers blos- somed into series production of their distinctive marque. (*The Motor*)

wheelbase version. Collectors lust after this marque; only twenty were built.

Not to hit his stride until after the war, Sidney Allard built his first special in 1937–38. The components came from the wreck of a V-8 Ford; his backyard was his workshop. The result was an open 2-seater with cycle fenders. Success in trials and hill climbs brought requests for similar cars and the marque Allard was born.

Like the foregoing, the Jensen evolved from a rebuilt Austin "Seven" that was given to Richard and Allan Jensen by their father when the boys were 16 and 19 years old respectively. After disassembling the Austin, they lightened every component wherever possible, firmed the suspension, and rebuilt it into a fast 2-seat sports car that passed everything in sight includ-

ing a car driven by the flabbergasted chief engineer of Standard. Hired immediately, the Jensens worked their magic on several Standard models during the late '20s and '30s.

Wolseley "Hornet" chassis were their next project and the word spread to Hollywood from whence came an order from Clark Gable. In 1934, the open Jensen-Ford V-8 tourer was shipped to the film star. This project received the blessing of the late Edsel Ford who went to the little factory in West Bromwich. As a result, the Jensen was recognized in 1936 as a marque; the model was produced in a small series powered by 3.6-litre, Ford V-8 engines. These "S" models were followed by the "H" series of 1938–39 with 120 and 131-inch chassis powered by 4.2-litre dual ignition straight-8 engines made by Nash. With coachwork made in the traditional manner, saloon, touring or cabriolet models were available to order, and prices ranged from 810 to 1,135 Pounds Sterling. Several coupes were also built with Lincoln V-12 engines. With the 4.2-litre Nash engines, the heavy Jensens were capable of sustained cruising at 85 mph, and could achieve 90–95 mph. Jensens expanded their production after 1945 and, when this was being written, were producing the world's only four-wheel-drive passenger car, a high speed grand turismo.

Inevitably, someone's favorite English car will have been omitted from this book. Such omission is regretted, but, as mentioned, England has produced more than 700 makes of cars since 1896, and it is impractical to include them all.

Finland

FINLAND'S AUTOMOTIVE INDUSTRY has had problems commensurate with and parallel to that little nation's efforts to become and remain independent. Before 1918, Finland was a fief of Imperial Russia and automobiles, while not unknown or unwanted, were a distinct curiosity. The government of the Czar did not encourage Finnish industry. Roads suitable for cars were a rarity and the few cars were mostly from Sweden and Russia.

The Finns, however, are a technically adept people and there were some competent engineers, machinists and small factories in the Helsinki to Viborg area. Frans Lindström of the firm, Mynämä Kone & Sähkötehdas, began in 1912 to build the one and only Lindström car. Construction required nearly a year. A small two-seater powered by a 2-cylinder, 4-cycle, air-cooled engine, the Lindström had wire wheels and, in its original state, pneumatic tires. The overall design and suspension were up to date for 1913. It was successful but never went into series production because of the demands of Finland's War of Independence which precluded further car development until after 1920. Used by its maker for around ten years, the little car was last licensed for road use in 1924. In 1954, the Lindström was dusted off and participated in a parade of veteran cars in Helsinki where it ran on cleats rather than rubber tires. The Lindström, as Finland's first car, is a national treasure.

The next verifiable Finnish attempt to manufacture cars occurred in 1921 when Yrjö Horsman, owner of a small factory named Sortavalan Konepaja, designed and built a 4–5 seat open tourer. The engine, an L-head, 4-cylinder unit insofar as can be ascertained, was not built by Horsman nor were the artillery wheels. It is quite possible that the engine, generator, electric headlights and the like were purchased from Scania-Vabis in neighboring Sweden. The car was successful, so much so, in fact, that it was named "Riemu" which means "Delight." Used for several years, the Riemu eventually fell into disuse when the engine was converted for marine use. The little car was a "one-off" of conventional design.

The years between the two world conflicts were hard for Finland and industry was financially handicapped. Coachbuilding firms, a dozen or so, eventually sprang up to

Finland's oldest car, the Lindström of 1913, during a parade of veteran cars in Helsinki in 1954.

(Lehtikuva Oy courtesy Oy Suomen Autoteollisuus AB)

fit imported chassis with bodies. One coachbuilder, P. J. Heikkilä, decided to build chassis as well. Heikkilä reasoned that a proper chassis of medium size could be used for both large passenger cars and small trucks. The cars and trucks were named Finlandia. Late in the twenties, at least four chassis were built. One was completed as a fire engine and was delivered to the Fire Brigade in Helsinki where its top speed of 56 mph brought it considerable fame as it served through two wars; it was retired

The Riemu was built in 1921 by Yrjö Horsman, an industrialist who is standing at right in this old photo. (*Oy Suomen Autoteollisuus AB*)

Only the emblem remains of one of the Finlandia cars. (*Oy Suomen Autoteollisuus AB*)

in 1956. Two of the chassis were fitted with powerful engines of unknown make and well-designed touring coachwork as illustrated. Heikkilä was unable to obtain the means to enter into series production so he retained both Finlandia tourers for his own use. One of them was used extensively in racing and various motor sports. Of the two Finlandias, one is said to have been completely worn out from arduous use; its whereabouts is unknown. The other was finally scrapped at Terijoki in Keralia which became a part of the Soviet Union after

The Finlandia cars were large sporting tourers.
P. J. Heikkilä, the builder, is at the wheel. (*Oy
Suomen Autoteollisuus AB*)

First series-produced motor vehicle in Finland was
the 1931 Sisu light truck. (*Oy Suomen Autoteollisuus AB*)

the Second World War. Only one radiator emblem remains of the four Finlandia vehicles, the handsome device shown here displaying a martial lion in gold against a red background surrounded by blue and surmounted by Finnish flags.

Another firm, Oy Suomen Autoteollisuus Aktiebolaget of Helsinki, began automotive activities in 1931 and produced an excellent line of light trucks. Called Sisu, the first series model, a 4-cylinder, 2-ton-capacity truck is shown. Some controversy has surrounded Sisu vehicles. An English reference book * states that production of passenger cars was instituted in 1934. Efforts to confirm the existence of Sisu cars has brought a denial from this manufacturer. However, Sisu trucks of a wide variety for both on and off-the-road service are manufactured to this date and are exported to many other countries.

There is a possibility that a Finnish passenger car may yet go into production, for Finland now has three successful truck manufacturers.

* *The World's Automobiles, 1880–1955*, G. R. Doyle (Temple Press Ltd., London, 1957).

France

FRENCH AUTOMOBILES had attained world leadership by 1900 because of Gallic effervescence, skills and one important event: enactment of The Locomotive and Highways Act of 1896 in England. Finally emancipated as seen in Part II, English motorists celebrated the event with the historic first London-to-Brighton run organized by The Motor Club. Because of the scarcity of English cars, entries were invited from the Continent. Thirty-three cars were on tap at the start of the 52-mile run. Among the French cars were De Dion-Bouton, Peugeot, Panhard & Levassor cars with their "world's fastest" reputation, a pair of three-wheeled Léon Bollées driven by Léon and Camille, and others. The Bollées surprised everyone, and frightened hundreds with their ability to weave in and out of horse traffic at 30 mph, and won the top two places. A Panhard & Levassor came in third an hour later after a breakdown raised its elapsed time to five hours. This triumph was taken as "proof" of superiority and triggered an overwhelming demand for French cars. As a result, scores of new makes mushroomed around Paris.

The marque Panhard & Levassor had already pioneered the front-mounted engine in a specially built frame with a stabilizing diagonal member (the "Panhard rod") from the frame to rear axle. This "Systéme Panhard" included a 4-speed sliding gear change and chain drive, a vast improvement over all others in the early 1890s. It marked the break from other flimsy belt-driven cars and enabled France to progress rapidly in the automobile industry. Emile Levassor died in 1897 from injuries suffered while driving the firm's first 4-cylinder car in the 1896 Paris-Marseilles-Paris race which was won by another P&L. Although others have said that all Panhard & Levassor engines prior to World War One had four cylinders, the firm did produce a few 2-cylinder "Centaure" models in 1901 and some 6-cylinder cars as evidenced by the 1905 demi-limousine illustrated here.

The marque's reputation, however, was based upon 4-cylinder cars, performance and racing victories. For the 1901 Paris to Bordeaux race, Panhard & Levassor fielded a team of 40-horsepower machines (130 x 140 mm. bore and stroke) equipped with coil ignition systems; these captured second through sixth places. The same year a 90 x 130 mm. 12-HP (CV) racer like the one illustrated won the voiturette (light car)

After assembling at the Arc d'Triomphe in 1946, French enthusiasts held a race of veteran cars to celebrate the golden anniversary of French auto- mobiles. (*French Embassy Press & Information Division*)

class in the Paris-Berlin race. In 1902, several 70-horsepower racers were built. The example illustrated won the Paris-Vincennes race and other events. The huge tube type radiator was supplied with water from a large tank on the extreme rear of the chassis, the water being circulated by a flywheel operated pump. Attempts to set a world's speed record failed in 1902—a Mors eclipsed all others with 77.13 mph—so the factory built a 160 x 170 mm. racer that also developed 70 HP; with this the Chevalier René de Knyff, the firm's director since 1897, drove to second place in the 1903 Gordon Bennett race.

Panhards were popular in America where, in 1904, a big 90-HP racer driven by George Heath won the first running of the Vanderbilt Cup Race at Roosevelt Park.

Heath was back the next year with his bellowing monster—which had a square bore and stroke of 170 mm.—and placed second, close behind a Darracq. This particular car was the first of the marque to use shaft drive and magneto ignition. Curiously, after this success P&L continued to use chain drive for some time. P&L next built the largest engine ever to emerge from the Paris works, a monstrous 18-litre, 4-cylinder affair that developed 130 brake horsepower. Groomed for the world's first Grand Prix race—put on in 1906 by the Automobile Club of France—the big racer went down to defeat under the Renault onslaught.

As the expense of competition increased, Panhard & Levassor next concentrated on utilitarian cars which were sporting in concept. In 1909, arrangements were made to

306

The 14 CV Panhard & Levassor of 1901. (*Panhard S.A.*)

produce sleeve-valve engines based upon the patents of the American, Charles Y. Knight. Several other marques in neighboring countries were using sleeve valves and the public was impressed with the silent operation of such engines despite the clouds of oily smoke. Thus, while several series of cars with conventional poppet valves and up to 60 HP remained in production, a 20-horse-power, 4-cylinder "sans soupape" ("without valves" although this appellation was incorrect), as the sleeve-valve models were thereafter known, began the pattern pursued faithfully until 1940.

After the 1914–18 war, Panhard & Levassor was seldom concerned with racing although a 12.8-litre, chain-driven racer made several appearances. In 1925, a 6.3-litre sports model ran 116 miles in one hour, and in 1926, the slender 8-litre sleeve-valve

"Razor Blade" raced on the Brooklands circuit in England and occasionally on the continent.

Finally in 1934, the management decided that the marque's early high-performance reputation should be confirmed and Captain George Eyston was retained to show the colors in a record attempt. The vehicle was specially built, a slim job powered by an 8-cylinder heated-up version of the unit powering the firm's luxurious 35 CV tourers and limousines. Thus it was that Eyston established a one-hour record on the Montlhery circuit at 132.99 mph in 1934 with the machine shown.

From 1930 on, Panhard & Levassor concentrated upon production of quality cars for the middle and upper classes. The popular, though unspectacular and blocky, 6-cylinder 6DS model of 1930 evolved into

The Paris-Vincennes 70-BHP racing car of 1902. Note lower seat for mechanic, near side. (*Panhard S.A.*)

In 1905, Panhard & Levassor produced a small series of large demi-limousines with detachable tops. One of the last P&L cars to use chain drive. Owner: Lindley Bothwell. (*Joseph H. Wherry*)

the stylish "Panoramique" which was a sensation in the Paris Show of 1933. Instead of the usual A-post at each side of the windshield, there were two slender parallel posts with curved glass. Increasing the driver's visibility, this preceded modern wrap-around windshields by nearly twenty years. While not radical, the overall styling was pleasing and the all-steel bodies were sturdy. Sleeve-valve, 6-cylinder engines of 2.5 and 2.9 litres, rated at 14 and 16 HP for tax purposes respectively, were used in the "Panoramique" chassis with 124.8-inch wheelbase. More luxurious were the limousines, on 131.5-inch wheelbase, powered by 6-cylinder 4 and 4.8-litre engines rated at 23 and 27 HP. A larger 85 x 112 mm. (bore and stroke) 8-cylinder, 5-litre engine rated at 29 HP was offered optionally. This ele-

gant series lasted through 1936 until the "Dynamique" offered two 6-cylinder engines: a 10-HP, 1.2-litre and an 11-HP, 1.4-litre. Aerodynamic bodies with flush headlights, skirted wheels and curved glass at the front door posts were prophetic of post-war Dyna-Panhard styling, and a tubular backbone type frame—the central tube enclosing the propeller shaft—with independent suspension on all four wheels paralleled the technical advances of German and Czech cars. The "Dynamique Junior" was a two-seater coupé on a 102.3-inch wheelbase; the "Major" coupés and convertibles had a 110.2-inch wheelbase and the "Berline" was a five-six passenger model on a 118.1-inch wheelbase. The head-on view shows the unique centered location of the driver and the famous P. & L. initials

Each of the 6 cylinders in the rare 1905 Panhard & Levassor demi-limousine was separately cast. (*Joseph H. Wherry*)

Engine oiling tubes and gauges kept the driver of the big 1905 Panhard & Levassor well occupied.

Accelerator pedal is between clutch and brake. (*Joseph H. Wherry*)

with an "S" on each side for "sans soupapes" indicating the sleeve-valve engines. The "Dynamique" was the last pre-war model.

After beginning as a steam car as seen in Part II, the De Dion-Bouton became a gasoline vehicle. The 1900 model, a single-cylinder, was popular despite its outmoded design. Widely exported, the 1-cylinder, 80-mm.-square engine was one of the few high-speed units at that time. Largely designed by the Count Albert de Dion himself, the basic secret of this engine's efficiency was careful machining to close toler-

ances. Other manufacturers in Europe and America purchased De Dion engines for their own cars. Running at the then unheard-of speed of 1,800 rpm, the engine developed 4 HP and was water cooled. Early in the century, bore and stroke were enlarged to 90 and 110 mm. respectively and larger 10-HP racing versions were also built.

Not a racing enthusiast, Count de Dion gave little support to such pursuits despite having helped to found the Automobile Club of France in 1895. Primarily, de Dion and his partner, Georges Bouton, were in-

310

The 12.8-litre, 4-cylinder Grand Prix Panhard of 1918. Bore and stroke were 155 mm. and 170 mm. Speed was 92 mph; fuel was consumed at the rate of 8 miles per gallon. (*Panhard S.A.*)

A sleeve-valve engine was used in the 1926 Panhard "Razor Blade" 10 CV racer. (*Panhard S.A.*)

George Eyston established a one-hour record on the Montlhery circuit at 132.99 mph, with this sleeve-valve Panhard special in 1934. (*Panhard S.A.*)

The 1933 P&L Panoramique "La Parisienne" was a large 6-cylinder, 4-litre sedan rated at 23 CV. (*Panhard S.A.*)

Introduced at the 1936 Paris Auto Show, the Panhard "Dynamique" had driver's position in the center, triple windshield wipers, and a tubular backbone type chassis. (*Panhard S.A.*)

Aerodynamic, stressed-steel body, flush headlights and curved glass in front door posts were futuristic features of the 1936 P&L "Dynamique." (*Panhard S.A.*)

The 1908 De Dion-Bouton during a stop in the astonishing New York to Paris Race via Siberia. One of five cars entered, the De Dion withdrew at Vladivostok because of mechanical troubles after covering 8,700 miles. A Thomas Flyer won. (*Automobile Manufacturers Association*)

1911 De Dion-Bouton roadster was imposing on a 129-inch wheelbase. A large V-8 engine developed 26 CV. (*Henry Ford Museum*)

The world speed record of 75.05 mph was held briefly in 1902 by a Serpollet flash-boiler steam racer like the one in the foreground. Serpollets were produced until 1907 and were France's most successful steamers. In the background is a contemporary Renault racer. (*French Embassy Press & Information Division*)

novators. They patented the De Dion axle in 1894 while still making steam cars. Not so successful was a peculiar arrangement of expanding clutches inside drums on each rear wheel; these permitted smooth gear changing but were so complicated that they were discontinued about 1907 in favor of the conventional clutch behind the engine flywheel. On the other hand, the De Dion axle with two swinging half-shafts and the transverse tube (which positions the rear wheels) were used on most De Dion-Bouton cars and were adopted by other marques after 1920 when independent rear suspension systems gained popularity. Even today the De Dion rear axle is employed in many variations around the world. With a shovel nose much like a dozen other marques, the

1-cylinder De Dion-Bouton was modernized into a range of runabouts and coupés and was continued until 1915.

The works did sponsor entries in two races, despite an aversion to such events. A pair of 2-cylinder, 8-HP models were entered in the 1907 Peking, China to Paris race and they captured second and third places. With this encouragement, a production 4-cylinder, six-passenger touring car developing 30 HP was outfitted for the even more stupefying New York to Paris race in 1908. Big and tough on its 128-inch wheelbase, mechanical troubles forced the De Dion's withdrawal at Vladivostok, Siberia, after having negotiated 8,700 grueling miles.

The finest pre-war De Dion-Bouton was the 26-HP, V-8 model of 1911. On a 129-

One of the first Berliet cars was this stylish, rear-engine voiturette of 1895. Note leg shelter for front passengers instead of the usual lap robe. (*Automobiles M. Berliet*)

inch wheelbase, this series was built in a wide variety of body types. In a rare racing attempt, a V-8 tourer placed fourth in the Targa Florio. Actually De Dion-Bouton had been making V-8 engines for several years and was the first manufacturer to series produce this type engine. After 1919, the firm manufactured 4 and 8-cylinder quality cars in the medium and upper price ranges on wheelbases up to 136 inches, but the economic slump of the '30s ended this pioneer make.

Of the more than six hundred distinct makes of cars produced in France, those built by the Bollée family were of early importance although they rarely are remembered today. Founder of this industrial dynasty was Ernest Sylvain Bollée who established an iron foundry near Le Mans in 1842. In 1873 his son, Amédée, built the steam carriage, "L'Obéissante," shown in Part II. Amédée had three sons, Amédée Jr., Léon and Camille, and with typical French individuality Amédée *fils* and Léon, both trained engineers, manufactured cars independently of each other, using their full names to identify them.

The marque Amédée Bollée started as a steam runabout in 1885 but, after a few were made, Amédée turned to gasoline engine development and by 1895 was producing four-wheelers with steering wheels. A talented engineer, Amédée soon was licensing his patented designs to de Dietrich

& Company and other firms, but he continued building his own costly, high-quality cars in limited numbers until the mid-'20s when the marque disappeared.

Léon Bollée cars also included a few steamers but the gasoline powered three-wheelers of 1896 London to Brighton fame, mentioned earlier, quickly made him a fairly wealthy young man by 1900 when he was just 29 years old. Léon strived for the ultimate in technical perfection and quiet operation. His finest car was a large 45-HP model built before the 1914–18 war. Of unassailable quality, this car in chassis, cost more in England than a Rolls-Royce in similar condition according to David Scott Moncrief in his *Veteran and Edwardian Motor Cars*. Unfortunately, Léon died in 1913 but the firm survived under the management of his widow. Various models on wheelbases from 118 to 138 inches powered by 4 and 6-cylinder engines of from 2 to 4 litres displacement were technically excel-

lent but rather unexciting and sales withered. Finally in 1924, Madame Bollée sold out to W. R. Morris of England and the Léon Bollée was discontinued in 1927 after a brief revival with 4, 6 and 8-cylinder Morris engines.

More exciting and famous was the Mors created by Emile Mors in 1895. In 1898, Mors built the first successful V-4 engine. Made in Paris, the Mors cars were slandered in England as being named for "death" because of their speed and the frightful noises emitted. In 1901, a big blustery 2-cylinder, 60-HP Mors won the Paris to Bordeaux race, averaging 50 mph, and overnight became the most serious rival of Panhard & Levassor. With his appetite thus whetted for more racing publicity, Emile Mors decided to attack the world speed record which had been established in 1899 by the Jenatzy electric car (see Part II). Under development was a large 4-cylinder racer with a sloping bonnet and friction

A 4-cylinder (100 x 120 mm.) 3,775 cc. engine with shaft drive powered the 22-HP Berliet landau-let of 1907. Wheelbase was 118.5 inches. (*Automobiles M. Berliet*)

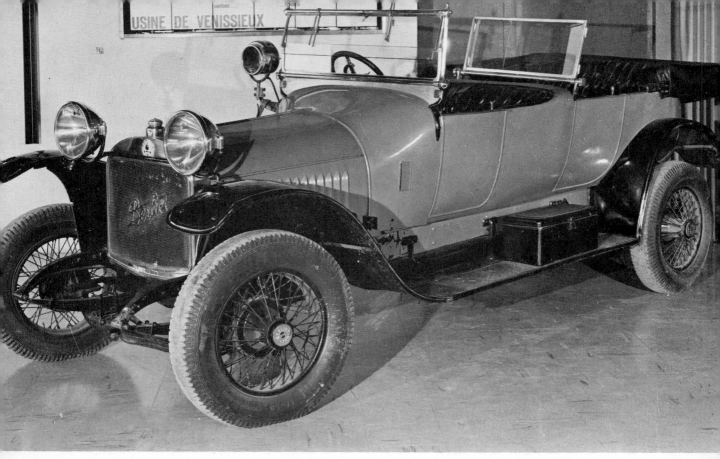

French elegance—the 4-cylinder, 4-litre Berliet dual-cowl torpedo on 126-inch wheelbase. Note high position of acetylene lamps. 1911. (*Automobiles M. Berliet*)

shock absorbers—the latter was a first for Mors who also developed the first magneto electric ignition and a compressed air starter. Before a Mors could tackle the world speed record, a Serpollet steamer captured the prize with a timed run of 75.05 mph. However, William K. Vanderbilt, the racing American who had already placed well in several races on Mors, established the marque's supremacy by raising the record to 76.08 mph in 1902. Vanderbilt is often credited with 76.5 mph on a 60-HP Mors; such a claim is erroneous but a driver named Dourdan did raise the world record —and on a Mors—to 76.6 mph later the same year. Moreover, before 1902 ended, Dourdan raised his own mark to 77.1 mph. The next year was the peak for Mors when

a 4-cylinder, 80-HP racer, with a pointed body looking like an inverted speedboat, won the tragic Paris-Madrid road race. Spectator and driver casualties during the first stage to Bordeaux were so high that French officials stopped the race and prohibited such future events on public roads. Fernand Gabriel drove his Mors, which had a top speed of nearly 80 mph, the 342 miles of the shortened race over horrible roads at an average of 65.3 mph in a fraction less than 5 hours. Mors lost its sporting temperament soon after this race and the works produced 122 to 130-inch-wheelbase passenger cars with 4-cylinders into the '20s. Of high quality and advanced design with shaft drive from about 1908, the early Mors are remembered for their unusual clutch which,

318

This five-passenger Darracq phaeton of 1904 cost $5,500. The 4-cylinder engine had a double ignition system combining magneto and coil. Wheel-base was 110.8 and overall height was 90.5 inches. (*Henry Ford Museum*)

with shoes expanding against the inside rim of the flywheel, was much like a drum type brake.

Andrè Citroën (of which more shortly) was the manager of the Mors factory for a few years and in 1927 he absorbed Mors and the pioneer marque was no more.

Beginning in 1895, the Berliet cars were built by locomotive manufacturers in Lyon but were little known until after 1900. Some electrics were made but quality gasoline phaetons and limousines, most of them with 4-cylinder engines, were built for the silk stocking trade from 1906. In 1907, a 2.5-litre model on a 110-inch wheelbase had its four 80 x 120 mm. cylinders cast in pairs. Known in England as the 10/14 HP model and by the works as the Type BD-2, it had

a magneto ignition system and a 4-speed gearbox. In 1909, the 4-litre 40-HP Type P on a 126-inch wheelbase would have fared well in the Prinz Heinrich Trials in Prussia had Marius Berliet had the foresight to use detachable rim wheels which the Michelin tire people developed about 1907. Even so, the Type P interested the American Locomotive Company which built it under license in the United States as the Alco (see Part V). After the war, quality 4-cylinder cars of 1.2, 2.5, 2.6 and 4-litre capacity were manufactured until 1930, some of them luxury models on wheelbases of 146 inches. There were few Berliet sports cars but a 2.6-litre sports four-seater called the "Silver Arrow" ran without success at Le Mans in 1923. In 1929, a 1.8-litre, 6-cylin-

319

Finest of the pre-war Talbot-Lago cars was the 1939 "Record" with 4.5-litre engine Grand Turismo coachwork by Figoni & Falaschi. (*Henry Ford Museum*)

The elegant, 4.7-litre, straight-eight Delage D-8 of 1930. Double phaeton coachwork by Franay. (*VU courtesy of Consulate General of Belgium*)

This post-war Delahaye was an almost exact duplicate of the 1938–39 Type D8-120 in appearance. Van den Plas coachwork. (*Joseph H. Wherry*)

der passenger series, the 14 CV, appeared on a 112-inch wheelbase and the marque continued until 1940. Berliet now makes some of the world's largest trucks.

Almost unknown today, the Chenard-Walcker began as a three-wheeler in 1895 and evolved into a 4-wheel machine with 2 cylinders in 1901. In 1904 the marque competed in hill-climbs and trials with 4-cylinder two-seaters. The firm made all of their own engines, designed a successful carburetor, was probably the first to employ forced lubrication through a drilled crankshaft in 1910, and in 1911 pioneered aluminum pistons in production models. After World War One, the marque bloomed and became highly individualistic. For several years, the front wheels alone carried brake drums assisted by a transmission-actuated boosting device. Styling was eccentric with slab sides sometimes ending in streamlined tails on tourers as well as on the competition models. Their appearance caused the C-W

sports cars and racers to be called "Warthogs" and "Tanks" and by other appropriate nicknames. Very low with frames underslung beneath the rear axle, they were fast and efficient.

At the initial running in the Le Mans 24-hour Grand Prix d'Endurance in 1923, a pair of 130-inch wheelbase Chenard-Walckers placed first and second with the leading car, piloted by Lagache and Leonard, averaging over 57 mph for a winning 1,372 miles. The long-stroke engines had four 80 x 150 mm. cylinders displacing 3 litres and single overhead-camshafts. Straight 8-cylinder, single-overhead-camshaft 4-litre models, and dual-overhead-camshaft 2-litre fours followed in 1924, and in 1925 a little 1.1-litre single-overhead-camshaft four appeared. In 1926, the 101-litre model was fitted with a supercharger and in the Spanish Grand Prix, a 12-hour event at San Sebastian, the tiny upstart with the "tank" body, defeated everything including the favored 7-litre

A 3.5-litre Lorraine 23 CV with four-passenger cabriolet coachwork of about 1930. (*VU courtesy of Consulate General of Belgium*)

blown Mercedes to score one of racing's great upsets. Two and four-seater sports models were then marketed with modified "tank" coachwork that was beautifully finished and tastefully appointed. Four-wheel brakes were standardized about 1928 when new 1.5-litre engines became available. More reserved family sedans were introduced in 1929 on wheelbases of 104, 122 and 132 inches with 1.5 or 1.8-litre fours or 2.9-litre 6-cylinder engines. For the enthusiast the "tank" styling was retained on open and closed 1.5-litre, 96-inch-wheelbase two-seaters. In 1930, an L-head, 2.2-litre sportster set an 82.5 mph, 24-hour record at Montlhery and a front-wheel-drive model was marketed briefly in the mid-'30s. Since 1945, Chenard, Walcker et Cie. has manufactured parts and components for the industry.

One of the most promising of the early French cars was the Darracq which first appeared in 1896. A shrewd industrialist and pioneer of mass production, Alexandre Darracq sold his cars throughout Europe and in America. A batch of them became New York City's first taxicabs shortly after 1900, and Darracqs were built under license in Italy and Germany. In 1900, the Darracq introduced tubular steel frames when most marques were still using hardwood. Two years later Darracqs had pressed steel frames. In the same year Darracq also built and sold more than 1,000 light 6.5-HP cars. Chain final drive was abandoned in favor of propeller shafts in 1900 and simultaneously the inadequate rear wheel brakes were supplemented by a hand-operated brake acting upon the differential. This device caused many a broken rear axle.

Darracq confirmed its reputation as a high-performance car by pioneering pushrod-

The 1905 Peugeot quadricycle was throwback to earlier designs. Driver sat behind passengers on a modified motorcycle seat and steered front wheels by handlebars. Speed was about 17 mph with the 510-cc., single-cylinder, 7 CV water-cooled engine mounted over rear axle. (S.A. *des Automobiles Peugeot*)

actuated, overhead valves in 1904 and raising the official world speed record to 104.5 mph with a big, 100-HP, 4-cylinder racer. Passenger cars with one, two and four cylinders were built from 1900 on. The finest in the 1904 line was the 5,122 cc. phaeton illustrated, a quality car with steering column gear change lever. In 1905, Darracq built a V-8-engined racer which developed 200 brake horsepower. Tube type double radiators arranged in a "V" to cut wind resistance gave these racers a fierce visage. One of these cars quickly boosted the speed record to 109.6 mph and then dramatically improved on its own mark in 1906 with 122.45 mph. That record was short-lived, however, when a Stanley Steamer shocked the gasoline car builders the same year with 127.66 mph.

A force to be reckoned with in European racing, Darracq invaded America in 1905 where Victor Hemery won the second running of the Vanderbilt Cup Race in an 80-HP, 4-cylinder type. This was the year the sponsor, W. K. Vanderbilt, stopped the race after the first four cars came in because the spectators became unruly and swarmed over the track. More than a quarter-million fans saw Wagner romp into first place in 1906 on another Darracq with a pointed-nose, 110-HP four. More racing victories kept Darracqs in the news when Louis Chevrolet campaigned successfully all over the United States on the marque, and the firm prospered with a moderately priced four, called the "Flying Fifteen" (15 CV—horsepower), one of the most dependable cars of 1905–06 and able to sustain 40 mph with ease.

The Lion-Peugeot of 1908 had a 4-cylinder, 2,211-cc. 16 CV engine coupled to a 4-speed gearbox. (S.A. *des Automobiles Peugeot*)

1912–13 Peugeot "Bebe" was designed by Ettore Bugatti: 856 cc. displacement developed 6 CV and gave nearly 35 mph. The "Bebe" was exported widely. (S.A. *des Automobiles Peugeot*)

Equally popular was a 2-cylinder, 12-HP car; one of these starred in the famous "Genevieve" motion picture.

In 1919, Darracq became a part of British-owned Clément-Talbot, the Clément part of which began in 1898 when the Paris bicycle and motorbike maker, Gustav Adolphe Clément, decided to enter the automobile fray. The resulting Clément-Bayard owed much to Panhard & Levassor, for Adolphe Clément was also a major stockholder in that firm for several years. In 1904, the Clément-Bayard (named for the "fearless" French knight who lived 1473–1524) was unusual, however, in having an 8/10-HP, T-head engine with dual camshafts located high in the block driving valves on opposite sides of the two 85 x 110 mm. cylinders. Apart from the engines, this marque conformed to the styling of the times.

To further complicate the Darracq story, the Talbot-Darracq combine merged with Sunbeam of England in 1921 and Clément eventually went its own 4-cylinder way a couple of years later only to be swallowed by Citroën in 1932. Darracq cars were also known in France as Talbot-Darracq after 1921 and became 4 and 8-cylinder cars in a wide variety on wheelbases varying from 96 to upward of 136 inches. A fine 4.6-litre, 62-HP, V-8 was produced in limited numbers during 1921–22. In the early '20s, overhead-camshaft, 4-cylinder, 1.5-litre models won their share of class victories in racing. In 1926, a 2.5-litre six (70 x 110 mm. bore and stroke) on a 132-inch wheelbase was produced; the bore was increased in 1927 to 75 mm. raising the capacity to 2.9-litres. This model, along with a smaller 2-litre six and a 1.7-litre four on a 123-inch wheelbase, kept the French branch of the Sunbeam-Talbot-Darracq firm in Suresnes

active on the continent until the combine came apart in 1935 when the Rootes Group took over the assets in England.

At this point Antonio Lago, the manager of the Darracq works, purchased the French facilities. Lago, a competent engineer in his own right, brought out the exquisite Talbot-Lago. For the 1936 Tourist Trophy Race in England, Lago fielded a team of sports cars with 6-cylinder, triple carburetor engines displacing 3,996 cc. A single camshaft high in the block drove inclined valves in hemispherical combustion chambers by means of angled pushrods (similar to BMW) and the output was 165 brake horsepower at 4,200 RPM. A 4-speed pre-selector gearbox increased flexibility. Managed by René Dreyfus, recently a restaurateur in New York City, the Talbot-Lagos won the top two places in the TT. Lago next improved on his winning recipe by increasing the engine capacity to 4.5-litres and adding double overhead-camshafts. Streamlined coachwork by Figoni & Falaschi graced new 104-inch-wheelbase chassis. All up weight was just over 3,200 pounds and top speeds of 115–120 mph were attained in tests. Lack of success in the 24-hour Le Mans in 1938 and '39 did not dampen the ardor of enthusiasts who snapped up the limited numbers produced. After the war, the Talbot-Lago GT coupés returned to racing circuits, one placing first overall in the 1950 Le Mans race while another raced the same year at Watkins Glen, U.S.A. Later, the revived Talbot-Darracq facilities in France were taken over by Simca to end a half-century of triumphs and mergers.

Another pioneer, Emile Delahaye, had a thriving farm machinery and brick works when he decided to cash in on the demand for French cars in 1896. The first Delahaye ran in the famed Paris-Marseilles-Paris race,

1911 Peugeot, beautifully restored, belongs to Mr. Donald Baker. Seen at an old car meeting on the green at Greenfield Village, Dearborn, Michigan, in late fifties. (*Joseph H. Wherry*)

its builder driving, and is covered in Part II. In 1902, Delahaye deserted single cylinders and belt drives in favor of 4 cylinders and chains and, like several others, mounted the gear change lever on the steering column. Magneto ignitions were adopted in 1904. At about this time, Delahaye had an intriguing wrinkle—a water-cooled muffler erroneously calculated to reduce noise; the device did not last. Delahaye engines were used for a year or two after 1910 in White cars in America (see Part V). From the first to last Delahaye, the chief engineer was Charles Weiffenbach who may have designed the first V-6 engine in 1911, and a 30-degree "V" at that.

From 1919 until 1935, Delahayes were refined 4 and 6-cylinder passenger cars on extremely rugged chassis with wheelbases of 120 to 136 inches. Sports and touring cars used 4 and 6-cylinder engines up to 3 litres capacity. In 1935, Delahaye took over Delage but both marques retained separate identity. Louis Delage, born to humble parents in Cognac, worked hard for his engineering degree and became chief designer of the obscure Turgan-Foy (1900–1906). When that marque folded, Delage set up his own small shop in the Paris suburb of Levallois-Perret where he powered his high-quality cars with De Dion engines until about 1910 when he designed his own 4-cylinder units. In 1911, a 15-horsepower, 6-cylinder car was produced and in 1914 a pair of special Delage fours placed first and third at Indianapolis, driven by René Thomas and Guyot. Four-wheel brakes were installed for the 1914 French Grand Prix and after the 1914–18 war, when Delage cooperated with Nieuport aircraft, this improvement was offered on all models. Although he had experimented with overhead-camshafts in 1914, Delage fitted side valves in 1919 and went to pushrod overhead valves in 1921 on 80 x 150 mm. bore and stroke fours and sixes on wheelbases of 126 to 144 inches. These luxurious tourers with speeds of around 80 mph were designated DO,

326

Jules Goux, victor in many races, on one of the long 192-mm. stroke, 2-cylinder, 3-litre Peugeot racers in 1908. Note chain drive and brief mud-guards. Maximum speed about 90 mph. (S.A. *des Automobiles Peugeot*)

GS and CO types. During the mid-'20s, Delage achieved racing fame with 2-litre V-12 and 1.5-litre 6-cylinder cars. The most elegant of all were the D8 types, expensive large cars fitted with fine coachwork and powered by superb 4,744 cc., straight-8 engines developing about 140 BHP. Though weighing upward of 4,000 pounds, the D8 had a sporting performance of nearly 100 mph and handled excellently with light, fast steering of 2½ turns lock-to-lock. Under Delahaye management, new independent front suspensions with transverse leaf springs plus Cotal electric gearboxes were introduced in 1936 on the 100 BHP 3-litre, 6-cylinder D6 which was marketed alongside the D8. Both models continued until Hitler's invasion and were marketed again briefly after the war.

Delahaye blossomed as a genuine sports car in 1936 with a tough 3.5-litre engine in the new Model 135. With pushrod-operated overhead valves and 7.0 to 1 compression ratio, this engine's six 84 x 107 mm.

cylinders were fueled by three carburetors and developed 130 BHP at about 3,800 rpm. A similar 3.2-litre engine was used in a series of fast open and closed two-seaters that won the Monte Carlo Rally twice and a coveted Coupés des Alpes. The competition model 135-M used a tuned version of the 3.5-litre engine with 8.3 to 1 compression ratio. With more than 150 BHP on tap and lightweight, cycle-fendered coachwork, the 135-M placed first at Le Mans in 1938. Handling was superb with transversely sprung, independent front-suspension and quick 1¾ turns lock-to-lock steering. The most popular model marketed during 1938–39 was the splendid D8-120 with Van den Plas or Chapron coachwork on 115-inch-wheelbase chassis with the 3.5-litre engine and either a Cotal electrically operated gearbox or a manual 4-speed unit. After the war, this model was continued as the Type 175 with few changes.

Most powerful Delahayes of all were the limited production 4.5-litre, V-12 racers with

327

Riding mechanic leans into curve as Giuppone corners his Lion-Peugeot in a voiturette race on the Turin circuit in 1908. Poor traffic control— note boy on motorbike in rear. (S.A. *des Automobiles Peugeot*)

overhead-camshafts and 200 brake horsepower. One of these, driven by René Dreyfus, triumphed over a 4.5-litre Bugatti to win one million francs in a 200-kilometre event on the Montlhery circuit in 1937. A very limited series of the V-12s was built with elegant coachwork by Figoni & Felaschi. Niceties included unique retractable windshields on open models. One of these, originally owned by ex-King Michael of Roumania, is said to be somewhere in the Soviet Union.

Another distinguished pioneer French marque was the de Dietrich made by a large steel firm of Lunéville in Lorraine. For obvious reasons, the car's name was changed to Lorraine-Dietrich just before the First World War and the famous Cross of Lorraine was incorporated into the emblem. Amédée Bollée designed the first model which appeared late in 1896, that magic year for French cars. Early emphasis was on racing although high-quality touring cars, noted for smooth operation, were marketed about 1900. Several de Dietrichs were entered in the terrible Paris-Madrid race of

1903. The intrepid Madame du Gast represented the fair sex in a 30-HP, 4-cylinder racer while the English pioneer driver, Charles Jarrott, manhandled a 45-HP example into third place before the toll of livestock, donkey carts, unruly spectators and drivers caused French officials to call off the race.

One would have expected steel manufacturers to specify all-steel frames for their cars. Curiously, however, de Dietrich frames were the customary hardwood sheathed with steel until 1905 when all-steel frames were standardized. That year, incidentally, saw the last running of the classic James Gordon Bennett Trophy races and de Dietrich's most ambitious racing attempt was of no avail. The race, held in the Auvergne area near where Michelin tires originated, was an uncontrolled shambles right from the drop of the starting flag because light-fingered representatives of the traditionally unruly natives are said to have appropriated most of the pre-arranged telephone lines for their own purpose.

In 1909, de Dietrich lost a designer and

Through a village street, in the grand old way, Boillot slams his Lion-Peugeot sans mudguards in the 1910 circuit of Boulogne race. Boillot won, followed by Giuppone and Goux on other Peugeots for a clean sweep. (S.A. *des Automobiles Peugeot*)

the automotive world gained an independent genius when Ettore Bugatti, after four years in the firm's engineering offices, struck out on his own. Bugatti, of whom more later, was partially responsible for the varied line of 2, 4 and 6-cylinder passenger cars which sustained the marque until well into 1914. These developed from 10 to 70 HP and cost the equivalent of $900 to around $4,500 in chassis form. At about this time, the works entered a big 12-litre racer with four 146 x 180 mm. cylinders in the tremendously rugged St. Petersburg to Moscow race and won on the home ground of the Russo-Baltique which was subsidized by the Tsar. With this 70-mph racer, de Dietrich pioneered the switch to L-head (or side-valve) engines at a time when valves on opposite sides of each cylinder (T-head) were believed most efficient. High scores in the Targa Florio and elsewhere next convinced the works that a displacement boost to 15 litres would be even better, but Peugeot proved otherwise in 1912 as we shall see.

From 1920 until the mid-'30s, the Lorraine-Dietrich was a luxury car costing $4,000 and more in the worthier currency of the time. All of the engines were oversquare, had six cylinders with overhead valves operated by pushrods, most of them 3.5 litres in displacement. Wheelbases ranged from 114 inches on fairly sporting open models to 132 inches for limousines and town cars. The marque returned to competition in 1924 with a team in the Le Mans 24-hour race. After a hot battle with a Bentley, the pair of Lorraine-Dietrichs took second and third places. In 1925, Lorraine, as the marque was known popularly, returned and captured first place, lost second to a Sunbeam but held third place against an Italian car. The Lorraines had their finest hour in 1926 when they swept Le Mans by capturing the top three places against a determined team of Bentleys.

The giant-killing competition Lorraines were powered by 6-cylinder (75 x 30 mm.), 3.5-litre engines. The blocks had wet cylinder liners, heads were fixed, and the overhead valves were operated by exposed pushrods. Dual carburetors, external oil coolers

329

Jules Goux and his Peugeots were a familiar sight on the Indianapolis Speedway. A pit scene in 1914. (*S.A. des Automobiles Peugeot*)

The smoky start of the Indy 500-mile race in either 1913 or '14. Note pits in foreground, racks of spare tires, and the official pagoda, right background. (*S.A. des Automobiles Peugeot*)

Dario Resta drove this Peugeot to victory in the 1916 Indianapolis Memorial Day Race. Note massive, finned, four-wheel brakes. Still fit, historic blue car is owned by Lindley Bothwell. Same car and driver won the 1916 Vanderbilt Cup Race at Santa Monica. (*Joseph H. Wherry*)

and cantilever rear springs were other features of the cars. Oddly, the gearboxes had only three speeds but the long stroke provided high torque as well as good low speed characteristics while reliability and maximum speed, at full tap, was right on 100 mph. Coupled with high quality and silence, when fitted with touring exhaust systems, Lorraine-Dietrich chassis were popular with coachbuilders. Dignified and reserved, the marque substituted craftsmanship and refinement for technical innovations during the 'thirties. Cars were discontinued just before the war but the firm is still active in heavy industry.

Even before the boom of 1896, French cars possessed a mystique. Second in early importance after Panhard & Levassor, was Peugeot. A large producer and a lively contender in the world marketplace today, Peugeot is still a ruggedly independent, family-owned enterprise which began about 1790 when an iron works was founded. Automotive activities began in 1889 as discussed in Part II. By 1900 Armand Peugeot had adopted tubular water cooling and battery ignition and was making his own 2-cylinder engines in 4, 10 and 30-HP versions, the latter having a bore and stroke of 140 x 190 mm. respectively. Magneto ignition was introduced in 1902 on two 4-cylinder, over-square engines: a 120 x 94 mm., 16-HP model and a 50-HP unit measuring 155 x 150 mm. Honeycomb radiator cores were adopted at the same time.

Emphasis was on racing and the long-stroke, high-torque Lion-Peugeot cars gave good accounts of themselves. Strokes as long

331

Open pushrods and well arranged power department of Ernest Hemery's double-valve, dual-over- head-camshaft engine in the 1916 Indianapolis winner. (*Joseph H. Wherry*)

as 300 mm. made some engine bonnets incredibly high from around 1906 on. Passenger cars like the type 81-B family cars with their 80 x 110 mm. engines, 4-speed gearboxes and chain drives paid the racing bills. Even more popular was the "Bebe" two-seater which started life about 1902 as a shaft-driven open model. In 1911 the legendary Ettore Bugatti was hired to redesign the "Bebe" and in 1912 it reappeared in open and closed versions powered by a long-stroke 4-cylinder (55 x 90 mm.) engine rated at 6 HP for taxing. A mere 103 inches long overall, the diminutive "Bebe" had a radiator shell not unlike the inverted horse-shoe design which became the hallmark of Bugatti's own marque. The "Bebe" was popular all over Europe and many still re-main in collectors' hands like the one in the Soviet rally in 1966 (see Russia).

Soon after Ernest Henry, a talented Swiss engineer, joined Peugeot, the marque soared to fame. Quickly a sensational range of dual-overhead-camshaft, 4-cylinder engines—the first of their kind—with four valves per cylinder was introduced with the valves inclined on opposite sides of the cylinder. The hemispherical combustion chamber was born. Today, nearly 60 years later, this type of combustion chamber is promoted as the "Hemi." Henry was also responsible for dry sump lubrication—oil was contained in a tank on the firewall and pumped to and from the crankcase—in 1913. The same year the works sent a 4-cylinder (110 x 200 mm.), 7.6-litre, dual-overhead-camshaft

The diminutive 1921–23 Peugeot "Quadrilette" Type 161 had 91-inch wheelbase. Driver and passenger sat in tandem. L-head, four 50 x 85-mm. cylinders cast en-bloc, 8 CV, electric lamps. Little car was a frequent racer in voiturette events. (S.A. *des Automobiles Peugeot*)

The 5 CV Peugeot cabriolet coupé of 1924 with 4-cylinder, 50 x 85-mm. engine, Type 172 BC. (S.A. *des Automobiles Peugeot*)

The 1929 Peugeot 201 "Coupé d'affaire" had a long stroke, 63 x 90-mm., 1,122 cc. engine. Knight-type double sleeve-valves gave the four cylinders a silent smoothness. Tax rating was 6 CV. (S.A. *des Automobiles Peugeot*)

In 1932 this 4-cylinder, 1.5-litre Peugeot 301-C set a Class F international record for 24 hours by covering 1,646.46 miles at an average of 68.8 mph. (S.A. *des Automobiles Peugeot*)

Grand Prix type racer to Indianapolis. Developing around 160 BHP at 2,250 rpm, this machine startled the natives by winning the Memorial Day classic with Jules Goux at the wheel, the first foreign car to do so. The next year, 1914, saw a pair of Peugeots driven by Duret and Goux place second and fourth respectively. In 1915, the Peugeot team placed again by capturing second and seventh places. Peugeot had already raced in Europe with four-wheel brakes and in 1916 the team tried the system at Indianapolis where Dario Resta piloted his blue car to first place with an average, for the 500 miles, of 84.05 mph while another Peugeot placed third. America's entry into the war prevented another Indy 500 until 1919 when Howdy Wilcox drove a new formula 4.5-litre Peugeot to first place while Goux placed third on another. Similar Peugeots had campaigned the European circuits during 1912–14 and one, a 5.6-litre

version, helped Georges Boillot become a national hero in 1913 when he won the Grand Prix of France. Boillot went on to set a 17-minute, 38-second mark on the chassis-busting 13.4-mile Mont Ventoux hill climb; this latter record stood intact until 1925.

Peugeot's emphasis, after 1918, was on passenger cars although light sporting coachwork often permitted competition by owners. Adoption just before the 1914–18 war of the then popular double-sleeve valve engines, patterned on the Knight designs, brought silky silence to large 4 and 6-cylinder cars with only slight performance penalties. In 1926, a 4-litre sleeve-valve Peugeot was running second to a Bentley in the Le Mans 24-hour race when it was ruled off the course due to a broken windshield caused by a pebble. Another 4-litre Peugeot also dropped out for minor mechanical reasons. Just about every wallet was catered to by

The 1934–36 Peugeot 301-D limousine was a development of the 1932 record car. The 8 CV, 4-cylinder engine displaced 1,465 cc. Dignified styling contrasted with the times. (S.A. *des Automobiles Peugeot*)

The Peugeot 401 cabriolet of 1934–35. (S.A. *des Automobiles Peugeot*)

In 1936, Peugeot introduced a revolutionary all-steel convertible on the Type 601 chassis. The "Eclipse" was 20 years ahead of its time. (S.A. *des Automobiles Peugeot*)

Open six-passenger coachwork on the 1938 Peugeot 402 with 4-cylinder, 2,142-cc. engine. (*S.A. des Automobiles Peugeot*)

The open 5-seater Peugeot 402 became an all-steel closed car when the electrically-actuated steel top was raised. (*S.A. des Automobiles Peugeot*)

The 1938 Peugeot 402-B was a five-passenger cloth top drophead. (*S.A. des Automobiles Peugeot*)

Concealed headlights, streamlining, and modern styling on the forward looking Peugeot 202N-2 four-passenger sedan. Introduced in 1938, the 1.1- litre, 4-cylinder car resumed production after the war until 1949. (*S.A. des Automobiles Peugeot*)

Peugeot during the vintage years. To bolster sagging sales in 1932, the works ran a special stripped version of their popular type 301, a 1.5-litre model, at Montlhery. Shown here, the 301-C racer set a new Class F international record for 24 hours by covering 1,646.46 miles at an average of 68.6 mph. The type 301-D sedan and open sports cars, some with stylish cycle fenders, were developments of the record car.

In 1936, Peugeot scored another first when the world's first all-steel folding convertible top (or hood) was developed. Preceding the 1957 Ford steel drop-head by twenty-one years, Peugeot's types 402 and 601 all-steel convertibles were produced alongside conventional fabric cabriolets and closed sedans. Just prior to W.W. II, Cotal electrically actuated gearboxes were fitted optionally to some Peugeots. In 1938, a Cotal-equipped sports model participated in the Le Mans race. Quality and conservative design dominated the Peugeot philosophy as war approached. The venerable French firm has consistently retained worm drive rear axles of their own design and has produced unusually fine, moderately priced passenger cars which are recognized by the knowledgeable as among the world's best built without regard to cost.

A late start in comparison with several other French pioneers, as observed in Part II, did not prevent the Renault from becoming a major marque by 1900. Along with the income from a vast range of small closed and open cars, the royalties from Louis's patented propeller shaft and other inventions such as a military searchlight enabled the brothers to indulge in racing. Use of 2-cylinder De Dion engines was supplemented by 4-cylinder engines designed by Monsieur Viet, who was a brother-in-law of Georges Bouton, the Comte De Dion's

partner. One such 30-HP engine in Renault's first all-out racer, driven by Marcel and illustrated here, won the tough Paris-to-Vienna race in 1902 by arriving at the finish line (two hours ahead of the officials) against a formidable field of Panhards, Mors, Mercedes and Napiers. Next, Renault entered the 1903 Paris-to-Madrid race where Marcel lost his life in one of the many accidents. Soon, they were building their own engines and in 1904 a monstrous 60-HP racer with four oversquare 160 x 150 mm. cylinders was ordered by Gould Brokaw, an American, who entered the 1904 Vanderbilt Cup Race. Probably the only shaft-driven racer in this event, the raucous machine left the race with mechanical trouble in the second lap. The next year, a similar racer with four 166 x 160 mm. cylinders developing 90 HP driven by the Hungarian, Szisz, won the first genuine Grand Prix race. Sponsored by the Automobile Club of France, the event was run near Le Mans; this was probably the first race to see extensive use of mudguards, or fenders, as well as the demountable rim wheels developed by the Michelin tire firm. Stubbornly Renault clung to the unusual behind-the-engine radiator location.

Kings and presidents used the 20, 30 and 45-HP, 4-cylinder limousines and landaulets on wheelbases up to 132 inches while more modest people bought the smaller 8, 10 and 14-HP models with 2 cylinders as fast as the expanding works could produce them for the home and world markets. Fernand Renault died in 1909 about the time that Louis developed the large 120 x 140 mm. 35-HP luxury type AR on a 145-inch-wheelbase chassis. Now responsible for the firm's destiny, Louis withdrew from all racing—a fascinating career told elsewhere in detail.

Most famous of the early Renaults were

the types AG, sturdy 2-cylinder, 80 x 120 mm., 8-HP vehicles on 100-inch wheelbases. Popular all over the world in various body styles, the AG "Taxi de la Marne" achieved immortality when hundreds of them were organized to shuttle an infantry division to the front late in 1914 when Paris was threatened by le Boche. This was history's first motorized division. Even this Renault achievement, plus developing the first successful light army tank, could not save Louis from eventual disgrace when he was accused of collaboration and imprisoned years later after another world war, nor his industrial empire from nationalization by a resurgent France.

After the First World War, the famous models 40 and 45 were developed from the big pre-war six. On wheelbases as long as 158 inches, the 110 x 160 mm. long-stroke engines displaced over 9 litres. Brake horsepower was about 140 at 2,750 rpm and despite all up weights of around 5,000 pounds, some versions did 90 mph. The wide radiators were still placed behind the engines against the fire wall and used thermo-syphon cooling—no water pump as had become common—and the shovel-shaped bonnet noses sloped down to meet frames that were among the industry's heaviest and strongest. Mechanical brakes on all four wheels were about the only modern touch. Finally in 1929, the radiator was moved to the conventional front location permitting the styling to be brought up to date. As smaller, more efficient engines became popular throughout Europe, the Renault production of 4-cylinder models increased with a successful range of 1.5-litre smaller family cars, while to recoup the performance reputation, a range of 7.1-litre straight eights was introduced in 1928. Called the "Reinastella," this type had the

first downdraft carburetors. In 1930, a new 4.2-litre eight, the "Nervastella," set a record of 101.98 mph average for 48 hours, and in 1935 an ultra-modern streamlined, single-seater "Nerva" won the Liége-Rome-Liége Rally. Renault entered another Nervastella 8 in the 1935 Monte Carlo Rally and won.

In the same year, the 4-cylinder, 1.5-litre "Celtaquatre" small sedans were introduced. Smaller cars for the middle classes now led in production at Billancourt. The excellent 11CV "Primaquatre" was developed from the 4-cylinder "Vivaquatre" taxicabs of 1933.

Very well known up until about 1914 was the Unic, manufactured in Suresnes from 1904 by Georges Richard who first built the Belgian Vivinus under license and who intended to produce a single model for all markets. Until the 1929 recession swamped the enterprise, 2 and 4-cylinder Unics of conventional design and high quality did gain limited popularity. Within a few years, Unic chassis, mostly on 126-inch wheelbases, were carrying various kinds of bodies from coachbuilders. In the Scandinavian nations and British Isles they were popular as taxicabs and, with more ornate coachwork, as illustrated, among the gentry. After 1919, a few 2-cylinder economy cars were built alongside fairly advanced 2-litre fours; the latter, at around $2,000 in chassis form, were hardly for the masses. Early in his career, Richard collaborated with Henri Brasier in building racing cars which won the 1904 and 1905 James Gordon Bennett races. After 1905, the Richard-Brasier cars were medium-large 4-cylinder machines, generally of 4 litres capacity; like the Unic, this marque also faded away with the economic slump in 1929.

Of the nearly seven hundred separate makes of French cars, surviving records of

In 1902, Marcel Renault won the 800-mile Paris-Vienna race. In 1965, two Frenchmen ran the route with the same Renault racer. (*Regie Renault*)

Elegant brougham coachwork on a 136-inch-wheelbase, 1907 Renault chassis. Note typical radiator behind the 4-cylinder 80 x 120-mm., 35/45 CV engine. (*Thompson Products Auto Museum*)

the majority are so sketchy that the automotive historian is often frustrated. Even official agencies in France are coy and plead their archives contain no photos. Many of these marques were, of course, obscure anyway.

One of the most interesting of the obscure marques was the Gobron-Brillié, made in

Levallois-Perret from 1898 to about 1930 by Gustave Gobron and Eugène Brillié. From the first surrey-topped tourers, this car employed a unique engine with two pistons in each cylinder. The pistons reciprocated in opposite directions with the crankshaft being actuated, directly, by the bottom pistons while the upper pistons acted upon the crankshaft through a complicated maze of cross-shafts and extremely long connecting rods. Initially this remarkable powerplant was mounted transversely in the chassis; later it was repositioned longitudinally. Despite its mechanical complexity, a 110-horsepower Gobron-Brillié held the world speed record on four occasions: twice in 1903 with 83.5 and 84.7 mph with Duray at the wheel and twice again in 1904 with 94.8 and 103.5 mph with Rigolly driving. A 6-cylinder 90-HP sports tourer was built in 1908–11 after which a 50-HP, 4-cylinder version enjoyed some popularity despite a very high chassis price of over $3,000. After 1919, some models with conventional engines were built but the marque gradually lost its glamour and fame and disappeared in the Depression.

Interesting eccentrics like the Crouan of 1901–04 powered by a 6-HP compressed air engine driving through a 5-speed gearbox, and the Louet of 1903–08 are even less remembered. The latter was one of a scant handful of marques with a 6-cylinder engine in 1903. On the other hand, the beautifully named Delaunay-Belleville, built from about 1902 at St. Denis, was a favorite among the wealthy and was prominently displayed by the nobility of Russia. Adorned with expensive coachwork on up to 146-inch-wheelbase chassis and powered with handmade 4 and 6-cylinder engines displacing upwards of 5 litres, this on-order-only marque was a mere memory by 1930. The

works revived itself by returning to the manufacture of industrial steam boilers but the manufacture of cars, although attempted, was never resumed.

The Hotchkiss, also made in Levallois-Perret from 1903 to its demise in 1956, deserves a book of its own. An American, Benjamin B. Hotchkiss went to France and organized the famous armaments works at the start of the Franco-Prussian War in 1870. Hotchkiss rapid fire guns, made in the U.S.A. under license, helped to win the West in many a battle against poorly armed Indians. After a 4-cylinder, 18-HP passenger series, a big 100-HP racer was built about 1905 but victories in racing eluded the marque. An innovation was the enclosed propeller shaft drive—the torque tube—which is used throughout the world today. The firm specialized in arms, and cars were actually a sideline. In 1908, a magnificent 9.5-litre, 6-cylinder model featured dual camshafts in the block; the valves, on opposite sides of the combustion chambers in T-head locations, were actuated by pushrods. Excellent engines, Hotchkiss units often employed ball bearings rather than the common (and cheaper) plain bearings. Though very rare, the most famous vintage Hotchkiss was the magnificent type AR of 1922, a sporting tourer with a 6-cylinder, single-overhead-camshaft engine of 6.6 litres and rated at 130 BHP at 3,000 rpm. If the marque failed in races, it succeeded marvelously in tortuous competitions like the Monte Carlo Rally which it won several times between the two big wars. The Hotchkiss shared honors with the superb Bugatti for doggedly retaining beam type front axles. Hydraulic brakes were finally adopted in 1936. It is worth noting that a branch factory was established in England early in this century and that the firm's 4-

1911 Renault 8 CV, 2-cylinder cabriolet. Note the wicker coachwork. (*Regie Renault*)

cylinder engines powered the first Morris cars (see England).

Though out of the picture since the early thirties, the Sizaire-Naudin—born in 1905 near Paris—deserves brief mention. Initially a lightweight single-cylinder car, this marque was the ingenious product of two brothers and M. Naudin. First to introduce a practical independent front suspension system utilizing sliding pillars in 1907 and upper and lower transverse leaf springs, the marque was a diligent competitor in voitu-rette races in the early years. Sizaire-Naudin engines used a long stroke and the engine hood was generally characterized by an unusual contour. After 1919, there was a range of dignified 4 and 6-cylinder passenger cars on wheelbases of 112 to 144 inches. Unfortunately, the early innovative urge had no effect on these vehicles which had reverted to conventional, rigid, beam-type front axles, and conformed in other technical areas. In England, the marque, assembled by F. W. Berwick, a noted coach-

A treasured survivor of the 8 CV, 2-cylinder Renault taxis, 700 of which were mobilized by General Gallieni to rush troops to the Marne front in September, 1914, when Paris was threatened. (*French Embassy Press & Information Division*)

A 1921 Renault formal landaulet on a 147.4-inch wheelbase. The 6-cylinder, 110 x 160-mm., 9-litre 45 CV engine was still forward of the radiator although the cowl was smooth; an air intake was on the sloped nose. (*Regie Renault*)

The big 7-litre, straight-8 Renault limousine of 1933. (*Regie Renault*)

builder, was registered as the Sizaire-Berwick.

During the 1914–18 war, most competent automotive engineers and manufacturers found outlets for their talents in the booming aviation industry. One such was Ernest Ballot who had manufactured thousands of automobile engines for car builders as widely separated as Argentina's pioneering Annasagasti and Europe's Delage and others. When Ballot decided to enter a car in the 1919 Indianapolis race, Ernest Henry was retained to design the machine and the marque Ballot was born. Henry forthwith—because time was short—adopted his revolutionary pre-war Peugeot designs incorporating dual-overhead-camshafts actuating four inclined overhead valves per cylinder in hemispherical combustion chambers. However, Henry made a change which influenced Grand Prix engines for the next two decades: the new Ballots had straight 8-cylinder (74 x 140 mm.) engines. Displacement was just under 5 litres; the camshafts were gear-driven;

roller bearings were used on the mains; dry sump lubrication was used; and there were two big carburetors. Despite impressive power and high performance, the cars were geared too high and had only two-wheel brakes. The effort at Indianapolis came to nothing.

The Ballots were reworked by decreasing bore and stroke to 65 x 112 mm. to conform to the 3-litre maximum for the 1920 Indy race; and a new four-wheel brake system was installed. These new engines developed 107 BHP at 3,800 rpm for brief bursts but this speed could not be maintained due to the small bronze connecting rod journals; thus the effective output was about 80 BHP at 2,500 rpm. To make matters worse, the gear ratios in the 4-speed box were poorly chosen and, this in conjunction with the outmoded leather cone clutch, caused low speed torque to be inadequate. With acceleration thus limited, the Ballots made a bad showing despite excellent flat out speeds. The latter characteristic was of no help at

346

Unic cars were popular in Norway where the 4- and 6-cylinder chassis were fitted with Norwegian coachwork. This 1914 town car and limousine was built by Karrosseri Carl Heffermehl in Oslo. (*Kongelig Norsk Automobilklub*)

The 1939 Hotchkiss 17 CV "Cabourg" saloon, a high-quality, 6-cylinder luxury car. (*French Embassy Press & Information Division*)

Indianapolis but the marque later came through in 1921 by winning the Grand Prix of Brescia in Italy.

Despite the Brescia victory, Ernest Ballot gave up racing and produced touring sports cars with 2-litre, 4-cylinder (70 x 130 mm.) dual-overhead-camshaft engines which developed 75 BHP at 4,000 rpm; the official French tax rating was 12 HP. On excellent 110-inch-wheelbase chassis with nice

The 1922 Amilcar had longitudinal cantilever springs, a 7.5 CV 4-cylinder engine and light-weight body. Wheelbase was 92 inches. (*Henry Ford Museum*)

The 1934 Avions-Voisin 3.8-litre "Aero Sport," an 85-brake-horsepower, fast tourer by Gabriel Voisin. Where fenders are wings, it is fitting that they should be graced with struts on a car built by the pioneer aircraft manufacturer. (*Joseph H. Wherry*)

coachwork, and with a top of 90 mph, this was a rare model, only 50 of which were made. It led to the exquisite 2LT powered with the same basic engine but with side valves which reduced speed to no more than 65 mph. Very sporting in handling, the 2LT

Finned cylinder head cover and exhaust manifold, and chain-driven fan and "dynastarter" were typical Voisin touches. The 1934 sleeve-valve, 3.8-litre "Aero Sport." (*Joseph H. Wherry*)

Roof slid back on rails along edges; doors were hung on piano hinges. The 1934 Voisin "Aero Sport." (*Joseph H. Wherry*)

The first Citroën, the 1919 Type A 10 CV torpedo with a 4-cylinder, 65 x 100-mm. engine and wheelbase of 113 inches. (*Société Citroën*)

The 1922 boat-tailed 10 CV, 1.5-litre Citroën "Caddy" type B2 was popular in trials and rallies. Top speed was 56 mph. (*Société Citroën*)

The 1924 Citroën 10 CV six-window B2 sedan introduced crowned fenders. (*Société Citroën*)

A stylish lady of 1925 enters her new Citroën coupe. Note the adjustable windshield, the round side windows, the rakish mudguards, the pointed nose. The 4-cylinder, 1,452 cc. engine had a two-bearing crankshaft; wheelbase 92.5 inches. (*Société Citroën*)

models sat on 110, 122 and 127-inch wheelbases depending upon the body style and cost up to $7,000 in 1923. Production eventually decreased the price by about two-thirds for open models when the 2LT was dropped in 1928. The final 2-litre fours of 1927–28 had overhead-camshafts but recession was in the wind and even the few magnificent 8-cylinder, 2.6-litre and the 80-mph, 2.9-litre models of 1928–31 could not stimulate sales enough to prevent absorption by the French branch of Hispano-Suiza.

The limited production Bignan was manufactured in a Paris suburb from 1920 to 1929 by a concern that made engines prior to the war. All of Jacques Bignan's creations had four cylinders, rugged 120-inch-wheelbase frames with semi-elliptical springs on all corners, and were unique in having the two-wheel mechanical brakes in front. Ahead of their time, the brake drums were deeply finned to facilitate heat dissipation. Most of the 3-litre engines had single overhead-camshafts and four valves in each 85 x 130 mm. cylinder, were rated at 17 HP (taxable) and powered rather clean-lined sports cars, some with boat-tailed bodies. Running in the first Le Mans 24-hour race in 1923, the Bignan's speed gained a fourth place tie with a 3-litre Bentley. Class wins in the 1924 Grand Prix of Belgium at Spa and a 24-hour endurance run at 74 mph average on the Montlhery circuit brought more prestige to this car which offered two and four-seater sports versions, fit for road or track, at less than $3,000. Throughout most of its short life there were also 2-litre (75 x 112 mm.) versions rated at 13 HP and

Citroën's popular 5 CV two-seater of 1922 was affectionately called "the little lemon" because of the standard color. (*Société Citroën*)

1.6-litre (70 x 104 mm.), 10 HP models for the economy minded.

Of the legions of lesser French makes, the Amilcar of 1921–39 was the best known in America. Two industrialists named Akar and Lamy bankrolled Amilcar and the principal designer during the twenties was M. Morel. The first model, as illustrated, had a 55 x 95 mm. long-stroke, L-head, 1-litre, 4-cylinder engine in unit with a 3-speed gearbox on a very light 92-inch-wheelbase chassis with tiny rear wheel brakes and quarter elliptic springs mounted in the cantilever position. Cornering was fierce—there was no differential. The flywheel, more like a waterwheel, had cups which lifted the oil to lubricate the bearings. Despite apparent fragility, the little car quickly made a name by winning light car—voiturette—races. In 1923, engine capacity was increased to 1,078 cc., and a 6-cylinder 1,093 cc. engine with dual overhead-camshafts was produced later with an optional supercharger giving 83 BHP at 6,000 rpm. A tough 1,580 cc. four was also offered as was an 8-cylinder (63 x 80 mm.) engine. The latter powered a series of closed cars on 96-inch wheelbases with 4-wheel brakes, a proper differential, and semi-elliptical springs while the 1.6-litre four powered 117-inch-wheelbase open sports tourers with 4-speed gearboxes and stylish coachwork.

Known as the G-6, the little 1.1-litre six weighed less than 1,500 pounds in road trim on a brief 74-inch wheelbase and was good for nearly 100 mph unblown and 120–125 mph with the supercharger operating. Racing in their classes during the vintage years,

353

The Citroën 5 CV "Cloverleaf" of 1923 got its name from the seating arrangements. Wheelbase, a tidy 88.5 inches. (*Société Citroën*)

Amilcars won many races—first and second in the Italian Grand Prix, the top three places in the Brooklands 200-mile race, established a class record for 24 hours at approximately 85 mph, and the like. In the thirties, a range of 2.5-litre fours was produced, but the depression caught this popular marque and Hotchkiss absorbed it. The last Amilcar was designed by J. A. Gregoire, a brilliant designer and an exponent of front-wheel drive; this "Compound" model had FWD and a lightweight alloy frame. Sad to say, few Compounds were built before the Second World War which finished this high performance small car.

From the sublime to the ridiculous is seldom more than a half-step. The Leyat, built in Meursault during 1922–24, was ridiculous with its aircraft propeller driven by a di-

minutive 3-cylinder, 10 HP engine, and its fate was predictable. At its top of 70 mph, the shrouded propeller did not inspire confidence. Intriguing as air drive was between the wars, it never succeeded despite the claims made for it in several countries including our own. More practical were several remarkable marques produced by three major aircraft manufacturers who understood the proper place for airscrews.

Most talented, and eccentric, of the aircraft designers, when it came to cars, was Gabriel Voisin whose single and multi-engine aircraft had been the backbone of the bombardment squadrons of the French Air Force. Early fame attached to this pioneer aircraft designer-builder: the first German airplane shot out of the skies fell to the nose gunner of a Voisin near Verdun, and

Paris traffic in front of the Grand Palais in 1923 reveals the popularity of the Citroën within three years of introduction. (*Société Citroën*)

Citroën built formal and commercial vehicles on the 1.5-litre type B14 chassis in 1926. This is the classic Parisian taxi with wicker paneling. (*Société Citroën*)

by 1919 when the first Avion-Voisin car went on sale, Gabriel's reputation as a self-assured artist-engineer was on a par with that of Bugatti. From his first to last car, Voisin was wedded to the silky quietness of C. Y. Knight's double-sleeve-valve engines. Voisin, though head of his large factory in Issy-les-Moulineaux, in fact as well as name, did most of the design work on his first car, a 136-inch-wheelbase sedan with disc wheels, servo-assisted mechanical brakes front and rear, a single plate clutch with a 4-speed gearbox driven by a long stroke (95 x 140 mm.), 4-litre, 4-cylinder engine. A finned aluminum cover over the peculiar cylinder heads, a combined generator and starting motor—a "dynastarter"—and full pressure lubrication for the five main bearings were Voisin features. No other car maker obtained the refinement with sleeve-valve engines as did Voisin. This 18 HP (taxable) model was supplemented by a 2-litre, 60 x

110 mm. model on 112-inch-wheelbase chassis which featured a single aluminum casting housing the crankcase, clutch and a 3-speed gearbox. It was designated the C4. In their initial contest, a team of C4s took the top three places in the 1922 Grand Prix for Touring Cars.

Beautifully built, luxuriously appointed, sometimes a bit bizarre in appearance, almost always with the heavy chassis frame in unit with hardwood-framed, aluminum-sheathed bodies designed by Voisin himself, this marque was a favorite with individualists.

Through the thirties, a wide range of 4, 6 and straight 8-cylinder Voisins appeared. In the upper price bracket, all were as picturesque as the 1934 "Aero Sport" saloon illustrated. This model, restyled, was the leader of the line until 1939. Engines of up to 6 litres and wheelbases as long as 141 inches carried all manner of coachwork.

Citroën's first 6-cylinder car was the 2.5-litre C6 introduced in 1928. (*Société Citroën*)

Struggling through a pass in the Himalaya Mountains, one of the Citroën "Kégnesse" halftracks of the Syria-to-Peking expedition of 1931–32. (*Société Citroën*)

By 1932, the "double chevron" had become famous as Citroën's emblem. The "Rosalie" 6-cylinder, 15 CV sedan. (*Société Citroën*)

Voisin even built several experimental 7.2-litre, V-12 models in the twenties, but a series of straight 12-cylinder cars in the early thirties was the strangest of all: a pair of 3-litre 6-cylinder blocks bolted end to end over a common crankcase intruded into the front compartment. The precedent for this monster was a famous early Lanchester (see England). At 4,000 rpm, no less than 180 BHP was generated and the top speed was right on 125 mph.

During its heyday, Voisin held scores of records. On one occasion, in 1927, a big

Voisin shattered the 24-hour record of the Renault 45 by doing the same stint at Montlhery but at 115 mph. At various times Voisin offered Cotal electric gearboxes, six speeds by means of 3-speed gearboxes torque-tubed to 2-speed rear axles, magnesium alloy pistons, and he even experimented with hydraulic brakes actuated by lines protectively enclosed inside hollow axles. An exponent of safety, in a carefree era, he claimed his cars could be depended upon to negotiate any surface offering traction providing the driver had the capability to handle his machinery properly. After the war, Gabriel Voisin helped to get the reborn Spanish auto industry on its feet by designing the little Autonacional "Biscuter," the sort of straightforward economy car so urgently needed in Spain.

Two other pioneer aircraft manufacturers of World War One fame, both situated in Billancourt on the Seine, entered the automotive free-for-all when conditions settled down after the war. The first, the pioneer flying Farman brothers, Henry and Maurice, had come over from England and established themselves in France during the century's first decade. In 1920, the first Farman car appeared, an impressive, expensively luxurious machine of conventional format on a 141-inch wheelbase, the type AG. A single overhead-camshaft distinguished the 6,597 cc., 6-cylinder (100 x 140 mm.) engine which had a fixed cylinder head. The taxable rating was 40 CV, and the engine drove through a 4-speed transmission with constant-mesh third and fourth. In the same price league as the Renault 40/45, the Hispano-Suiza and Rolls-Royce, Farmans were fitted by the finer coachworks like Kellner of Paris with socially acceptable bodies ranging from cabriolets to the most formal town and brougham types.

In 1927, the type NF appeared with stroke increased to 150 mm. thus raising the volume to 7,069 cc., while the wheelbase expanded to a massive 145 inches. Patrician in every respect, silent and quietly chic, the Farman appealed to a select few who could afford a bare chassis price of $6,000 and more, plus coachwork. In 1933, the marque disappeared and the Farman works returned to the more lucrative production of bombing aircraft.

The Société des Moteurs Salmson had been the French agents, and assemblers, for the English marque, G. N. During the 1914–18 war, the firm boomed with the development of one of the world's first successful high powered radial aircraft engines— not a fussy rotary, be it noted, but a 250 horsepower air-cooled stationary engine. Wide acceptance by the Allied air services including our own, brought prosperity.

Such technical sophistication prompted a most unique first Salmson, the type E, of 1921. Two chassis lengths were catalogued, 98 and 107-inch wheelbases. There was no differential and the rear axle was slung beneath cantilever, quarter-elliptic springs; up front semi-elliptics were used. Steering was light and quick—just a shade over one turn lock-to-lock. A 3-speed gearbox, leather cone clutch and a 1,087 cc., 4-cylinder, 62 x 90 mm. engine rated at 10 HP (taxable) completed a specification devised for lightness and speed. What appeared to be a conventional L-head four with the normal two valves per cylinder was unique in having only four pushrods operating off the camshaft which was in the block; a special system of springs closed the valves. Initially the E-type Salmson's appearance was a bit reminiscent of the charming pre-war Hispano-Suiza Alfonso XIII sports car. By 1924, though, V-windscreens, crowned fenders, and less scanty roadster bodies were fitted. Driving the type E was often a hair-raising project. The lack of differential action caused cornering problems, and the two small brakes on the rear wheels operated in a most unorthodox manner: a foot pedal braked the right rear wheel, a hand lever the left. In addition, friction shock absorbers were fitted only to the rear axle. High power-to-weight ratio gave excellent acceleration, however, which more than compensated for a comparatively low top

359

speed, and the car was an immediate success in class racing.

In 1924, the Salmson type AL appeared on an improved though technically similar chassis with the same choice of wheelbases. Dual overhead-camshafts on the same 1.1-litre block increased the flat out top speed to 65–68 mph and Amilcar, this marque's chief rival, was hard put to match it in class and voiturette competitions. Adaptable to speed tuning, the AL's engine could be "hotted up" to the point where it could attain more than 100 mph for short bursts, the first 1.1-litre car to achieve this rate. In 1926, the bore was opened to 65 mm. thus increasing the displacement to 1,195 cc., a development eventually leading to a capability of a scorching 110–120 mph. By this date the longer wheelbase option had decreased to 103 inches. Small sedans were marketed from late 1928 on, some of them having the stylish Weyman-type fabric covered coachwork, powered by either the 1,195 cc. four or an optional 62 x 90 mm., 1,630 cc., 6-cylinder engine developed by adding another pair of cylinders to the 1.1-litre block. These saloons evolved into quite refined cars offering economy with speed, a normal differential and 4-speed gearboxes, but at a price above the small Citroëns and other mass-produced contemporaries. Sports models could also be bought with the six.

With the thirties came a mighty 2-litre, supercharged, straight 8-cylinder competition sports car capable of around 130 mph which won its class at Le Mans, Spa, on the Targa Florio circuit in Sicily, and other courses and etched the name of Salmson on the record books for all time. The marque struggled through the lean thirties, rose again briefly after 1945, then was taken over by Renault in 1955 only to disappear completely two years later.

With more inherited money and enthusiasm than practical common sense, the brothers Angelo and Paul Albert Bucciali tried all through the twenties, and until 1932, to launch a long, low, high-powered car that would have cost a king's ransom had it gone into production. Their only achievement was the attraction of large crowds in a succession of Paris Salon shows and the dissipation of a fortune although they must have delighted parts suppliers and employees.

Several intriguing features of the last show model merit brief mention. On an immensely long, underslung chassis, the 1932 model—rumored at the time to have been inoperable—displayed an aristocratic body hardly more than 4 feet high, and obviously inspired by the matchless Bugatti Royale. Half the length was engine bonnet. Underneath were a pair of 3.7-litre, American-made, straight-8, Continental engine blocks mounted, side by side, in a 30-degree Vee, on a single crankcase. This V-16 had two radiator cores, one per block, but just one grille. Front-wheel drive was employed as was all-around independent suspension. By far the most practical parts of the monster were the aluminum alloy wheels with integral cast-in brake drums, a feature no doubt also inspired by Ettore Bugatti whose stature as the master designer of the vintage period was in no danger from the Buccialis who had shown their final statement with their 1932 dream car.

We look now at André Citroën, the man who brought mass-produced cars within reach of the average family man in France. From the time he began manufacturing double helical gears in 1913, Citroën thought in terms of mass-production. Once the manager of the Mors works as previously observed, this engineer-industrialist did not

At speed on the Montlhery circuit in 1933 is "La Petit Rosalie," the Citroën 8 CV special. More than 199 records were shattered in this demonstration of stamina. (*Société Citroën*)

share the viewpoint of most car makers that automobiles were only for the financially comfortable. In fact, André Citroën has been compared with Henry Ford and the Englishman, William R. Morris.

Just seven months after World War One ended, the first Citroën was shown publicly, the 1919 Type A touring car with the popular, smooth-sided "torpedo" styling on a 113-inch wheelbase. The tread was 45 inches, and the 4-cylinder, 68 x 100 mm. bore and stroke engine developed 20 BHP at 2,100 rpm. The taxable horsepower was 10 and the car was called the 10CV. The crankshaft had but two bearings, a single plate clutch controlled a 3-speed gearbox and the cylinder head was removable. In spite of seeming frail, the little 1,452 cc. car proved exceptionally tough. Even the foot-operated propeller shaft braking—the hand brake controlled the drums on the rear wheels—was no more troublesome than the usual insufficient braking that other cars had. An immediate success, annual production exceeded 10,000 units by 1921 when the Type B2, a refined version, came out with enclosed bodies. Inverted quarter-elliptic springs were used in front and double quarter-elliptics at the rear, and were engineered to eliminate the need for shock absorbers. Variations quickly included the "Caddy Sport" with a third seat in the boat-

Citroën's famous "traction avant"—front-wheel-drive—cars were introduced in 1934. The "Light Eleven" model. (*Société Citroën*)

The "Fifteen-Six" of 1938 brought 6-cylinder performance to the world famous "Traction Avant" Citroëns. Maximum speed: 80 mph. Note vertical bonnet louvres and other detail differences from the "Eleven." (*Société Citroën*)

Pre-war Simca cars were license-built variants of Italian Fiats—here a Simca "Huit." (*French Embassy Press & Information Division*)

tail and a speed of 55–56 mph which owners found right for rallies and trials. Other variants of the B2 were the Coupé de Ville, a small town car of 1923, and four-door sedans and tourers.

Most famous early Citroën was the Type C3, popularly known as the 5CV due to the taxable horsepower, introduced in 1922 with a side valve, 55 x 90 mm., 856 cc. engine. Weighing just under 1,300 pounds, the C3 had semi-elliptic springs front and rear and a 92.5-inch wheelbase. Called "Little Lemon" because of the standard yellow enamel finish and not because of its full bore maximum of 37 mph, the two-seater roadster was supplemented in 1923 with the "Cloverleaf," so called because of the arrangement of the three seats. In 1922, Citroën half-tracks crossed the Sahara and the marque's popularity boomed to the point where Opel across the Rhine negotiated for license rights.

While the 10CV and smaller 5CV continued to sell well in France and nearby countries, the works scored a first—possibly a world first—in 1925 with a revolutionary all-steel body in one piece produced in Citroën's own new steel pressing plant at Saint-Ouen. Prior to this date, Citroën bodies were wood framed in the manner of the time. The new Type B12 had an improved 1.5-litre, L-head engine, efficient 4-wheel brakes, and appeared in open and closed models. The next year, 1926, saw the finer B14 which became the basis for fleets of taxicabs that swarmed on the boulevards of Paris throughout the thirties. The C4 of 1927 had a 1,538 cc. engine and led to the firm's first 6-cylinder (72 x 100 mm.) model in 1928, the C6 "Rosalie," a sturdy 2.5-litre (42 BHP at 3,000 rpm) car on a 116-inch wheelbase chassis. Branches were established in England and Belgium. The 400 cars-per-day production rate gave Citroën 36 percent

A French-built, 6-cylinder, 1931 Hispano-Suiza H6B formal landaulet with coachwork by Carros-sier Kellner of Paris. (*French Embassy Press & Information Division*)

A magnificent Hispano-Suiza type 68 coupe de ville. Despite 144-inch wheelbase, or more, the 9.5-litre V-12, 220-brake-horsepower engines pro-pelled the heavy cars at 100 mph. Acceleration was electrifying and roadability rivalled smaller sports cars. (*French Embassy Press & Information Division*)

of the home output and helped vault France into number two position, internationally, just behind the U.S.A. Finally in 1929, Citroën went to water pumps after stubbornly holding to thermo-syphon cooling.

To prove the marque's mettle under extreme conditions, the works sponsored the Central Asia expedition. From April, 1931 to February, 1932, forty adventurers in fourteen "Kégresse" half-tracks powered by the 2,442 cc., C6-type engines fought their way from Beirut, Syria, across Iraq, Iran, Afghanistan, through Himalayan passes, around the Pamirs, across Sinkiang, and the inhospitable Gobi Desert to Peking, a distance of 7,500 miles. Meanwhile, the C6 "Rosalie" was restyled, the engines were mounted flexibly in relation to the frame, and a stripped version broke a score of world records at Montlhery by running continuously for 85,000 miles at an average of 65 mph. The next year, 1933, a 1.5-litre, 4-cylinder "Rosalie" 8CV special shattered another batch of records by an amazing endurance run of 187,500 miles at 58 mph average. Citroën's fame thus established, the firm prospered notwithstanding the universal slump.

The turning point in Citroën's technical progress occurred in 1934. In April, the world's first, mass-produced, front-wheel-drive passenger car was introduced and an old design philosophy was re-established once more: the wheels would be located at extreme front and rear thus increasing interior space, making a more comfortable ride and providing maximum road-holding. Consequently the new "Traction Avant" 7CV and the "Eleven" (11CV) sedans utilized the proven 1 and 1.6-litre engines, respectively, set well forward with a 3-speed gearbox. The latter was in unit with the differential driving the front axle half-shafts.

Suspension—independent in front, of course —was by torsion bars, the first such serious application in France, and 4-wheel hydraulic brakes were standard. The five-passenger 7CV and "Light Eleven" sedans sat on wheelbases of 114 inches while that of the six-seater 11CV "Normal" was 121.6 inches. With less power on tap, the five-passenger "Traction Avant" 7CV would do around 50 mph while the two "Elevens" could top out at 60–65 mph. Body and chassis were in unit providing an extremely rigid structure.

Even today a thirty-year-old Citroën Eleven, decently maintained, has fantastic roadability and is a distinct pleasure to drive. In 1938, installation of the 2.5-litre, 6-cylinder engine, based on the larger "Rosalie" model's powerplant, went into the 121.6-inch-wheelbase model and the new "Fifteen-Six" resulted so the family man requiring higher performance had an 80 mph machine. Interiors of all these revolutionary cars were cavernous, exceptionally well appointed, and all would deliver well over 20 miles per U. S. gallon at high average speeds. Thousands of them are still treasured in Europe. The "Eleven" and "Fifteen-Six" were produced in large quantities through 1955. Except for the war years, the "Traction Avant" Citroëns that looked something like a 1934 Ford (but were immeasurably better) enjoyed the longest production run of any French car, before or since. The modern "DS"—very safe and unappreciated in America—is the direct descendant of this remarkable series which was decades ahead of its time.

Seeing the success of Citroën, Renault and Peugeot in the mass market, Henri Pigozzi, a prominent importer of Italian cars, began the assembly of the Fiat "Ballila" in 1932. Quite successful, Pigozzi (who had

Bugatti type 35T with supercharged 2,270 cc. engines were the nemesis of opponents on the grand prix circuits. (*Henry Ford Museum*)

emigrated from Italy) organized the Société Industrielle de Mecanique et Crosserie Automobile and the Simca was born in 1934.

The incomparable Hispano-Suiza types built in the ever more important French branch of that firm are, due to space limitations, dealt with in the section devoted to Spain. Suffice it to say, the elegant H6B models of 1931 and those magnificent giants, the 9.5-litre, V-12 types 68 were among the finest cars built anywhere during the all too brief "golden age" of the automobile. These jewels are illustrated here because they rightly represent the French branch which became the effective head-

quarters of the venerable firm which began in Barcelona in 1901. Since 1945, Hispano-Suiza has concerned itself with armaments, the automotive interests being confined to military vehicles.

Equally without compare were the cars made by Ettore Bugatti who was born in Italy, trained in the fine arts, then fell under the spell of the automobile and worked for several Italian firms. He designed cars for Lorraine-Dietrich, Peugeot, and others, as already observed elsewhere. An artist all of his life, "le patron" created works of art in Bugatti cars. Attention here will be devoted to the most significant Bugattis built for

366

Converted for road use, this Bugatti 35T has wire wheels. Note finned brake drum, spring through front axle, and friction shock absorbers. (*Joseph H. Wherry*)

connoisseurs and private owners intent on winning races. Distinct types were numerous even though production amounted to the relatively low total of around 9,000 cars from 1912 until effective production ceased late in 1939. An indication of technical excellence is that Bugattis garnered more than 3,000 racing victories between 1919 and 1940, and continued to frighten opponents until Bugatti's death in 1947.

Born into a family of artists and sculptors in Milan in 1881, the young Bugatti turned to engineering where his exceptional talents led him to design and build cars of technical perfection. After a scant year of engineering training, Ettore built a twin-engined, three-wheel car in 1899 and immediately won a batch of races in the Milan area. The next year he built an overhead valve, 4-cylinder, four-wheeled car that went 40 mph; with this he won a prize in the 1901 International Exposition in Milan. When De Dietrich bought production rights for his car, Bugatti spent the next seven years in Alsace, under German rule since the Franco-Prussian War. This connection and design contracts with other car builders after 1907 enabled Bugatti to establish himself near Molsheim. Through the years, Bugatti built a self-sustaining industrial king-

Naked gearbox, uncluttered instruments and stark cockpit details of the type 35T Bugatti in the Henry Ford Museum. Note remote-control gear change lever (with knob), handbrake outboard of body, and the steering mechanism. Headlights are not original. (*Joseph H. Wherry*)

Bugatti engines are a feast to the eyes—a magnificent straight-8, single overhead-camshaft, dual-ignition powerhouse in this case. (*Joseph H. Wherry*)

dom including foundries, machine shops, his own electric generating plant, vineyards and winery, a large farm, an employees' village and even an excellent hotel. Today, the Bugatti factories build no more cars but are actively engaged in engineering, developing superb railroad powerplants and industrial machinery.

But back to le patron's cars. The first marque Bugatti, built in 1910–11, was a tiny, 4-cylinder, 65 x 100 mm., 10 CV racer that, with Ernest Friederich driving, proceeded to polish off almost all of the big machinery in the 1911 Grand Prix of France by placing second behind a 10.5-litre Fiat. The little 1,327 cc. Type 13 was a sensa-tion. With a chain-driven overhead camshaft, the engine developed 25 BHP which drove a smooth 4-speed gearbox through a multiple-plate wet clutch; maximum speed was around 60 mph. By 1914, the engine was improved with double valves—two inlet and two exhaust per cylinder—and the speed increased to 95 mph. Several were produced on 94.5-inch wheelbases. The little giant-killing Type 13 began a string of Bugatti racing victories.

During the German advance in 1914, Bugatti buried two prototype engines in the ground, closed his Molsheim works, and went to Paris with his family and key workers. Since 1909 or so, a 5-litre, 8-cylinder

369

A Bugatti 57C coupé with coachwork by Gangloff of about 1939. The engine was a 3,257 cc. 8-cylinder, dual-ignition unit developing 135 BHP un- supercharged; with blower, output increased to approximately 200 BHP depending upon the requirements. (*Harrah's Automobile Collection*)

car, "Black Bess," had been under development; in 1915 it ran in the Vanderbilt Cup Race and a few were built, one for the French air ace, Roland Garros. For the duration of the 1914–18 war, Bugatti built aircraft engines; some of them, V-16 types of 500 HP, were built in the U.S.A. by the Duesenberg brothers.

After the war, the Type 13 engines were exhumed and placed in limited production with slightly enlarged 68 x 100 mm. (later 69 mm. bore) capacity. A team of the new 1.5-litre, Type 22 models with roller bearing crankshafts captured the first four places in the 1921 Brescia race and Type 22 and Type 23, on wheelbases of 100.5 and 126 inches, respectively, were marketed. The Type 22 was for owners who wanted to race, as the "Brescia-modified" and Type 23 was

a touring sports car. Both "Brescia" derivatives were produced until 1926.

In 1923, a 2-litre straight-8 with a single overhead-camshaft was produced and in 1926 the Type 30, a fascinating open four-seat touring sports car, was introduced. Both of these 1,990 cc. (60 x 88 mm.) 8-cylinder cars were very fast. On a 113-inch wheelbase, one of the two-seaters achieved 117 mph in 1923. Three bearing crankshafts, polished like jewels, three valves per cylinder, and integral blocks and heads were used.

From 1924 to 1930 Bugatti's production was centered around the famous Type 35. A prolific family of competition and sports cars, there were five principal versions of this model. Frames were tough, rigid with heavy longitudinal and cross members to re-

The Type 57S Bugatti is distinguished, externally, from the 57C by pointed radiator grille; produced during 1936–38. (*Joseph H. Wherry*)

sist torsional stresses, and were beautifully finished by hand. Wheelbases and treads of all variants were 94.5 and 47.4 inches respectively. Suspension was by half-elliptic springs which passed through the partly hollow front axle, and by reversed quarter-elliptics in the rear with friction shock absorbers at each end. The competition models had Bugatti's patented aluminum alloy cast wheels with integral finned brake drums of impressive size while the sports versions were usually fitted with wire wheels bought in from Rudge-Whitworth. Le patron is often quoted as saying that he built his cars to run and "not to stop" and, consequently, he eschewed hydraulic brakes with their plumbing and valves. Thus the brakes were mechanically operated but they were excellent and as near fade-proof as any drum type brakes had ever been.

While the weight of all road-ready 35-types was rarely more than a bare ton, and while all were single overhead-camshaft straight-eights with fine 4-speed gearboxes and multi-plate iron and steel clutches designed and made by Bugatti, there were considerable differences in the engines. The unsupercharged Grand Prix Type 35 (1924) and Type 35A (1926) and the supercharged Type 35C (1927) with Roots type blower had the 60 x 88 mm., 1,990 cc. displacement engines. Initially Type 35 had roller bearings. Dual Solex carburetors were used on unblown 35-types. In 1927, the stroke was increased to 100 mm., thus boosting the displacement to 2,262 cc. resulting in the Grand Prix Type 35B which was supercharged and the Type 35T which was not. The 35B came to be called the "Targa Florio" after awards gained in Sicily

371

Only seven examples of the Bugatti "Royale" were built. Officially Type 41, the huge cars were powered by 300-BHP, straight-8 engines displacing 12,-760 cc. In 1958, owner Charles Chayne presented this incomparable car to the Henry Ford Museum, during ceremonies at Greenfield Village, where it is now on display. (*Joseph H. Wherry*)

and, with the 2-litre Type 35C, marked the end of Bugatti's reluctance to incorporate superchargers which he believed to be basically immoral because they had the effect of increasing the engine's capacity. Bugatti was a puritan, a technological autocrat, a man of integrity; he loathed insincerity in people or machines.

Leading to minor confusion in Bugatti lore, the Type 43 appeared in 1927. Dubbed the "Grand Sport," the Type 43 was a production sports car, the "civilian" model of the 2.3-litre Grand Prix Type 35 variants in Bugatti's view. Supercharged, it could top 100 mph with ease and was one of the first such high performers offered to the European public. It usually appeared with folding top and a side-mounted spare wheel. Despite "civilian" status, 42 types raced everywhere. There was also a small batch of 52 x 88 mm. Grand Prix cars built during 1925–26. These 1.5-litre models conformed to the then current engine formula in the G.P. events. In 1927, the further modified Type 39, without supercharger, appeared with a shorter stroke 60 x 66 mm., 1.5-litre engine; with blower, this became the Type 39A.

The unblown Type 37 and the supercharged Type 37A were current during 1926–32. On chassis similar to the Type 35, and with the same tread and wheelbase, this model's engines were like those of Type 35 in layout—that is triple valves operated

To buy a new Bugatti "Royale," the client was required to prove a suitable pedigree. (*Joseph H. Wherry*)

by single overhead-camshafts—but had only four 69 x 100 mm. cylinders displacing 1,496 cc. Rather than roller bearings, plain white metal bearings were used.

In 1930, one of the least known Bugattis was marketed, the 3.3-litre, straight-8, dual-ignition Type 49, which was popular with professional men as everyday transport. One of these is known to have served over 700,000 miles without a breakdown of any kind. As a matter of fact, the reliability and durability of all Bugattis enabled even the Grand Prix types to be used successfully on roads and streets providing the detuning was properly accomplished. In 1930, the

Type 50 appeared. A powerful, 4.9-litre, 8-cylinder (86 x 107 mm.) car capable of 110–120 mph with 200 BHP at 4,000 rpm, the Type 50 is probably the only post-World War One Bugatti model with just three speeds (other than the seven examples of the Type 41 "Royale"). Incidentally, the gearbox was integral with the differential in the rear. The Grand Prix Type 54 (1931) was developed from the Type 50, had dual overhead-camshafts and developed 300 BHP.

The year 1930 also saw the introduction of the little-known—perhaps rare would be a better term—Type 47, a very expensive

This Bugatti "Royale" was built for a royal customer; now it can be viewed in Reno, Nevada. The formal cabriolet coachwork—a "Berliner de Voy- age"—was works-built. (*Harrah's Automobile Collection*)

16-cylinder competition car with a pair of the 1,990 cc., 8-cylinder engine blocks mounted side by side on a single alloy crankcase (shades of Bugatti V-16 airplane engines of World War One). Louis Chiron used a 4-litre Type 47, catalogued as the "Grand Sport," victoriously in several hill climbs, and one was built for Le Mans but little more is known of this model.

Dual overhead-camshafts were used also in 1931 on the Type 51, a further variant of the Type 35B. The hemispherical combustion chambers increased output to 180 BHP. Oddest of all Bugatti creations, however, was the experimental Type 53, a four-wheel drive, all independent suspension speedster which, on the Avus ring in Germany, was timed at 133 mph in 1931.

By 1932, Bugatti's son, Jean, was taking an active part in the design department. He was largely responsible for the Type 55 with a 2.3-litre, dual overhead-camshaft engine modified with two valves per cylinder in a 108-inch Grand Prix Type 54 chassis. Weighing only about 2,500 pounds, the Type 55 had 135 BHP at 5,000 rpm and could reach nearly 100 mph in a standing quarter-mile. On one occasion, a Type 55 was clocked at 124 mph on the Brooklands track in England. Bugatti's triumphant years in Grand Prix events were coming to a close but in 1934 the Type 59, with a 3.3-litre DOHC engine won several events; this was a rare model. At Spa, a 59 driven by René Dreyfus won a smashing victory and was said to have a flat-out potential of more than 175 mph. A unique feature was a divided front axle.

It is useless to attempt to correlate type numbers with the year of their introduction where Bugattis are concerned. The extensive design studios at Molsheim were always busy with a vast number of designs, some

of which materialized while others did not. New models were designed for diverse reasons. For example, the Type 41 "Royale" was catalogued from about mid-1927 until 1939 and was conceived because of a challenge of sorts. This most magnificent Bugatti—probably the world's most elegant and technically perfect car—is reported to have resulted from an opinion voiced by an English lady during a formal affair at Molsheim. Wearing her automotive chauvinism like a Union Jack, the fearless woman is said to have observed that, while Bugattis were admittedly the fastest cars one could buy, a Rolls-Royce was still the finest, or something of that nature. Ettore Bugatti promptly set about to remedy the situation.

Le patron's solution was the enormously elegant "Royale." The two illustrated are publicly displayed in museums, one in the Henry Ford Museum at Greenfield Village in Dearborn, Michigan, the other in Harrah's Automobile Collection at Reno, Nevada. The engine shown is a "Royale."

The initial example of this superb car sat on an immense wheelbase of 180 inches; the tread was also generous, 66 inches front and rear. From grille to rear deck, Type 41 was pure Bugatti in every line and detail. No less vast was the 8-cylinder, single overhead-camshaft engine which was more than 4½ feet long. There were the usual three valves per cylinder. Bore and stroke were 125 x 150 mm.—14,726 cc. displacement, 14.7-litres. While personally testing Number One, Bugatti nearly lost his life; the accident hospitalized him. Slightly smaller dimensions characterized the six succeeding production chassis: wheelbase and tread, respectively, were 170 and 63 inches. Piston stroke was also reduced to 130 mm. which brought the swept volume down to a still massive 12,760 cc. In American par-lance, this is approximately 765 cubic inches. Machined with painstaking care from a single billet of steel, the massive crankshaft ran in nine water-cooled main bearings. Of light alloy and hand-finished to a satin smoothness—as were all Bugatti engines—the cylinder block and crankcase were in one piece, and the valves were made of a secret formula metal which Bugatti claimed should never require grinding. Dual ignition and a single double-choke Strom-berg carburetor were used. So great was the care in fabricating "Royale" engines that no tolerances were permitted. Bugatti per-fection! Despite its great size, these engines, complete with all accessories, weighed con-siderably less than 800 pounds which made them lighter than the powerplants of many other fine cars in the luxury class.

The chrome steel chassis frames were, of course, of large proportions; the longitudi-nal members were 10 inches deep at the mid-section. The gearbox, on the rear axle, had just three speeds because the enormous torque of this 300-brake-horsepower en-gine was sufficient to propel the car from a walking speed to its 125 mph maximum in top gear, in silence and without shudder. Second gear ratio was good for 90–95 mph while first gear top speed was more than 50. Maximum peak power was developed at 1,700 rpm while the tachometer was red-lined at 2,000 rpm. Even at top speed, the engine was loafing along effortlessly; no wonder that "Royale" was guaranteed for the lifetime of the original buyer. With the ultimate in stressed aluminum coachwork, weight of a complete Type 41 was in the neighborhood of 5,300 pounds—no more than a modern Imperial, Lincoln or Cadil-lac. The ride was exceptionally smooth and noiseless with Bugatti's traditional suspen-sion system and, despite its size, perfect weight distribution and worm and roller steering gear assured positive control and precise handling with none of the wallow and rolling of most out-size cars. True to his convictions, Bugatti clung to his own mechanical brakes which were servo-assisted. Just as on his Grand Prix cars, the "Roy-ale" had cast, integral brake drums and wheels of light alloy, proof that even a heavy, large car can have a minimum of un-sprung weight with beneficial results and in-creased safety.

Ready for the body, the bare chassis scaled about 3,500 pounds and cost around $20,-000. Coachwork added another 10 "grand" or more. In the late twenties and until 1939 there were few who could afford a "Royale." Only six were built after the first which was wrecked; each was built to order after the applicant was screened and approved by Et-tore himself—just any ordinary millionaire could not qualify. "Royale" was the world's most exclusive—and expensive—automobile. King Carol II of Romania owned one with an additional two tons of armor plate around H.M.'s plush compartment; he ap-parently desired to test the written "life-time" guarantee. The speed was still in ex-cess of 100 mph but the poor chauffeur had to risk the Transylvanian wilds without protection.

When the Type 41 "Royale" was laid down, Bugatti intended to build twenty-five cars. This left around eighteen of the mag-nificent engines which had to be disposed of; Ettore sold them to the National Rail-ways of France as powerplants for railcars in which these engines set new standards of speed and durability.

The last Bugatti production model con-ceived by le patron was Type 57 which had its debut in 1934. No less magnificent but more practical than the "Royale," this model's 120 and 117.5-inch wheelbase frames were enlarged versions of those used on the Grand Prix Bugattis and the tread was 53.2 inches. Suspension, brakes, the 4-speed gearbox and clutch, and combination exposed propeller shaft with torque tube at the rear followed the classic Bugatti pattern. Weight of the chassis was just over one ton ready for coachwork and while the price was high it was considerably less, by about half, than that of the "Royale." Consequently a fair number were built. Engines were the usual in-line eights with two inclined valves per cylinder in hemispherical combustion chambers actuated by dual overhead-camshafts. With 3,257 cc. displacement, single ignition was standard as was a double throat carburetor; bore and stroke were 72 x 100 mm. Block and crankcase were of alloy and the crankshaft had five main bearings.

The basic Type 57 developed 135 BHP at 4,500 rpm and, being strictly an even-tempered road machine, had mild tuning with 6.1 to 1 compression ratio and a top speed of around 90 mph. In 1935, the Type 57S appeared with timing changes and a much higher 8.3 to 1 compression ratio. Output was increased, accordingly, to 185 BHP at 5,500 rpm and full tap performance was well over 100 mph. Almost all of this type were on the shorter wheelbase, and one of them set a new 24-hour record at Montlhery with 124 mph average. The very limited production Type 57T appeared during the same year and, fitted with higher ratio rear axle gears, was much lighter because it was intended for endurance events.

Types 57SC and 57C followed in 1937 and '38 respectively. Basically both of these were standard Type 57 models, the 57SC having a Roots-type supercharger which increased the brake horsepower to 200–220. Acceleration is said to have been little short of phenomenal and the top speed of similar nature. Victory in the 1937 Le Mans race went to a Type 57SC. High ratio rear axles, tuning and external oil coolers were the main modifications to the unblown Type 57C which won the 1939 Le Mans 24-hour race with its maximum straightaway speed of more than 135 mph. The victory in the 1939 Le Mans was more notable than it sounds: averaging over 86 mph for the twenty-four hours, the Bugatti's mark was not exceeded for nearly two decades until the C-Type Jaguar, a post-war development, arrived on the scene.

To recount the impact of the marque Bugatti on the racing scene and in technical innovations, even briefly, would require more space than is available for this entire section on the historic cars of France. Even this lengthy look covers only the most important models. To cover completely the remarkably diverse cars of that nation would occupy, in turn, a volume in itself and then there would be inevitable omissions. In France, the modern automobile took form —*not* in Detroit as millions of Americans seem to think. Only the high spots have been covered, and of these, the treatment accorded the superb Bugatti has been all too brief, for this car is held by many to have been the finest produced anywhere at any time. There have been many extraordinary makes of cars, but none has been more remarkable than the Royale made by an Italian who found his opportunity and fame in France.

Germany

BECAUSE Gottlieb Daimler and Karl Benz are most responsible for creating the first successful automobiles, so were the firms they founded dominant in shaping the industry in their country. We pick up Daimler and Benz activities where we left off in Part II.

Late in 1899, Gottlieb Daimler introduced his famous racer, the 28-horsepower "Phoenix" which was also known as the Constatt-Daimler to distinguish it from the related Austro-Daimler model (see Austria). Touring models with tonneau bodies were built on the same chassis. This monster was so high and heavy—around 1,700 pounds—on its short 70-inch wheelbase and 55-inch tread that it was nearly impossible to manage at speed. The "Phoenix" was fatal to several drivers including Daimler's foreman. The "Phoenix" did, however, bring Emile Jellinek, the Consul-General of the Austro-Hungarian Empire in Nice, France, into a close association with the works in 1900. Jellinek had already obtained distribution rights for Daimler cars outside of Germany.

Daimler died the same year at the age of 66 and was succeeded by his son Paul while Wilhelm Maybach, an associate, continued as chief engineer. Paul had already designed an improved racer with a 4-speed gearbox controlled by a lever on the steering column and an engine with the crankcase cast integrally with the cylinder block. He also had developed one of the first foot pedal accelerators. This car impressed Jellinek who ordered a batch of thirty-six improved models designed by Maybach.

Jellinek would have been highly amused had he foreseen the future rise of Hitler who preferred Mercedes cars over all others—amused because Mercedes Jellinek, for whom all Daimler cars were named after 1901, was the granddaughter of a Jewish rabbi. At any rate, the first Mercedes, Maybach's design, had a safer, longer chassis and, upon introduction in 1901, was certainly the most advanced motorcar of its time with a pressed steel frame and a compact honeycomb radiator core. The four 116 x 140 mm. cylinders were cast in unit with the cylinder head, and aluminum alloy was generously used for the crankcase and gearbox housing to reduce weight. When other manufacturers were still using automatic inlet valves—relying upon piston suction on the down stroke to open the valve—Maybach fitted the more efficient mechanical in-

The 35-HP, 4-cylinder Mercedes-Simplex tourer of 1901–02. (*Daimler-Benz AG*)

let valves operated by the camshaft. The engine developed 35 HP and was a T-head with inlet and exhaust valves on opposite sides of the cylinders. The final drive was by sprocket chains and basically the same chassis was used with a variety of coachwork for several years culminating in the 18 HP "Kettenwagen" tonneau coupé of 1903–04. The first Mercedes won the first of many racing awards in the mountainous 280-mile race at Nice in 1901. An improved longer wheelbase model, the 35-HP, 5.3-litre, 4-cylinder "Simplex" of 1901–02, was built under license by the Steinway piano people in New York and is believed to have inspired the American marque Simplex of later vintage.

Daimler and Maybach had tried everything worth trying before the marque became Mercedes. They were first with gate change gearboxes and successful float-fed spray carburetors. The latter, a Maybach innovation of 1893, was copied by other manufacturers. In 1895, coil springs were tried

but were soon discontinued in favor of leaf springs. As early as 1902, the firm also built some "mixt" petrol-electric runabouts and tourers.

In 1903, a big, noisy 60-HP Mercedes racer won the Gordon Bennett Race, and in 1904, a 9-litre, F-head model driven by the Belgian, Camille Jenatzy, won the same race in County Kildare in Ireland by averaging 49.2 mph over the 327-mile course. A 90-HP, 12.7-litre racer was used by W. K. Vanderbilt in 1904 to set a new world speed record of 92.3 mph, and in April, 1904, the same car raised the record to 97.3 mph.

In 1907, Porsche designed another "mixt" car for the Daimler works; this one differed from the Lohner-Porsche electrics still being built in Austria by having electric motors in the rear wheel hubs only. A team of the Mercedes "mixt" cars failed to place well in the 1907 Grand Prix of France.

Maybach left Daimler in 1907 and Paul

378

18 PP 4 Zylinder Mercedes Kettenwagen Coupé 1903.

759

The 18-HP, 4-cylinder Mercedes "Kettenwagen" —chain wagon—tonneau door coupé of 1903 was developed from the first Mercedes of 1901. (*Daimler-Benz AG*)

The 1905–06 Mercedes grand prix racer. A big, 6-cylinder engine developed 120 HP. Exceptionally successful, a similar racer won the 1908 Dieppe Grand Prix. Note huge chain sprocket. Otto Salzer is at wheel. (*Daimler-Benz AG*)

The 1910 Mercedes-Knight was so named because of the double sleeve-valve engine developed under license. Though smooth and silent, engine consumed quantities of oil. (*Daimler-Benz AG*)

Daimler took over as chief engineer. He designed a chain-driven 120 HP racer, a 4-cylinder, 155 x 180 mm. machine, that won the 1908 Grand Prix of France. Propeller shafts replaced the chain drives. The works also experimented with the double sleeve-valve engine about this time and built a series of silent, smoky touring cars powered with Knight-based engines in 1910, probably the first Mercedes with pointed nose. Other similarly styled models appeared with pushrod-operated overhead valves permitting decreased displacements. In 1912, a Mercedes racer placed third in the Indianapolis Memorial Day Race. About this time

water-cooling was tried for the brakes but was not continued. Paul Daimler's most successful design was the 4.5-litre, 4-cylinder racer illustrated. Developing 120 brake horsepower with a single overhead camshaft and four valves per cylinder, this machine won the first three places in the last pre-war Grand Prix of France in 1914, won the Vanderbilt Trophy Race the same year at Santa Monica, California, with Ralph de Palma driving, placed first in the 1915 "Indy" classic and triumphed in several other events in the United States until 1917.

Simultaneously with the 4.5-litre racer, 6-cylinder sports and touring cars displacing

The 4.5-litre, 4-cylinder, 120-HP grand prix Mercedes of 1914 triumphed on European circuits and placed first at Indianapolis in 1915. In the 1914 Grand Prix of France, this model won first three places for Lautenschlager, Louis Wagner and Otto Salzer. Top speed capability was approximately 115 mph. (*Daimler-Benz AG*)

8 litres were produced along with a big 4-cylinder, 9.5-litre model with three valves (two were exhaust) per cylinder. Just before the war, several 4-litre racers with sleeve-valve engines were raced in Europe without success. During the war, the 4-cylinder, overhead-valve 28/60 model was produced with most of the output going to the army for staff use; this car looked almost exactly like the Mercedes-Knight of 1910.

Mercedes racers began to triumph across Europe beginning with victory in the 1921 Coppa Florio in Sicily when Max Sailer drove an 8-litre, 28/95 HP six from the Stuttgart works immediately prior to the race. Ferdinand Porsche took over as chief designer when Paul Daimler retired late in 1921 and he reworked several supercharged 4-cylinder cars of 1.5 and 2-litre which had failed at Indianapolis and on the Brooklands circuit because of bad brakes and other deficiencies. Porsche improved these racers with four-wheel brakes and engine tuning and entered them in the next Targa Florio which they won. This feat was repeated in 1924. Another early Porsche-designed Mercedes was the 2-litre, flat-nosed eight which ran in the 1922 Monza Grand Prix.

Meanwhile Benz cars were being produced in Mannheim where Karl Benz had

The 2-litre, 8-cylinder Mercedes racer at Monza in 1922. Design consultant Ferdinand Porsche stands, bareheaded, second from right. (*Porsche Werkfoto*)

The 40-horsepower, chain-driven 1905–06 Benz "Prinz Heinrich Wagen" was an accomplished trials performer; in 1907 it placed first in the Herkomer Trials for speed and construction. (*Daimler-Benz AG*)

In 1911, the "Blitzen Benz" set a world speed record at 141.4 mph over a measured mile. The four 185 x 200 mm.-cylinders were cast in pairs. With 21.5 litres displacement, engine developed 200 BHP at 1,650 RPM. (*Daimler-Benz AG*)

The Benz "Rennwagen" of 1921 had a 6/18-HP, 4-cylinder, overhead-valve engine. (*Daimler-Benz AG*)

The 24/100/140 Mercedes K-Wagen of 1925 earned itself the unhappy nickname of "Death Trap." Sports and tourers with works-built bodies were most common. (*Joseph H. Wherry*)

concentrated upon refining his original motor carriages until about 1901 without concerning himself with new models. Benz, incidentally, outlived his early rival and died in comfortable retirement in 1929 at the ripe old age of 85. Early racing efforts with a succession of rear-engined cars were disappointing until Benz hired Hans Nibel as chief designer. He gave up the 2-cylinder rear engine layout. The first Benz to successfully challenge Mercedes and other makes was the chain-drive 40-HP "Prinz Heinrich" model which placed second in the 1906 durability trials sponsored by Adolf Herkomer, an artist who reasoned that comfort and sturdiness of the entire structure, including the coachwork, was of equal importance with speed.

In 1907, an improved 50-HP "Prinz Heinrich" tourer with four 115 x 180 mm. cylinders won the Herkomer trials outright.

The "Prinz Heinrich" tourer was series produced and a factory entered example won the Prinz Heinrich Trial in 1908. The same year Victor Héméry drove a big 12.5-litre Benz racer to victory in one of the toughest, chassis breaking races of all time —the torturous 380-mile Russian race from St. Petersburg to Moscow. Over the virtually roadless route, Héméry averaged nearly 51 miles an hour. Later in 1908, the 120-HP, 12.5-litre monster placed second to a Mercedes in the Grand Prix of France at Dieppe where it showed a top speed approaching 100 mph.

Such racing victories helped sell the passenger cars, so the next step was a 4-cylinder, 150-HP racer of 15-litres which established a speed record of 109 mph on the sands of Daytona Beach, Florida. Benz had turned the engineering department under Max Wagner on a search for speed records. Consequently, one of the most incredible racers in history was built in 1909 on a compact 112-inch wheelbase. With its four 185 x 200 mm. cylinders cast in pairs, the displacement was an astonishing 21.5 litres— about 1,300 cubic inches. Overhead valves were operated by long pushrods and the output was 200 horsepower at a rather lazy 1,650 rpm. A speed of 140 mph at 1,400 rpm was the goal. The large radiator was

A Mercedes type K of 1926 with Saoutchik cabriolet coachwork. (*Daimler-Benz AG*)

The Mercedes-Benz car for the middle class market in 1926 was the "Stuttgart 200" 5-passenger sedan with a 2-litre, 6-cylinder engine designated as the 8/38 HP. (*Daimler-Benz AG*)

12458

Long hood, four-seater sports touring coachwork on the 6.8-litre supercharged Mercedes-Benz Type "S" chassis of 1927. (*Daimler-Benz* AG)

Four-seat touring sports body on a 1927 Mercedes-Benz SS chassis. With Kompressor the output was 180 horsepower. Note enamelled grille with a pair of three-pointed stars. (*Joseph H. Wherry*)

This magnificent 1928 Mercedes-Benz "SSK" two-seater sports car has a 116-inch wheelbase. Finished in gleaming white, this restored example belongs to the Henry Ford Museum. (*Joseph H. Wherry*)

topped off with a huge header tank that protruded forward like a beak and the streamlined body extended aft of the cockpit to a point. A 4-speed gearbox and heavy brass sprocket chains were used. During tests its speed reminded the works crew of lightning and the car was called "Blitzen Benz." Héméry took the Blitzen to England's Brooklands track where he set a new mile record at 115.9 mph.

Needing long straight stretches, the car was shipped to Florida where Barney Oldfield scorched the smooth sands from Daytona to Ormond Beach before spectators who were enthralled with the unheard of speed the monster delivered. Oldfield next set a flying mile mark of 131.7 mph and demonstrated acceleration by attaining 88.8 mph for a standing mile. The Blitzen Benz toured the United States with Oldfield setting new records at every demonstration. The car's speed limited it to long straightaways—tight tracks like the brickyard at Indianapolis brought on tire troubles—but on the Brighton Beach track at Brooklyn, Bob Burman drove a flying mile at 141.4 mph to establish a world speed record that stood for thirteen years. Still in existence, the Blitzen Benz is believed by many enthusiasts to be one of the greatest sprint cars of all time and to be capable still of setting records.

387

The 7.1-litre, 6-cylinder engine is supercharged with a Rootes-type blower; horsepower is 225. Speed, 125–130 mph. (*Joseph H. Wherry*)

With the "Blitzen" proving the quality of Benz engineering, the works produced a variety of sports cars in series from 1910 on beginning with a 40-HP, 5.7-litre which had dual exhaust and inlet valves, dual ignition by magnetos and final drive by propeller shaft rather than chains. This model established a class speed record of approximately 104 mph and inspired larger 60 and 75-HP models and luxury limousines and phaetons for wealthy customers.

On the eve of the 1914–18 war, the Benz works was experimenting with rear engine layouts which resulted in the marque's most advanced sports car in the early '20s, the "Tropfenwagen" (teardrop), a streamliner. The Tropfenwagen's 2-litre engine had aluminum pistons, a crankshaft turning in roller bearings, dual overhead camshafts and a 3-speed gearbox constructed integrally with the differential. A backbone type chassis with transverse front springs and rear suspension by swinging axle half shafts and inboard-mounted rear brakes were other features ahead of their time. Developing 80 horsepower, the revolutionary Tropfenwagen averaged 85 mph in the 1923 Grand Prix of Italy at Monza

Instrumentation of the Mercedes-Benz "SSK" includes manifold and supercharger pressure gauges; would baffle most modern drivers. Wire wheels have knock-off hubs. (*Joseph H. Wherry*)

to capture fourth place. Several were built and raced throughout Europe having their greatest success in hill climb events. This Benz design led to a successful line of passenger cars in 1934.

From 1919 until 1926, Benz passenger cars were large, many having 144-inch wheelbases. Both 4 and 6-cylinder engines were used, all of them cast en bloc, ranging upward from 2.6-litres displacement. The post-war inflation wreaked havoc throughout Germany and from 1923 the Benz and Daimler firms cooperated increasingly until they merged in 1926.

As already observed, Porsche was in charge of engineering at Daimler and the merger with Benz increased his responsibilities. Porsche's cars were as distinctively individualistic as was their designer. The K-wagen (K for Kompressor, supercharger) Mercedes of 1925 was a case in point: on a massive 136-inch wheelbase (some tourers were on a huge 149-inch chassis) powered by a 6,245 cc., 6-cylinder, long-stroke (94 x 150 mm.), supercharged engine, this machine's nose heaviness, bad handling and poor brakes won it the sobriquette of "Death Trap." Weighing up to 5,000

The ultimate in high speed touring in 1928, a
Mercedes-Benz SS 27/140/200 HP cabriolet with
coachwork by Castagna. (*Daimler-Benz AG*)

One-of-a-kind "Kaiserwagen" was built in 1930
for the exiled Kaiser Wilhelm II. The supercharged 8-cylinder engine turned out 230 HP. The
ultimate in luxury, the car had an elaborate push-
button and signal light system by which the ex-
emperor flashed his commands to chauffeur, Walter Lange, seen here at the wheel. (*Daimler-Benz
AG*)

Coachwork by Saoutchik graces this splendid Mercedes-Benz 500S double phaeton owned by Robert Burkholder. (*Joseph H. Wherry*)

The beautifully preserved supercharged 1935 Mercedes-Benz 500K owned by Matthew Post. A consistent concours winner, this car's coupé body is works-built. (*Joseph H. Wherry*)

Favorite Nazi parade car was the "Grosser Mercedes" cabriolet "F" powered with the 8-cylinder 155/230 HP engine; 1938. (*Daimler-Benz AG*)

The 1936 Mercedes-Benz 170-V had its 4-cylinder 1.7-litre engine in front; the same engine was also used in the rear-engined 170-H. (*Daimler-Benz AG*)

pounds with touring coachwork, it was officially denominated as the 24/100/140 HP model—24 HP taxable, 100 HP without supercharger operating and 140 HP with the blower howling. Able to pound out nearly 100 mph, the K-wagen was not popular but it led to the "S" and successive types.

Actually, the immediate result of the Daimler-Benz merger, the first car to be officially named Mercedes-Benz, was the 8/38 HP type listed as the "Stuttgart 200." Introduced in 1926, the "200" signified a 2-litre engine (six 65 x 100 mm. cylinders) and ushered in a type designating system still used today by Daimler-Benz AG. On a rather short 112-inch wheelbase chassis, the Stuttgart 200 was a moderately priced high-quality, utilitarian car for the lower middle class. Production problems coincidental with the merger, however, produced strife between the hot-tempered Porsche and the management, and the fiery Austrian resigned and returned to Steyr (see Austria) in January, 1928, soon after the 3-litre, 137-inch wheelbase "Mannheim"

model was introduced. The latter was an enlarged version of the "Stuttgart" model.

Porsche's mark and that of Benz engineer Max Wagner was on Mercedes-Benz, however; before departing he had directed the design of the excellent S-type which was introduced in 1927. Unlike the unfortunate K-type, the S sat on a 134-inch wheelbase and the improved 6.8-litre engine (six 98 x 150 mm. cylinders) was located well behind the front axle for better weight distribution. Roadability was improved and the lighter steering was quicker with 2½ turns of the steering wheel from lock-to-lock. Listed as the 36/220 model for the maximum horsepower with the supercharger operating, the S-type could reach 60 mph in about 14 seconds and a top speed of 110 mph. The whir of the blower, which could be operated continuously no more than 20 seconds, and the blast through the external exhaust headers were enough to awaken the dead. Despite a weight of around 5,000 pounds, the S-type won the first race on the new Nürburgring circuit in 1927, the Ger-

In 1939, Caracciola drove this 12-cylinder, 3-litre, supercharged Mercedes-Benz "Rekordwagen" to a class D standing mile record of 127.099 mph. (*Daimler-Benz AG*)

The 1910 Horch 17/32 HP 4-cylinder "Sport-wagen." (*Verband der Automobilindustrie EV*)

man Grand Prix and races all over Europe when pitted against pure competition cars, a remarkable achievement for a car designed as a touring vehicle and a lasting credit to the genius of Porsche.

Further development led to the SS—the "Super Sports"—which had a 7.1-litre (100 x 150 mm.) supercharged engine with a magnesium block and a single overhead camshaft. Designated as the 38/250 model,

The 1932–36 Horch 850 had sporting features and a 120-horsepower, 8-cylinder, 5-litre engine. (*Walter J. Spielberger collection*)

Favored as a parade car by Nazi officials, the 1936 Horch was a huge car on a wheelbase of 140.5 inches powered by an 8-cylinder, 4-litre engine with overhead camshaft. Front and rear independent suspensions and as many as eight gear ratios gave heavy car high performance. (*Henry Ford Museum*)

the SS could manage approximately 115 mph. On these supercharged types, the blower cut in with full application of the accelerator pedal. Torque was terrific, the 4-speed gearboxes were tough, but it was a rare driver who escaped frequent clutch replacements. Even fiercer was the 27-170-225 SSK—the "K" stood for Kurz, short—on a 116-inch wheelbase. Appearing in 1928, the improved supercharger increased the output to 225 HP and the short burst top speed to 125–130 mph.

Hans Nibel succeeded Porsche as technical director in 1928 and in 1931 he placed the SSKL in production. On the 116-inch chassis, the "Super Sports Kurz Leicht" (light) had a frame lightened by drilling and higher engine tuning that resulted in a maximum burst output of 300 horsepower with the blower operating. Although intended as a touring sports car, an SSKL was timed at 156 mph. Rudolf Caracciola blooded the SSKL by winning the 1931 Mille Miglia and the type went on to pile

up victories in grands prix and other events through the '30s.

The supercharged 3.8-litre type 380K appeared in small numbers in 1933. With pushrod overhead valves, this 8-cylinder sports-tourer developed 120 HP, and the 123.5-inch-wheelbase chassis featured 4-wheel independent suspension, but the type served mainly as the forerunner of the magnificent and luxurious type 500. A favorite chassis for custom coachbuilders such as Saoutchik, these were 5,000-pound cars with straight 8-cylinder engines displacing 5-litres. The unblown 500S was often seen with double-phaeton or limousine coachwork while the supercharged 500K was most popular as open and closed two-seaters as illustrated. Developed from the latter were the fabulous 540K roadsters of which about 300 were built for wealthy customers, huge 5,800-pound giants on fully independent 130-inch-wheelbase chassis. With 8-cylinder, 5.4-litre powerplants, these were rated at 115 HP unblown and 180 HP with super-

A contemporary magazine advertisement for the 1931–32 Audi "Dresden" model. Engine: in-line, 8-cylinder, 5.1 litre, 100 HP. (*Walter J. Spielberger collection*)

The 4.4-litre, V-16 rear engine Auto Union P-Wagen of 1934 designed by Dr. Porsche. (*Porsche Werkfoto*)

The 1937–38 Auto Union P-Wagen developed more than 400 HP. In this car Bernd Rosemeyer set a 10-mile world speed record of 223.9 mph in 1937. (*Porsche Werkfoto*)

chargers cut in. The 540K was capable of more than 110 mph. Despite their size, ponderous steering and cost, around $12,000 and more, the types 500 and 540 were of sporting character and roadability. Large as they were, however, they did not match the "Grosser Mercedes" of 1937–39.

Reaching a pinnacle of opulence, the "Grosser" was an updated version of the "Kaiserwagen" built in 1930 for Wilhelm II. Favored as parade cars by Nazi officials including Hitler, the Grosser's 148-inch wheelbase tubular steel X-frame chassis was independently sprung all around on coil springs. The big 7.7-litre, straight-8 engine delivered 280 horsepower at 2,700 rpm. Im-

pressive speed (said to have been nearly 140 mph even with seven persons aboard) was effectively controlled by an advanced servo-equipped brake system.

While the big luxury cars garnered the publicity, the bread and butter emphasis of Daimler-Benz AG during the thirties was on quality passenger cars. In 1931, the 4-cylinder, overhead-valve, 1.7-litre Type 170 appeared. Experiments, inspired by Ferdinand Porsche, who seemed to be everywhere at once throughout Central Europe, resulted in the Type 130H in 1934. The "H" stood for "Hinterseite" or rear, the location of the 1.3-litre, 4-cylinder engine at the end of a central tube type frame not unlike that

Dr. Ferdinand Porsche, Rosemeyer and Auto Union "Rekordwagen" during the 1937 Grand Prix of Holland. (*Porsche Werkfoto*)

of the Tatra cars of Czechoslovakia. Front, independent suspension was by double transverse leaf springs while the rear swing axle half-shafts were suspended by positioning links and coil springs. This development led to a similar passenger car with the Type 170 engine located in the rear, the 170H. From 1936 on, the front-engined model was designated as the 170V (V for "Vorderseite"—front location) and all body types from convertibles to 4–5 passenger sedans were built in comparatively large numbers. Though reasonably good, the rear-engined 170V was not popular.

On the eve of World War Two, passenger car production in the Daimler-Benz plants approximated 30,000 cars per year while commercial and military vehicles were produced in greater numbers. A 1937 Daimler-Benz racer developed 645 HP and in 1939 the W165 racing cars powered with 1.5-litre, V-8 engines fitted with a two-stage supercharger and the 3-litre, 12-cylinder racers were being groomed for assaults on various standing records. Caracciola drove the 3-litre racer to a new Class D mile record of 127.099 mph and Lang and Caracciola captured the top two places in the

In 1932, Dr. Porsche designed this prototype for Zündapp. The rear engine was a 5-cylinder radial. In this design, the germ of the future Volkswagen was born. (*Volkswagen of America*)

The 1906 NSU runabout had a 6/10-HP, 4-cylinder engine and was a popular car at a moderate price. (*Verband der Automobilindustrie EV*)

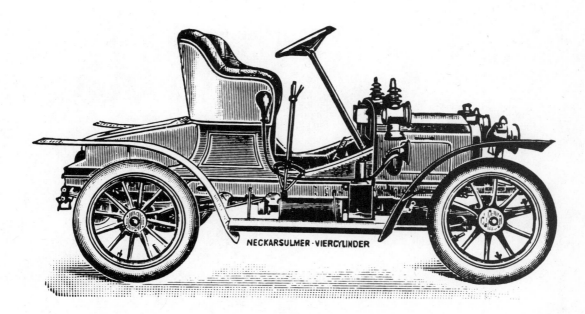

NECKARSULMER·VIERCYLINDER

The 1.5-litre, air-cooled rear engine prototype designed by Porsche in 1933 for NSU accurately prophesied the future course of his Volkswagen development. (*Volkswagen of America*)

Volkswagen prototypes of 1936 (right) and 1937 (left). The design was well developed at this stage. (*Porsche Werkfoto courtesy of Volkswagen of America*)

The 1939 special VW built by Dr. Porsche for the Rome-Berlin distance rally which never occurred because of the outbreak of war. (*Porsche Werkfoto courtesy of Volkswagen of America*)

H. M. King Christian IX of Denmark and Prince Hans were seated behind the driver of this 1906 Adler. (*Verband der Automobilindustrie EV*)

Miss C. Rosborough of Dublin at the wheel of her 1910 Adler. The 1,300 cc. 10-HP engine has 4 cylinders. Seated next to the owner is Mr. Casey, Lord Mayor of Cork; Mr. Coughlan of the "Cork Examiner" is seated in back. The occasion was preparations prior to departing for England to compete in the Fourth International Rally in 1963. (*Cork Exchange courtesy of the Irish Veteran & Vintage Car Club*)

Adler "Diplomat" of 1935, an expensive, 3-litre, 6-cylinder, grand turismo model with front-wheel drive. (*Walter J. Spielberger collection*)

1939 Grand Prix of Tripoli on a pair of W165s to defeat the new type 158 Alfa Romeos. Thus ended a decade that saw Mercedes-Benz battling Auto Union and Alfa Romeo right down to the moment when blackout curtains fell across Europe.

Next in importance in the German automobile industry before 1940 was Auto Union which came into being in 1932 with the merger of Horch, Audi, Wanderer and D.K.W. The senior marque in this combine in point of years was the Horch, originated by August Horch who left Benz in 1902 to begin making his own cars in Zwickau, now in East Germany. Although meaning "listen" in German, little was heard of the marque until a 5.8-litre, 4-cylinder Horch won the 1906 Herkomer Trials. Then an improved model won the 1906 Prinz Heinrich Trials. A quality machine, the winning car had an F-head engine—the

overhead inlet valves were operated by push-rods—and the crankshaft, connecting rods and most other moving parts of the engine worked in ball bearings. The next year, Horchs won three more gold medals in the Herkomer Trials but lost first place to a Benz. Until the 1914–18 war, fours and sixes were manufactured, most of them having aluminum crankcases, dual ignition systems with coil and magneto, water pumps in the cooling system when many marques employed thermo-siphon circulation and final drives by propeller shafts inside torque tubes.

After the war, Horch cars rivalled Mercedes-Benz in the luxury field (but not in numbers) with 8 and 12-cylinder in-line engines. The 8-cylinder cars had 3.1-litre engines and 136-inch wheelbases in the late '20s and were designated as 20/56 HP models. In the '30s, Horch engines had over-

The 1934–38 Adler "Diplomat" was made in cabriolet and sedan models. A 60/65-HP, 6-cylinder engine had overhead valves, displaced 2,916 cc. Transmission had four speeds. Wheelbase was 126 inches on cabriolet shown; sedans were longer. (*Walter J. Spielberger collection*)

Outstanding performance of the front-wheel-drive, 4-cylinder, 1,697 cc. Adler special won it the Index of Performance award in the 1938 Le Mans 24-hour classic. (*Joseph H. Wherry*)

head camshafts and fully independent suspension systems with swing axles in the rear. A few 4-litre eights were built but the 3,517 cc. V-8, developing 82 horsepower at 2,500 rpm when equipped with dual Solex carburetors, was the mainstay after 1936. On a wheelbase of 122 inches and with 4-speed gearbox, this Type 930V had a top speed of just under 80 mph with sedan coachwork and a bit more as two-seater roadsters. Much larger on 140.5-inch wheelbases, the finest Horchs had either the V-8 engine or a 5-litre, 12-cylinder powerplant and were favored by the elite and by military and government officials as parade cars. Eight-speed transmissions and firm suspensions gave these 5–6,000-pound vehicles speeds over 100 mph and handling qualities which were quite sporting despite gargantuan dimensions.

The Audi (also meaning "listen" but in Latin) was next in rank in the Auto Union lineup and was also built in Zwickau beginning in 1909. Light cars of conventional design were built until the First World War; afterward the marque enjoyed limited popularity with attractive 4 and 6-cylinder cars, mainly roadsters. As early as 1920 Audis had V-windshields and sporty lines but the cars were rarely seen in sporting events other than tours. In the early '30s, the "Dresden" was the marque's mainstay, a medium large 8-cylinder car powered by a 100 HP, 5.1-litre engine. After the merger into Auto Union in 1932, the Audi was modernized in style and ranked just below the Horch in the combine's catalog. As a current note of interest, the Audi is again in production in Germany as the top car from Auto Union.

Wanderer was first built in1910 in Chemnitz by the Winklhofer & Jaenicke AG. Called the "Puppchen" (little doll), this little 89-inch-wheelbase tourer was a narrow

The 1934–35 BMW Type 315 had a 6-cylinder, overhead-valve, 1.5-litre engine. (*Bavarian Motor Works*)

Type 326 BMW sedans of 1936–40 had 2-litre, 6-cylinder engines. (*Bavarian Motor Works*)

First BMW sports car was the 1.5-litre Type 315 of 1935–36. (*Bavarian Motor Works*)

tandem two-seater with the passenger behind the driver who controlled a 4-cylinder, 1.2-litre, T-head engine that had magneto ignition, water pump cooling, a dual intake carburetor, a foot accelerator pedal and shaft drive. Reliable and popular, the Puppchen's 12 horsepower was sufficient to drive the 1,100 pound tourer at about 60 mph. When production resumed in 1919, the marque languished until 1931 when Ferdinand Porsche was retained to redesign the car, and in the same year the fabulous Austrian made the first known application of an all-torsion bar suspension system to the Wanderer. Porsche also designed an all-new model around a 1.9-litre, 6-cylinder engine which had an aluminum block with cast iron cylinder liners, and a larger 8-cylinder Wanderer. Unfortunately, the large car was never produced in series but the 6-cylinder car was a success.

With a more curious background, the D.K.W. car originated in 1916 as a lightweight steam car, the "Damp-Kraft-Wagen," the brainchild of a Danish engi-

neer by the name of Jørgen S. Rasmussen who resided in Germany. The steamers soon gave way to motorcycles powered by efficient two-cycle engines. Rasmussen next adopted the front-wheel drive system developed by Gregoire in France. Around 1927, the D.K.W.—by that time known as "Das Kleine Wunder"—was an attractive open two-seater with a ½-litre, 2-cycle engine with two cylinders. After being absorbed by Auto Union in 1932, production of a 3-cylinder model of ¾-litre capacity was undertaken in Zwickau in the Audi factory. This model became the pattern for the post-World War Two Wartburg copy still made in East Germany and for the modern D.K.W. which is made in the Federal Republic.

When Hitler came to power, subsidies were granted to Auto Union as well as to the dominant Daimler-Benz and other manufacturers like B.M.W. With their four lines of passenger cars barely holding their own, Auto Union management embarked upon a racing program which bore first fruit

406

The BMW Type 327 of 1936–38 was a sensation. Camshaft high in block operated inclined overhead valves in hemispherical combustion chambers. Maximum speed was about 90 mph. (*Joseph H. Wherry*)

in 1934 with rear-engined cars designed by Porsche. Called the P-Wagen (for Porsche), the 1934 racer had a 295-horsepower, 4.4-litre, V-16 engine located immediately forward of the rear axle. Breaking a trio of world speed records, the P-Wagen slaughtered all opposition to win the Swiss, Czechoslovakian and German Grand Prix events. The weight of the engine provided increased traction for the rear wheels while the fuel tanks, centered on the chassis, eliminated any ill effects from weight changes as the fuel was consumed. The driver, poor soul, sat in front of everything with his feet over the front suspension. With most of the weight in the rear, the P-Wagen was a skidding demon and even seasoned racing drivers like Tazio Nuvolari were less than happy sitting in front of, rather than behind, the engine.

Most successful on the monster was Bernd Rosemeyer who had cut his racing teeth on motorcycles which had sliding pro-

clivities more akin to the P-Wagen. During 1936, therefore, Rosemeyer was much seen in Porsche's latest Auto Union design, an improved 6-litre, 16-cylinder V-type. He trounced the rivals from Daimler-Benz three times in five grands prix. In 1937, the P-Wagen, with more than 400 horsepower on tap, won the Vanderbilt Cup Race in the United States with Rosemeyer driving at speeds of more than 155 mph on the straights. A Mercedes-Benz and an Alfa Romeo took second and third while the other P-Wagen placed fourth. Before the year was out, Rosemeyer established a new world's speed record for ten miles at 223.9 mph. The monsters went on dueling with Mercedes-Benz racers until Rosemeyer tried to exceed 268.3 mph—to beat a new Mercedes mark—in January, 1938, on the Frankfurt to Darmstadt autobahn. As his car emerged from an overpass at full throttle, a cold wind, a blown front tire, or both—the exact cause remains a mystery—caused the

407

Displacement of the BMW 6-cylinder, Type 327 engine was 1,971 cc. With 7.5 to 1 compression ratio and three carburetors, power was 80 BHP at 4,600 RPM. (*Joseph H. Wherry*)

Auto Union to skid wildly, flip over twice and then to hurtle 200 yards through the air. Rosemeyer, just 27 years old, was thrown out and died instantly. The Auto Union versus Mercedes duels came to an end with his death which is commemorated with a monument on the autobahn.

On the first day of January, 1931, Ferdinand Porsche had established his own design bureau in Stuttgart. No longer would he be beholden to boards of directors but could utilize his talents independently wherever they were needed which seemed to be everywhere in Germany and Austria. Porsche had nurtured the desire, for many years, to design a reliable car that the average working man could afford—a "people's car." His first big chance came when Wanderer retained him in 1931. Although his transverse torsion bar suspension system did not go into widespread production by Wanderer, rights to the Porsche patents

Owner John Hallberg shares cockpit of BMW 327 with a friend. Note concealed spare wheel. (*Joseph H. Wherry*)

BMW Type 327/28 coupé was developed from two-seater sports roadster. (*Bavarian Motor Works*)

The BMW Type 328 sports car of 1937–40 was
a refinement of 327. Top speed was 100 mph.
(*Bavarian Motor Works*)

BMW Type 328 specially fitted with lightweight
aluminum body and supercharger developed 120
BHP at 5,800 RPM. Weight was 1,500 pounds.

Speed of 135–140 mph enabled type to win 1940
Mille Miglia. Latter event was shortened to 100
miles because of the war. (*Bavarian Motor Works*)

1902 Opel 10/12-HP "Tonneau" model had stern door for rear seats, 2-cylinder engine with three forward speeds. In advance of its time, automatic chassis lubrication was standard. Note steering column gear change lever. Speed was about 30 mph. (*Adam Opel AG*)

This 1908 Opel 10/18-HP, 4-cylinder model was the "Double Phaeton." (*Adam Opel AG*)

Opel 1909 "Doktorwagen" with 4-cylinder, 4/8-HP engine gave light two-seater top speed of about 33 mph. Popular with country doctors, the removable steel rims minimized tire changing time. (*Adam Opel AG*)

The Opel 6/16-HP "Torpedo" model of 1911 was a high quality car at a moderate price. Crowned fenders, dual cowl, and 4-speed gearbox were features. Speed was 40 mph. (*Adam Opel AG*)

Tulip body and pointed radiator shell on 8/25-HP, 4-cylinder 1920 Opel shows influence of pre- war Prince Henry styling of competitive marques. (*Adam Opel AG*)

Opel's "Laubfrosch" 3/12-HP, two-seater of 1924 was license-built copy of André Citroën's 1922 5 CV model. This popular economy car had 4- cylinder engine with electric starter, full pressure lubrication, and 3-speed gearbox. (*Adam Opel AG*)

During 1927–28, Opel built the first known rocket-powered cars: "Rak 2," second in the experimental series, starts down the Avus track near Berlin on May 23, 1928, with Fritz von Opel at the wheel. Stubby wings, fixed with negative incidence, helped keep the car on the ground. The cluster of twenty-four rockets produced 125 mph. (*Adam Opel AG*)

were licensed out to Alfa Romeo, Lancia, Citroën, Volvo and others. In all fairness, Porsche might have benefited by studying the 1878 designs of Anton Lövstad (see Norway). At about the same time, the Soviet government made overtures to Porsche and he visited Russia but chose instead an offer by the Zündapp works, a Nuremberg motorcycle maker. Thus it was that in 1932 Porsche designed and built three prototypes of a car that eventually evolved into the Volkswagen. Rear-engined by a 5-cylinder, radial, air-cooled powerplant and suspended all around on transverse torsion bars, the Zündapp-Porsche was successful but never reached production.

But the seed was planted and in 1933 the Neckar SU works in Neckarsulm in Württemberg called upon Porsche to design new life into their marque, which was born in 1903. By 1906, the NSU was a competitive 4-cylinder machine. The 1933 Porsche-designed NSU looked remarkably like the 22-HP Steyr of 1936–40 (see Austria) and even more like the modern Volkswagen with its 4-cylinder, air-cooled, horizontally-opposed type engine of 1.5-litres capacity. Overhead valves were used and

Fritz von Opel receives congratulations after historic run; beside Opel, in black hat, is Max Valier, rocket pioneer. (*Adam Opel AG*)

cooling air was rammed around the cylinders by a belt-driven blower. Porsche designed the model (illustrated) to maintain a true 55 mph all day long without undue stress, and its roadability was unsurpassed due to the torsional suspension sytem. Again only three prototypes were built, one of which survived the 1939–45 war to reappear in Stuttgart in 1950, having been rescued by a former NSU engineer. Later, a government grant enabled Porsche to develop his project further and in 1936 the KDF cars ("Kraft durch Freude"—Strength through Joy) were unveiled in prototype form. How Porsche's people's car, the famous VW, finally got into production is a story too well known to be repeated herewith. The high point of pre-war Volkswagen development, however, was the beautifully streamlined VW special built during 1938–39 to compete in the Rome-Berlin distance Rally, an event which was cancelled due to the war. More than any other person, Dr. Ferdinand Porsche was responsible, along with his son, Ferry, for the miraculous resurgence of the automobile industry in shattered post-war Germany.

Named for the German "eagle," the Adler was the product of Heinrich Kleyer who built bicycles in Frankfurt before 1900. In that year Kleyer obtained production rights to the 1-cylinder De Dion-Bouton cars (see

415

Tests of Opel-Raketwagen "Rak 3" involved large tow car and rails. (*Adam Opel AG*)

France), but by 1906 he was building 4-cylinder models of his own design and was exporting them with some success. The 10-HP, 1909–10-model had a 1.3-litre engine and sold well, but a big 75 horsepower, 5-litre sports model failed to place in the 1910 Prinz Heinrich Trials and was, consequently, produced in very small quantities. The same year, however, a 3-litre model went into production for the luxury market, and with the 1.3-litre four, continued until 1915.

Motorcycles filled out the Adler line along with large cars on wheelbases up to 134 inches until 1932 when a small front drive car of advanced design was introduced with independent suspension and a fully synchronized 4-speed gearbox. Weighing barely a ton and named "Trumpf" (Triumph), this car had an all-steel body integrated with the frame. A 1.7-litre, 4-cylinder engine developed 40 horsepower and drove the car 90–95 mph. The front drive system, though, was so similar to that patented by J. A. Gregoire of France that the latter brought legal proceedings against Adler, but the litigation finally came to nothing with the Trumpf being built under license in France and marketed there as the Rosengart Supertraction. The Trumpf was a splendid car for both sports and touring, light on the wheel with its rack and pinion steering, and superbly roadable. By 1938, the Trumpf was available in open and closed models seating up to five persons. Some of them are still in use; one competed in a Leningrad-to-Moscow rally as recently as 1966 (see Russia).

416

Engineer Volkhart at the wheel of "Rak 1" during tests May 12, 1928. Note quarter-elliptic rear springs in cantilever position. (*Adam Opel AG*)

In 1934, Adler introduced the "Diplomat" model, a luxury car powered with an overhead-valve, 6-cylinder engine displacing 3 litres and developing 60 HP at 3,000 rpm. On wheelbases of either 126 inches or 132 inches, the "Diplomat" had centralized chassis lubrication, was available in six-passenger open tourers, convertibles and closed limousines and, in a limited production version, as a streamlined two-seat front drive grand turismo model with cycle fenders over the front wheels.

The little 1,697 cc. "Trumpf" had, by 1936, made a name for itself in roadster form by winning a fair share of races, so Dr. Porsche was called in to give it a measure of his special treatment in the form of a tubular chassis containing a supertuned version of the same engine with dual carburetors which raised the output to 105 BHP at approximately 4,200 rpm. Aerodynamic, lightweight aluminum bodies accommodated four persons. With driver only aboard, this special Adler achieved 122 mph in tests on the Nürburgring. In 1938, a pair of the 105-HP specials placed first and second on the Index of Performance classification in the Le Mans 24-hour race, the top car averaging 108 mph. The car illustrated here is one of the famous Le Mans pair and, until recently, was in everyday service in this country. Also built under license in Belgium by Impéria, the Adler "Trumpf" was probably the finest all around small car to come out of pre-war Germany and it is a pity that the marque did not survive after the war.

World War Two finished many a Ger-

The little 1925, 4/14-HP Opel was the economy 4-seater sedan companion of the "Laubfrosch" roadster. (*Adam Opel AG*)

The finest Opel for 1931–33 was the 6-cylinder, 1.8-litre model. Rated at 32 HP at 3,200 RPM, top speed was 50–54 mph. General Motors styling influence is evident. (*Adam Opel AG*)

man make. The division of the nation into Western and Eastern regions very nearly did in the Bayerische Motoren Werke, makers of the B.M.W. Originally established early in the First World War to manufacture aircraft engines in Munich, the firm turned to motorcycles in 1919. In 1928, the works marketed its first car, a license-built version of the Austin Seven (see England) after acquiring the Eisenach factory in the city of the same name. Eisenach (see Part II), a pre-1900 marque also known as the Wartburg, was renamed Dixi in 1902 and, until 1914, was manufactured in a fairly expensive 5-litre, 4-cylinder series of tourers and limousines. The first true B.M.W. cars were small 800 and 900 cc., 4-cylinder machines of 1932 designed by Dr. Fritz Fiedler. With independent front suspensions, the fours paved the way for the 1.1-litre, overhead-valve, Type 303, 6-cylinder model of 1933 which was improved by enlarging the engine to 1.5-litre displacement in 1934.

Known as the Type 315, the 1.5-litre six was produced in family cars and in a sports car version with triple Solex carburetors and 6.8 to 1 compression ratio. Developing 40 horsepower at 4,500 rpm, the 315 sports car was light, and fast. It began a successful though brief racing career by winning a race in 1935 on the Nürburgring.

The 2-litre Type 319, developing 65 HP and capable of 95–97 mph, followed and this model quickly evolved into the Types 327 and 328 in 1936 and 1937, respectively. Fiedler, with the Types 327/328, scored by placing the camshaft high in the cylinder block enabling him to incline the valves in hemispherical combustion chambers for greater efficiency without necessitating overhead camshafts. It is quite possible that Fiedler was inspired by the 1914 engine designed by Jan Hagemeister, builder of the JAN cars (see Denmark). At any rate, the new camshaft and valve gear, plus cylinder bores enlarged by 1 mm. and compression

Introduced in 1935, the Opel Olympia had a 1.3-litre, 4-cylinder engine rated at 26 HP. Body and chassis frame were of unit construction and brakes were hydraulic. Speed was 60–63 mph. (*Adam Opel AG*)

The 1936 Opel Kadet styling and its 1.1-litre, 23-HP, 4-cylinder engine strongly influenced the struggling Soviet Russian automobile industry. (*Adam Opel AG*)

ratio raised to 7.5 to 1, shot the output up to 80 horsepower at 4,600 rpm on the very sporting three-carburetor engines.

In the popular 2-seater sports Type 328, a bit lighter than the 327, a maximum of 100 mph was easily achieved, and from a dead stop, an honest 60 mph was reached in less than 11 seconds. That was exceptional performance for a 2-litre car in 1937 —or to put it another way, that is good performance today for a 120-cubic-inch touring sports car, a tribute to an engine design that was years ahead of its time. Victories in the Le Mans classic and a host of other races made the B.M.W. 328 a favorite up to the outbreak of war in late 1939. In 1940, a special 120-HP, supercharged version with an aluminum body of envelope design had a top speed of 135–140 mph and easily won the shortened Mille Miglia in Italy. A 3.5-litre car, the Type 355, was introduced on the eve of the war but

few were built. In 1945, the factories in Eisenach were confiscated by the occupying Soviets and production of B.M.W. cars resumed only after facilities were reorganized in Munich in 1951.

Soon after acquiring the Lutzman car in 1899, the Adam Opel A.G. (producers of bicycles and sewing machines in Rüsselsheim) also obtained rights to build the Darracq (see France) under license. By 1907, however, Fritz Opel had designed a distinctive, but conventional, 4-cylinder tourer with shaft drive. One of them won the Emperor's Prize in a race in the Taunus Mountains and the Opel had become a make in its own right. When the 4/8 HP "Doktorwagen" was introduced in 1909, success was assured. The two-place roadster had a peppy L-head, 4-cylinder engine; time-saving, demountable, steel wheel-rims; and proved popular with professional men. To appeal to the family trade, the 6/16 HP

The 2.5-litre, 6-cylinder, 55-HP Opel Kapitan of 1939 was capable of over 75 mph. Two and four-door sedans looked like scaled-down American GMC models. (*Adam Opel AG*)

touring model was marketed in 1911. Speed was increased to 40 mph and a 4-speed gearbox improved acceleration but fixed wheel-rims represented a retrogression. Styling was better, though, with smooth-sided "torpedo" coachwork and crowned fenders. Production had increased to about 500 cars annually by late 1914.

With allied occupation troops swarming over the works, production did not resume

Finest pre-war Opel was the comparatively large 3.6-litre Admiral. The overhead-valve, 6-cylinder engine delivered 75 BHP. (*Adam Opel AG*)

Guido Thost placed first in a German Automobile Club trial covering 415 miles. Winning time was 16½ hours for his 1910 Hansa, 7-HP sports tourer. (*Verband der Automobilindustrie EV*)

until 1920 when the very clean 8/25 tourer was introduced with full pressure lubrication, an electric starter and body styling reminiscent of several "Prinz Heinrich" sports tourers of other pre-war marques. But post-war inflation prompted an attempt to produce a "people's car" and the Citroën 5CV (see France) was produced under license as the Opel "Laubfrosch" (tree frog) from 1924 until 1928 when works production had soared to approximately 250 cars per day. The "Laubfrosch" initially cost upwards of $1,000 but mass production brought the price down. A similar two-door sedan, the 1.1-litre 4/14, was also produced.

In 1928, the 4/14 sedan was restyled, other models were built, some on 128-inch wheelbases, and in 1929 General Motors purchased Adam Opel A.G. Though retaining the Opel name, GMC initiated styling and engineering changes that reflected Detroit thinking. During the '30s, overhead valves and coil spring "knee action" front suspension were used on all models. Opels enjoyed considerable success in Germany, and abroad where they exceeded the exports of all other German firms combined. The 4-cylinder, 1.1-litre "Kadet" and 1.3-litre "Olympia" were best sellers. A "Super Six" of 1938 looked like a miniature 1936 Chevrolet and was an improved version of the 1.8-litre six of 1931–33. Largest of the pre-war Opels were the 6-cylinder 2.5-litre "Kapitan" and the "Admiral" of 1939 and 1938 respectively. With its 3.6-litre, 75-brake-horsepower engine, the "Admiral" had a maximum speed of nearly 85 mph and was on its way to a large share of the medium priced family market when the war brought a halt to production for the public.

There was a Taunus car in Germany as long ago as 1913 and it survived into the '20s; it was built in small numbers in Frankfurt. The name was revived early in 1939 by Ford which had established a factory in Berlin in 1926 where models "T" and "A"

Germany's finest marque, Maybach was built to the ideal of perfection—cost was no object. This 1922–26 Type W3 had powerful 6-litre, 6-cylinder engine. (*Walter J. Spielberger collection*)

were assembled. In 1931, Deutsche Ford G.m.b.H. moved to Cologne and the next year commenced manufacture of the "Köln" model (named for the city), open and closed four-seaters powered by a simple yet reliable 4-cylinder, L-head engine of 933 cc. displacement. Structurally the small German Fords were like the British models, but the styling was better, virtually duplicating American Fords on a smaller scale. Conventional frames were used with a solid front axle slung beneath a transverse leaf spring. In 1938, the "Köln" was restyled to look for all the world like the famed 60 HP V-8 of 1937. A slightly larger model that could seat five persons in a pinch was named the "Eifel" and had a flat-head, 4-cylinder, 1,172 cc. engine that, with a 4-speed gearbox, gave good performance and was adaptable to tuning, extra carburetors, etc. Also looking like the 60 HP V-8, the "Eifel" had rather Germanic looking front fenders with a more pronounced sweep and freestanding headlights. The V-8 Ford was also

built in Cologne from late 1937 until the war. Most of the V-8s had excellent coachwork by the Gläser firm, cabriolets having the customary headliners which made the interiors as snug as the all-steel sedans. A restyling of the 1.2-litre Köln in early 1939 resulted in a small version of the 1939 full size American Fords and this model resurrected the name "Taunus." Ford's German enterprise was destroyed in wartime raids, but bounced back afterwards and today is a leader in the industry in Central Europe.

The remaining large German manufacturer prior to 1940 was the Carl F. W. Borgward G.m.b.H. of Bremen. Borgward merged the assets of three old marques in 1938. Oldest of the three was the Hansa which began in 1905 with a small series of 2-cylinder tourers of straightforward design. By 1910, 4-cylinder models had won several trials and club events but the marque never prospered and in 1914 merged with the Lloyd, a line of electric and gasoline cars dating back to 1904. In the '20s, the Hansa-

423

Lloyd cars were comparatively large 4 and 6-cylinder vehicles for those of means. Though of sturdy, quality construction with solid Teutonic lines, they were not particularly distinguished. In 1929, Carl Borgward purchased all facilities. Borgward had built the Goliath since 1926, a tiny, 3-wheeled, two-seater powered by a single-cylinder, 20 cc., two-cycle engine, which in 1934 became an advanced, 2-cylinder, air-cooled, two-seater with fully independent suspension. A "people's car," this Hansa 500 had a rear engine but was too small. After the total merger in 1938, no more Goliath or Lloyd cars were built but there were two 4-cylinder Hansas, a small 1.1-litre four-passenger car of conventional design and an ultra-modern, fully streamlined 1.5-litre model featuring swing rear axles and fine performance. They probably would have succeeded but for the war. The Borgward combine brought back all three marques after 1948.

Some have accused the German automobile industry of having been, and being, a cutthroat dog-eat-dog affair. In many respects it has been but the way in which scores of marques have been submerged and merged into oblivion is reminiscent of the course of auto making in the United States where only four mass-producers remain.

There have been other marques in Germany: the Brennabor (1909–29) built in Brandenburg by the Reichstein brothers; the Dürkopp (1900–28) began with license-built, 2-cylinder Panhard & Levassor cars; the Hanomag (1913–52) of Hanover, made in a works famed for its 1914–18 aircraft but most notorious for its boxy "Kommissbrot" rear-engined, 1-cylinder, "paint and tin" coupe of 1925 and for finer streamlined

4-seaters of 1938–39; the Phänomen (1912–29), initially a 3-wheel overgrown motorcycle; the Piccolo (c.1907–33) made in Thüringia in a variety of single to 4-cylinder models; the Stoewer (about 1898–37) of Stettin, excellent cars, some models with front-wheel drive; and nearly two hundred more like the Mauser of c. 1920–29 by the armaments firm, which are unknown today.

Of all the non-surviving German cars, though, the magnificent Maybach was perhaps the finest. When Wilhelm Maybach left the Daimler works, he became a designer of airship engines in Count Graf von Zeppelin's factory. Maybach's engines powered the huge hydrogen-filled gas bags that bombed Britain during World War One. After that war, Maybach produced cars until 1939 with one thought in mind: quality. The first series of 1921 had 6-litre, 6-cylinder, overhead-valve engines. These were followed by 3.8-litre sixes developing 140 HP at 4,000 rpm and a beautifully hand-crafted 12-cylinder, V-type of 8-litres turning approximately 220 HP at 3,000 rpm. Town cars and giant limousines on wheelbases of 12 feet and more were delivered to wealthy patrons for prices exceeding $25,000. As on other fine cars, the frames and invisible parts were finished with as much care as were the leather and brocade upholsteries, and the leather tops on cabriolets and broughams. In the late '30s, Maybachs had four-wheel, independent suspensions and, though the cars weighed 5,000 to 6,000 pounds, they had speeds approaching 100 mph and handled with the fleetness of many smaller cars. Maybach chassis were as eagerly sought by the finest coachworks as were those of Bugatti and Hispano-Suiza. They were Germany's contribution to the golden age of the automobile.

Hungary

VERY LITTLE is known about the Hungarian automobile industry prior to the 1939–45 war. Because Hungary was associated with Austria under the Hapsburg dual monarchy prior to 1919, some have assumed that automotive developments were inextricably linked with Vienna. Such belief is only partially warranted. As early as 1875 Magyar inventors were laboring to create their own cars.

The records of many of the achievements of Hungarian automobilists were destroyed in two World Wars. Were it not for the devotion of Lajos and Ottó Haris, the automotive history of their countrymen would probably not be in evidence today. In downtown Budapest, the Haris Testvérek—Haris brothers—operate what is probably one of the world's most unique museums. The Haris brothers have emphasized that their museum "is not one established or helped by the state. It is definitely a private, amateur museum." While a few, full-sized cars are displayed, the vast majority of the exhibits are highly detailed scale models built by the Haris brothers.

Of the more than one hundred exhibits, about three dozen are concerned with Hungarian-designed and built motor cars dating from 1875 to 1940. Unfortunately, the active production years of the various marques have proved difficult to trace. The development of Hungarian cars, however, is facilitated by the sketchy data and photographs.

The history of Hungary's automobiles began in 1875 when György Wessely secured a patent on his ornately gilded, self-propelled coach. With an unidentified engine —probably a paraffin burner—powering the rear axle, the "Colonet," as it was named, is preserved in model form in the Haris brothers' remarkable museum. How the "Colonet" performed, or if it was satisfactory, is not known. The driver sat on the high front coachman's bench and steered the centrally pivoted front wheels by a lever and handle mechanism. Brakes were the usual external shoes acting upon the steel tires of the large rear wheels, but there were additional prong-like devices which were apparently levered against the ground to prevent rolling backward on grades. Wessely's patent drawings also included designs for more practical motor carriages of smaller size.

For the next twenty years, Hungarian mechanics seem to have satisfied themselves with a few Daimler and Benz motor carriages. There is evidence that some engines

In 1875 György Wessely powered an ornate coach with an internal combustion engine. This was the "Colonet," Hungary's first horseless carriage. (*Haris Testvérek Autó Múzeuma*)

Donát Bánki and János Csonka constructed this pioneer carburetor in 1892 in Budapest. (*Haris Testvérek Autó Múzeuma*)

from those pioneer factories in Germany and from De Dion in France were imported and built under license in and around Budapest. By 1890, however, some important indigenous developments were coming to the fore.

In 1892, Donát Bánki and János Csonka built the first carburetor in Hungary. Illustrated here, the carburetor appears to be a simple gravity tank with a metering device. Four years later in 1896, the first Csonka car is said to have appeared. From the photographs of the model available, the car was a small two-seater with an advanced type frame, semi-elliptic springs, and what appears to be a differential housing for a shaft drive on the rear axle. A single-cylinder engine developed 4 horsepower and the implication is that a small series was produced. In all fairness, the vintage of the 1896 Csonka seems to be open to argument because there were no known shaft and differential axle drives at this early date (see Renault). In 1902 and 1904 the Bánki-Csonka combine built several series of 2 and 4-cylinder cars, a number of which were used by the Postal Service.

Repair shops were being established throughout the Budapest area to care for the needs of owners of imported motor cars. The first shop is said to have been established by Nándor Hora. In addition to repairing motor cars and bicycles, Hora assembled the 1898 car illustrated with a modern Budapest street scene in the background. This car built by Hora is known in Hungary as the 1898 or 1900 Aurore because of the trademark, and also is referred to as the Aurore-Klement. Because of the latter name, it is believed that Nándor Hora had the cooperation, and probably the technical assistance, of the manufacturers of the Laurin & Klement which was being produced in Prague. According to Lajos and Ottó Haris, however, the Aurore is the "first" Hungarian marque. Evidently mechanic Hora built several similar vehicles, voiturettes on fully-elliptic springs and quite attractive. Nándor Hora continued to build cars until at least 1905.

The marque Podvinecz-Heisler does not appear in any known register of the world's cars. Nevertheless, a machine factory by the same name introduced their first motor vehicle in 1900—the six-eight seater shown.

The first Csonka was this 1-cylinder, two-seater said to be of 1896; the overall design appears to be of a much later vintage. (*Haris Testvérek Autó Múzeuma*)

The Bánki-Csonka 3-HP, 2-cylinder car of 1902 had a curved dash and a luggage box. (*Haris Testvérek Autó Múzeuma*)

In 1904, János Csonka built a series of 4-cylinder vehicles for the Postal Service. (*Haris Tesvérek Autó Múzeuma*)

In 1898, mechanic Nándor Hora constructed his first car, this 1-cylinder voiturette seen here on the museum grounds in downtown Budapest. (*Haris Testvérek Autó Múzeuma*)

This vehicle was powered by a 1-cylinder, 8-HP engine and was placed in public service as a bus. The final drive was by a ring gear on the left rear wheel. The Podvinecz-Heisler marque continued for several years. The same firm also built a line of luxury cars named Phönix. Of fairly conventional design, very high to accommodate the head-gear of the aristocracy and nobility, Phönix cars used chain drive and were powered by 4-cylinder engines. Whether an actual example of a Phönix car exists today is not known. The 1/5 scale model illustrated is on display in the Auto Múzeuma in Buda-pest and depicts the 15-horsepower, 1910 landaulet owned by Princess Augusta von Hapsburg. The automobiles built for the Hapsburgs were as ornate as any horsedrawn coach for the royalty of the old empire who spared no expense as they traveled. As a

The 1900 Podvinecz-Heisler. Note the gear drive mechanism on the rear wheel. The Tauril tires were also of Hungarian manufacture. (*Haris Testvérek Autó Múzeuma*)

distinct marque, the Phönix seems to have disappeared with the Hapsburgs.

Another obscure marque was the Géza Szám which seems to have enjoyed limited popularity from 1902 for a few years. With obvious resemblance to the Renault of the period, the scale model by the Haris brothers discloses a 1-cylinder, 4-HP, water-cooled engine and a propeller shaft final drive. Relatively small two-seaters, most of this marque appear to have been built for the Hungarian State Postal Service.

In 1907, an engineer named István Bory experimented with single-cylinder, air-cooled engines and the same year introduced a 7-HP, two-seater roadster. From the information available, the little Bory had a tubular frame, semi-elliptic leaf spring suspension and a chain drive. A single large headlamp, raked steering column and a high seat behind a very low dashboard gave the tiny runabout a dashing look for its time. The Bory, built by the Josef Bory Automobilfabrik in Budapest, survived, intermittently, until

This is a skillfully built (1/5 actual size) model of the 1910 Phönix landaulet which was owned by Princess Auguszta von Hapsburg. (*Haris Testvérek Autó Múzeuma*)

about 1923 when it disappeared as an independent make.

One of the better known Hungarian marques was the Magomobil. Sometimes called the MAG, this make had its beginning before the 1914–18 war and survived well into the '30s. Manufactured in series by the Magyar Altalanos Gépgyár, the 1913–14 five-passenger touring cars were straightforward in design, had electric lighting, and were powered by 4-cylinder engines of unknown specification. A fairly large concern, the M.A.G. works survived the war and produced fairly conventional brougham, se-

dan and open cars during the twenties. In 1926, an attractive model was produced and many of these saw service in Budapest as taxicabs. The 1.2-litre engine had four cylinders. Styling was conventional as was the chassis structure although the engine hood and radiator shell resembled some Italian Fiats of the period. In 1928, a luxury Magomobil was produced with a 50-HP, 6-cylinder engine. Fairly large, there were seats for six persons. Also called the "Magosix," this larger sedan had a maximum speed of 55–60 mph. Some were fitted with open sporting coachwork. More than likely, few, if

Géza Szám single-cylinder cars were used by the
Hungarian Postal Service in 1902–04. (*Haris
Testvérek Autó Múzeuma*)

The 1907 Bory was the first air-cooled car built in Hungary. (*Haris Testvérek Autó Múzeuma*)

any, Magomobils survived the war and the examples shown are Haris-built scale models of superb detail.

Another prestige car in Hungary was the Raba which lasted from 1904 until after 1943 when hostilities caused its demise. Even then the Raba works continued to build trucks for military use until the automotive industry was nationalized in postwar years. Raba is significant for having manufactured the first automotive diesel engines in Hungary in 1923 when 40 HP, 4-cylinder units were installed in cars and trucks. The heyday, however, was between 1912 and 1918 when the luxurious Raba "Grand" was the pride of the Raba-Györ works. Again, details are lacking but an examination of the 1914 type modeled by the Haris brothers discloses a gold-trimmed

formal brougham of undoubted quality and, most likely, fair performance. This particular "Grand" was an official car for Hungary's last king, Charles IV. There were some smaller Raba cars also, and the factory produced another little known marque called the Stolz.

Hungary's troubled history during much of this century has militated against widespread industrial development. There were, however, other Hungarian makes of cars. Manfred Weiss built some cars called the M.W. but specialized in trucks from 1920 to the mid-'30s as did the Szilvay-Mávag works which became locally famous for fire trucks and lasted until World War II. The Röck was built by a machinery factory beginning about 1905 and continued for several years, finally manufacturing large cars and

Magomobil cars were well known in Hungary. The 1913–14 type touring car is shown. (*Haris Testvérek Autó Múzeuma*)

A 1926 Magomobil taxicab (front) and a pair of
1913–14 Mag tourers. (*Haris Testvérek Autó
Múzeuma*)

Raba cars were prestigious like the 1914 "Grand"
parade car which belonged to Charles IV, the last
king of Hungary. This exquisitely detailed (⅕ scale) model is complete to the royal ensign on
the front fender. (*Haris Testvérek Autó Múzeuma*)

Master model builder, Lajos Haris, with several of the models built in partnership with his brother, Ottó. The large limousine is a 1908 Csonka. (*Haris Testvérek Autó Múzeuma*)

busses. Other obscure marques were the Lorenc & Lorenc of 1901–05, and the Méray Loránt which was built in limited numbers from about 1907 until the late '20s. The Magyar Automobil R-T works produced Marta cars and commercial vehicles in co-operation with Austro-Daimler from around 1912 until the depression years. During the years when Hungary was establishing its independence after the 1914–18 war, there were many attempts to establish a progressive auto industry. The Fejes earned some popularity in the '20s and '30s and may have been one of the last independent private car marques in Hungary before the war. Other manufacturers assembled cars of Czech, German and French origin. Since nationalization, new vehicles have appeared; most have been trucks and other urgently needed commercial types.

435

Italy

CENTURIES AGO the great Leonardo da Vinci turned his thoughts to diverse types of propulsion. Not until 1854, however, did a self-propelled Italian land vehicle materialize which could pass muster as an automobile. In that year Virginio Bordino built a steam carriage which is now a treasured exhibit in the Museo dell'Automobile in Turin. The first successful attempt to harness the internal combustion engine to a vehicle in Italy was in 1895 when Michele Lanza built ten or twelve powered wagons. At about the same time, a Professor Enrico Bernardi built a car. Lanza gave up the effort and returned to his candle factory. Bernardi also soon lost interest. But cars filtering into Italy from France, Switzerland and other neighbors were whetting the appetites of industrialists in a country where craftsmanship was traditional.

One of these industrialists was Giovanni Agnelli of Turin who secured backing in July, 1889, to found an enterprise expressly to manufacture automobiles—the Fabbrica Italiana Automobili Torino. Thus was born F.I.A.T. Within a few years, Fiat cars outnumbered all other Italian marques; today this dominance still prevails. The first Fiat cars were high-riding, 2-cylinder, 3.5-HP carriages. These rapidly gave way to 4-cylinder closed broughams, town cars and tourers with piston displacements approaching 4-litres.

Agnelli attracted capital and developed his firm as a joint stock company. He had the industrialist's talent for securing top engineering and production personnel, and he also understood the value of publicity which—in those days as now—meant racing victories. As early as 1902, Agnelli fielded racing teams and in that year a Fiat driven by Felice Nazzaro won the Tour of Italy, a 1,300-mile event, at an average speed of 23 mph. Fiats were raced all over Europe and America. The big red cars were achieving amazing speeds: in 1906 a 179 HP Fiat did 155 mph, and in 1908 a 200 HP racer won the American Grand Prix in Savannah, Georgia. With this victory came a demand for Fiats in the United States and a factory was established in Poughkeepsie, N.Y. where they were built under license until 1917. Fiats won the Grand Prix of France before the 1914–18 war and a score of other events of similar rank with special racers. Those huge, 4-cylinder engines displaced as much as 16.5-litres and had pushrod-operated, inclined overhead valves.

436

Ancestor of all modern Fiats were the high-riding
1899–1900 carriages powered by 679-cc., 2-cyl-
inder, 3.5-HP engines. (*S. A. Fiat*)

Passengers entered through a rear door in the 12-
HP semi-brougham of 1902–03. The 3,770 cc.
4-cylinder engine indicates a rapid development.
(*S. A. Fiat*)

The Type 4 of 1910–18 was the most luxurious early Fiat, an extension front landaulet. The 5,699-cc. engine developed 45 HP at 1,600 RPM. A similar Type 2 had a 28-HP, 1.8-litre engine. (S. A. *Fiat*)

Sporting coachwork with "mother-in-law" seat on the 1912–15 Fiat Type 3 "Ter" chassis. With 4-cylinder, 4,396-cc., 40-HP engine, the top speed was nearly 60 MPH. (S. A. *Fiat*)

By 1912, Fiat efforts were concentrated upon producing a wide range of cars for the marketplace in Italy. Fiats were increasingly popular in other European countries, too. Fiat produced cars and trucks for the Italian Army and developed a range of aircraft engines and complete aircraft as well. Most Fiats tended to be large, in fact the Type 520 "Super Fiat" of 1921–23 was a huge, expensive luxury vehicle with either open or closed coachwork on a massive 152-inch wheelbase. The engine of the "Super" was a V-12 with 85 x 100 mm. bore and stroke and a displacement of 6,805 cc. Weighing well over 5,000 pounds without passengers, this giant's 50/60 HP engine propelled it at 80 mph, a respectable speed for powerful cars of half the weight.

During the '30s, Fiat began to produce cars of more moderate size and cost for the masses and this program was sharpened with the introduction of the 4-cylinder, 1-litre "Ballila" models which rolled off the assembly lines by the scores of thousands up to the outbreak of World War Two. For the family man who wanted more performance and space, there was the 1934–37 "Ardita" with a 2-litre engine in a 106.3-inch-wheelbase chassis. In between was the 1.5-litre, Type 1500 series brought out in 1935. These three ranges of 4-cylinder models set the pace for Fiat's resurgence in 1945 after the factories were virtually wiped off the landscape during Allied bombing.

Fiat absorbed several smaller manufacturers beginning in 1900 when Fiat bought out Giovanni and Matteo Ceirano who were producing bicycles and light cars named Welleyes in Turin. The two principal employees of the Ceirano brothers were Vin-

This large, 7-passenger, 1913 Fiat Type 3-3A tourer is in the Lindley Bothwell collection. (*Joseph H. Wherry*)

Type 501 was exceptionally popular and remained in production from 1919 through 1926. The four cylinders (65 x 110 mm.) displaced 1,460 cc. Rating was 23 HP. An overhead-valve model 501-S was also available and, with nearly 70 mph on tap, won many sports car races. Wheelbase was 104.3 inches. (S. A. *Fiat*)

Type 505 Fiat of 1919–25 was a larger 120-inch-wheelbase, 2.3 litre, 4-cylinder chassis on which a variety of coachwork was fitted. (S. A. *Fiat*)

Type 520, the "Super Fiat" of 1921–23, was a 6.8-litre, V-12-cylinder giant on a 152-inch-wheelbase chassis. This 40/60-HP model reached about 80 mph. Chassis alone cost upwards of $8,000. (S. A. *Fiat*)

cenzo Lancia, then just nineteen years old, and Claudio Fogolin; both of them took positions with Fiat when the Welleyes enterprise was purchased. The Ceirano brothers re-entered business in 1902 and built the limited production Ceirano cars until about 1927, the final model being the 4-cylinder, 1.5-litre Type S-150; they also built the SCAT cars from 1906 to 1927 as the second marque of their Società Ceirano Automobili Torino. The marque SCAT was a sporting vehicle and gained fame by winning the Targa Florio in 1911, 1912 and 1914. Had it not been for the first Ceirano effort of 1898–1900, Vincenzo Lancia might have become an accountant as his father had wished. Instead, Lancia found his life's work at Fiat.

The young Lancia became famous as a racing driver on big, red Fiat racers; in his spare time he tested Fiat passenger cars. His first victory was in July, 1900, when he won at Padova in a 6-HP racer. Reckoning his apprenticeship completed in 1906, Lancia entered into partnership with Claudio Fogolin, established Lancia & C., and introduced the first Lancia a year later in Turin after a fire nearly wiped out the small factory.

All Lancias, from the first, have borne Greek alphabet names, thus the 1907–09 "Alpha" which in prototype form developed 14 HP at 1,450 RPM. The third "Alpha" prototype, illustrated, was an 18/24 HP, 4-cylinder, 2.5-litre, double phaeton fitted with coachwork by Carrozzeria Locati & Torreta. The 90 x 100 mm. cylinders were cast in pairs, side valves were used as was a high tension magneto and a 4-speed gearbox. From the first, Lancia employed propeller shaft drive although the majority of cars were still using chains and sprockets. The "Alpha" was successful and was put into production. In 1908, the "Dial-

441

Chassis price alone of the Type 519 Fiat catalogued in 1922–24 was around $4,400. The 6-cylinder, 4.8-litre, overhead-valve engine developed 77 HP at 2,600 RPM. Pistons were aluminum and there were five main bearings. Wheelbase was 142 inches, 4-wheel brakes were hydraulic and speed was about 75 mph. (*S. A. Fiat*)

On a wheelbase of 133.9 inches, the 1928–29 Fiat Type 525 was another in a vast array of luxury models. An overhead-valve, 6-cylinder, 3.8-litre engine developed 68.5 HP at 3,200 RPM. Speed was about 65 mph. (*S. A. Fiat*)

1773

While serving in Asmara, Ethiopia, with the U. S. Army in 1963, Sgt. James R. Daniel purchased this circa-1932 Fiat 524C from its original owner. A 6-cylinder sports sedan, the rear doors have interior handles only. Identification was made from chassis and engine numbers. (*James R. Daniel*)

The "Ballila Sport" of 1932–34 was one of a wide range of small, 995-cc., 4-cylinder Fiats on wheelbases around 90 inches. With 30 HP at 4,000 RPM, this 508S would do about 68 mph. (S. A. *Fiat*)

Fiat Type 518C "Ardita" of 1933–34 was a 65-mph, 106.3-inch-wheelbase family sedan. The 4-cylinder, 1,944-cc. engine developed 45 HP at 3,600 RPM. Type 527 was a similar 2.5-litre model. (S. A. *Fiat*)

Varied coachwork was installed on Fiat 1500 chassis. A 6-cylinder, 1,493-cc. engine developed 45 HP at 4,400 RPM and gave speeds around 70 mph. Introduced in 1935, the "1500" was brought back after World War Two and remained available through 1948. (S. A. *Fiat*)

Fiat's small car, the 500 "Topolina" had a 569-cc., 4-cylinder, 13-HP engine on a 78.74-inch wheelbase. Produced from 1936–39 and after the war through 1948, this tiny two-seater inspired many similar small cars. (S. A. *Fiat*)

The first Lancia was the "Alpha" 18–24 HP of 1907–09. The 4-cylinder, 2.5-litre engine developed 28 HP at 1,800 RPM and drove car at over 55 mph. More than 100 were sold. (*Lancia & C.*)

pha" appeared with a 3,815 cc., 6-cylinder engine developed from the "Alpha" engine. Although the 6-cylinder car had a speed of 68 mph, there was scant market in Italy for such a vehicle and it was not continued.

In 1909, Lancia again took to the racing circuits but in his own cars and in 1910 he set a mile record on the Modena circuit with an average of fractionally more than 70 mph. Production cars were built in a bewildering array—the 4-cylinder, 3.1-litre "Beta" of 1909 had a monobloc followed in 1910 by the "Gamma," a 3.4-litre of which more than 250 were built and quickly sold. In 1911, Lancia and Fogolin acquired larger facilities in anticipation of the orders which seemed inevitable when their cars were displayed in the many motor shows of the period. The "Delta" was followed by the "Didelta," the "Epsilon" and the "Eta" which had a 4-litre, side valve engine and a

dry single plate clutch. Up until the "'Eta," Lancias had the leather cone clutch. In 1912, Lancia built a series of cars which first used steel disc rather than wood artillery type wheels; called the "IZ," a large batch were built for the Italian Army. The "Theta" followed in 1913. Known also as the 25/35 Lancia, some 1,700 were built.

On the 5th of June, 1915, Lancia secured patents on an advanced V-8 engine with the cylinder banks arranged at an angle of 45 degrees. But Italy had entered the war and the Lancia works expanded again and built military trucks for the duration. Late in 1918, the V-8 engine was dusted off and a new V-12 engine was developed and displayed at the London and Paris Shows of 1919. The cylinder banks were staggered and set at a narrow 20 degrees and, the first time on a Lancia, the valves were overhead as was the single camshaft. Bore and stroke

446

Vincenzo Lancia in one of his 1909 racing cars. (*Lancia & C.*)

were 80 x 130 mm., the displacement 7,837 cc. Due to economic conditions, however, neither the V-8 nor the V-12 models were produced. The new 4-cylinder, 5-litre "Kappa" was an immediate success, though, and it introduced a variable rake steering column, electric starter, and an interior gear change lever. Kappa's 35 HP (taxable rating) engine gave these clean torpedo tourers a top speed of 75 mph; it was produced during 1919–20. An improved version, the "Dikappa" of 1921, had overhead valves, lightweight coachwork of walnut and acacia framing and aluminum panels. In 1922, the "Trikappa" appeared with a 4.6-litre V-8 engine that developed 98 BHP at 2,500 RPM.

The most famous of all Lancia types was the "Lambda" introduced at the London and Paris Shows in 1922 after prototypes had undergone three years of development. A narrow, 20-degree, V-4 engine of 2,120 cc. displacement initially developed 49 HP. In all, nine series of the "Lambda" were produced through 1930 while the power progressively increased to 69 HP and the speed to a maximum of 78 mph. The "Lambda" pioneered the integrated body-frame type of structure. Sporting open Lambdas had a wheelbase of 122 inches. This model also pioneered independent front-wheel suspension using coil springs concentric with hydraulic shock absorbers in a unique pillar design, illustrated, which gave phenomenal steering control and unexcelled handling. Four-wheel brakes and a variety of coachwork for luxurious town cars and limousines on 132.5-inch wheelbases made the Lambda an all-time favorite with the wealthy and enthusiasts. Some 13,000 were built. For the customer requiring luxury during the early '30s, the "Dilambda" offered

Lancia built nearly 1,200 cars in three series during 1911–12. A mono-bloc, 4-cylinder engine powered this luxury landaulet on 128-inch wheelbase. (*Lancia & C.*)

The Lancia "Lambda" 2nd series V-4, 2-litre, 14/60-HP chassis with superb formal coachwork. Lambdas were built from 1922 through 1930 and introduced unit construction of body and chassis. (*Lancia & C.*)

Front view of Lancia "Lambda" prototype shows pillar type independent front suspension, a revolutionary development in 1922. (*Lancia & C.*)

The Lancia 35-HP "Kappa" of 1919–20 had 5-litre, 4-cylinder engine and speed of 75 mph. A large luxury car, pedal-operated electric starting was standard. (*Lancia & C.*)

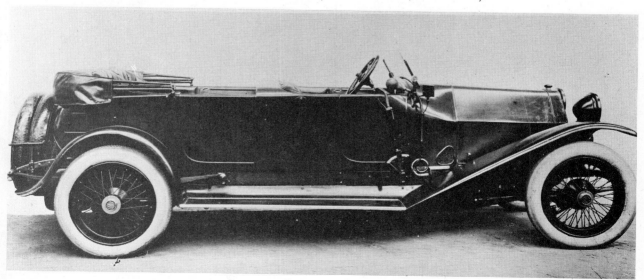

The Lancia "Lambda" 5th series with sporting 5-seater coachwork on 144-inch wheelbase. (*Lancia & C.*)

The Lancia "Lambda" 8th series long-wheelbase, 2.6-litre, V-4 luxury sedan. (*Lancia & C.*)

The Lancia "Dilambda" series 1 of 1931 had a 24-degree V-8 engine displacing 3,960 cc. Output was 100 HP at 4,000 RPM. Speeds ranged from 75 to 80 mph or more depending upon wheelbase and coachwork. (*Courtesy of Harrah's Automobile Collection*)

custom coachwork on a separate X-type frame. A 3,960 cc., narrow, 24-degree, V-8 engine with pushrod-operated overhead valves developed 100 horsepower at 4,000 RPM. The long 100 mm. stroke gave high torque through a 4-speed gearbox and top speeds of 75–80 mph. In all, 1,685 were built on wheelbases of 129.5 and 136.6 inches.

Independent front suspension was used on the 2-litre, V-4, 52-HP "Artena" and the 2.6-litre, V-8, 68-HP "Astura" models introduced in 1931. Engines were mounted on leaf springs which were secured to the frame as vibration dampeners. The Artena's maximum speed was 68 mph, the Astura's around 75 mph. Enclosed bodies only, works-built or by coachbuilders, were mated with the frame. Production lasted through 1937. The integral body-frame of the "Lambda" was scaled down in 1932 and in 1933 the "Augusta" was marketed with a lovely little 1,194 cc., V-4 engine which developed 35 HP at 4,000 RPM. Pillar-type independent front suspension was used with leaf spring rear suspension. The gearbox had four speeds and the propeller shaft employed flexible disc couplings rather than conventional universal joints. Moderately priced, three series of the "Augusta" were produced through 1935. On the small side and seating four persons, the "Augusta" was often entered in sporting events winning class victories several times in the Mille Miglia and other races.

The final Lancia types prior to the Second

Lancia "Dilambda" wheelbases were 129.5 and 136.6 inches. Production started in 1929 and con- tinued for four years. (*Lancia & C.*)

The Lancia "Artena" of 1931 had 1,924 cc., V-4 engine developing 52 HP at 4,000 RPM. Wheel- base was 117.60 inches. (*Lancia & C.*)

Lancia "Augusta" of 1933–35 was lightweight, 1.2-litre V-4 which had 35 HP at 4,000 RPM and 65 mph speed in basic touring form. (*Lancia & C.*)

World War were the 1,351 cc. "Aprilia" of 1937–40 and the 903 cc. "Ardea" of 1939–40; each model had V-4 engines. The "Aprilia" was the last of Vincenzo Lancia's creations. He died unexpectedly in February, 1937, at 55 years of age. Both models were reintroduced after the war as the foundation for the continued success of the enterprise founded by the soup maker's son who was trained to be an accountant, but turned racing driver and engineer.

The exploits of Italian cars on the world's racing circuits have become legendary, and no marque has contributed more than Alfa Romeo. The first of this marque, then A.L.F.A., was the 4-litre, side-valve Type 20–30 of 1910 which materialized when the Darracq firm of France found that it was useless to pour more francs into their Italian subsidiary in Portello after a batch of cars assembled from French-made parts proved unsuccessful. From the outset, engineer Giuseppe Merosi developed the new cars around monobloc engines. The A.L.F.A.

was first seen in competition in the 1911 Targa Florio when a 20–30 HP racer came close to winning. The 6-litre, 40–60 HP model of 1913–15 sat on a 126-inch wheelbase and seemed destined for success. With lightweight bodies, speeds of 70–75 mph were common and when the Count Ricotti had Carrozzeria Castagna build a fully streamlined and closed body on a 40–60 chassis, speeds of 85 mph gave A.L.F.A. widespread publicity.

Merosi was ready to field a grand prix racer in 1914, a 4-cylinder machine of 4.5-litres with dual overhead camshafts, when war preparations submerged the Portello factory in military production. In 1915, Nicola Romeo brought industrial experience and capital to the struggling remains of the Darracq fiasco, reorganized the enterprise and changed the car's name to Alfa Romeo. In 1919, Romeo resurrected the 1914 grand prix racer which won several minor events and was entered in the Brescia Gentleman's Grand Prix in 1921; Campari led the race

The first all-Italian car from the ex-Darracq works in Portello was the A.L.F.A. 24 HP of 1910. Power was by a side valve, 4,084 cc., mono-bloc engine. Racing debut was in 1911 Targa Florio. (*Alfa Romeo Milano*)

In 1914, Count Ricotti had Castagna build this fully enclosed, streamlined body on a 40–60-HP A.L.F.A. chassis. Top speed exceeded 85 mph. (*Alfa Romeo Milano*)

Berlina coachwork on the 1921–22 Alfa Romeo 20–30 ES Sport 114.2 inch-wheelbase chassis. (*Alfa Romeo Milano*)

The 1923 Alfa Romeo P1 had a 6-cylinder, 2-litre, dual overhead-camshaft engine. With supercharger, 118 BHP was developed at 5,000 RPM. Intended as a grand prix racer, it was not successful. (*Alfa Romeo Milano*)

The 1923 Alfa Romeo 3-litre RL racer was named for the Targa Florio which it won the same year.

Enzo Ferrari won several of his early victories on this type. (*Alfa Romeo Milano*)

In production from 1922 to 1928, the Alfa Romeo RL-SS chassis had a 3-litre, DOHC engine developing from 71 to 83 HP at 3,500–3,600 RPM.

Two-seater boat-tailed Bertone coachwork shown. (*Alfa Romeo Milano*)

Pirola and Guidotti in the Alfa Romeo 6C 1,500 SS in which they won their class in the 1929 Mille Miglia. The 6-cylinder, 1,487-cc., supercharged engine developed 84 BHP at 5,000 RPM; speed 95–100 mph. (*Alfa Romeo Milano*)

Alfa Romeo's 6C 1,750 dominated sports car racing in the early thirties. Dual overhead-camshaft, 1,752-cc., 6-cylinder engines had outputs upward of 46 HP. (*Courtesy of Henry Ford Museum*)

for thirteen laps when a leaking radiator forced retirement. Despite this, the sporting tradition of Alfa Romeo was established.

Sporting, sedan and formal coachwork was fitted during 1921–22 to the 20–30 ES Sport models, fine 4.25-litre, 67 HP machines. In 1923, the first all-out racing car of modern design from Portello was unveiled. Designed to the then-new international Two Litre Formula, the P1 had 6 cylinders with dual overhead camshafts operating the valves in hemispherical combustion chambers. Merosi's finest design to date, the P1 was withdrawn from serious competition when Ugo Sivocci was fatally injured in an accident during tests on the Monza circuit before the Grand Prix of Europe in 1923. The P1 was capable of 112 mph and one of the three built turned faster speeds later when tested with a supercharger.

Alfa Romeo's first big racing victory was in the 1923 Targa Florio with the 3-litre RL sports type stripped for maximum performance. Soon Alfas were placing high in other events and raising havoc with the well laid plans of Bugatti, Mercedes and other potent marques with longer experience.

About this time a gifted engineer, Vittorio Jano, left Fiat and joined Alfa. His first Grand Prix design, the famed P2 with an amazing 2-litre, 8-cylinder engine was readied for the 1924 season. With dual overhead camshafts and a supercharger, the P2 developed 175 BHP at 5,500 RPM. Throughout 1924 and 1925, a team of P2s piloted by Campari, Antonio Ascari, Count Brilli-Peri and others won enough races to capture the world's championship for Alfa Romeo. The P2 cars remained active through 1930 and an accounting of their successes would require a volume.

Dual overhead camshafts, superchargers and racing victories became a virtual way of life for Alfa Romeo right up to the 1939–45 war. In Alfa Romeo parlance, the designation "6C" means 6 cylinders, "8C" indicates 8 cylinders, etc. The 6C 1,500, a basic 1.5-litre type produced during the '30s, in many variants, won the Mille Miglia in 1929 and went on to dominate sports car events. They were followed by the 6C 1,750 (1¾ litres), the 8C 2,300, 8C 2,600 and 8C 2,900 (2.3, 2.6 and 2.9 litres) which also were built for racing and touring in all body styles from open two-seaters to expensive cabriolets with coachwork by the finest Carrozzeria. In 1938, the 8C 308, a supercharged 3-litre delivering 295 BHP at 6,000 RPM, paved the way for the fantastic 1.5-litre Type 158 and the post-war Type 159 monopostos that brought two more world championships to Alfa Romeo and vaulted drivers like Fangio of Argentina and Giuseppe Farina, a racing driver with a Ph.D., to international fame.

Few marques anywhere have incorporated more engineering knowledge won on the racing circuits into passenger car design than has Alfa Romeo. The war prevented the racing world from seeing what twin-engined Alfas could do or whether up to 16 cylinders were worthwhile. The modern racing marque, Ferrari, stems directly from the close cooperation between Enzo Ferrari and Alfa Romeo.

All told, Italy has seen some 100 separate makes of cars come and go. There were few better cars anywhere than the Brescia-Züst which thrived from 1906 to 1914. In 1908, a 4.5-litre Züst placed third in the New York-Siberia-Paris race behind the winning Thomas Flyer. The products of another of those Swiss engineers who seemed to pop up in Spain, Russia, the U.S.A. and elsewhere, the Züst range also included larger models with 4.7-litre engines. All were sporting in nature.

Diatto, made in Turin from 1907 to 1930,

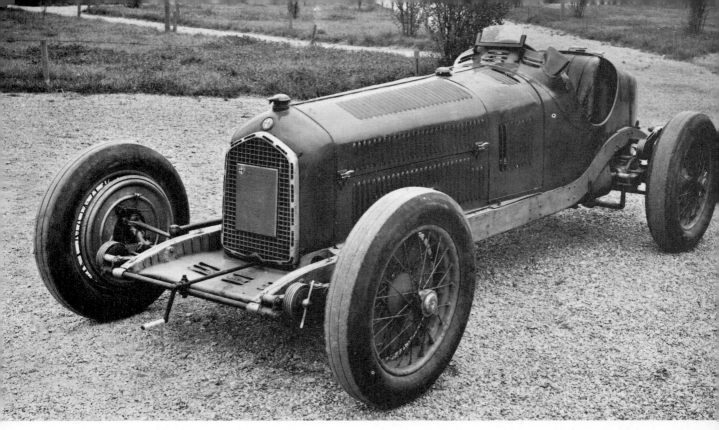

The great 1932 Alfa Romeo type B (later called P3) had a 2,654-cc., 8-cylinder, DOHC engine with two superchargers and dual propeller shafts. (*Alfa Romeo Milano*)

Alfa Romeo built the 8C 2,300 from 1931 through 1934 in grand turismo, racing and grand prix versions. This is the long chassis—122-inch wheelbase—cabriolet with Castagna coachwork. The 142-HP at 5,000 RPM, 2.3-litre engine had eight cylinders and dual overhead-camshafts. (*Courtesy of Henry Ford Museum*)

Only eighty-six of these 6C 2,300 B grand turismo Alfa Romeos were built in 1936–37. The dual overhead-camshaft, 6-cylinder, 2.3-litre engine developed 76 HP at 4,400 RPM. Maximum speed was over 80 mph. (*Alfa Romeo Milano*)

The 1935–38 Alfa Romeo 6C 2,300 B "Mille Miglia" took fourth place overall and first in touring classification in the 1937 event of the same name. Only a limited number were built. (*Alfa Romeo Milano*)

One of the most beautiful of the supercharged Alfa Romeo grand prix, single-seaters was the 8C 308 of 1938. The 8-cylinder, blown, 3-litre engine delivered 295 BHP at 6,000 RPM, provided a top speed of 160–165 mph. (*Alfa Romeo Milano*)

A 1908 Brixia Züst similar to this model placed third in the 1908 New York via Siberia to Paris race. The 4-cylinder 1,495 cc. engine developed 10 HP (tax rating) at 1,000 RPM. Production lasted from 1907 to 1914. (*Museo dell 'Automobil, Turin*)

Reputed to have been built for Rudolph Valentino at a cost of $35,000, this Isotta-Fraschini Type 8 of 1924 had eight 85 x 130 mm.-cylinders and delivered 80 HP. The 145-inch wheelbase-chassis cost around $7,000 minus coachwork. The owner is Tony Luther. (*Joseph H. Wherry*)

often used Bugatti engines built under license in the early years. In the '20s, Diattos had 2-litre, overhead camshaft and 4-cylinder, 3-litre engines of high quality.

Bianchi went back even farther, to 1900 when Edoardo Bianchi added cars to his line of bicycles. Very limited in number, the Bianchi limousines of pre-World War ·One days eventually gave way to special modifications of Fiat and other makes.

The Ansaldo cars were a hand-built side-line of the well-known aircraft and armaments firm based in Turin. The Type 4CS sports cars of 1923–26 were perhaps the finest Ansaldos. On wheelbases ranging from 109 to 128 inches, 1.8-litre, 4-cylinder engines were used. Later 2-litre, 6-cylinder engines with many aluminum components powered the 6BN and 6BC types. In 1930, the Type 18 had a 2.8-litre, overhead camshaft, 6-cylinder engine.

Other sporting marques included the OM which was made in Brescia from 1919 to 1948. Despite the use of an outmoded L-head, 6-cylinder, 2-litre engine, an OM captured the first three places in the Mille Miglia in 1927. Hit and miss, OMs showed up in occasional races in the '20s and '30s, sometimes with overhead valves and superchargers.

There was also the SPA, built in Turin from 1906 to 1948. In 1909 an SPA won the Targa Florio. In the 1920s, a small series of 2.7-litre, 4-cylinder and 4.5-litre, 6-cylin-

The magnificent 6-litre, Type 8 Isotta-Fraschini engine. (*Joseph H. Wherry*)

der sports car was built, some with rather sensational custom coachwork by firms like Bertone.

The Itala survived in Turin from 1904 to 1935. Large tourers and limousines with T-head engines on wheelbases around 120 inches predominated but there were racing Italas as well. A famous example of 1908 had a 12-litre, 4-cylinder, F-head (overhead inlet and side exhaust valves) engine developing 100 horsepower and had a flat-out speed of 100 mph. The Italian prince, Scipione Borghese, was a great Itala exponent and driver and in 1907 he won the Peking to Paris race in an 8-litre model with dry sump lubrication. Itala's experiments with rotary valves—used on team cars in the 1913 Grand Prix of France—and economic troubles brought on by World War One led to the marque's eventual decline in a world where low-priced cars were needed.

Temperino, made by a small Turin firm, valiantly tried to capture the low-priced mass market being tapped by Fiat with an attractive car powered by a 2-cylinder air-cooled engine of 1.2-litres. Though simple and cheap, the Temperino lasted only from 1921 to 1924.

Almost alone of all the quality Italian marques that began in the '20s, Maserati has survived. The Maserati brothers set up shop in 1926 in Bologna to build racing and grand turismo cars and their first car, a 1.5-litre, straight-8 was a source of constant irritation to Scuderia Ferrari and their allies in Alfa Romeo. The "Masers" came up fast and have the distinction of winning the 500 mile Indianapolis Memorial Day Race for

463

two years consecutively in 1939 and 1940 with Wilbur Shaw at the wheel. After the war, the Maserati brothers lost control to the Orsi combine but Neptune's trident still marks the "Maser" noses.

Finest of all Italian cars was the Isotta-Fraschini built in Milan from 1900 when Oreste Fraschini and Cesare Isotta secured technical assistance from French interests. In 1905, Fraschini's racers had overhead-camshafts and in 1907 Fernando Minoia—later to win fame on Alfa Romeos—won the Coppa Florio in an overhead-cam Isotta. In 1910, Isotta-Fraschini cars were the first production models anywhere with four-wheel, drum-type brakes. As late as 1913, racers of the marque were still using chain drive. After World War One, the marque became competitive with Hispano-Suiza as an elegant, expensive carriage for the aristocracy and celebrities. From 1920, until the late '30s the Types 8, 8A and 8B were marketed in chassis form with 144–145-inch wheelbases. Most famous, the Type 8A had straight-8, 7.4-litre engines with overhead valves and nine main bearings and cost upwards of $8,000 without coachwork. Beautifully built and quite fast, the Isotta-Fraschini is regarded by many enthusiasts as one of the world's fine cars. For the customer requiring more than 85 mph, the "Spinto" and "Super Spinto" were available on order.

Japan

By the turn of the century, the automobile had arrived in Japan where rapid strides were being made in heavy industry. A world power was in the making. Despite this, it is not likely that an automobile was made in Japan prior to 1902. Even that date is open to question. Archives at the disposal of the Jidosha Kogyo-Kai—the Automotive Industrial Association—do attest that Japanese engineers were beginning to design experimental cars. The first bonafide evidence of a Japanese-built automobile concerns the large steam car built by Torao Yamaba in 1904, a car examined and illustrated in Part III.

The technical knowledge was available, however, and the island empire's expanding trade was providing the necessary materials. Internal combustion gasoline engines had been produced in Japan before 1900 for industrial applications and all of the various systems and components of cars were understood. Two and 4-cylinder engines with air and water cooling were available in either two or four-stroke versions. The recent Pacific war wrote *finis* to many archives so we are faced with sketchy data and little photographic support when we review Japanese cars built prior to 1940.

The earliest gasoline car, for which undeniable documentation exists, is the 1907 Takuri type 3. Presumably types 1 and 2 were prototypes. In style, there is some resemblance to several European cars, particularly to the Laurin & Klement which was imported in the early 1900s. About one dozen Takuris were made—a small but noteworthy series—by the Tokyo Motor Car Works, which was headed by Shintaro Yoshida. Chief Engineer for car development was Komanosuke Uchiyama. The 2-cylinder, horizontally-opposed engine was water cooled by a core type radiator and thermal siphoning. Bore and stroke, respectively, were 4 and 4.5 inches giving a displacement of 113.1 cubic inches (1.9 litres). The output was 12 HP driving through a cone clutch and a 2-speed transmission. Final drive was by dual chains and sprockets.

Takuri coachwork was wood-framed and bolted to a basic steel frame of longitudinal and cross members. The seats for four persons were upholstered in leather. There were no windows other than the windscreen. Semi-elliptic springs were used over each wheel. A single large carbide headlamp was supplemented by a pair of smaller lamps fixed to the windshield frames. Tires were

First "all-Japanese" petrol car, the 1907 Takuri type 3. The water-cooled, horizontally-opposed 2-cylinder engine developed 12 horsepower. Final drive was by dual chains. (*Jidosha Kogyo-Kia*)

Japan's first professional automotive engineer, Komanosuke Uchiyama in one of his cars in 1922. (*Jidosha Kogyo-Kia*)

Obviously rugged construction characterized the 1910 Kunisue cabriolet. Note speedometer drive mechanism in front of axle at right front wheel. (*Jidosha Kogyo-Kia*)

The 1911 Tokyo was one of Japan's first 4-cylinder passenger cars. Closed and open models were built. (*Jidosha Kogyo-Kia*)

Japanese-built military lorries used in the campaign against the German enclave at Tsingtao on the China coast. Note the deeply lugged, hard rubber tires, the chain drive. (*Jidosha Kogyo-Kia*)

Ancestor of the modern Datsun cars was the 1916
Kwaishinsha D.A.T. model 41. (*Jidosha KogyoKia*)

pneumatic. The car was as rugged as it had to be for there were virtually no surfaced roads in the Empire outside of a few large cities. Perhaps the most unusual feature was water cooling for an engine layout that was usually air-cooled. Like its competitors, the Tokyo Motor Car Works soon turned its attention to producing trucks and lorries.

In 1910, the Kunisue Automobile Works built the first Kunisue in Tokyo. A 4-seater cabriolet type of relatively small size, the Kunisue engines were also water-cooled 2-cylinder units developing 8 HP at about 1,800 rpm. Of extraordinarily sturdy construction, as shown by the size of the front beam axle, this car must have been quite heavy for its size. How it performed is not revealed in the scanty data in the surviving records, nor are production figures known

other than that the number built was limited to a small series.

In 1911, the Tokyo Motor Vehicle Works Ltd. (not to be confused with the manufacturer of the Takuri car) brought out the Tokyo car in cooperation with Kunisue. With "full limousine" coachwork, the Tokyo was one of the first Japanese cars of record to be powered by a 4-cylinder, in-line engine. An L-head, water-cooled, with 3.5 by 4.5 inches bore and stroke, this engine was comparatively powerful developing 16–18 HP at 1,800 rpm. Magneto ignition was used. The most luxurious car built in Japan up to 1911, the Tokyo was built in a small series—"in some numbers"—for more than a year but the exact number is not a matter of record. An interesting, but not exclusive, feature was the windshield which could be

469

The "first trial model Datsun" was this two-seater of 1917. Note the loose brake cables beneath the stubby body. (*Jidosha Kogyo-Kia*)

folded upward and secured beneath the roof. Shaft drive was used with a 3-speed transmission, conventional longitudinal leaf springs and two-wheel brakes.

Fewer than fifty passenger cars of all marques and types were built in Japan prior to 1912. After this date, efforts were increased and by 1916 the Kwaishinsha Motor Car Co. Ltd. had introduced the ancestor of the modern Datsun cars. Named the D.A.T. type 41, the limousine models had a 99-inch wheelbase and a tread of 45 inches. A 4-speed gearbox was coupled by a multiplate clutch to a water-cooled, L-head, 4-cylinder engine (3.125 x 4.5 inch bore and stroke, 1.5 litres) that developed 15.8 HP. The D.A.T.'s ignition system utilized a battery and generator, and the final drive was by shaft and bevel gears. Series production of open and closed models was instituted after satisfactory tests.

In 1917, Kwaishinsha was reorganized, renamed the DAT Motor Vehicle Manufacturing Co. Ltd., and relocated in Osaka where production was resumed with the addition of a new model, the first Datsun. This was a sporty little two-seater on pressed steel wheels. Cycle type fenders and a stubby, bathtub-shaped, all-steel body on a wheelbase of about 85 inches made this car suitable for a variety of uses including military. The engine and power train were derived from the preceding D.A.T. type 41 and performance is reported to have been excellent. There was, in fact, a hint of the lines of contemporary small European sports cars; the rear of the body reflected the then popular "tulip" shape and the spare wheel was mounted on the right side.

Mass production was just around the corner in 1922. Another Osaka-based firm, the Jitsuyo Automobile Co. Ltd. introduced the Lila and Lila Peaton models, closed sedan and open tourer types respectively. Both were four-seaters of all-metal construction and used 4-cylinder engines of approximately 2-litres displacement. Employing conventional rail frame and leaf spring sus-

470

Lilla and Lilla Peaton cars, sedans and tourers respectively, were built in Osaka from 1917 to 1940. Doors on this model were located on left side only. Front wheel guards were unusual feature. (*Jidosha Kogyo-Kia*)

pension systems, the Jitsuyo cars were strictly utilitarian and were designed from the start for mass production, having flat sides and no built-in complexities. A unique feature was the individual protective U-shaped iron on each front wheel. Jitsuyo also prepared a slightly more stylish car, the Gorham but it was short-lived.

When the great earthquake of 1923 devastated Japan, automobile production facilities were all but destroyed. Mitsubishi, the huge shipyard enterprise which later engaged in aircraft production, was just getting into volume production of five-passenger limousines and touring cars. When the various plants were rebuilt, Jitsuyo and Datsun enterprises were merged and their models were continued, with varying degrees of success up until the outbreak of war in 1941.

Mitsubishi also rebuilt and resumed activity. Lesser known marques active from about 1921–24 to 1938–40 were the Ohta made by Ateliers Kotsuku in Tokyo and the Ohtomo, a very light-weight, air-cooled series designed by J. Toyokawa who was educated in the United States, and built by Hakuyosha Automobile Co. Ltd.

By 1940, the Datsun was clearly in the ascendancy while the Toyopet made in Koromo and the Toyota, built in Nagoya, were coming rapidly into prominence. These two marques had their genesis in 1936 and 1937 respectively. When the war of 1941–45 began, the Japanese automobile industry had achieved a large measure of maturity although all the marques were small in size, low in power and of moderate performance.

The Netherlands

BEFORE THE TURN of the century, as already observed in Part II, Dutch engineers were busily replacing the horse as prime mover. By 1900, there were at least nine firms making automobiles for sale in the land of dikes.

As elsewhere in Europe, Dutch coachbuilders adapted their art to the new power source. One such firm in Arnhem, in Gelderland province, six miles from the German frontier, built the first motor busses in The Netherlands. The very old photo of a Bij't Vuur autobus reproduced here was taken in 1903 by Mr. G. Riemer when he was a youngster. Still an active enthusiast, Mr. Riemer is now the Director of The Netherlands' National Museum of the Automobile in Driebergen. No technical details are known of this marque; however, this photo is the only one existing of this type which soon faded from the automotive scene.

"Two-plus-two" seating was old hat by 1900 in Amsterdam where Maatschappy Simplex turned out double chain-driven carriages with rear engines. Steering wheels and landaulet-type folding hoods were features of the early Simplex which continued as a marque until about 1912. There is no known connection between the Dutch marque, Simplex, and those in other countries with the same name.

Arnhem was also the birthplace of the Gelria which more or less conformed to the style of the time, as evidenced by the 1901 model shown here weighted down with a large family. Outside of the single-chain drive powered by a 2-cylinder engine mounted low at the rear, and the steering column gear change lever, little more is known of the Gelria which was in production only a few years.

Amersfoort, about 25 miles southeast of Amsterdam, was the seat of the D. H. Eysinck Fabrieken which manufactured bicycles. In 1900, the first Eysinck car appeared. The engine and core-type radiator were in the front beneath a bonnet and the gear change lever was on the steering column which was topped with a steering wheel. Final drive was by two sprocket chains. Smaller than either the first Simplex or Gelria cars, the Eysinck originally accommodated a driver and one passenger. A measure of success enabled this little known Dutch marque to stay in production until the mid-'20s when all production reverted to bikes and motorcycles. The rare photo of the 1908 six-passenger tourer shows the

In 1900, the height of automotive fashion in Amsterdam was this Simplex landaulet. One passenger shared the driver's seat; two more sat up front facing toward the rear. Note the steering wheel. (*Nationaal Museum van de Automobiel*)

Gelria cars were among the earliest marques in The Netherlands. This is the 1901 model with gear-change lever on steering column. (*Nationaal Museum van de Automobiel*)

This photo, taken in 1903 by G. Riemer, is from the prized collection in The Netherlands National Museum of the Automobile, and shows a circa-1900 Bij't Vuur autobus in Amsterdam. (G. Riemer)

Eysinck in one of its best years after it had come of age with 6-cylinder engines, semi-elliptic springs, a conventional 3-speed gearbox, drive-shaft and hypoid final drive. The round radiator has occasionally caused the Eysinck—also produced in limousine form in limited numbers—to be confused with the most famous Dutch make, the Spyker.

In all The Netherlands, the most famous firm of coach and carriage makers was that of H. J. and J. Spyker, brothers of Trompenburg, an Amsterdam suburb. Among the Spyker clients was the Royal Family; a coach they built for Queen Wilhelmina is still used for state ceremonies. In 1898, the brothers reorganized as the Fabrik Nederlands de Automobiel. Their reputation for quality coaches soon brought them an order for a 1-cylinder, two-seater from an importer in Bradford, England. The first Spyker was an immediate success and, from sometime in 1899 for the next two years, the entire output of the Trompenburg enterprise was eagerly purchased by the English firm and the Spyker, as a consequence, gained its early fame in England. That Spyker produced cars in series prior to 1902 is not generally recognized.

It is not clear just when the far-seeing Belgian engineer, Josef Laviolette, was hired as chief designer by the Spykers. The year was probably 1902. At any rate, the world's most advanced car, for its time, rolled out of the Spyker works in mid-1902. Delays prevented H. J. Spyker from driving it in the Paris to Madrid Race. The 1902 Spyker two-seater was a sensation: it had six separately cast cylinders with 91 and 128 mm. bore and stroke (8,676 cc. displacement) and a tough, 7 main bearing crankshaft. The world's first 6-cylinder automobile, this Spyker's engine had splash lubrication for the

474

The prototype Eysinck car of 1900. Manufacturer D. Eysinck is at the wheel. (*Nationaal Museum van de Automobiel*)

connecting rods and pistons and the crankshaft bearings were lubricated by cotton wicks fed from the sump. The valves were operated by a unique worm gear drive, and a low tension magneto supplied current to the make-and-break ignition. The output was 50 brake-horsepower transmitted through a big leather cone clutch and a 3-speed gearbox. Other interesting features were the all-steel frame and four-wheel drive.

475

A large car, the 1908 Eysinck had a 6-cylinder engine. The bracket on the steering column located the rubber horn bulb at the driver's right hand for instant use. (*Nationaal Museum van de Automobiel*)

The latter innovation—also a world first—incorporated a front differential braking device which, with the rear drum brakes, resulted in four-wheel brakes. In 1903, a Spyker 6 was demonstrated at the London Motor Show.

Thus inspired, Napier (see section on England) introduced a 6-cylinder car late in 1903 which, with greater resources behind it, became the first production 6-cylinder marque. As a result, it got the lion's share of publicity while the Spyker brothers had to be content with the honor of showing the way. Now in a place of honor in the National Museum of the Automobile in Driebergen, the 1902 Spyker "Six" is The Netherlands' most prized automotive possession.

Spykers gained more prestige by competing in the 1,000 Mile Reliability Trial in England in 1903 with one of their series-produced 2-cylinder, 10-horsepower two-seaters. Although the Spyker failed to win first place, it did rank well up the list. "The few marks lost were for tire punctures and a 5 minute stop to adjust a trembler (coil) and another 5 minutes for fixing a water hose on the cylinder block. These in no way affected the reliability," stated a Spyker works representative. The 2-cylinder series was continued until about 1912 and ushered in the round radiator.

Family-sized, 4-cylinder Spykers followed. Most of these had 2½-litre engines with bore and stroke of 90 x 100 mm. respectively. Stylewise, the larger 4-cylinder models followed the lines of the 2-cylinder two-seaters. Because the taxable horsepower was 12 and the brake horsepower around 18, these are known as the 12/18 model. Technical details included improved lubrication systems, 3-speed transmissions with sliding gears, conventional rear-wheel drive by a propeller shaft, expanding drum-type brakes on the rear wheels only and high-tension magneto ignition. Semi-elliptic springs were used, front and rear, and the front suspension was years ahead of its time: the pat-

ented one-piece front axle was hollow throughout its length and featured unique "ball joints" at each end rather than the usual kingpins. These ball joints were enclosed in spherical bronze cups which sealed them against dust and other foreign substances. These innovations were examples of the genius of Laviolette who also devised an advanced pressed steel frame incorporating what is now called a "belly pan." Some of the series-built, 4-cylinder Spykers were thus equipped; they are said to have been unusually quiet at speed because of the decreased air turbulence beneath the bodies.

One of the 1905 Spyker "Four" 12/18 models achieved international fame in the motion picture, "Genevieve," produced by Henry Cornelius in 1952 for the J. Arthur Rank Organisation.* A 1904 Darracq had the starring auto role. The Spyker, owned

* *Veterans of the Road* by Elizabeth Nagle, pp. 139–144; Arco Publishing Co., Ltd., London, 1955.

Most important of all of The Netherland's historic cars is the 1902 Spyker. The Museum sign says: "4 Wheel Drive, First 6-cylinder car in the World." (*Nationaal Museum van de Automobiel*)

This Spyker racer was demonstrated outside of the Crystal Palace at the 1903 London Motor Show. The spectators evidently approved of the "SIX CYLINDERS DRIVEN ON FOUR WHEELS" as the sign says. (*Nationaal Museum van de Automobiel*)

Most popular of the early Spyker cars was the 2-cylinder model. This is the 1906 two-seater. Round radiators, not exclusive with Spykers, were adopted in 1904. (*Nationaal Museum van de Automobiel*)

The 1906–07 Spyker 12/18 tourer had a 4-cylinder engine displacing 2,546 cc. (*Nationaal Museum van de Automobiel*)

by Veteran Car Club of Great Britain member, Frank Reece, and driven in the film sequences by actor, Kenneth Moore, was a worthy and colorful adversary in the movie which was a fictional commemoration of the London-to-Brighton runs in Edwardian years. Said to be the only Spyker extant in England, the "Genevieve" competitor has three horizontal ventilating louvres on each side of the round engine hood rather than the more numerous vertical vents on the 1907 family tourer illustrated.

A more powerful 4-cylinder vehicle, the 15/20 model, was developed and one was entered in the classic Peking-to-Paris Race in 1907. Shown here, this special Spyker had the four-wheel drive mechanism that was so successful on the 1902 Spyker "Six." The rigors of the "hairy" race from Peking to Moscow over roads that were hardly more than trails failed to daunt the Spyker or its

crew. Despite several mishaps including two complete turn-overs in the wilds of Siberia, the 15/20 Spyker placed second behind Prince Borghese's 7.5-litre Itala in this historic event against a starting array of five of Europe's best on the 10th of June, 1907. (The 2-month race avoided Mongolia's Gobi desert which was crossed first by an American car as we shall see in Part V.)

In 1913, Spyker cars played a vital part in the "Vrijwillig Militair Automobiel-Korps" —the Voluntary Military Automobile Corps —which became a part of the military field forces when the First World War began. By late 1914, Spyker's principal competitors in The Netherlands were the Hillen and Stokvis cars. These two makes, built in Pays-Bas and Arnhem, respectively, had been introduced in 1911 and 1912. Unlike the Spyker, however, they were not continued after

479

The 15/20 HP Spyker as prepared for the Peking-Paris Race in 1907 in which the Dutch car won second place. (*Nationaal Museum van de Automobiel*)

the war although they were produced in series. Another obscure make, the Groninger, made in Groningen, unfortunately failed to survive the pre-war years as did the Omnia of Voorburg, the Held of Rotterdam and the Aarts made in Dongen.

Though The Netherlands was neutral, the war's aftermath depressed the Dutch economy and Spyker barely survived against the dozens of post-war makes exported by other nations to The Netherlands. One of the Spyker brothers was lost in a shipwreck off Harwich, England, and the surviving brother was financially unable to continue produc-

tion. New financial interests took over the Spyker works and reorganized it as the N.V. Industrieele Maatschappi Trompenburg under the management of a famous Dutch flyer named Winjmalen. The latter got off on the wrong foot by firing Spyker's greatest asset, the engineer Laviolette. The wings of the "flying Dutchman" turned auto maker were soon clipped, however, and the equally foolish financiers forced the production of a series of large, expensive cars powered with 6-cylinder, 5.7-litre Maybach engines imported from Germany. Although the latter-day Spykers were beautiful, aris-

A 1906–07 Spyker 12/18 all set for a family outing. Note the tie rod location in front of the axle. (*Nationaal Museum van de Automobiel*)

481

This is either a Hillen or Stokvis serving as a military staff car in 1914. (*Royal Netherlands Army*)

tocratic and properly luxurious, they did not fill the needs of the average Dutchman who turned to inexpensive English, French and American cars. The engineer, Laviolette, disappeared in obscurity, his proven talents unappreciated by the financiers who knew little about the business of making cars for the biggest share of the market. In 1926, the Spyker—once great—also faded away. The Dutch did not build another car until the modern Daf appeared.

482

Norway

AUTOMOTIVE PIONEERS in Norway were severely hampered, during the late years of the nineteenth century, because difficult topography and discouraging economic conditions militated against large-scale commercialization of mechanical developments. Had Norway been in the mainstream of European industrial development rather than on the fringe, there is little doubt that Anton Løvstad's fame would be worldwide today.

A civil engineer, Løvstad sought to improve the ride of horse-drawn vehicles. Experiments with spring rates and the torsional effects of metal under stress led to an astounding invention. On the 2nd of April, 1878, Løvstad was granted a patent for a system of transverse torsion bar springs. His discoveries led directly to similar systems on modern cars. Dr. Ferdinand Porsche and others—around fifty and sixty years later—based many suspension developments on Løvstad's patents. When longitudinal torsion bars were first used in the 1930s most engineers studied Løvstad's findings and were then, as now, in his debt.

Curiously, when a few pioneers did begin to tinker with automobiles in Norway, Løvstad's torsion bars seem to have been overlooked.

The first automobile in Norway powered by an internal combustion engine was imported late in 1895. A four-passenger Benz, it stimulated some of the Norwegian engineers and mechanics. One such was Paul Henning Irgens who already had designed in 1883 a promising vehicle with a fully enclosed passenger compartment. On this design, the driver sat on the front of the platform-type frame. Immediately behind the driver was an engine of the Otto type mounted transversely. It is not clear whether the small front wheels were pivoted centrally or turned individually; the larger rear wheels were chain-driven. A single half-elliptic spring was used in front and full-elliptic springs, mounted longitudinally, were at the rear. It is believed, however, that nothing came of the design which on paper compares very well with contemporary machines in other European countries.

Irgens travelled widely and as a competent mechanic, instrument maker and all-around technician by profession, he knew what was happening on the roads of other countries. Determined to build a car, he

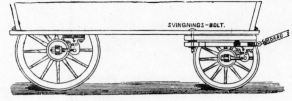

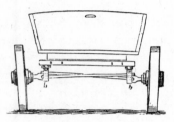

Side, bottom and end view diagrams of the amazing transverse torsion bars application for horse-drawn wagons patented in 1878 by the Norwegian inventor Anton Løvstad—the direct ancestor of numerous automotive installations. (*Kongelig Norsk Automobilklub*)

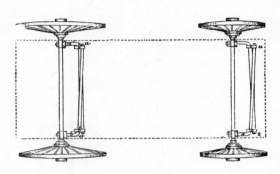

In 1883, Paul Henning Irgens of Christiania, Norway, designed this motor vehicle. (*Norges Tekniske Høgskole*)

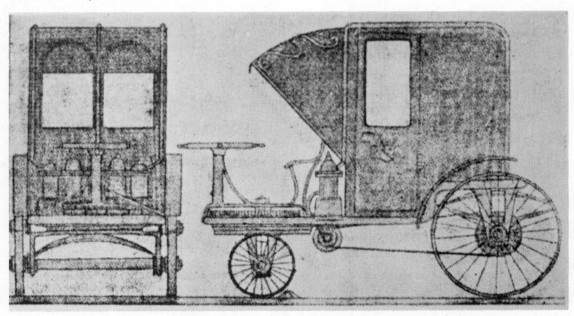

Jacob Irgens about to test drive his car in 1898; note the carriage-type central pivoting, tiller-operated steering. Irgens's workshop, in background, was in Bergen. (*Kongelig Norsk Automobilklub*)

Restored by enthusiast Arthur Moe, seated at the tiller, this 1905 Fossum is possibly earliest Norwegian car still in existence. (*Kongelig Norsk Automobilklub*)

Fossum cars in front of the builder's workshop in Oslo. The 1906 machine (left) has transverse springs while the 1907 model (right) has longitudinal springs. (*Norges Tekniske Høgskole*)

Carl Hantsch at the wheel of the first NAV car in front of the factory in 1908. A straight forward, 8-horsepower, single-cylinder design. (*Norges Tekniske Høgskole*)

Carl Hantsch of Norsk Automobil & Vognfabrik, examining the second NAV car during a test run in the countryside. (*Norges Tekniske Høgskole*)

A 1928 Geijer 8-cylinder sedan in front of the Royal Palace in Oslo. "*Norwegian Geijer, Norwegian-built*" states the side-mounted spare wheel cover. (*Kongelig Nørsk Automobilklub*)

moved from Christiania to Bergen in 1895 where his brother, Jacob Irgens, had a workshop. About a year later—more probably sometime in 1897—Paul and Jacob Irgens rolled out their motor vehicle. The Irgens had its single cylinder gasoline engine underneath the body driving the rear wheels by chains. The tiller acted directly upon the front wheels which were pivoted in the center of the axle in the horse-wagon manner.

The Irgens firm built no more gasoline-engine cars but devoted their attention to steam-powered omnibuses capable of carrying twenty passengers in some models and as few as ten in other versions. These Irgens steam busses were used in Bergen, Trondheim and other cities in 1899. One of them—quite fittingly—was named "Alpha" and was truly the beginning of self-propelled public motor transport in Norway. Paul Irgens was an unappreciated genius. Born in 1843, he is probably best known as the inventor of a successful marine engine in 1880 and of a gasoline turbine engine which he patented in 1898. He died in 1923—the undoubted father of the motorcar in Norway.

The next serious effort to produce cars in Norway was by Markus Hansen Fossum. The owner of a machine shop in Oslo, Fossum repaired motors of all kinds. By 1903, the Oldsmobile was fairly popular and Fossum was regarded as the authority on the marque. In 1905, Fossum decided to build his own motorcar. Little is known of this car, but it was followed in 1907 by another resembling the "curved dash"

Geijer saloon and open tourers on display in 1929. (*Norges Tekniske Høgskole*)

Olds according to Geir Hvoslet, editor of *Motorliv*, the official organ of the Royal Norwegian Automobile Club (KNA). Fossum built several cars between 1905 and 1908 but exactly how many is not known, nor is it clear whether Fossum offered them for sale or whether they remained his property for experimental purposes. Fortunately a 1907 Fossum has been discovered and restored by an enthusiast, Arthur Moe; it is illustrated here.

The first firm organized expressly to build and market home-grown cars was the Norsk Automobil & Vognfabrik A/S. Carl Hantsch, a master mechanic with considerable engineering ability, seems to have been the moving spirit behind this venture which was established in 1907 in Oslo on Bernt Ankers Street. The first NAV, a four-seater open tourer, was a straightforward 8-horsepower, 1-cylinder vehicle. Ignition was by high-tension magneto. The final drive appears to have been by chain and sprocket. After a series of tests and public demonstrations, a second improved tourer was built and equipped with shaft drive and carbide lamps. But, public support was lacking and the NAV did not go into series production.

In 1909, the Norsk Automobil Vognfabrik became a car repair and body-building shop. A score of European and American makes were being imported and Karrosserie —coachbuilding firms—were springing up in Norway as in other countries.

Carl Hantsch departed and joined the Kolberg, Caspary A/S which was already well established as importer of Darracq,

Unic, Daimler, Cadillac and other marques which they distributed. This firm also built bodies. Another well-known Karrosserie was that of Carl Heffermehl whose coachwork on Unic cars is illustrated in the section devoted to cars of France. From the early years of the century to the Nazi invasion, various firms assembled a number of foreign makes such as the Tidaholms Bruk and Scania-Vabis of Sweden, the Hupmobile, Overland, Hudson, Studebaker, Rockne, Plymouth, Dodge and other makes found to be dependable in the rugged Norwegian winters. The Belgian marque, Vivinus, was popular during the first two decades, the Ford "T" was a sensation, and German, French and British cars were popular. There just was not sufficient public interest or investment to make an all-Norwegian marque a worthwhile proposition.

A shortage of cars during the 1914–18 war led to the last big effort to produce a native car when the A/S C. Geijer & Co. was set up in 1921 in Oslo. For bread and butter, busses were built, but soon a line of attractive, well-built Geijer touring and saloon cars were coming out of the works. The engines were 6 and, later on, 8-cylinder, L-head, Lycoming engines imported from the United States. The gearboxes, axles and wheels were also "bought in" from various suppliers, mostly American. However, the frames, springs, radiators, bodies, and interiors were fabricated from the ground up in the Geijer factory.

The Geijer was well liked, proved to be exceptionally rugged and, with four-wheel brakes and 4-speed transmissions, was well matched to Norway's terrain. But the competition of literally dozens of imported cars supported by vigorous sales organizations finally drove the Geijer from the market in 1930 after nine years of production. A quality car, the Geijer was awarded prizes for coachwork and the marque was often seen at the Royal Palace. It was Norway's most ambitious and last home-built car to reach the marketplace.

Russia

THE NEW EMPHASIS on consumer goods in Russia is accompanied by an apparent rise of enthusiasm for the preservation and display of the automobiles of yesteryear. Some Soviet citizens are reported to be restoring cars dating back to the early days. Perhaps, one day soon, Soviet citizens will be taking part in international rallies and other motor sports.

The crowds lining the streets of Moscow to view a "parade" of old cars in the early autumn of 1966 signified a potential for future automotive contacts. Many of the cars, restored and treasured by Russian enthusiasts, came from as far away as Leningrad. Details are skimpy, but the owners "rendezvoused" on the Lenin Hills; from the hills the cars paraded through Moscow streets and alongside some of the public parks. Although most of the participating cars—dating from 1892 to 1940—were makes originating outside of the Soviet Union, this vintage and antique car event was of considerable importance in the light of the post-1960 announced effort to increase production of family type automobiles.

It is extremely difficult to obtain photographs of Russian-designed and manufactured automobiles of pre-World War II vintage. Consequently, the inclusion of the best cars in the 1966 Moscow old car parade in this section, without regard to the national origin of the cars concerned, is deemed worthwhile. Of course, the few pre-war Russian-built cars make this previously unheard of event all the more interesting.

Widespread destruction of archives during the various periods of war, and reticence on the part of Soviet authorities increase the difficulties facing the automotive historian. However, there were several attempts at producing cars in Russia prior to World War I. The Tansky and the Seawronsky were built in St. Petersburg (now Leningrad) between 1901 and 1905. The dates and other "facts" about these cars are open to question because of lack of documented proof. This applies to the following also: the Marck built in Moscow 1906–10; the Leutner built in Riga, Latvia (then and now a component part of the USSR), 1911–15; and the Stetysz, made in Vilno, Lithuania (now a part of the USSR), from about 1924 to 1928.

Somewhat better known are the several marques built in the Soviet Union, between the two world wars, by the state-owned Autotrust in the Moscow area; the Amo (1926–29), the Nami (late '20s to well

491

The Russo-Baltique won several competitions including the 1912 Monte Carlo Rally. (*Sketch by L. D. Sutton*)

The crest of the House of Romanov was used as a medallion on the Russo-Baltique cars by order of the Tsar Nicolas II. (*Joseph H. Wherry*)

Taking part in a 1966 *"parade"* of old cars through Moscow streets is this small open tourer. The car's lines resemble those of the Opel or Russian NAMI of circa 1929–31 or it could be a variant of the license-built Ford Model A, the GAZ-A. The supplying agency states: *"This machine, a gift of British workers, used to carry Vladimir Lenin."* However, Lenin died in 1924. (*Novosti Press Agency*)

"A column of Soviet-made cars. The machine in the foreground is GAZ M-1 built in the middle of the '30s." The Soviet-supplied data fails to identify number 119 following an American-built Ford Model A. (Y. A. Dolyagin and Novosti Press Agency)

The KIM-10, a "small displacement car" of 1940, shows the influence of small German cars of the period. (A. Nevezhin and Novosti Press Agency)

into the mid-'30s), the Penza (about 1926 to 1940), and the Yaroslav (about 1926–35). In addition, the state-owned Gorkovskii Auto Zavod in Gorki (formerly Nisvi Novgorod) has built several series of cars since the early '30s beginning with the GAZ-A which was a slightly modified Model A Ford built under license. In 1935, the GAZ-M.1, a license-built variant of the 1934 Ford, was placed in production; our accompanying photo shows that the Soviets modified the Ford design.

Before World War II, passenger car production in the Soviet Union probably never exceeded 30,000 units annually, and the majority of these were for official use. Trucks and industrial vehicles were critically needed and were given production priority.

Undoubtedly, there were a few other Russian marques not mentioned above. One particularly achieved a measure of fame throughout Europe, the Russo-Baltique. Research indicates that the original decision to produce an "all-Russian" car must have been made sometime late in 1905 by the management of the Russko-Baltyskij Waggonyj Zavod in Riga. According to hearsay —and possibly quite true—the Tsar Nicholas II was the moving spirit behind the decision to make the car and the Russian-Baltic Wagon Factory, a well-established industrial concern, was the logical manufacturer. The Riga builder of railroad rolling stock

Leading the excellent Moscow parade of old cars in 1966 was an 1892 Benz Velo, the entry of a group of Leningrad enthusiasts who restored the vehicle. (*Y. Dolyagin and Novosti Press Agency*)

Two Soviet citizens in their beautifully restored 1912 Baby Peugeot. Of uncertain vintage is the GAZ truck. (*Novosti Press Agency*)

This happy family drove their 1926 Fiat type 503 from Leningrad—"*a distance of about 700 km*"— to participate in Moscow's old car parade in 1966. (*Novosti Press Agency*)

"The owner of this Rolls-Royce maintains that, every year, he goes on long tours driving to the Black Sea coast of the Caucasus and to the Soviet Baltic republics." This appears to be a variant of about 1924 with a special all-weather top. (*Novosti Press Agency*)

had a difficult assignment and went shopping for help in Western Europe. A Swiss engineer, Julien Potterat of Lausanne, was hired as production manager of the new automotive department while the Belgian automobile designer and manufacturer, Charles Fondu, was induced to supply basic designs for a range of engines. The managing director, Kritzky, was a Russian engineer, and he and Potterat were jointly to design the new cars.

The Tsar gave his moral backing to the project and probably furnished a generous financial subsidy. At any rate, no effort was spared to produce all parts of the Russo-Baltique cars in Russia. This aim included tires, ignition components—everything. That such ambitions were not wholly realized is not surprising. As matters developed, various small parts, magnetos and the like, had to be imported.

The 1905 war with Japan had made one thing crystal clear to Russia's rulers—modern industrial development on a wide scale was an urgent need. There was no time to waste, and preparation of assembly facilities began immediately when Potterat arrived in Riga late in 1905. Included were foundries and tin-smithing shops. Gearboxes and crankcases were to be of aluminum. Production started sometime in 1908—the exact date is not known. The first cars were powered by big 4-cylinder, L-head engines with 105 mm. bore and 130 mm. stroke. A medium size two-seater, this model was the 24/30 (24 HP taxable formula, 30 brake horsepower). One was entered in a 1909 race from Riga to St. Petersburg and return. The Russo-Baltique came in third behind a 50-HP Mercedes and a big 70-HP Opel. Potterat drove a fast race, but the road was far from the best in Europe,

497

"This Ford used to belong to Antonina Nezhda-nova, the famous Russian singer." Most likely this is an imported Ford Model A. (*A. Nevezhin and Novosti Press Agency*)

Spectator interest in this Opel of about 1931 is evident. Most likely this is a 1.3-litre, 4-cylinder model of the popular German light car. (*A. Neve-zhin and Novosti Press Agency*)

Two passing cyclists seem to sympathize with the plight of this enthusiast whose front-wheel-drive Adler "Trumpf Junior" of 1938 vintage *"failed to reach the rallying place on Lenin Hills"* for the 1966 old car parade in Moscow. (*N. Sharanda and Novosti Press Agency*)

and his time was 8 hours, 5 minutes for some 380 miles.

The initial performance so pleased the Imperial court that the Tsar granted the works the honor of using the crest of the House of Romanov as the medallion of the car. Large sedans and touring cars were developed and many were purchased by wealthy customers and by the Imperial government. Various engines were built with bore and stroke dimensions of 80 x 110, 100 x 140 and 120 x 160 mm. in addition to the first 24/30 HP models. In 1911, a Russo-Baltique sports two-seater placed first in the Riga-St. Petersburg-Riga race, and in 1912 defeated Europe's best to capture first place in the classic Monte Carlo Rally driven by André Nagle, a Russian engineer. Nagle next took a Russo-Baltique on the marque's greatest feat in 1913 and, starting from Paris, drove eastward completely around the Mediterranean Sea and back to his starting point. The route included the Swiss Alps and the wilds of North Africa.

According to Alec Ulmann of Indianapolis Raceway and Sebring fame, the Russo-Baltique remained in production in Riga until that city was captured by German forces in 1917.

Maximum production of the Russo-Baltique eventually reached a few more than 500 per year. None is known to remain. It is possible that a few were equipped with 6-cylinder overhead camshaft engines for

499

such a powerplant was developed by the works early in World War One. This engine, however, was produced under the direction of General Shidlovsky primarily for use in Sikorsky bombing aircraft which went into action in 1915, the world's first 4-engine bombers. Even more likely, this overhead camshaft engine probably benefited from the engineering experience of another famous Swiss engineer, Marc Birkigt, whose Hispano-Suiza cars (see Spain) were license-built by the Russian-Baltic Wagon Factory before the outbreak of the war. Prior to World War Two, the Russian automobile industry showed little original thinking, a situation continuing until very recent years. Tests of Russian cars of 1948–58 vintage, the Zis, Moskvitch, Pobieda and Volga, all reflected strong European and American influences. There is little doubt that the Russo-Baltique was the first important Russian step toward developing an automobile industry.

Scotland

ALTHOUGH THE BIRTHPLACE of James Watt, who brought the steam engine into practical being, is Scotland, that country, curiously enough, made little progress with steam cars. However, Scotland has a lively automotive history, and produced some cars of distinction. The Beardmore, Madelvic and Salveson were among a dozen or so Scottish marques that came and went without creating much of a stir, and so were the Robertson, the Galloway and the Rob Roy.

Of greater importance were the Albion, the Argyll, and the Arrol-Johnston. The latter two makes were among the first in the British Isles to employ four-wheel brakes with several mechanical applications prior to the 1914–18 war. Financial mismanagement and poor distribution caused the Scottish automobiles to founder after some successful years. The Albion lasted from 1900 to 1915; the Argyll from 1899 to 1932; and the Arrol-Johnston from 1895 to 1931. Scottish cars had their golden years before World War One and production gradually diminished after that conflict. Some of Scotland's historic cars have been preserved in the famous Sword Collection in Ayrshire and others are in the Museum of Transport in Glasgow.

Production was never on a par, in point of numbers built, with English cars to the south of the border. Glasgow was the home of the Albion and the Argyll; the Arrol-Johnston was initially produced by the Mo-Car Syndicate in Paisley and later was moved to Dumfries.

The first Albion cars (the A-1 model of 1900) typified the Scottish sturdiness and inclination toward economy. The hard rubber tires and full-elliptic springs were not unusual, but high front mounting of the fuel tank, the location of the gill-type radiator beneath the frame plus the spade grip on the steering tiller were out of the ordinary. Transversely mounted inside the frame rails at the rear, the engine had two horizontally opposed cylinders with bore and stroke of 4 and 5 inches respectively. A large cubical oil tank was rearmost on the frame. The output was 8 horsepower which, with light total weight, should have provided comparatively good performance. The Albion Motor Company, Ltd. made its own motors and single jet carburetors for the most part. Inlet valves were automatically

The collection of Scottish cars in the Glasgow Museum of Transport includes, from front foreground to rear: 1927 sleeve-valve Argyll 12/40; the 1924 Beardnore 12.8-HP, overhead-camshaft model with "all-weather top" by Richard Mays; the 1920 Arrol-Johnston 15.9-HP drophead coupé; 1910 Albion 13-HP tourer; 1907 Argyll tourer and a mixed quintet of Albion and Arrol-Johnston dogcarts of about 1900. (*George A. Oliver*)

actuated and the very large flywheel type magneto—on the left side looking forward —was a unique Albion feature for many years. Nearly as wide as long—the wheelbase was 66 while the widest tread was 54 inches —the Albions were reasonably popular in the highlands and enjoyed a reputation for durability.

By 1905, Albions were no longer "dog-carts" but had developed into stylish 6-seater touring and limousine types. Engines still had but two cylinders but were nearly

502

The prototype chassis of the 1900 Albion model A-1. Note fuel tank high at frame front, radiator core beneath center of frame, and huge flywheel-type magneto on engine in rear. (*George A. Oliver*)

square with 4.875 x 5 inch bore and stroke and developed 16 horsepower. The early cars had two speeds forward and one reverse; those from 1905 on had three speeds forward with a sliding gear transmission. Chain drives and cone clutches were used for most of the marque's life.

The typical Argyll of 1900 used 1-cylinder, coil ignition De Dion engines imported from France. Short and high as was the vogue at the turn of the century, most Argylls had pneumatic tires and used the continental type vertical steering column incorporating a 3-speed gear change lever. Most models in 1900 were basically similar.

Within a few years, the Argyll had become a full size family car with semi-elliptic springs and two-cylinder engines of about 1¾-litre displacement. Engines, if not made in the Argyll works, were often purchased from Aster, a Scottish parts manufacturer of Dumfries. This firm brought out a car of its own in 1924 only to see it go the way of so many others after five years or so. Transmissions for the Argyll were generally "bought in" from other specialty manufacturers. The 1907 Argyll shown had a Govan gearbox using one shift lever for the three forward ratios and another lever for reverse gear. Just before the 1914–18 war, single-sleeve valve engines of

The 2-cylinder, horizontally-opposed, 8-HP engine of the prototype 1900 Albion A-1. Note wagon-type wheel rim brakes and the single chain drive far below. Rear wheels are 35.5 inches in diameter. This prototype covered 50,000 miles in service before being retired to the Museum of Transport in 1908. (*George A. Oliver*)

During an RSAC rally from Glasgow to Lanark and return: the 1914 Argyll 15/30 "Streamlined Torpedo" followed by the 1910 Albion 24/30-HP tourer. (*George A. Oliver*)

A pair of 1900 Argyll dogcarts in the Museum of Transport in Glasgow. Basically alike, car on left is powered by a 2¾-HP De Dion engine and has a horizontal tube radiator while car on right has a 5-HP M.M.C. engine and a larger capacity vertical tube radiator. (*George A. Oliver*)

Mr. Knollys Stokes of Dublin, Eire, with his 1905 Argyll. (*Irish Press courtesy of Irish Veteran & Vintage Car Club*)

This 1907 Argyll 10/12-HP tourer formerly belonged to the famous "Sword Collection" in Ayrshire. (*George A. Oliver*)

Burt-McCullum design had a considerable vogue in the British Isles. The 1914 "Streamlined Torpedo" models, large, attractive touring cars, used such a silent though oily sleeve valve power plant and —best of all—had four wheel brakes actuated mechanically.

From inception in 1895, many Arrol-Johnston cars were of family size; but most were of the small, two-seater, powered-cart variety in much the same concept as that of their highland competitors. The 1901 model (license SB 2) and the 1902 runabout (ST 52) are particularly fine examples of the maker's and restorer's art. Moreover, the steering wheels indicate the early Arrol-Johnston advantage over the opposition. Around the turn of the century, this marque was usually powered by engines with horizontally opposed cylinders, each of which concealed two pistons working on cranked

levers on a common crankshaft. A bore of 4.25 inches and stroke of 3.375 inches was common. Magneto ignition, water cooling, cone clutches with four gear speeds forward and quadrant type fore-and-aft gear change levers were standard. The rear wheels were chain-driven. Hard rubber tires on 36-inch-diameter front and 41-inch rear wheels could cut through the mud, on the trail-like roads, to get a firm grip on more solid ground.

By 1905, the Arrol-Johnston had evolved into a more comfortable conveyance with all-weather protection for the passengers. The driver, however, took the rain in his face although he did have a roof over his head. The top was detachable and the rear compartment was heated by the exhaust. Transversely mounted 3-cylinder engines, with exposed valve gear and huge magnetos, delivered power to the rear

Produced near the close of 1913 to 1914 specifications, this 15/30-HP, sleeve-valve Argyll "Streamlined Torpedo" is from the "Sword Collection" in Ayrshire; now owned by the Glasgow Transport Museum. Note the large brake drums. (*George A. Oliver*)

wheels by a single chain. Of note to collectors, the 1905 Arrol-Johnston (license SH 103) shown here brought nearly $9,000 in 1965 at the second Sword Collection auction in Paisley.

One of Arrol-Johnston's early triumphs —possibly the marque's greatest—was defeating a Rolls-Royce and winning first place, overall, in the first running of the classic Tourist Trophy Race in the Isle of Man with an average speed, over a rough course, of 33.9 mph. The year was 1905 and an 18-horsepower model driven by J. S. Napier did the trick.

Arrol-Johnston, as a marque, was considerably hampered by financial juggling—a prerequisite to staying in business—but did develop into a range of fairly fine large tourers and medium size coupe and saloon models. Within a few years, the designers

This Arrol-Johnston is either a 1901 or 1902 model. Possibly the oldest of the marque existing, it was restored by the staff of the Transport Museum. The engine is the usual 2-cylinder, horizontal type with 2 pistons in each cylinder. The quadrant gear change for the 4-speeds-forward, 2-reverse gearbox is on the near side behind the horn bulb. (*George A. Oliver*)

had taken a leaf from the Renault style book and had placed the radiator core behind the 4-cylinder in-line engine which was mounted longitudinally. This arrangement allowed for a steeply sloped hood, and provided excellent forward visibility. (In America, the Keeton was an almost exact style copy.) Shaft drives were used. According to George A. Oliver of Glasgow, an artist-author of note, the restored 1911

508

This 1902 Arrol-Johnston 10-HP "dogcart" was built in Paisley by the Mo-Car Syndicate. (*George A. Oliver*)

model illustrated is "not a particularly interesting car to drive: it is unresponsive and its controls lack sensitivity. It was, however, reliable in its day and sold reasonably well." Of rather elegant appearance—the bathtub shape of the rear of the body was calculated to reduce the swirls of dust at speed—this 80 x 120 mm., 4-cylinder, 16-HP model, with rear-wheel brakes only, had performance out of all proportion to its ability to stop safely. Oliver has written that when the Scottish racing driver, Jack Stewart, drove this 1911 Arrol-Johnston recently, "its lack of brakes worried him." A

year or so later, four-wheel brakes were standardized.

After the First World War, the Arrol-Johnston had the radiator core in front of the engine; the 1920 drop-head coupe 12/40 in the accompanying group photograph is an example.

Probably the most mechanically advanced Scottish car was the Beardmore. Produced in a variety of body styles, many with coachwork by specialty houses, this marque was a high quality, limited production vehicle by Beardmore Motors, Ltd. of Glasgow. During the war, thousands of

509

This type of 1905 Arrol-Johnston is exceptionally rare and is preserved in the Museum of Transport in Glasgow. Heat from the exhaust made the rear compartment comfortable in winter. For warm days, the tonneau top was removable. (*George A. Oliver*)

Beardmore engines powered a variety of Allied military aircraft. This technical background was evidenced in the 2.4-litre 4 and 6-cylinder automobile engines used in this marque. Overhead camshafts made the Beardmore a relatively fast machine during its short span of existence from 1920 to 1928. Now the once promising Beardmore is, like a thousand others, a collectors' item to be cherished.

Scotland still has several custom body builders, some internationally famed racing groups, and several active truck manufacturers.

The 1905 Arrol-Johnston 3-cylinder engine is transversely mounted. Note the exceptionally large magneto. Formerly in the Ayrshire "Sword Collection," this car is now in the Transport Museum. (*George A. Oliver*)

The 1911 Arrol-Johnston 15.9-HP tourer has a body design reckoned to reduce dust swirls. Fairly fast, the car had 2-wheel brakes that were not known for stopping ability. (*George A. Oliver*)

Spain

Sometime during 1895, Captain La Cuadra of the Royal Artillery visited Paris where he fell under the spell of the automobile. Returning to his home in Barcelona, he immediately set to work organizing personnel and means for "la fabricación del automóvil." La Cuadra and his associates agreed it was high time that Spain should have an automobile industry, since the efforts of Señor Bonet del Rio to series-produce an electric-powered three-wheeler in 1890 had come to nothing. Thus it was that Spain's first gasoline-engined car, the La Cuadra, was eventually produced in Barcelona late in 1899. A five-seater touring car of rather good proportions, the car was propelled by a 2-cylinder (80 x 110 mm.), water-cooled engine of 4.5 HP and double chain drive. Front and rear compartments were covered with a folding canvas top. A smart bonnet concealed the engine and the tube-type radiator was behind a sloped nose. Front doors were lacking. A small series of La Cuadra touring cars was built but the marque faded from sight early in 1901. Extremely rare and little known, one example is believed to exist in Madrid. Photographs, however, have proved impossible to obtain.

Señor La Cuadra's efforts were an inspiration to others, for he later became vaguely associated with Señor J. Castro who had, in 1901, entered into an agreement with Marc Birkigt, one of automobiledom's all-time greats. Born in Switzerland and educated as an engineer, Birkigt prevailed upon Sr. J. Castro to finance a factory and in 1901 the enterprise "J. Castro S. en C. Fábrica Hispano-Suiza de Automóviles" came into being. Birkigt, who had worked on railroad locomotive designs and on electrical projects, was the chief engineer and production manager. Contrary to some published reports in recent years, the first products of the new concern were not Hispano-Suiza cars by name but the 1902–04 Castro 10-HP, 2-cylinder tourer. Birkigt designed everything on and in the car including the 100 x 120 mm. bore and stroke engine. Very soon an improved 4-cylinder, 14-HP model was built. Both of these cars had large carbide headlamps, vertical brass radiator grilles of a design consistent with later Birkigt designs, and shaft drives rather than sprocket chains.

In 1904, the firm was reorganized—and here is where the pioneer La Cuadra became associated—as the Sociedad Hispano-

The last word in luxury touring in its day was the 1907–10 Hispano-Suiza. The middle bucket seats increased capacity to seven persons. Note the side-mounted carriage lamp, tool box beneath running board and the dashing dragon head horn tube in brass. (*Miarnau Studio courtesy Empresa Nacional de Autocamiones SA*)

Specialty shops marketed fitted trunks made to order like this one on a 1907–10 Hispano-Suiza. Full-length side curtains—rolled up here—were unfurled for all-weather touring. (*Miarnau Studio courtesy Empresa Nacional de Autocamiones SA*)

A sensation in its time was the 1912 Hispano-Suiza 15 T "Alfonso XIII." A paragon of sports cars, this 3.6-litre machine's speed was 90 mph. (*Joseph H. Wherry*)

Suiza Fábrica de Automóviles, the Spanish-Swiss Automobile Factory Company. Thus, the first marque Hispano-Suiza cars were born. The emblem was composed of stylized wings surrounding the white Swiss cross on a red circle.

Catering to wealthy patrons, Birkigt turned out a succession of limousine, landaulet and formal models including town cars and "bridal brougham" types. The latter, called the "true brougham" in the early '20s, was characterized by an additional fender on each side midway between the wheels, a feature that emphasized the isolation of the high-born occupants of the luxurious coach body.

From 1904 to 1910, Hispano-Suiza engines had a variety of cylinders and displacements. The 4-cylinder units had bores and strokes of 100 x 120 and 130 x 140 mm. although Birkigt was hopefully experimenting with "square" designs with equal bore and stroke. Birkigt's 6-cylinder engines which powered the 1906 tourers and closed cars ranged from 115 x 115 to 130 x 130 mm., and in 1907–08 to 100 x 120 and 130 x 140 mm. bore and stroke, respectively. The smallest 4-cylinder engine had a displacement of 3.75 litres. In virtually all of these the cylinders were cast in pairs. From his earliest designs, Birkigt employed aluminum alloy extensively, having mastered efficient means of casting the light metal. As early as 1906, most Hispano-Suiza crankcases and gearboxes were cast in an integral unit.

Though powerful and reliable, these engines did not please him entirely. Consequently, Birkigt pioneered the T-head engine layout in which the intake and exhaust valves were on opposite sides of the block. A perfectionist, the famed Swiss engineer insisted that frames and all other

514

chassis components—the engines and all parts not generally exposed to view—be as carefully finished as the exteriors of his cars. From the first Hispano-Suiza of 1904, the marque was always a work of art. Wheelbases from 1906 on were rarely less than 117 inches and as often as not were in excess of 130 inches on the 6-cylinder models. The works in Barcelona built some bodies but usually the wealthy buyers ordered chassis, only, which were then sent to the coachbuilders.

Perhaps the spur to Birkigt's perfectionist philosophy was supplied in 1904 by a small, obscure firm in Cadiz province which had supplied King Alfonso XIII with a 24-HP Anglada. Despite the royal endorsement, the Anglada soon fell by the wayside and no details remain other than of its auspicious beginning.

In 1909, a Hispano-Suiza branch factory was established in the Bois Colombes, a suburb of Paris. Cars were assembled in this works, and during World War One, aircraft engines—magnificent Birkigt-designed overhead camshaft V-8s—were turned out by the thousands. Our own ace of aces, Captain Eddie Rickenbacker, flew to fame on a "Hisso"-powered S.P.A.D. type 13 as did many other American, Belgian and French

The no nonsense, functional construction of the Hispano-Suiza "Alfonso XIII" has a magnetic appeal even to the youthful. The emblem contains the Swiss cross combined with symbols indicating its dual heritage with Spain. (*Joseph H. Wherry*)

Restored and owned by the Montagu Motor Museum in Beaulieu, this "Alfonso XIII" was shipped to Peacock Gap, Marin County, California for a one-time showing in the U.S.A. at the Concours d'Elegance in 1966. (*Joseph H. Wherry*)

Lord Montagu of Beaulieu obtained his rare Hispano-Suiza "Alfonso XIII" in 1961, the first Spanish car in his museum. The Hissp's original Irish owner was killed by a sniper's bullet during the 1916 Rebellion. Note the damaged rim of steering wheel (arrow) which the bullet struck before ricocheting into driver. (*Joseph H. Wherry*)

aces. Despite the eventual importance of the French plant, the home office remained in Barcelona, where the marque originated, until after World War One, and for this reason the Hispano-Suiza cars are considered, in this volume, to be Spanish.

In 1910, Birkigt prepared a special racing car for the Grand Prix of France. Going all out for torque, Birkigt ignored his previous preference for closer affinity between bore and stroke and designed a racing engine with a stroke of 200 mm. while the bore was a modest 65 mm. The four cylinders were cast in one piece—en bloc. A smashing success, the tiny racer with the high bonnet, to accommodate the stroke, won the Voiturette (light car) class in the Grand Prix of France; placed first and third in the Ostend International Race; swept

Most "Alfonso XIII" models were two-seaters like this elegant example; a few, however, were built as four-seaters. (*Joseph H. Wherry*)

first, second and fourth places in the Boulogne Voiturette Race—all in 1910. Birkigt then turned his attention to superchargers and successfully raced 4-cylinder, 3-litre machines with a unique blower mounted on the front of the block which assisted the exhausting of burned gasoline by means of a third valve in each cylinder. This racer led to one of the most eagerly sought gems of motoring history, the type 15T "Alfonso XIII" sports car introduced in

1911 according to old archives, not in 1912 as has been recorded in recent years.

The "Alfonso XIII" had four 80 x 180 mm. cylinders, developed 64 brake horsepower at the then high engine speed of 3,200 rpm (15.9 HP tax rating) and was a two-seater with the barest coachwork on a lightweight, short chassis with high tension magneto ignition, a leather cone clutch and shaft drive. The first "Alfonso" had 3-speed gearboxes; later 4-speeds were stand-

517

The 4-cylinder, T-head engine of the "Alfonso XIII" was built integrally with the transmission. Engineer Marc Birkigt aimed at perfection and he achieved it to a degree rarely obtained. (*Joseph H. Wherry*)

ardized. Maximum speed was close on 90 mph, fast in 1912 for an over-the-counter car. When S. M. el Rey don Alfonso XIII visited the works in Barcelona, he ordered one and granted permission for his name ·to be used as the model designation. Subsequently, sporting four-seater bodies were also available on the 15T as it was listed in the catalogs.

Sometime in 1917, the great French flying ace, René Fonck, was presented with an Alfonso XIII model by admirers. In 1918, Hispano-Suiza cars adopted the La Cigogne Volante de Lorraine—stork of Lorraine—as the mascot and henceforth that emblem adorned the radiator cap. The 1914–19 catalogs listed a 4-cylinder, T-head engine with bore and stroke of 100 x 150 mm. This larger engine had a taxable rating of 24.8 HP and it is believed that some of the

"Alfonso XIII" models were so equipped.

After the 1914–18 conflict, Hispano-Suiza activities were centered increasingly in France where the firm concentrates on armaments today. However, the Barcelona works continued to produce cars until the early '30s. The success of the overhead camshaft aircraft engines, with threaded steel cylinder liners screwed into aluminum blocks, led to a new series of 6-cylinder, 100 x 140 mm. engines in 1919. Developing 130 brake horsepower at 3,000 rpm, these 6,597 cc. engines had dual ignition and twin-choke carburetors. Known in most countries from its British Treasury Rating, for tax purposes, as the 37.2 HP model, it was also produced in single ignition versions. Though a large car with wheelbases up to 145 inches, it was exceptionally light and weighed less than 3,000 pounds in

518

Rare, even in the first decade of this century, was the exotic *"bridal brougham"* coachwork, with the extra mudguards forward of coach door, such as graces this Hispano-Suiza of about 1908. (*Miarnau Studio courtesy of Empresa Nacional de Autocamiones SA*)

sporting versions because of widespread use of aluminum in the engine and coachwork. Finned-aluminum brake drums lined with steel on all four wheels and a brake servo system driven off the transmission plus ultra-quick steering—a mere 2½ turns of the wheel, lock-to-lock—gave the 6.5-litre Hispano-Suiza superlative handling qualities. The chassis alone cost upward of $9,500 making the elegant "Hisso" a car for the wealthy connoisseur. Reliable and smooth—the compression ratio was 4.5 to 1 —the 4-speed transmission took the huge car to maximum speeds in excess of 85 mph remarkably quick.

All in all, there were some three dozen distinct models of the Hispano-Suiza. Except for the Alfonso XIII model, the most famous was the "Monza" with the bore increased to 102 mm. while the stroke re-mained 140 mm. On a 133-inch wheelbase with sports touring coachwork, the Monza would do 90 mph with ease. On a Monza equipped with one of his own fabric-covered bodies, C. T. Weymann dueled a Stutz on the brickyard in Indianapolis in 1928. What was supposed to be a 24-hour match brought mechanical disaster to the Stutz, which had so many troubles it was forced to retire after some 19 hours. The Hispano-Suiza, a veteran of thousands of hard miles before the duel, was as fresh as a daisy and racked up an average of more than 70 mph.

In 1924, an 8-litre Hispano-Suiza—with a bore and stroke of 110 and 140 mm.— won the Boillot Cup at Boulogne and was produced afterwards as the Boulogne model.

In post-war years, most of the Spanish factory's cars had 4-cylinder engines. In later years, pushrod-operated, overhead

519

1914/16

Cost was no consideration when ordering a Hispano-Suiza around 1910 with "extension front brougham" coachwork. Aristocratic occupants were sheltered from the elements and communicated with the chauffeur via the speaking tube terminating behind his ear. (*Miarnau Studio courtesy of Empresa Nacional de Autocamiones SA*)

valves replaced overhead camshafts to reduce costs. For the same reason, the threaded steel cylinder liners gave way to cold steel sleeves. Still there were occasional limousines with gold-plated fittings for kings and maharajahs.

To compete with other builders of expensive cars for the wealthy and royalty, the French factory brought out the magnificent V-12 on a 12-foot wheelbase in 1934. Seven bronze-bushed main bearings, tubular connecting rods, overhead camshafts, dual ignition, aluminum pistons and luxury coachwork at ready-to-roll prices upward of $25,-000 caused this model to be short-lived. (Much the same fate doomed the Bugatti Royale.) Finally in 1936, a 5.2-litre, pushrod, 6-cylinder model, the Type K-6, was introduced. A smart "grand turismo" type, the K-6 weighed 4,500 pounds and up, developed 145 bhp, and could maintain around 90 mph. By this date, the Spanish factory in Barcelona had been pre-empted by the Republican government and was producing no cars at all, but the French plant made cars on order until World War II. Since 1940, a very few Hispano-Suiza cars have been assembled in Argentina from im-

On occasion Hispano-Suiza chassis were fitted with four-seater sports coachwork and pointed noses. This is a 1914 or '15 model. (*Miarnau Studio courtesy of Empresa Nacional de Auto-camiones SA*)

The chauffeur of a 1922 Hispano-Suiza town car had a folding canopy but still lacked side curtains or windows. This well preserved example is in the Lindley Bothwell collection. (*Joseph H. Wherry*)

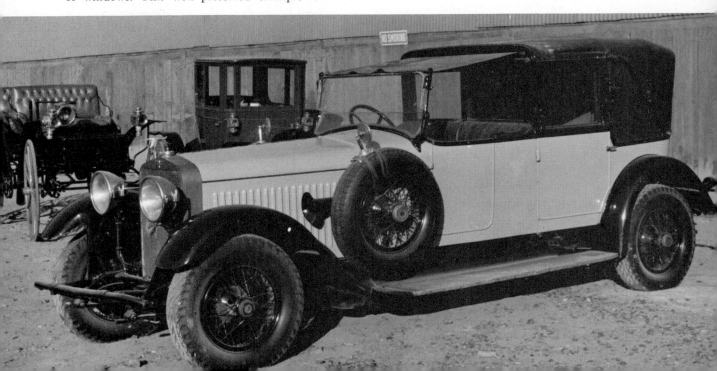

The 6.5-litre, 6-cylinder, single-ignition, overhead-camshaft engine in the 1922 Hispano-Suiza passenger cars were rather modestly rated at 135 bhp. (*Joseph H. Wherry*)

ported parts. The Hispano-Suiza is but a nostalgic memory in Spain. The facilities in Barcelona and Madrid are now the properties of the state-owned Empresa Nacional de Autocamiones SA where the marque Pegaso was built in the fifties.

While the automotive industry of Spain was always primarily concerned with the risky business of catering only to the very rich, there were occasional efforts to build low-priced cars. One such marque was the David, small two and four-seat cyclecars built between 1907 and 1922. Spanish accounts say that some 1,500 Davids were built, most of them powered with small engines made in Switzerland. One David, named "Duke of Montpensier," raced often in provincial events. In 1922, a David won

a voiturette race from Barcelona to Madrid and return, but this victory could not prevent the end of the little car.

A more ambitious project was that of the Barcelona firm of Talleres & Hereter which produced the 4-cylinder, 12 to 15-HP Ideal cars from 1915 to 1920 with brief success. Technically, they were interesting, especially a few with the then very high 9.5 to 1 compression ratio. T-H interests quickly turned to aircraft engine design and eventually the firm was absorbed into a state-owned corporation.

Similarly in Barcelona, the Diaz & Grillo sports two-seaters were built in small numbers between 1917 and 1922. Smartly styled and powered by 4-cylinder, 60 x 100 mm. engines of L-head design, they failed simply

522

Adopted as the radiator mascot during World War One, the "Stork of Lorraine" graces the nose of this long-wheelbase Hispano-Suiza cabriolet of about 1930. (*Miarnau Studio courtesy of Empresa Nacional de Autocamiones SA*)

because there was no market. Matyas & S.R.C., also based in Barcelona, built a few Matyas cars between 1915 and 1920; most were four-seat tourers with rakish, pointed noses.

An effort on the island of Majorca also came to nothing between 1924 and 1928 when a handful of enthusiasts produced limited numbers of the Loryc and Euskalduna cyclecars powered by 2-cylinder, 2-cycle engines. The Izaro, Storm, Landa, Hisparco and others were victims of over-optimism.

Long before establishing his reputation with Alfa Romeo, Wilfredo Ricart and a Señor Pérez established a works in Barcelona in 1922. The Ricart y Pérez 4-cylinder sports cars were streamlined with aluminum bodies, ran well in the Peña Rhin Grand Prix in 1922 against Alfa Romeo, Bugatti and other top machines. They were powered by efficient 4-cylinder engines with dual overhead camshafts in finned aluminum covers. Some four and five-seater tourers based on the racing model were also built. Again there were few buyers because Ricart made the old mistake of catering to the affluent few. In 1928, the firm reorganized as Ricart España, survived until 1930, and built a few very expensive luxury cars, most of them dual cowl phaetons powered with dual overhead camshaft, 2,400 cc., 6-cylinder engines.

All told, Spain has had some two dozen marques. The best known, after the unforgettable Hispano-Suiza, was the Elizalde

523

A clean, overhead-valve, 4-cylinder Elizalde engine, the only available photograph relating to this forgotten marque. (*Juan Aymerich archives*)

which survived in Barcelona until 1930, another luxury vehicle in a country where the masses had hardship incomes. Founded by Don Arturo Elizalde in 1913, the Fabrica Española de Automoviles Elizalde announced successful tests of 4-cylinder prototypes early in 1914. In 1916 the patronage of King Alfonso XIII made possible the development of the 8-cylinder Type 20 which was produced in racing sports car versions, limousines and town cars. The competition Type 20 acquitted itself well in 1916

The competition Nacionale Pescara sat on a wheelbase of 102.4 inches. Huge magnesium-alloy brake drums were integral with 28-inch wheels. To decrease weight, even the body, firewall and fuel tank were of electron. This is the factory team at Shelsley Walsh in England for one of the events in the 1931 European Mountain Championship which this marque won after triumphs in France, England, Germany, Czechoslovakia and Spain. (*Juan Aymerich archives*)

in the Peña Rhin Grand Prix in Barcelona, as well it should have for most of Europe was at war and there were few topnotch opponents. A few cars a month were produced at astronomical prices until 1917 when contracts were received for 150-HP, V-8 aircraft engines for the Air Force.

In 1919, the King—a great motoring enthusiast—ordered an attractive brougham on the Type 20 chassis, illustrated here by an artist's sketch. The works next prepared the huge Type 48—probably one of the largest cars anywhere—for display in the Paris Salon of 1921, a monstrous limousine about 8 feet high with engine hood higher than a man of average height. The 8-litre, 8-cylinder engine with bore and stroke of 90 x 160 mm. must have had impressive power. With the *ultimo* in luxurious appointments, it

was priced at around $30,000. Elizalde next developed the Type 51, a single-seater racing car with a 4-cylinder engine. This evolved into the Type 518, an 8-cylinder competition car which excelled in Spanish events but was rarely seen elsewhere. Always secondary to other industrial interests, car production ended in the Elizalde works in 1930.

Although time was running out for the Spanish aristocracy during the closing years of the 1930s, most industrialists still failed to read the signs of the times. With Hispano-Suiza and Elizalde no longer viable enterprises in Spain, there were still those who sought to build luxury cars. It appears that industrial and economic realism were lacking.

One scarcely known engineer, Raul Pate-

In the lead during the 1933 Spanish Grand Prix until the experimental blower failed. Boat-tailed and weighing well under a ton, the 3-litre DOHC Nacionale Pescara straight-8 did nearly 130 mph in racing trim. (*Juan Aymerich archives*)

In one of the Pescara's last competitions, the famed Zanelli placed a remarkable second in the racing class to Hans Stuck on the massive 16- cylinder Auto Union at the Kesselberg hill climb in 1935. (*Juan Aymerich archives*)

ras Pescara, the Marquis de Pescara, had built and briefly flown (in 1922) a helicopter with counter-rotating rotors and other even more successful aircraft. When Pescara turned to automobiles, he secured the patronage of King Alfonso XIII (as everybody seemed to do) and established the Fábrica Nacionale de Automoviles in Barcelona.

The prototype Nacionale Pescara of 1928 was a roadster with open bucket seats and a pointed tail on a deep box-section frame with semi-elliptic springs, solid front axle, piston type hydraulic shock absorbers and worm and roller steering. Extensive use of aluminum and magnesium alloy was made to reduce the weight to approximately 2,100 pounds. The proto' was tested on the Terramar course near Barcelona. The engine block was aluminum; bore and stroke of the eight in-line cylinders were 72.2 x 90

mm. respectively. Wet steel liners were specified. Competition models had dual overhead camshafts while a single overhead camshaft was specified for touring cars. In each case the camshafts were driven by bevel gears and a vertical kingshaft at the front of the block. Statically and dynamically balanced, the connecting rods were of duralumin. The carburetor was a single, dual-choke Zenith, the magneto was by Vertex, and dynastarters (combined generator and starting motor) were standard. A pump circulated the water and full pressure lubrication protected the bearings. The intake manifold was on the left, exhaust ports on the right. Cylinder heads and camshaft covers were also of aluminum, the latter highly polished.

Three wheelbases were catalogued: 102.4 inches for competition cars, 118.1 inches for the 4/5-passenger tourers and 128 inches

526

In the Pyrenees, a five-passenger touring Pescara with 118.1-inch wheelbase. Extensive use of magnesium and aluminum alloys held curb weight to 2,640 pounds. The single overhead-camshaft version of the 3-litre engine developed 80 BHP at 3,600 rpm. (*Juan Aymerich archives*)

on the big 7-seat model. All had unique, lightweight, magnesium alloy (electron) wheels with integral brake drums—in effect the drums were the wheels; 28-inch tires were used. Electron was also used for the crankcase, clutch and gearbox housing.

Production costs were not considered—the usual Quixotic Spanish attitude—because the King would assure success. One of the three surviving Pescara cars, an appetizing two-plus-two roadster on the original prototype chassis, was owned briefly by

Alfonso XIII until the fall of the monarchy in 1931, then passed to an army officer when the factory was confiscated by the Republican government, was used throughout the 1936–39 civil war, and recently came to grief on an ocean voyage due to careless handling aboard ship. Literally bristling with technical innovations and beautifully built down to the last metric capscrew, this Pescara is now being reconditioned by its owner, who has generously allowed the use of old negatives for the accompanying illustrations.

The normal 2,960 cc. single camshaft engine for touring developed 80 BHP at 3,600 rpm. Output was increased to 125 BHP at 5,500 rpm with dual camshafts. A vast range of rear axle gears permitted quick changes to accommodate requirements but, strangely, it seems, the gearbox contained only two gears. Top gear provided direct drive; the original ratios are not known. The records show that the competition models illustrated won the European Mountain Championship—hill climbs in our lingo—in 1931 against formidable opposition which included 7-litre Mercedes, Maseratis, Bugattis, Alfa Romeos and the like. There were times when triple-lobe blowers were fitted to the Pescaras. Whether or not the team cars were so equipped for the 1931 hill climb season is not known but, considering the limitations of just 3 litres and two gear speeds, the winning Pescaras must have been blown.

Also catalogued was a larger bore eight displacing 3,550 cc. And there was yet another Pescara engine, an almost unbelievable in-line, 10-cylinder affair with 71.3 x 100 mm. bore and stroke. Reportedly, two of these 4,100 cc. engines were made for installation in long-wheelbase, 7-passenger luxury models; their output is not known nor are details of firing order or valve timing available. The artist's catalogue drawings are most interesting.

Some fourteen Nacionale Pescara cars were built. Of these only three remain: the roadster once owned by the king, one of the 1931 Mountain Championship team cars without its engine, and an extremely fast supercharged racer modified to single-seat format.

During the mid-thirties, the Marquis developed a 60 x 80 mm., 3.6-litre, V-16 engine while associated with an industrial concern in Switzerland. With a single overhead camshaft on each cylinder bank and pressurized by a Roots-type blower, it is said to have developed 150 BHP at 5,200 rpm, but this figure seems to be on the low side considering the displacement and other factors. Pescara also experimented with free piston engines, tried to promote a jet engine design for aircraft long before World War Two, and even considered nuclear power and air cushion vehicles for use over any terrain—a man in the wrong country at the wrong time.

Sweden

Up near the Northern Lights automobile manufacturing is an old story. There's much more background to Swedish cars than meets American eyes in the form of modern Volvo and Saab cars which were first imported about 1955. The history of Swedish cars, according to an official of the Technical Museum in Stockholm, "is a story which has never been told in an internationally understandable language."

The Tidaholm Bruk is one of the oldest Swedish makes. Unfortunately, the archives disclose too little on this firm's automobiles which were produced in limited numbers from about 1903 to 1935 in Göteborg. Rugged, all-purpose machines, they combined characteristics of passenger cars and off-the-road trucks. Before World War One, vehicles like the Tidaholm Bruk shown were highly favored in the rugged North country. This particular 4-cylinder machine was slated for a buyer in St. Petersburg (now Leningrad), Russia, but the outbreak of hostilities prevented delivery. Tidaholm Bruk A.B. is said to have "made the first all-Swedish car," whatever such a phrase means. There are precious few countries able to produce everything needed to fabricate as complex a machine as an automobile in all of its technical requirements from tires to lighting filaments.

As late as 1910, the Atvidabergs Vagnafabrik, literally a "wagon factory," built high-wheeled cars by the relatively simple and expedient means of modifying horse-drawn wagons with the installation of 1-cylinder gasoline and paraffin burning engines and steering mechanisms. The anachronistic Atvidabergs cars were much like the Hollsmann cars in the U.S.A. Available information does not disclose whether automobiles were built from the ground up in series production by this firm. Atvidabergs is now an important supplier of component parts to Volvo.

Little known outside of the Scandinavian nations is AB Thulinverken, a pioneer aircraft maker. From 1919 to 1928, Thulin cars were manufactured in limited numbers —often to customer order—totalling about 300 cars. Made in Lansdskrona, the 1924 Thulin Type A tourer illustrated was distinguished by a sharply pointed radiator shell. Styling and general arrangements were fairly typical for cars of the period. Weighing about 1,720 pounds, the car's 4-cylinder, L-head 20-HP engine provided a maximum speed of just over 40 mph. As might be

As late in the automobile age as 1910, Atvidabergs Vagnafabrik was building gasoline-engine-powered wagons like this one; of course, horseless carriages and wagons were common in other countries, too. (*Tekniska Museet, Stockholm*)

From 1903 to 1935, Tidaholms Bruk AB of Göteborg built specialized vehicles in a wide variety. The 1911 chassis, shown herewith on a postal van body, was employed for passenger cars as well. (*Tekniska Museet, Stockholm*)

Typical of the Tidaholms Bruk automobiles was the 1914 heavy duty vehicle built for a buyer in old St. Petersburg, Russia. Sweden's rugged terrain required particularly sturdy cars. (*Tekniska Museet, Stockholm*)

Thulin cars were built to special order in limited numbers in Landskrona. The 1924 model tourer has a 4-cylinder, 1,420-cc., 20-HP engine, full pressure lubrication to three main bearings, and a pointed radiator shell in the European tradition of the time. (*Tekniska Museet, Stockholm*)

Thulin cars for 1928 had flat radiator grilles and other styling changes. Semi-elliptic springs were retained but the dumb iron frame extensions were deleted in favor of a horizontal front cross member carrying the spring shackles. (*Tekniska Museet, Stockholm*)

expected in a nation of master wood craftsmen, selected and seasoned hardwoods were employed with metal sheathing in body building—an almost universal practice until the late '20s. A 4-seater, the Thulin was updated in 1928, given restyled fenders curving

The first Volvo was the 1927 model P4 dubbed "Jacob" by the Göteborg concern. The 4-cylinder engine displaced 1,940 cc. (118.5 cu. in.), developed 28 horsepower. Styled by artist Mas-Olle, the new car was an immediate success. (AB *Volvo*)

far over the front wheels, and the radiator shell was blunted to a flat surface. The Thulin's builders turned to tool production in 1928.

About this time Volvo entered the automobile picture. It was in 1927 that the first Volvo car was rolled out of the factory in Göteborg, the result of a decision in 1924 by industrialist Assar Gabrielsson and engineer Gustaf Larsson to challenge the domination of imported cars on the home market. The pioneering 1927 model touring car had a wheelbase of 112.24 inches and a 4-cylinder 118.5 cubic inch engine developing approximately 28 HP at 2,000 RPM. The top gear maximum speed was 37 mph. A 4-door sedan was built the same year. Both types had full leather interiors and

body frames built of selected ash and red beech. The open tourer was sheathed in metal and the sedan body, aft of the hood, was covered with leatherette, a feature on many cars of the period. The next year, 1928, Volvo entered the export market with a shipment to Finland. Exports to Norway followed.

By 1933, the PV-653 model had an all-steel body and a higher performing 6-cylinder, 3.6 litre engine of 80 HP. This engine was continued in its basic form in the more stylish 1939 sedan with flush headlights and contemporary streamlining. The Volvo models known so well in America have quite a lineage. Incidentally, the Saab cars, products of the Svenska Aeroplan Aktiebolaget, are a post-war product.

"Jacob" from the side, the first Volvo of 1927.
(AB Volvo)

The sedan version of the 1927 Volvo had leather-ette covered body. The radiator adornment is of interest; the small circular device refers to the Latin meaning of Volvo: "I roll." (AB Volvo)

The spacious leather interior of the 1927 Volvo.
(AB Volvo)

The Volvo model PV653 of 1933 had an all-steel
body and an 80-horsepower, 6-cylinder engine.
(*AB Volvo*)

The 1937 Volvo reflected the semi-fastback styling of American influence. (*AB Volvo*)

The Volvo model PV801 of 1938 was a roomy car of compact size; note the far aft position of the rear seat. (*AB Volvo*)

The 3.6-litre, 6-cylinder engine had reached high efficiency by this 1939 Volvo model PV36; styling was modern with flush headlights. (*AB Volvo*)

The first series produced passenger car built by Scania works in Malmö was this 1902 model with the uniquely curved dash; the 1-cylinder, water-cooled engine was an imported Kemper, 6 HP, from Berlin, Germany. (AB *Scania-Vabis*)

Long a builder of fine cars, some deserving "classic" or "thoroughbred" status, the present firm of Scania-Vabis in Södertälje near Stockholm no longer builds passenger cars; however, trucks and busses by this firm are marketed in some forty-five countries. Today Scania-Vabis trucks are also built in a subsidiary plant in Brazil for the Latin American market. Prior to 1911, Scania cars were built in Malmo in a long series. Shown here are those of 1902 and

1903 and the quality landaulette models of 1907 and 1908. The 1907 model had a 4-cylinder, 15-HP engine. Other body styles included family tourers and a few models with runabout bodies.

In 1911, the Vabis firm—mentioned in Part II as an active car builder prior to 1900 —and Scania merged forming Scania-Vabis. In 1901, Scania runabouts were the world's first cars to have ball bearing wheels and, in several races, they beat the Vabis cars

Even in the early days of the automobile in Sweden, color choices were offered as indicated by this 1902 Scania; the lamps are also varied. (*Tekniska Museet, Stockholm*)

to the finish line. The year of the merger, the new firm produced the world's first motor bus on a specially designed chassis; previously, rehashed truck chassis were used with bodies and bench seats cobbled onto the rough-riding platforms.

The first joint Scania-Vabis effort was a briskly performing, fairly large, 2-litre, 36-HP Phaeton, Type 3-S of 1911. Sweden's Royal Family soon owned several Scania-Vabis cars including a 1914 Type 2121

Phaeton equipped with the firm's own 4-cylinder, 22-HP engine and a body entirely sheathed in metal. By 1915, Scania-Vabis Phaetons with engines of from 22 to 50 HP were the favored staff cars for the military services, and the limousines were gaining in public popularity. Of the latter, the Type 2,154 of 1,919, was of especially fine design with an interior like a miniature drawing room. A notable feature of this 4-cylinder, 5-litre vehicle, which is preserved in the

For 1903, Scania passenger cars had a 2-cylinder, 8-horsepower engine with 3-speed transmission plus reverse; though the rear axle was built integrally with gearbox, chain drive was used. Rear seat passengers entered the tonneau via rear door; the tonneau could be removed and replaced with a cargo box. (*AB Scania-Vabis*)

A restyled engine hood with vertical lines and a longer tonneau, and redesigned, more steeply angled steering gear were the marks of the 1904 Scania. The engine was not changed; the chain drive is clearly visible here. (*AB Scania-Vabis*)

The finest Scania for 1907 was the limousine powered with the Type "M," 4-cylinder, 15-horsepower engine engineered and produced in the Scania works in Malmö. (*AB Scania-Vabis*)

The attractively contoured fenders of the 1907 models were continued in 1908 by Scania, but a new Type "L" engine developed 20 horsepower in this phaeton. (*AB Scania-Vabis*)

Flat-crowned front fenders, more easily produced, were fitted to the 1908 Scania line which featured an improved Type "H" 4-cylinder engine in the landaulet. (*AB Scania-Vabis*)

In 1909, the Vabis works in Södertälje produced the fine Type 2S landaulet; the factory's own Type G4 engine provided 14 horsepower. (*AB Scania-Vabis*)

Side-mounted spare tires without wheels or rims are first seen on the 1910 Scania phaeton; power was the Type "H" 18-horsepower engine. (*AB Scania-Vabis*)

With the merger in 1911 came a joint series, the Type 3S phaeton, first to be called Scania-Vabis. A new Type F4A engine delivered 30—36 horsepower. (*AB Scania-Vabis*)

Sweden's finest phaeton in 1914 was the Scania-Vabis on the type 2,121 chassis powered with a 22-horsepower engine. Smoother body lines with all controls moved inside complemented the V-radiator shell of shiny brass. (AB *Scania-Vabis*)

Accentuating the V-radiator shell was a torpedo body on chassis type 2,154 and a new, powerful type 1,546 engine which developed 50 horsepower. Fenders and dumb irons were also fully valanced in 1915. (AB *Scania-Vabis*)

This 1917 Scania-Vabis Type "I" phaeton served as staff car for the General commanding the 6th Division of the Royal Swedish Army until 1924. The flat-nosed styling was more utilitarian. Preserved today in the works museum in Södertältalje, the still operable 4-cylinder engine has bore and stroke of 78 x 110 mm. and a 4-speed transmission. The foot brake operated a strap mechanism on the propeller shaft while handbrake actuated expanding shoes in rear wheel drums. (*AB Scania-Vabis*)

Also built upon the type 2,154 chassis, and powered with the 50-horsepower, 5-litre engine (100 x 160 mm.) were these luxury Scania-Vabis models. The "Limousine de luxe" had V-windshield and radiator topped off with a steel roof with rounded edges—an advanced car for 1919. (*AB Scania-Vabis*)

firm's museum, is the roof with rounded sides of steel. Scania-Vabis cars were of technical excellence considerably above the average for the 1919–20 period and were, for a time in the twenties, assembled and marketed in Norway.

About the beginning of 1925, Scania-Vabis entered the truck and bus field in which they are presently active in many nations. The firm increased their line of marine engines, and, regrettably, built their last passenger car, an art in which this firm excelled although their automobiles are virtually unknown outside of Scandinavia.

Other Swedish marques were launched with less success than those described and shown: the Hockenström from around 1914 to the mid-'20s; the Lidköping of 1922–23; the Self of 1916; the Söderbloms of uncertain early date; the Swensen (with a Danish-sounding name) of the century's first decade; and no doubt others that have disappeared. Automotive graveyards and shattered dreams are worldwide phenomena and —like the rosters of inventors—are not the exclusive heritage of the large nations.

Preserved in all its elegance is one of the 1919 Limousine Scania-Vabis models on the type 2,154 chassis. The luxurious interior with curtains, strap-operated sliding windows, footrests, mohair upholstery and dome light speaks for itself. The jump seats increased total passenger capacity to seven. (AB *Scania-Vabis*)

Switzerland

MORE THAN TWENTY different makes of automobiles were produced commercially in Switzerland before 1931. In Geneva alone, there were ten car manufacturers early in this century. Many of these were small enterprises like their counterparts in other countries including the United States where more than 3,000 separate name-makes of cars have come and gone. However, the pioneer automotive industry lives on today in three large manufacturers of trucks and busses. Saurer, Berna, and FBW makes are well known in Central Europe.

Rudolf Egg is regarded as the first to take up in Switzerland where Isaac de Rivaz left off early in the 19th century. By 1905, Egg's cars were in series production including runabouts that were the mechanical and style equals of those in Germany and France. Egg was at one time associated with Weber & Company in Uster where he was engineer in charge of automobile design. One of his designs was the 1900–1902 Weber four and six passenger carriages. In the 1902 model illustrated, the driver and two persons sat in front; there was a steering wheel on an angle rather than the period's usual straight column, four control levers, and a large water-cooled 1-cylinder engine with a nearly square bore and stroke of 160 and 170 mm. respectively. The fuel tank was high in the rear for gravity flow. Beneath a leather top fitted with landau irons sat three passengers. This pneumatic tired automobile is said to have been able to speed 35 mph for short bursts.

Later Rudolf Egg became engineer for the manufacturers of the Rapid cars in Zurich.

One of the most elegant of the early Swiss cars was the 1902 Berna Ideal made in Bern by Josef Wyss (see illustration). One passenger sat sideways in front while the other, with the driver, sat behind. In Switzerland as elsewhere in the early days, it was stylish for the driver to sit in the rear—a hold-over from the design of some formal horse carriages. The Ideal had a large 1-cylinder, 5.5 HP square engine with bore and stroke of 100 mm. The water-cooling coils were low in the front. The De Dion drive system, employing two short axle shafts, was used. A lever on the vertical steering column—rack and pinion by the way—operated the 2-speed transmission through a sleeve clutch. The other column lever controlled the gasoline feed. With leather, formed wood fenders, and coachwork fin-

Rudolf Egg, pioneer automobile designer influential at the turn of the century in Switzerland, at the wheel of one of his cars in the Alps in 1905.

This roadster-runabout 3-seater rivals the designs of larger nations. (*Swiss Museum of Transport & Communications*)

ished in red with two gleaming black carbide side lamps and the single huge headlamp in front, the Ideal was a striking machine. The Berna works discontinued building cars in 1905 and converted all production to trucks, a business that continues today in Olten.

To become famous in later years as the inventor of the Magneta electric clock, Martin Fischer of Zurich began production of the very small and unique Turicum "Roller" car in 1904. This tiny car, scarcely more than 9 feet long, had a 1-cylinder engine driving the rear axle by chains. The unusual feature of the little Turicum was the lack of a steering column—something modern engineers are desperately trying to eliminate today. The car was steered by two foot pedals. The hands were occupied with

engine controls and brake levers. Fischer's Turicum cars, given the Latin name for Zurich, had the first "quick release" detachable wheels.

Fischer built cars of several series. Some of his later models, such as the 4-cylinder, 4-passenger 1908 Turicums built in Uster were exported to other European countries where, occasionally now, one shows up at a veteran car meeting. Fischer, who was his own chief engineer, invented an early friction drive which was very successful. In 1909, Fischer built another factory in Brunau. The large 1913–1914 Fischer models were particularly fine. This last series of Martin Fischer's cars seated six and had a 33-HP, 4-cylinder engine displacing 2,720 cc. This engine had sleeve valves and was

Between 1900 and 1902 the Weber works in Uster built four-passenger cars like this single-cylinder vehicle with an infinitely variable belt drive to the rear wheels; a Rudolf Egg design. (*Swiss Museum of Transport & Communications*)

The Berna "Ideal" motor carriages made by Josef Wyss had an air of elegance; the 1902 model. (*Swiss Museum of Transport & Communications*)

The two-seater Ideal, 1902, had straight dash and folding top. Josef Wyss, at wheel, was the founder of Motorwagen Fabrik Berna, still a prominent truck maker. (*Motorwagen Fabrik Berna A.G.*)

Josef Wyss (in cap) at controls of one of the several Ideal cars he manufactured in 1902; note side seating of front passenger. (*Motorwagen Fabrik Berna A.G.*)

On June 13, 1902, Wyss organized a mass road test of his cars. Here are three Ideals at the start of the run. (*Motorwagen Fabrik Berna A.G.*)

inspired by the Knight (American) design. Quite out of the ordinary for its time, the 4-speed transmission contained a primary wheel with four internal gears of various diameters which, when meshed with a shaft-mounted bevel gear, provided a selection of ratios. Chassis were of heavy box-section longitudinal rails. Fischer built both Fischer and Turicum marques at a combined rate of about four a day. Between 1911 and 1913 some 200 Fischer cars were exported to South America. Other interests took Martin Fischer away from cars late in 1914 and his two marques were no more. For a brief time around 1913, Fischer cars were built under license in the U.S.A. One wonders whether a Swiss Fischer will ever turn up at an antique car gathering.

Along about 1903, the automotive editors of European newspapers suddenly became aware of two brothers from Geneva. Frederick and Charles Dufaux were said to be grooming some powerful new cars for assaults on the then standing speed records for gasoline cars. Paris editions of the *New York Herald* newspaper headlined the Dufaux brothers in the December 1, 1904, issue and described the great cars they were building in Geneva—large 8-cylinder, 12¾-litre machines with the cylinders cast in pairs, each of which was surrounded by a rectangular water jacket. The reports proved correct for on the 15th of November, 1905, Frederick broke the official world speed record for gasoline cars—then held by a Panhard-Levassor at 144 Km per hour—with a flying kilometre run timed at 156.5 Km per hour, or 97.257 mph, in one of their 150 HP Dufaux two-seater specials. The brothers offered both 4-cylinder and 8-cylinder runabouts and four to six-passenger tourers with less potent engines varying from 15 to 120 HP. Series built, the Dufaux cars had chain drives, and used ball and roller

Turicum cars, built near Zurich from 1904 to about 1924, were often unique. The 1904 "Roller" designed by Martin Fischer, in driver's seat, was steered by foot pedals. (*Swiss Museum of Transport & Communications*)

The 1908 Turicum tourer, powered by a 1,940-cc. engine developing 16 horsepower, had a variable ratio friction drive. It continued in production until about 1913. (*Swiss Museum of Transport & Communications*)

The 8-cylinder 1905 Dufaux racing car that broke the world's speed record at 97.5 mph; cylinders were cast in pairs. Now restored, the car will still reach 87 mph. (*Swiss Museum of Transport & Communications*)

bearings plus light alloys in the engines which drove 4-speed transmissions through leather cone clutches. Semi-elliptic springs were employed, and aluminum was a favorite body material for the limited-production, high-performance Dufaux cars.

One of the finest of the early Swiss cars was the limousine version of the Ajax which was built in Zurich from 1906 through 1910 when bankruptcy ended the firm. Exquisitely detailed, Ajax cars were 5 and 6-passenger machines of a comparable quality to contemporary Rolls-Royce and Hispano-Suiza cars. Featuring large 4-cylinder engines, rich brass trim and luxurious interiors, Ajax cars had a reputation for robustness and durability. Built only on special order and expensive, only one is now known to exist, the town car illustrated here, a plush 4-cylinder prestige car. Other less exclusive Ajax cars were popular as taxis.

The lovely Stella was built from 1902 until late 1914 in Geneva by Voitures Stella. Less is known of this marque than of other Swiss cars, but it is believed that the noted Rudolf Egg had a hand in designing the 1910 limousine shown here. The circular radiator shell, the fenders, and overall functional simplicity of the coachwork were hallmarks of the Stella. Many of the Stella cars had multi-piece curved windshields, and were usually fitted with wire wheels when most other Swiss cars were using wooden artillery wheels. Stella was regarded as a quality car for the discriminating driver.

The largest producer of automobiles in Switzerland was Max Martini whose first car, in 1897, had a rear engine. In 1903, Martini set up production in St. Blaise near Neuchâtel. The first year 30 cars were built. In 1905, Martini set a record of 21 hours, 5 minutes in one of his own cars for the

554

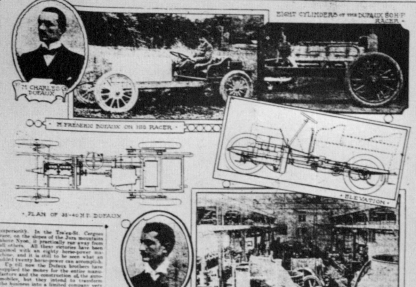

The Paris editions of the New York *Herald* featured the 150-horsepower, 12¾-litre Dufaux cars in December, 1904. (*Swiss Museum of Transport & Communications*)

A typical, luxury limousine-landau built by the Automobilfabrik Ajax from 1906–10. Six rode in comfort in this 1908 model powered by a 4-cylin-der engine. (*Swiss Museum of Transport & Communications*)

546 highway miles from London to Neu-châtel, a popular record attempt route of the day. Martini advertised his cars as "The first and oldest national make." When the 1914–18 war began, he produced cars and trucks for the Swiss Army.

The 1914 Martini was a high quality vehicle favored as a military staff car and also as a 5–6 passenger family tourer. This model was the most popular Swiss car of that year. A 4-cylinder L-head 90 x 150 mm. engine was standard while a 6-cylinder engine was optional with coachbuilt bodies of various styles. The Martini evolved into a long line of 4 and 6-cylinder prestige vehicles which continued in production through 1931. Production varied from about 300 to 350 per year, but approached 1,000 units annually on occasion between 1922 and 1931.

To Americans today, these annual production figures seem small. Even so, more Martinis were built than the more familiar Cords, Duesenbergs, Mercers and other more famous American makes. Chassis of Martini cars were rugged and beautifully built. Metal tubes with flexible rubber fittings were often used for the cooling system

556

The 1910 limousine by Voitures Stella had a 20-horsepower, 4-cylinder engine. One of Switzerland's major car builders, Stella lasted until the first world war. (*Swiss Museum of Transport & Communications*)

Most numerous of all Swiss cars was the Martini. In 1905, Max Martini drove this 40-horsepower tourer from London to Neufchatel, a popular speed run of the day, for a new record. Martini is at the wheel. (*Swiss Museum of Transport & Communications*)

The 1914 Martini 6-seater tourer was popular as a military staff car; was also extensively exported. The 4-cylinder engine with bore and stroke of 85 x 130 mm. had reputation for robustness. (*Swiss Museum of Transport & Communications*)

Sharply pointed radiator shell and exquisite craftsmanship characterized the Pic-Pic of 1919; the firm name was Piccard, Pictet & Company based in Geneva. A large sleeve-valve, 4-cylinder engine, 4-speed transmission and multi-plate clutch were features. (*Swiss Museum of Transport & Communications*)

The Saurer works in Arbon still makes quality trucks and buses. From 1898, Saurer cars were built in limited numbers. This 1902 model, laden with four passengers, ascends a rather steep grade. (*Société Anonyme Adolphe Saurer*)

The 1912 Saurer tourer had clean lines and enjoyed success in various competitive events. This marque figured prominently in the earliest experiments to adapt Diesel engines to automobiles and trucks. (*Société Anonyme Adolphe Saurer*)

where other manufacturers customarily employed rubber hoses. Martini cars were also among the earliest to have parking lights as standard equipment. In some respects, the 1914 model illustrated was several years ahead of its time. The handbrake lever acted upon the rear wheels and the footbrake lever upon the 4-speed transmission. The steel-spoked wheels had a center-lock device allowing quick changes.

An outstanding Swiss car was the elegant Pic-Pic tourer, the product of the engineering and craftsmanship of Paul Picard, an inventor of water turbines, and Jules Pictet. The first Pic-Pic was built in 1906—the date is uncertain—and was designed by Hispano-Suiza founder, Marc Birkigt. Production of this marque ranged from a minimum of 113 to a maximum of 639 cars annually. On occasion, Picard & Pictet fielded racing cars. In 1914, a pair of Pic-Pics were on tap for the Grand Prix of France. These racers were powered by 4½ litre, single sleeve valve engines which were based upon the system developed by the manufacturers of the Argyll in Scotland. Like several other marques by this date—Fiat and Peugeot for example —the Pic-Pics were equipped with four-wheel mechanical brakes and magneto ignition systems.

Regarded on the Continent by 1919 to have been on a par with the Rolls-Royce, the 1919 Pic-Pic Tourenwagen (illustrated) had a large, 4-cylinder sleeve valve engine and was undeniably a fine car. Just why Picard and Pictet chose to forsake the 6-cylinder format, which had distinguished their earlier models such as the 1907 tourers, is not clear. The sleeve valve engines were quiet but they gulped oil and were not given to high speed. From 1911 to 1914, the Pic-Pic engines were license-built in several countries where they were used in some racing cars. Some sources have stated that the Pic-Pic remained in series production as late as 1924. However, Alfred Waldis, director of the Swiss Museum of Transport & Communication in Lucerne, states authoritatively that production ceased in 1921 and that the last known example built was purchased in Switzerland by Gnome-Rhone Motors of France in 1924.

The Saurer works, the outgrowth of an iron foundry dating back to 1853 when Franz Saurer opened shop in St. Georgen, is today a leading manufacturer of diesel trucks and busses in a factory complex in Arbon on Lake Constance. In 1888, Adolph Saurer, son of the founder, began manufacturing internal combustion engines for industrial use and in 1898 the first Saurer automobile was built. Outwardly conforming to competitive makes of the time, these first Saurer cars had the high dash front and towered over pedestrians on full-elliptic springs. Beneath the carriage coachwork, though, the horizontal 1-cylinder engine had two opposing pistons which swept a displacement of 3.14 litres and developed 5 horsepower. By 1902 Saurer cars were noted for toughness and hill-climbing ability, a necessary prerequisite for a Swiss motorcar.

Dr. Rudolph Diesel, inventor of the engine type bearing his name, collaborated with the Saurer works in 1907 and 1908 with the result that the latter year saw the world's first diesel-powered truck. Three years later, a fully laden Saurer truck accomplished a truck first by crossing the United States from coast to coast. Saurer continued, according to works archives, to manufacture private touring cars in the early years of this century. By 1912, however, the major output was trucks, and cars like the tourer illustrated were becoming a sideline. During the

'30s, Saurer assembled Chrysler cars. Today the multi-factory firm makes aircraft engines and huge diesel engines for a variety of highway, railroad and industrial applications, as well as quality trucks and busses.

With a technical tradition out of all proportion to national size, Switzerland's automotive pioneers, from de Rivaz on have never received the accolades due them with the exceptions of Marc Birkigt, creator of the Hispano-Suiza, and of Louis Chevrolet.

The latter made his fortune in Detroit. In fact, many Swiss believe that Chevrolet used a perspective view of the cross on the Swiss flag as the outline of the emblem of the car that became a worldwide best seller.

Other Swiss marques were the Orion, Moser, Helios, Mobil, Sigma, Millot, Franz, Helvetia, Royal, Maximag, Hurlimann, Genève, Soller, Yaxa, Zürcher and a few others. Despite efforts, no photographs of these obscure cars have been found.

Part V

AUTOMOBILES OF THE TWENTIETH CENTURY

Our Own Automobiles Reach Maturity

T HE GREATEST OBSTACLE to early acceptance of the gasoline car was the consternation resulting from the sudden appearance of one of the noisy contraptions. Horses reared and bolted scattering bystanders and spilling riders or carriage passengers. One manufacturer, seeking to give a friendly appearance to his gas buggies, attached life-sized dummy horse heads to the front of the rigs.

By around 1902, however, word was out that if you owned a gas buggy, for instance, you could be well on your way before your neighbor's steam car had operating pressure —and you could make a non-stop round trip of more than 100 miles without waiting overnight to recharge the batteries. By 1900, literally thousands of blacksmiths, machine shop operators, and engineers of a dozen specialties across America fell under the spell of the gasoline carriage and began to build them.

Cars carried names of people, insects, animals, flowers, trees, and even words of endearment like Darling on their nameplates. The 1904 Calorie counted but one year of life and the Vim had vim enough only for 1914. Cars named for heavenly bodies like the Moon (1905–30), Star (1903–28), and Sun (1915–24) shone brightly a number of years but the Komet (1911) phased out quickly. Then there was the Comet, unrelated to the present compact from Ford Motor Company, which struggled along from 1917 to '25.

Names of mythological origin like Hercules (1914–15) and Vulcan (1913–15) failed to impress the public. The Vogue stayed in vogue from 1917 to '23, but the Havoc could cause hardly any in its single year, 1914. Cars named for states—Oregon, Ohio, Rhode Island, New York, Kentucky, California, Nevada, and more—failed to excite the patriotism of their own citizens.

Cities like Kankakee, Toledo, Milwaukee, Tulsa, Reno, Menominee, Los Angeles, Hartford, Holyoke, Elkhart, Allegheny, Chicago, Fostoria, and more, had cars named for them but their chambers of commerce didn't take the cue.

The Preferred of 1920 wasn't, nor could the Mutual of 1919 outdo the horses on the track any more than could the Equitable of 1901–03 get its share of the market. Car buyers failed to spark to advertisements for Old Reliable in 1912, and the unhealthy

One of the most popular of all carriage-based automobiles after the turn of the century was the "curved dash" Oldsmobile which was built in Lansing, Michigan, from 1900 to 1904. The 1-cylinder, horizontal engine put out 7 horsepower; bore and stroke were 5 and 6 inches; wheelbase, 67 inches; tread 55. Transmission had spur gears with two speeds forward plus reverse. Note the large flywheel. Radiator was cooled by water from 5 gallon tank; fuel capacity was also 5 gallons. Original finish was black with red pin striping. Price was $675. (*Henry Ford Museum*)

sounding Ricketts in 1902 and again in 1909 inspired nobody. Some names, it would seem, just weren't appealing.

Names familiar in the years of Dobbin's decline occasionally thrived for a time, like the Orient Buckboard which lasted six years. On the other hand, the Queen of 1902–07 was an excellent full sized tourer, and well named, but few have survived.

In 1903, Henry Ford got into production with the first Model A, and Cadillac, in its second year, was becoming a good seller

although the firm purchased most of their engines from other manufacturers.

Advertising claims were frequently as far-fetched as are some today. Franklin had many good years between 1901 and 1935, but, before World War One started, claimed that water-cooled cars were successful merely because their makers had had the wisdom to follow Franklin's example and adopt the 4-cylinder engine. Franklin cars were always air-cooled, of course, but so were many others—about ninety of them.

1901 Crestmobile (1900–05) cost $550; had single-cylinder, air-cooled engine with self-starter; remarkably simple, body was a sturdy craft-built wood box; side lamps held candles. (*Henry Ford Museum*)

In the early days, most manufacturers did not have proving grounds. Although most builders gave every car a brief test drive, some conducted far-ranging road tests over a prescribed route covering terrain of every sort. Other manufacturers had agreements with municipal authorities to use fairground race tracks for speed and roadability tests. At least one car builder had an elaborate oval with steeply banked curves about 1914 —the entire surface was planked with hardwood boards.

If any single gas buggy fired the public's imagination in the early years, it was the curved dash Olds which was produced from 1900 to '04. The Lansing firm's first big break came in 1903 when the government purchased a large batch of a delivery version of the straight dash model for the Post Office Department—three years after officials in some overseas British dependencies adopted the motor car.

In 1903, the automobile conquered the vastness between the Golden Gate and New York City using old stage routes and military trails. The driver was a young doctor, H. Nelson Jackson of Vermont. Visiting in San Francisco, Jackson covered a $50 wager

1902 Franklin (1901–35) lets go with a cloud of smoke as it parades past spectators after taking part in the revived Glidden Tour of 1959. The drive-past took place at the termination of the Tour, the Henry Ford Museum in Greenfield Village at Dearborn, Michigan. William C. Wright is the owner of this roadster. (*Photo by Author*)

that an automobile could never make the journey. Dr. Jackson bought a new Winton, and, accompanied by Sewell K. Crocker of Tacoma, Washington, did the job between May 3 and July 27.

Advertisements, as now, were aimed at the ladies. Clothing designers turned out fetching regalia for every season, climate, and type of journey anticipated. Women were cajoled with special hats guaranteed to protect hairdos even when "speeding along at 20 miles an hour."

Only the most expensive cars were closed so there were many "motoring accessories." Advertisements extolled the need for weather-proof face masks with built-in goggles and sheepskin-lined "bundlers"—a sort of open-end receptacle—into which small tots could be laced. Then there was the dual-purpose auto lorgnette which looked like a miniature sidescreen with an isin-glass-covered window in the center. A wind-blown female passenger was advised to protect her face with this device when travelling; later when the car stopped she could employ the handy lorgnette as a fan.

One chilly designer came up with a muff which simultaneously covered the driver's arms *and* the steering wheel. Probably the hottest of all gimmicks was an oven lined with asbestos which could be mounted around the exhaust manifold of a Model T Ford. When the picnicking family arrived at their destination, the potatoes were baked.

Racing victories generally—though not always—meant sales and most of the manufacturers fielded entries in the big events like the Vanderbilt Cup Race. In 1906, J. D. Maxwell was at the wheel of an 8-cylinder powerhouse. The races paid off and the Maxwell was popular from the beginning in 1904 until Walter P. Chrysler bought the

568

Looking down through the top of the small hood, the transverse, 4-cylinder, air-cooled engine of the '04 Franklin is disclosed. In the two-seater runabout, the power developed was about 20 while the larger engine in the Light Touring Tonneau developed 30 horsepower. Cylinders were cast singly; valve springs were on the heavy side. The oil smudge around top of second cylinder from left indicates a leaky gasket. Franklins were manufactured in Syracuse, New York. (*Photo by Author*)

Henry Ford built famed old "999" in 1902, won the Manufacturer's Challenge Cup race the same year, and set a new world speed record of 91.4 mph. Cylinders of the monstrous, 4-cylinder engine were cast singly; note the unusually thick radiator core. (*Henry Ford Museum*)

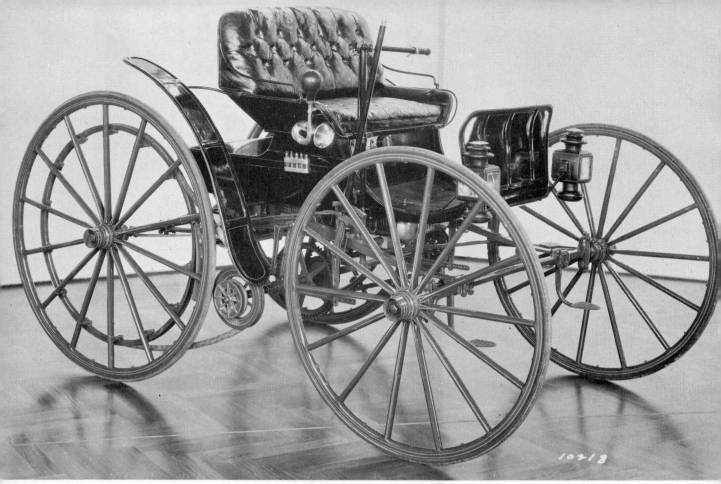

The 1903 Holsman Auto Buggy (1902–09) had a 2-cylinder horizontally-opposed engine, two forward speeds but no reverse. Weighing but 650 pounds, the Holsman's high, thin wheels were calculated to cut down through any mud to solid ground and to maintain traction; the wheels of the '05 model were 4 feet in diameter. Braided leather belt drive was employed. A leather top and side curtains were options. Prices began at $650. (*Henry Ford Museum*)

prosperous firm in 1924 and merged "the good Maxwell" into his own line which was introduced in 1921.

Next to a racing victory, an unheard of accomplishment sold cars. No doubt every car maker prayed for the first woman to drive across the continent—in his car. When four brave ladies did so, they drove a 1909 Haynes.

Newspapers and magazines editorialized on the pros and cons of being an "automobilist." One man in Alaska, who had never seen a car in his life, built one in 1905

in Skagway. A good car it was too—he even drove it over the old Richardson Trail from Valdez to Fairbanks and used it several years. Robert E. Sheldon is now a member of the Alaska Legislature and his car—first of any kind in Alaska—still survives.

The car called Success was a fleeting commodity. The 1906 Success counted on its already obsolete carriage design for popularity in rural areas. The 1-cylinder, 3-HP, air-cooled engine was mounted on the right side of the carriage body box, and drove the rear axle by a chain. The vehicle lasted just

This 1902 Holsman Auto Buggy belongs to the Lindley Bothwell collection and is the four-seater model; rear passengers entered through a tonneau door; the leather upholstery was of a high order in this early open horseless carriage. Note the carriage step. (*Photo by Author*)

three years from 1906 to '09. The name was back on the hood of a car briefly in 1920, then vanished from automobiliana.

Before the first decade of the 20th century was over, most cars closely resembled each other in appearance and performance except for high-priced machines. Engineers with distinctive ideas and the means to proceed along individual lines were becoming scarce for the most part.

Two men had a more burning determination than most of their contemporaries to build the best possible cars with available technology and materials. They were Lee Sherman Chadwick and H. A. Lozier. Chad-

wick caught the bug while an engineering student at Purdue University and Lozier succumbed while manufacturing a successful line of marine engines which, by 1902, had bested many of the best European engines in speedboat competition.

About 1901, Chadwick developed a new type of driving mechanism for commercial laundry machines. As a result, he came to the attention of a ball bearing manufacturing firm in Boston where he went to work as general manager. Chadwick soon had the ailing factory out of the red by changing the sequence of manufacturing operations. Next, he invented the world's

1903 Orient Buckboard (1903–09) had hand-painted trim in gold on gasoline tank, a 1-cylinder, 4-cycle engine, and was a mere 9 feet long. (*Henry Ford Museum*)

Elmore cars were built in Clyde, Ohio (1900–12). This 1903 model is one of the finest of the mark to be preserved. Cost $800. (*Robert E. Burke Studio, courtesy of Thompson Auto Museum*)

ELMORE 1903
THOMPSON AUTO MUSEUM
CLEVELAND OHIO

Overland cars were built in Toledo, Ohio, from 1903–29. This is the slope-nosed first model and is believed to have been made in Indianapolis just before the parent firm moved to Ohio. (*Willys-Overland Motors, Inc.*)

Henry Ford's first production model was this 1903 Model "A" shown here in front of the great man's birthplace in Dearborn, Michigan. With the tonneau seat installed, the price was $900 as shown here. This model had been preserved in its original condition with red body striped in gold with black fenders. Low average road speed obviated need for horn, lights or windshield. More than 200 of these were sold in 1903 justifying the advertised claim, "The Car of Satisfaction." (*Henry Ford Museum*)

As a "runabout" without the tonneau seat, the 1903 Ford Model "A" sold for $800. (*Henry Ford Museum*)

Leland's first model of the Cadillac, the 1903 model runabout shown, looked very much like the '03 Ford Model "A" and also carried the "A" model designation; Henry Ford and his friend Leland enjoyed early cooperation. The 1-cylinder engine was fueled with sufficient gas to travel some 200 miles without refueling. Price, $750. (*Henry Ford Museum*)

first centerless roll-grinding machine and then found the time to do what he wanted to—build a car. In 1903, Chadwick completed his first car working almost single-handedly; it is generally considered to be the world's first car with roller and ball bearings. Then to gain experience, he became production manager in Philadelphia for Searchmont Motors, makers of a buggy-auto. He built a 4-cylinder engine that sped the flimsy Searchmont at 35 to 40 MPH in 1903. The financial panic of the same year ruined Searchmont, and Chadwick, on his own again, hand-built another 4-cylinder car that went almost 60 MPH. Convinced that ball and roller bearings were the key to dependability, durability, and high performance, he sold this car, the first with the Chadwick name. With the funds obtained, Chadwick set up shop in a stable in the Quaker City.

By 1905, more than a dozen Chadwicks with 24 and 40-HP, 4-cylinder engines had been built and sold. In 1906, he built two dozen more cars which quickly sold and then he decided that six cylinders would be better than four. He was after power and performance, and the Great Chadwick Six was born enabling him to interest investors in order to move to Pottstown, Pennsylvania, and put his new car into production. He would use aluminum for many components where strength was not required. In 1907, Chadwick made a three-stage supercharger and advertised it as optional on all his cars which were built first, then priced, because he was more interested in quality than in quantity. Thus, Chadwicks were high priced, but eagerly sought by enthusiasts. The Fast Runabout of 1908 did an honest 100 MPH and cost $6,500, and the limousine, Type-16, cost almost $8,000. The lowest priced Chadwick, a tourer, cost $5,500.

Chadwick runabouts with superchargers were sensations on the race circuit with just 65 rated HP. One did 107 MPH and by 1909 had defeated just about everything, including a 300-HP, imported Benz, by doing 10 miles in less than 8.5 minutes.

The outstanding feature of the Great Chadwick Six was the engine with cylinders cast in pairs. A copper water jacket surrounding each pair provided about four times as much coolant circulation for each cylinder as was common at the time. The valves and guides were also water-cooled. When competitors scoffed at such an expensively constructed engine, Chadwick's reaction was to win races with no fan belt; his cars still cooled efficiently. Deep inside the engine were oil lines to each bearing and the splash system incorporated a shaft-driven, forced-feed oiling system. A patented lever controlled from the dashboard allowed the driver to synchronize the fuel jet in the carburetor with the accelerator setting. This enabled Chadwicks to idle smoothly at low speed but still accelerate rapidly.

Another Chadwick patent was for an exclusive covering on the chain drive which kept out foreign matter. Still another Chadwick patent was for the direct drive, double bevel gear transmission. Driveshafts were coming into prominence, but Chadwick reasoned that the chains were less complicated, stronger, and more easily maintained. Chadwick used chrome-nickel steel in his gears and frames—another first. Chadwick was also one of the first to build aluminum bodies. The lightweight sheets were formed over a body framework of selected and seasoned hardwood. The Chadwick bodies were built outside his own Pottstown factory but under his constant supervision and according to his designs. When bodies sometimes delayed completion of his cars, Chadwick

576

This gleaming 1904 Packard tourer (1899–1958) was a contestant in the '59 Glidden Tour and a winner of the concourse event held at the termination point, Greenfield Village in Dearborn, Michigan. The rear view shows the tonneau entry; the lady is in period costume. Owners: Mr. and Mrs. Richard Teaque. (*Photos by Author*)

built a body factory in Fleetwood, Pennsylvania, and put Harry Roumig in charge. General Motors eventually purchased the works, and this is how the Cadillac Fleetwood came into being.

In 1911, Chadwick had a serious disagreement with his financial backers who were unable to understand why he had built only some 260 cars. Chadwick explained that he could expand, create a large organization, and still build the best cars on the road but that profits, instead of being extracted, would have to be reinvested. This perfectionist wanted to further improve his cars —another dream the stockholders could not understand. The money-people believed that the Chadwick was the country's best car and that it did not need to be improved. Thus rebuffed, Chadwick walked out taking his name and patents with him, retired to the quiet Connecticut countryside where he invented a device which could have eliminated road maps. This was the "Road Guide" that attached to the dashboard; by gearing to the wheels, it recorded the miles and signalled by bells, pointers, and a printed drum where the motorist should make his next turn. Chadwick produced disks for popular routes between major cities and had the Road Guide manufactured.

The Road Guide was a limited success, but Chadwick soon left the automobile industry and entered the stove manufacturing business. However, Chadwicks survived in small numbers. Many enthusiasts believe Chadwick to have been the genius of the first decade of the century; the quality of his cars makes a good case.

Lozier, the other "great" of the period, had more immediate financial support available. From his marine engine factory, Lozier sent an engineer, Perrin, to Europe in 1902 to scout the secrets of quality car produc-

tion. This research resulted in the second claim for the world's first all ball and roller bearing engines. (In France the great Ettore Bugatti later adopted ball and roller bearings but Lozier—or Chadwick—was first.) Establishing his car factory in Detroit, Lozier first produced fine touring cars, and introduced the famed T-head, 6-cylinder engine about 1906. Eventually this powerhouse displaced 560 cubic inches. Some Lozier runabouts had a wheelbase of 131 inches and weighed 5,000 pounds. At the first Indianapolis 500-miler, a Lozier almost won, and probably would have, had it not been for a slow pit crew. At the 450-mile mark, the Lozier had broken all records for that distance but lost to a Marmon Special. After the race, the Lozier, a stock machine, showed no mechanical wear at all and quickly sold as a used car.

Lozier put increased effort into racing while Chadwick had trouble with his directors. The Lozier lasted only a few years longer than the Great Chadwick.

By 1910, General Motors was growing rapidly having acquired Buick, Cadillac, Oakland (which gave way to Pontiac in 1932), and Oldsmobile. But another combine, the U. S. Motor Car Company, was also forming with Columbia and Maxwell as the basis; this firm was under the guidance of Walter P. Chrysler whose genius was in corporate management. Rambler, too, was booming—one of the first to introduce spare tires and windshields as standard equipment.

In Indianapolis, Marion introduced the first American made 12-cylinder, V-type auto engine in 1909 preceding Packard— usually credited with the first V-12—by six years. Winton boasted of the world's lowest repair rate (29.2 cents per 1,000 miles). Friction drives threatened manual gear shift-

Tonneau doors for entry into the rear passenger compartment were common as on this 1904 Ford Model "A" tourer. Note the open sprocket for the chain drive and the full-elliptic leaf springs. (*Photo by Author*)

ing, and the two-cycle engine had virtually disappeared in America. The Model T Ford, introduced in 1908, was doing more to popularize left-hand drive than all of the others, and in the same year pioneered magneto ignition in the U.S.A. The Hudson runabout in 1909 was the first quality car for as little as $900 equipped with a three-speed sliding gear transmission.

The first decade of this remarkable century ended with the Buick plant in Flint, Michigan, being the largest in the fledgling industry with more than 6,000 employees.

In every state of the Union, to own an automobile became the goal of every person, young and old. Manufacturers tried virtually every name imaginable calculated to entice the idealistic, the wishful thinker, the naive or the status seeker.

There was the *Washington, Revere,* and *Patriot;* the *Coyote, Gopher* and *Deere;* the *Emancipator* and the *Victory;* the *Harvard* and *Yale,* the *Princeton* and *Oxford;* the *Powercar, Sampson,* and the *Practical;* the *Shamrock, Western,* and *Flying Dutchman;* the *Supreme* and the *Wonder;* the *Able,* and the *Foolproof;* the *Club Car, Calvert, Annhauser-Busch, Empire,* and *Van Dyke;* the *Lad's Car,* and *Princess;* the *Tally Ho, Prudence,* and the *Pilgrim;* the *Buck* and

579

MARK TWAIN and the DOUBLE ACTION OLDS

By 1905, Mark Twain had become a convert to the automobile; here the famous writer-humorist takes the air in a Double Action Oldsmobile. (*Automobile Manufacturers Association*)

Robert E. Sheldon, now a member of the Alaska Legislature, built this two-seater "runabout" in 1905 without ever having seen more than pictures of automobiles; this is not only Alaska's first auto-mobile, but probably the only one built in the 50th state. Sheldon's car is preserved in the university of Alaska's Museum at College, Alaska. (*Dedman's Photo Shop, Skagway*)

This 1905 National (1900–24) was once owned by Death Valley Scotty but is now preserved in the Kings of The Road Museum in Cugamonga, California. The swivel-mounted brass spotlight was an accessory popular with motorists who lived in the wide open spaces and employed their motor cars for hunting and prospecting in the wilds. Youngsters love to sit in the high seats and try the monstrous steering wheels. Who doesn't? (*Photo by Author*)

A powerful, 70-horsepower, 5-litre, 6-cylinder engine drove this well worn National sports roadster of about 1918; the battery cover is conspicuous by its absence. Suspension by semi-elliptics; wheelbase 130 inches; performance in the 70s and price new over $2,000. Made in Indianapolis. (*Randolph Brandt collection*)

One of the greatest of all names in American cars was Duryea built from 1893 until 1917. This 1905 Phaeton was the car for the country squire. Still retaining the tiller steering and buggy styling, it had coiled-spring suspension and a 2-cylinder, air-cooled engine; a quality vehicle throughout. (*Robert E. Burke Studio, Inc., courtesy of Thompson Auto Museum*)

the *Dragon*; the *Runner* and *Walker*; the *Banker* and *Average Man's Car*; the *Intrepid* and *Thorobred*; the *Savage* and *Remington*; the *Gabriel*, *Anger*, and *Ranger*; the *Dial* and *Juergens*; the *Sharon* and *Jordan*; and even a *Hertz* and a *Step-N-Drive*.

Some names like *Wizard* didn't seem to work at all. There was actually—of all names —a *Waterloo*.

About 1910, advertisements in certain journals praised "The Champion Light Car" which was warranted to cover "a mile in 51 seconds or your money back." This was

the Mercer—really not very "Light" at nearly 2,500 pounds—but it would go. Until Mercer closed shop in 1915, only 800 or so were built to rigid standards of perfection in Trenton, New Jersey.

In 1913, "Ralph DePalma won the 302-mile Cobe Trophy Race at Elgin, Illinois, August 29, at an average speed of 66.8 miles per hour," the Mercer Automobile Company's ads trumpeted. In fact, Mercers took that important race three years in a row beginning in 1911. Not another car of the period beckoned to the coonskin coat crowd

582

Many were the early cars with frontal lines similar to the Renault of France. The 1905 Autocar (1897–1911) runabout had a 4-cylinder, water-cooled engine with radiator core slung low and between the dumb irons. When most other cars were chain-driven, Autocar had a drive shaft. Worth $900 new, this gem is now preserved in the Lindley Bothwell collection. (*Photo by Author*)

as loudly until the original Stutz Bearcat of 1914 came along.

What made the Mercer so great? Several reasons—not the least of which was supply and demand—the first was short and the latter tremendous. Over its entire 152-inch length, the lavish care of the makers was obvious. The 118-inch wheelbase gave good stance. To the top of the steering wheel on the $2,600 Raceabout was a low 51 inches—the monocle windscreen didn't count. The 4-cylinder engine had a bore of 4.38 and stroke of 5.0 inches, for a displacement of 300.7 cubic inches, dual magneto ignition, a compression ratio of a now low sounding 4.78 to 1, and was rated at a modest 34 HP. A Mercer Raceabout in good tune could easily turn in a speed of 75 MPH. The heavier Type-35, Series H touring car with five aboard did 50–60 MPH with ease which was over-driving most roads of the period. A long-range car, Mercer had a 40-gallon fuel tank.

When the Stutz Bearcat snarled into the

PATENTED

The Sturtevant (1904–08, Boston) of 1905 had a magnetically and centrifugally operated automatic clutch and performed extremely well with its 4-cylinder, 35–45-horsepower engine; it was a car ahead of its time. (*Automobile Manufacturers Association*)

By 1905, the automobile was becoming as important to Sunday afternoon outings as were the picnic baskets. If this photo looks familiar, it's because you've seen it on your TV screen. Circled behind the picnickers are a Packard, a Franklin, and two others not identifiable. (*Automobile Manufacturers Association*)

By 1905, the air-cooled Franklin, made in Syracuse, N. Y., was one of the most popular of cars in the United States. (*Robert E. Burke Studio, Inc., courtesy Thompson Auto Museum*)

The 1905 Cadillac coupe was one of the few completely closed cars manufactured in the U.S.A. Advertised then as the "Car of Economy," this example is owned by Miriam Woodbridge of Detroit proving that the ladies love old cars, too. The coupe body lines were identifiable with the stage coaches only so recently replaced. (*Photo by Author*)

The 1905 Maxwell (1904–24) runabout owned by D. E. DeRees of Battle Creek, Michigan, is an early model of this marque. A sought-after model, this one should be painted red trimmed with black. It is promenading past the spectators at the conclusion of a revived Glidden Tour in the late fifties at the Henry Ford Museum in Dearborn. (*Photo by Author*)

J. D. Maxwell, manufacturer of the marque bearing his name, was also an early competition driver of some note. Here he is behind the wheel of 8-cylinder racer which he entered in the 1906 Vanderbilt Cup event. The radiator core completely surrounded the cylinders. (*Automobile Manufacturers Association*)

Barney Oldfield and ever present cigar at the wheel of an early Maxwell racer. Note the asbestos wrapping around exhaust pipe to protect mechanic's arm. (*Randolph Brandt collection*)

picture in 1914, the Mercer had met its match. The Bearcat was poised on a wheelbase just 2 inches longer—120 inches—and it weighed about 1,000 pounds more. But the mighty Stutz had a 4-cylinder mill displacing 540.4 cubic inches. The Bearcat lived on in much modified form—even tamed somewhat for the ear-muffled streets of the early thirties—until the depression finally drove Henry Stutz's firm to the wall, as it had many others.

About 1911 or '12, a period perhaps most suitably described as one of refinement set in upon the American automobile industry. The 1911 De Dion V-8 from France had made a deep impression on the industry's leaders. No one has ever said so officially, but it is believed that some builders in this country decided to give Europe some competition in its own bailiwick. After all, a number of European makes were sold in the U.S.A., so why not sell American cars abroad?

Several American cars were being exported quite successfully as 1912 arrived: Buick to Europe, the American Underslung to Australia, and Ford's remarkable Model T everywhere, and everywhere included Mongolia.

The Mongolia caper happened this way:

American citizen Ethan LeMunyon was in Tientsin, China, with an export-import firm dealing mainly in animal hides and wool. Representatives of the Tasha Lama, the Bogdo of Mongolia, appeared unexpectedly one day making guarded inquiries about the "breath cart." LeMunyon was a mechanical engineer by profession and was assigned to the Mongolian dignitaries who explained that the Bogdo desired to own one

587

AUTOMOBILES OF THE WORLD

of the strange vehicles that ran by itself. LeMunyon was to select a suitably sturdy "breath cart" for the Bogdo who ranked second only to the Dalai Lama of Tibet in the Buddhist world.

LeMunyon selected the Ford Model T closed limousine as filling the bill—some 2,500 taels of Mongolian silver, about $2,000 imported—because it was rugged and relatively simple to drive. After transporting the Model T to Kalgan near the Mongolian border by railroad, LeMunyon drove it across the Gobi Desert accompanied by a missionary nurse on her way to her station in Mongolia and an assistant, one Almblad.

By caravan trails, river beds, and desert, the journey across the Gobi was susceptible to attack by bandits. The bandits never came close but LeMunyon and the Bogdo's Model T were attacked by a horde of wild black Gobi dogs. The timely arrival of a caravan eliminated the peril. The Model T became stuck several times in deep sand and again friendly Mongol caravaneers came

The 1906 Cadillac Model "S" had an aura of elegance with leather top and privacy for the "mother-in-law" seat occupants aft. The two carbide headlamps were supplemented by a pair of smaller lamps on the dashboard. (*Robert E. Burke Studio, Inc. courtesy Thompson Auto Museum*)

CADILLAC 1906
THOMPSON AUTO MUSEUM
CLEVELAND OHIO

The 1906 Cadillac, featuring a 30-horsepower, 4-cylinder engine, Model "D," cost a cool $2,800 new. One of the more picturesque advertising phrases was, "There is practically no energy lost in the Cadillac." As was the case with "practically" all cars during the first decade of the present century, however, considerable energy was required on the part of the driver—it wasn't "lost" but was enjoyed to the fullest. (*Photo by Author*)

The "horseless carriage" era was giving way to designs that looked like automobiles when the Success was introduced in 1906. Built in St. Louis, Missouri until 1909, the engine of this motorized buggy was mounted on the right side of the body just forward of the rear wheel. The box body and anachronistic lines contrasted interestingly with the steering wheel. (*Henry Ford Museum*)

Costing $4,000 in 1906, the Packard runabout had bucket seats and a detachable tonneau seat for one person. Cast in pairs, the four vertical cylinders developed 24 horsepower and drove through a three-speed gearbox. A fast and elegant roadster on 24-inch artillery wheels. (*Henry Ford Museum*)

In 1906, the Ford Model "K" was in the luxury class. The 6-cylinder engine had separately cast cylinders. (*Photo by Author*)

Dubuque, Iowa, was the home of the Adams-Farwell from the first model in 1899 to the last in 1913. In 1904, a 3-cylinder rotary aircraft type engine was used. This post-1906 model has a 5-cylinder rotary; owned by Harrah's Automobile collection. (*Joseph H. Wherry*)

to the assistance with horses or draft bullocks. Fuel had been sent ahead to three desert stations.

Once in Ulan Bator, LeMunyon learned that Mongolia had recently declared itself independent of China and that the "living God" was now also the Emperor. After a wait of seven days, LeMunyon was summoned to the palace and charged with instructing a servant in the fine art of driving. This, surprisingly, was accomplished with dispatch and LeMunyon and Almblad then took leave.

According to the lengthy account of this remarkable adventure with a Model T Ford as told in *Westways* magazine by Art Ronnie, LeMunyon delivered the keys to the god-emperor saying something fitting like, "Hello God, here's your car," certainly a heartfelt greeting after the harrowing tour across the Gobi Desert.

By horse carriage, river steamer, and railroad, LeMunyon returned to the hides and wool enterprise in Tientsin. LeMunyon had previously operated his own engineering firm and "had made the first transmission to be used on the Model T, also the first brakes" according to a communication from

text continued on page 680

Ransome E. Olds, already famed as the creator of the "curved dash" Olds, brought out the R.E.O. in 1903; the marque continued until 1936. A very advanced car in later years, this 1906 tourer had a 2-cylinder engine and chain drive. (*Robert E. Burke Studio, Inc., courtesy Thompson Auto Museum*)

592

The Metz (1907–21) was built in Waltham, Massachusetts. This '07 runabout had a 20-plus-horsepower, 4-cylinder engine with a gearless, friction type transmission. Priced under $700, the Metz was advertised as capable of 28–32 miles per gallon of gas and as being especially economical in oil consumption: "100 miles on one pint of lubricating oil" and that was low for those days. A frequent trials competitor—a team of three were victorious in a race from Minneapolis to Glacier National Park. This veteran is owned by Paul R. Jones of Belding, Michigan. (*Photo by Author*)

1907 Ford Model "R" was one of several versions of 4-cylinder models preceding the famed "T" model. (*Robert E. Burke Studio, Inc., courtesy Thompson Auto Museum*)

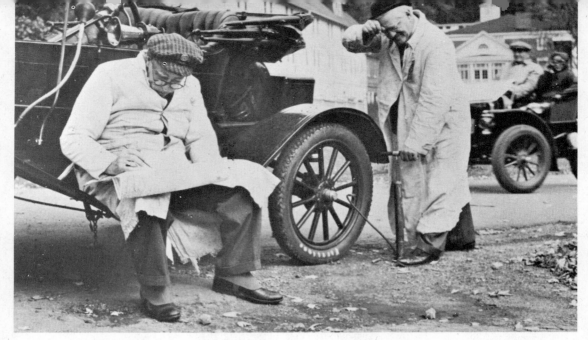

An adventurous and durable nature was needed to enjoy motoring in the early days of the automobile. "This is one time we should have skipped the Chowder Society's get-together." (*Firestone News Service*)

The 1909 Thomas Flyer (built in Buffalo, New York, 1899–1911) was of lower overall height than the standard Thomas touring cars. A big, 60-horsepower engine made the Flyer a competition favorite. Rugged and fast, an '08 Flyer won the great round-the-world race from New York to Paris and sales zoomed. (*Photo by Author*)

As imposing from the rear as from the front, the Thomas Flyer model of 1907 owned by Leonard A. Davis of Pontiac, Michigan sold originally for around $3,500. Chain drive was used. (*Photo by Author*)

Regardless of the year, the Thomas Flyer was a man's car. This is the 1908 model. (*Robert E.* *Burke Studio, Inc., courtesy Thompson Auto Museum*)

From 1902 to 1914, Thomas B. Jeffery built the original Rambler in Kenosha, Wisconsin; the firm became Nash Motors, revived the name in 1950, and is now American Motors. The 1908 model shown was made before Charles Nash joined the firm. The four cylinders delivered 32 horsepower. Unusual was the square bore and stroke of 4½ inches. Weight was about 2,800 pounds and the price of $2,250 was considered reasonable for the quality offered. (*American Motors Corp.*)

The 1908 Buick Model "F" had a 20-horsepower four and cost $1,250. The first of this marque was built in 1903. The firm originally made plumbing equipment, some of the early models had an adjustable steering wheel. (*Henry Ford Museum*)

In 1909, "Get a horse" was a popular way to taunt the automobilists. People were—and are—pretty much the same everywhere as we learn when we examine the attitude of the Mongolians a few short years after this dismal picture was taken. (*Automobile Manufacturers Association*)

Winner of the great race from New York City to Seattle, Washington, was Number 2 of the Ford team driven by B. W. Scott and C. J. Smith. Here they are shown awaiting the start of the event at New York City Hall on June 1st, 1909. Twenty-two days and 4,106 miles later Scott, Smith and their Ford reached Seattle. (*Ford News Department*)

In 1909, four brave ladies drove a Haynes (1898–1925) from Chicago to New York City. In 1894, Elwood M. Haynes made what is generally regarded as the first successful gasoline car in the United States, in Kokomo, Indiana. By 1909, the Haynes had a self-starter and was considered a suitable car for the distaff side. (*Automobile Manufacturers Association*)

The 1922 Haynes model 75 with expensive town car coachwork. A large 6-cylinder engine developed about 70 BHP. Wheelbase was 132 inches. This pioneer Kokomo, Indiana, car also had 12-cylinder engines from 1916–18; after the war all were sixes. Prices began at around $1,800. (*Randolph Brandt collection*)

Sporting open bodies, step plates and fairly high performance from 50 or 70 BHP engines, models like this were available in the Haynes range. The 1922 model with a determined looking driver. (*Randolph Brandt collection*)

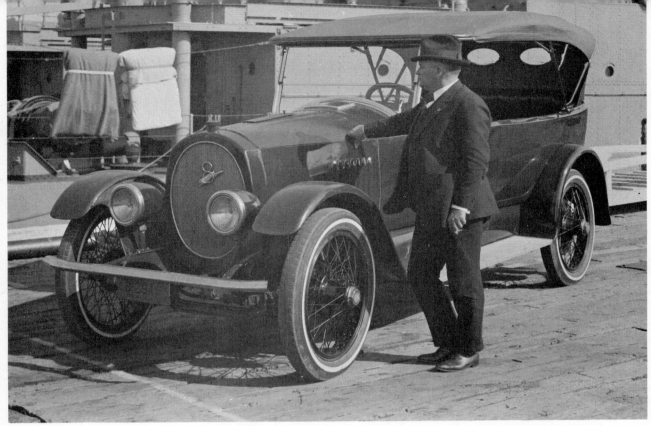

After earlier association with the Haynes car, the Apperson brothers of Kokomo, Indiana, began making their own cars in 1903. This model 8-21 "Jackrabbit" of 1921 had eight 3.25 x 5 inch-cylinders in-line, semi-elliptic springs and pleasant, distinctive styling on a 130-inch wheelbase. Note the rabbit in the "8" on the oval radiator core. Salesmen frequented military bases then as now. (*Randolph Brandt collection*)

The 1923 Apperson "Jackrabbit" changes were mainly in styling; note the rabbit had moved to the radiator cap. Two years later the marque was discontinued. (*Randolph Brandt collection*)

One had a choice of two body styles for the 1909 Simplex, a runabout or tourer like the model shown. Built in New York City—originally with the cooperation of Daimler in Germany—Simplex was a massive car. Chain drive was used to the end. Wheelbase was either 124 or 128 inches; engine was a large (5¾ inches bore and stroke) 4-cylinder developing 50 horsepower. Maximum speed was around 80 mph. The trunk above the huge fuel tank was covered with patent leather. Warren S. Weiant, Newark, Ohio, is the owner. (*Photo by Author*)

A 1909 R.E.O. on the green at Greenfield Village in Dearborn after a gathering of antique enthusiasts in 1958. This model had a 4-cylinder engine.

At the end of its career in 1935–36, R.E.O. had a semi-automatic transmission with change lever on the dashboard. (*Photo by Author*)

From 1902 to 1927, the J. Stevens Arms & Tool Co. of Chicopee Falls, Massachusetts, built this marque; originally there was a relationship to the original Duryea car. This is the 1909 Stevens-Duryea runabout. (*Robert E. Burke Studio, Inc., courtesy Thompson Auto Museum*)

Small boys today are as intrigued with a Model "T" Ford as they were when this 1909 model was built. Costing $850 in '09, the "T" came in "any color you want as long as it's black." Within a few years the price was cut in half with mass-production, then trimmed even more. With a wheelbase of 100 inches, width of 68 and height with top raised of 83 inches, the Model "T" was simple to drive, exceptionally rugged, and literally put the world on wheels. (*Photo by Author*)

The Bob Cummings television series with frequent appearances of Grandpa Collins' old Mitchell did much to make this marque famous. Built in Racine, Wisconsin, from 1903–24, they were notable competitors as is this example, a 1910 model, in the old time Glidden Tour. (*Automobile Manufacturers Association*)

The Marion (1904–15) was built in Indianapolis. 1909 runabout had 4-cylinder engine and performance over 70 mph with top down. This example is in the Lindley Bothwell collection. (*Photo by Author*)

This 1909 Mitchell in the Lindley Bothwell collection is about to undergo restoration; those were the years of right hand drive in the U.S.A. (*Photo by Author*)

The 1909 Cartercar (1907–16) had a friction drive which gave an infinite number of gear ratios. The foot brake pedal functioned as a parking brake when depressed, as shown here, and moved to the right where it locked in place by a ratchet device; the speedometer mounted outboard of the body on the armored cable was an added item in a later year. This car is in the Lindley Bothwell collection. (*Photo by Author*)

The 1909 Mitchell shown has participated in the revived Glidden Tours. Half-elliptic springs were used all around; car was built to carry heavy loads, was a magnificent tourer. (*Photo by Author*)

By 1909, the Maxwell runabout offered style, performance, and durability at a moderate price. (*Robert E. Burke Studio, Inc., courtesy Thompson Auto Museum*)

MAXWELL 1909
THOMPSON AUTO MUSEUM
CLEVELAND OHIO

The 1909 Hupmobile Speedster was an early success for this marque which was made from 1908 to 1941 in Detroit and Cleveland. (*Robert E.* *Burke Studio, Inc., courtesy Thompson Auto Museum*)

For 1910, the Hupmobile Speedster had doors and redesigned dashboard. In the Lindley Bothwell collection, the background of World War One recruiting posters adds to the nostalgic scene. (*Photo by Author*)

Sixty years ago, "Pathfinders" were dispatched to scout the trail to be followed by the competitors in cross-country trials. In 1909, the crew of the scouting car for the Glidden Tour blazed 2,600 miles of roads, mud, sand, and rock-strewn paths.

The official car was a 1909 E.M.F., a marque built from 1908 to 1912 in Detroit by the firm of Everitt-Metzger-Flanders, which was purchased by Studebaker. (*Automobile Manufacturers Association*)

The 1910 Flanders "Suburban Model" dispensed with doors. Built in Detroit (1910–12) by the Everitt-Metzger-Flanders combine, it too was to become a part of the Studebaker interests. (*Robert E. Burke Studio, Inc., courtesy Thompson Auto Museum*)

Mercers were built with fastidious care in Trenton, New Jersey, from 1910 to 1925. The first models were 4-seater tourers like the one shown, a 1910 model. (*Automobile Manufacturers Association.*)

One of the finest quality cars ever built in the U.S.A. was the Winton manufactured in Cleveland, Ohio, from 1897 to 1925. The first model had an electric starter. Each car was inscribed, "He wears the crown of excellence." It was this commitment to unexcelled quality that finally caused the marque to fade from the market. This 1910 tourer is in the Lindley Bothwell collection. (*Photo by Author*)

The sterns of cars of the first decade resembled the frigate of a previous era. Part of the Lindley Bothwell collection, the 1910 Speedwell, was typical although this was a quality machine. First manufactured in Reading, Pennsylvania, later in Dayton, Ohio, Speedwell's years were from 1903 to 1914. Note the two small diamond-shaped windows in the tail sheet. (*Photo by Author*)

Part of the great automotive empire built up by Colonel Pope was the Pope-Hartford (1903–12, Hartford, Connecticut). Often raced, the 1910 owned by Lindley Bothwell collection is still capable of turning a mile in well under the minute. (*Photo by Author*)

The 1910 Buick had a 4-cylinder engine, bore and stroke 4½ x 5 inches, 40 horsepower. Owned by Daniel C. Zabel of Denver, this beautiful veteran participated in the revived Glidden Tour in 1958. In light blue with burnished brass work and polished wood dashboard, car is striking. (*Photo by Author*)

"The Car That Satisfies" is the way the Regal of 1910 was advertised. The 4-cylinder engine had square bore and stroke of 4 inches, developed 25–30 horsepower. Wheelbase of the model "30" was 107 inches. A feature was a fourth ring on each piston to inhibit oil blow-by. At $1,450 up, Regal tourers and sedans were available as well as the runabout; thousands were sold between 1908 and 1922. Model shown is the "Underslung" speedster. (*Henry Ford Museum*)

Happy is the enthusiast who can claim ownership to a glistening pair of carbide headlamps such as these. John Hallberg displays such a pair from the Lindley Bothwell collection. (*Photo by Author*)

Here's one to identify as to make and year. The Automobile Manufacturers Association, from whose files this photo came, cannot identify. Car image appears to have been super-imposed upon a print showing a well known monument in the United States; however, car might be European from the costume of the young lady behind the wheel.

The first Chevrolet was the pointed-nose model of 1911 built by Louis Chevrolet, a talented engineer from Switzerland, shown behind the wheel of his first car. (*Automobile Manufacturers Association*)

The Lozier had few quality equals during its time (1901–17). For 1911, the well developed six gave 51 horsepower. (*Henry Ford Museum*)

Long air-cooled, the Knox by 1911 had changed to thermal syphon water cooling. A quality vehicle in middle price range, the Knox was built in Springfield, Massachusetts, from 1900 to '13. It was "Silent, Strong, Magnificent" as advertised. (*Photo by Author*)

Many owner-restorers of old cars prefer to transport them on trailers rather than to risk driving them on crowded highways. Between 1909 and '27 the J. I. Case Threshing Machine Co. of Racine, Wisconsin, built tough cars well suited to rural areas. This is the 1911 model tourer. (*Photo by Author*)

In 1911, a reasonable $600 purchased the snappy Maxwell Model A.B. roadster. A dark blue body striped with yellow topped the 86-inch-wheelbase chassis fitted with a water-cooled, 2-cylinder, horizontally-opposed engine of 22 horsepower. (*Henry Ford Museum*)

Antique car meetings generally conclude with a concours d'elegance where experienced appraisers of ancient vehicles give them a detailed examination. Here Christie Borth of the Automobile Manufacturers Association inspects a rare ALCO tourer of 1911. Built by the American Locomotive Company from 1909 to '12, an ALCO is seldom seen. (*Photo by Author*)

A 1911 Stevens-Duryea promenades at the con- owned by Morris E. Kunkle of Harrison City,
clusion of a recent Glidden Tour. The Massachu- Pennsylvania. (*Photo by Author*)
setts firm had a full line of cars. This tourer is

Overland built the Speedster runabout in 1911 West of Varysburg, Pennsylvania, this Speedster
with a 35 horsepower, 4-cylinder engine before is restored with a tan finish trimmed in brown.
moving into more staid lines. Owned by Burt G. (*Photo by Author*)

The 1912 Overland tourer had a 4-cylinder engine similar to that used in the Speedster. (*Photo by Author*)

When Ethan C. LeMunyon drove the 1912 Ford Model T Town Car across the Gobi to the capital of Mongolia, desert nomads helped him yank the car from deep sand. (*Copyright 1964, Automobile Club of Southern California*)

Model T Ford meets a camel caravan in the middle of the Gobi enroute to Ulan Bator for delivery to the Tasha Lama in 1912. (*Copyright 1964, Automobile Club of Southern California*)

On another occasion, Ethan C. LeMunyon was rescued by a quartet of oxen harnessed in diamond pattern to the Tasha Lama's Model T Ford Town Car in the middle of the Gobi. The scene is a rocky, dry stream bed. (*Copyright 1964, Automobile Club of Southern California*)

The 1912 White tourer was successor to the earliest steamers. From 1910 to 1918, the White Sewing Machine Co. built gasoline cars in Cleveland, Ohio. Originally advertised as having fewer electrical parts than other makes, White made their own electric starting and lighting equipment. Beautifully restored, this tourer is owned by Jack L. Tallman of Decatur, Illinois. (*Photo by Author*)

Model T Ford Town Car and LeMunyon arriving in Mongolia's capital in 1912. The last lap of the trying journey was made with the assistance of friendly nomads and their oxen. In the background is the "Temple of The Horse." (*Copyright 1964, Automobile Club of Southern California*)

T Ford and LeMunyon finally meet the Tasha
Lama of Mongolia. (*Copyright 1964, Automobile
Club of Southern California*)

Last of the fine White passenger cars was the 1918 model. This example was a parade car for nobles of the Mystic Shrine in San Francisco in 1932. (*Randolph Brandt collection*)

The 4-cylinder, five-seater Buick tourer of 1912. By this date the Buick plant in Flint, Michigan was one of the industry's largest. (*Robert E. Burke Studio, Inc., courtesy Thompson Auto Museum*)

James Scripps-Booth was one of the most unorthodox of engineers. This tandem two-seater cycle car of about 1912, powered by a 2-cylinder, V-type, air-cooled engine mounted transversely to drive the rear wheels by means of a rubberized belt, is an example of his effort to provide fast transportation at low cost. (*Automobile Manufacturers Association*)

The American Motor Car Co. of Indianapolis built the American Underslung from about 1904 to '15; the great Harry C. Stutz had a hand in the design of this marque in its later years. The 1912 model runabout was a great favorite in Australia as this portion of an old advertisement in a down-under journal indicates. The frame was below the rear axle, swept up and over the front axle, one of the earlier successful attempts to lower the overall height of automobiles. (*Wheels Magazine, Australia*)

The 1912 Flanders closed coupe, built under the aegis of Studebaker, achieved some popularity. Bright red trimmed with black, this rare refugee from automobile valhalla is owned by the Lindley Bothwell collection. (*Photo by Author*)

Bare chassis of pre-war, 20-HP Franklin discloses the full-elliptic springs, nearly vertical steering column and transversely mounted, 4-cylinder, 1.2-litre (about 72 cu. in.) air-cooled engine. The sedan is the 6-cylinder model of 1923. (*Randolph Brandt collection*)

The 1912 Franklin still employed full-elliptic springs after many other makes had switched to half-elliptics. This roadster, immaculate in dark blue, is owned by Sam DeBolt of Reno, Nevada, and has run on the revived Glidden Tour with complete reliability. (*Photo by Author*)

The 1927–28 Franklin's air-cooled, 6-cylinder, 3.9-litre engine resided behind a radiator similar to those of water-cooled cars. Wheelbases available were 119 and 128 inches. Forty years ago as now, most Americans preferred a frontal design like other cars. (*Randolph Brandt collection*)

The Mercer Model 35J Raceabout is one of about only 600 to 700 built by the famous firm. The 1913 model shown has a 4-cylinder, T-head engine with bore and stroke of 4⅜ and 5 inches respectively; output was rated at 30 horsepower. Though the Raceabout had a wheelbase of 118 inches, the overall length was compact due to the wheels being at the extremities of the frame which was swept upward over both axles. Owned by Benjamine F. Johnson of Connersville, Indiana, this 4-speed transmission equipped car can still turn a fair burst of speed. (*Henry Ford Museum*)

From 1906 to 1930–31 the Kissel Motor Car Co. built fine cars on Kissel Avenue in Hartford, Wisconsin. Advertised as "Every Inch A Car," various body styles were available with quality 4-cylinder engines developing 30, 40 or 50 horsepower. For genuinely high performance, there was also a large 60-horsepower "Six" with custom coachwork. The 1912 Kisselkar tourer shown is owned by S. H. Cooper of Reno, Nevada. (*Photo by Author*)

From 1912 to 1935, the most famous factory in Indianapolis built the mighty Stutz cars, "The Car that made good in a Day." This 1913 roadster used a 6-litre, T-head, 4-cylinder engine developing 60 horsepower. Not as light in weight as the Bearcat with its scantier coachwork, this roadster was, nevertheless, able to achieve around 70 mph with little effort. (*Robert E. Burke Studio, Inc., courtesy Thompson Auto Museum*)

Tony Koveleski of Scranton, Pennsylvania, owns this 1914 Stutz Bearcat. Between 1911 and 1914, the Bearcat was the standout competition sports car in the United States. The big, 6-litre, 4-cylinder, T-head engine developed 60 horsepower; the crankshaft was hollow and a magneto dual ignition system was employed. This was one of the few American cars of the era to use a torque tube around the propeller shaft. 80 mph was common in a Bearcat, even one equipped for touring as this one is. (*Photo by Author*)

By 1914, the Chevrolet had lost the European look given the original by its Swiss designer. The '14 Royal Mail model two-seater roadster in the Henry Ford Museum has a wheelbase of 106.5 inches and a 22-horsepower, 3.69 x 4-inch engine with one of the earlier thermo-syphon cooling systems. (*Henry Ford Museum*)

Accessory manufacturers boldly offered performance equipment and special bodies to owners of the Model T Fords; in 1915 this Ames body turned the modest roadster into a flashy runabout and there were engine items to supply performance to match the appearance. This restored model, seen on the green at the Henry Ford Museum in 1959, is owned by Leslie R. Henry of Newtown Square, Pennsylvania. (*Photo by Author*)

A Jackson, Michigan, product, the Briscoe had a checkered career from 1914 to 1922. The 4-24 model of 1916–20 had a 4-cylinder, L-head engine of 34 horsepower, full-elliptic springs front and rear, and a 103-inch wheelbase. Sturdiness and a price around $650 made it popular for a time. (*Randolph Brandt collection*)

The Packard tourer of 1916 had the fabulous "Twin Six" engine, the first V-12 cylinder engine in any American passenger car. With a wheelbase of 135 inches, this fine car helped give Packard its first 10,000-car year. Rated at 75 horsepower, the Twin Six could accelerate smoothly from 5 mph to around 70 in top gear without a tremble. For such magnificence, the 4,400 pound luxury car cost a reasonable $3,200. (*Robert E. Burke Studio, Inc., courtesy Thompson Auto Museum*)

The engine of a beautifully restored 1916 Packard "Twin-Six" during a concours d'elegance on West Coast. Note safety rim around fan blades. (*Joseph H. Wherry*)

One of the finest American makes was the Pierce Arrow built from 1901 to 1938. This 1916 Race-about, owned by Henry Austin Clark of the Long Island Automotive Museum, has a wheelbase of 147.5 inches and track of 57 inches. A massive 6-cylinder engine displacing nearly 14 litres developed 60 horsepower. Although a very heavy vehicle, the car handled easily, was fine for competition with its 4-speed gearbox, and could exceed 80 mph when fully extended. One of the few Pierce Arrow models with separate headlights, the big machine cost $6,000 new. Note the small jump seat fitted to the side of the body. Clark drives the machine after the concours in '59 at the Henry Ford Museum. (*Photo by Author*)

Rare and a style leader, the Daniels was built in Reading, Pennsylvania. The formal "true brougham" of 1919–20. Production was limited through its span from 1915 to '25. (*Randolph Brandt collection*)

Unkind jokes were frequent when George N. Pierce of Cleveland began making cars in 1901; he was a manufacturer of bird cages. Triple tail lights and headlamps on fenders were hallmarks of this dignified car. The big 1920 touring sedan. (*Randolph Brandt collection*)

That there's little new under the sun is shown by the 1916 Dodge two-door which had removable door posts—the "hardtop" look many years ago. (*Dodge Division, Chrysler Corp.*)

The R. & L. Baker Co. of Cleveland, Ohio, made the Owen Magnetic during the 1915–21 period from the designs of R. M. Owen & Co. of Lansing, Michigan. A large car with a 136-inch wheelbase, it was powered with a 6-cylinder, 50-horse-power engine which drove through a transmission controlled magnetically and operated by a small device on the steering wheel. Westinghouse shock absorbers were another feature of this $3,750 car. (*Henry Ford Museum*)

At one time, Hudson had the fastest car selling for less than $1,000 made in the United States. The Detroit firm, their sports cars behind them by the advent of this 1917 model, was in continuous production with cars better known for quality than for popularity from 1909 until 1955 when the marque was merged with Nash. The Super Six was big, fast, and in the medium price field. (*Robert E. Burke Studio, Inc., courtesy Thompson Auto Museum*)

This 1919 Packard landaulet has custom coach-work with unusual fenders. The owner is Martin L. Schaffer of Lafayette Hills, Pennsylvania. (*Photo by Author*)

Custom "true brougham" coachwork in the Euro-pean tradition on a Cadillac chassis of about 1918. The small mudguard forward of the passenger step distinguishes this formal body type. (*Randolph Brandt collection*)

Brewster & Company on Long Island were established coach builders. Upon order, the firm also built fine cars between 1915 and 1935 for celebrities; such a custom built car is this 1920 Brewster landaulet owned by William J. Mascol, Jr. of Cleveland, Ohio. Continental engines were generally employed. (*Photo by Glenn Kopp*)

The Model T Ford appeared in every conceivable guise; this "T" fire truck of about 1920, beautifully restored and trimmed with gold pin striping, was shown at a gathering at the Ox Bow Hunt Club near Westport, Connecticut, in 1953. (*Photo by Author*)

The 1920 Velie range included four-seat sports models with prophetic "hardtop" styling and shiny exhaust headers. Engine was an in-line 6 displacing 3.2-litres (about 190 cu. in.); wheelbase was 112 inches. Built in Moline, Illinois, 1908–29, later models had V-8 engines. (*Randolph Brandt collection*)

The Moline Plow Co. of Freeport, Illinois, built the Stephens during 1916–25. A medium priced, large, 6-cylinder car, this is the 1920-23 model. (*Randolph Brandt collection*)

Rarest 1920 Chalmers model was this racy two-seater, sports roadster, with bird beak nose and 6-cylinder, L-head engine. Was this speedster as fast as it looked? If so, it needed four-wheel brakes, but the lines were stunning. (*Randolph Brandt collection*)

1920 Chalmers had a 6-cylinder (83 x 114 mm.) engine and included all body types including luxury town cars at medium price. Wheelbase of all models was 117 inches. Prices began at $1,500. Built in Detroit from 1908 until absorbed by Maxwell in 1924. (*Randolph Brandt collection*)

Built in the Michigan city of the same name 1903–22, the Jackson had 8 cylinders in-line from 1916. Of better than average quality, this final 1922 model cost $2,000 up. Jackson also made 4 and 6-cylinder cars. (*Randolph Brandt collection*)

The Carroll was a moderately priced, 6-cylinder car made in Lorain, Ohio, during 1920–22. Not to be confused with the Carrol (Strassburg, Pa., 1912–20), the design was straight forward; good, but undistinguished. (*Randolph Brandt collection*)

Curtained privacy for bathing beauties (?) was thoughtfully provided in the 1920 Columbia, a 25-HP, 6-cylinder sedan on a 115-inch wheelbase. Built in Detroit during 1916–25, this gas car was not directly related to the Hartford, Connecticut, electrics of earlier years; cost $1,300 up. (*Randolph Brandt collection*)

Low priced comfort for 1921: the 4-cylinder, 100-inch-wheelbase Overland, ancestor of the famed Jeep. Note the seat-shaped apron below grill. Suspension was by transverse leaf springs. Built in Toledo along with larger Knight-engined cars. (*Randolph Brandt collection*)

Russell E. Gardner, "America's Buggy King," originated the Gardner in 1919 in St. Louis, Missouri. This is the initial 3.5 x 5.00 inch, 4-cylinder model on 112-inch wheelbase chassis of common type. Later 6 and 8-cylinder models on longer chassis were introduced. A line of luxury cars wrote finis to the marque, after a long struggle, in mid-thirties. (*Randolph Brandt collection*)

The King, produced in Detroit, 1905–25, graduated from a 115-inch wheelbase, underslung, long-stroke four in 1914 to a more conventional straight-8 on a 120-inch chassis costing $1,300 up. The 1920 touring model. (*Randolph Brandt collection*)

Honest, dependable but never a great success was the 1922 Barley, a 6-cylinder car built in Kalamazoo until 1925 when the firm was acquired by Roamer. (*Randolph Brandt collection*)

A colonel and his 1918 Roamer, a 6-cylinder, 128-inch-wheelbase car that changed little from the first 1916 model to the last in 1927. Advertised as the "Fastest stock chassis in the world—105 miles per hour," this car was famed for its Rolls-Royce type grille and excellent workmanship. Sports roadsters were also made; another Kalamazoo car. (*Randolph Brandt collection*)

Built in Philadelphia, 1917–22, the Biddle had rakish European lines, a 16-valve, 4-cylinder engine made by the Duesenberg brothers, a famous name, and was a quality, limited production sports car with a high price. The 1920 model. (*Randolph Brandt collection*)

Once a well known car, the Grant was manufactured from 1913 to 1923 in Cleveland, Ohio. Comfortable, dependable, durable but rather unexciting and lacking distinguished characteristics, the Grant went the way of hundreds of contemporaries. This is the 1920 Light Six. (*Automobile Manufacturers Association*)

The sporty Leach 6 was built in Long Beach, California, 1920–23. Production was limited and none is known to have survived. Note the golden bear emblem below the Motometer and the rack for golf clubs. Other forgotten West Coast petrol cars were the California (Long Beach), the expensive Heine-Velox (San Francisco, 1907–?) the 13-litre Fageol (Oakland, 1916–21), the Squier (Virginia City, Nevada, 1899), the Portland (Oregon, 1914–15), the Ajax (Seattle, 1914–15), and others. (*Randolph Brandt collection*)

The 3.8-litre Liberty six of around 1921 conformed, technically, with the popular makes. Built in Detroit during 1916–25, this 117-inch-wheelbase car underwent few changes. Price was medium-low. (*Randolph Brandt collection*)

There were numerous efforts to produce cars in Texas such as the Lone Star (El Paso in 1917 and San Antonio, 1920–21), the Texas (Fort Worth, 1918–22) and this 4-cylinder Ranger made in Houston during 1920–21; though competitive technically, it is forgotten. (*Randolph Brandt collection*)

From 1911 to 1930, James Cunningham & Sons built the exceptionally fine Cunningham in Rochester, N. Y. Whether touring model or town car like this 1919–20 pair in a showroom, on 132 and 142-inch wheelbases respectively, these splen-did 7.25-litre, V-eights were capable of 90–95 mph. Power was 90 BHP at an easy 2,200 rpm; torque was high. The 4-speed gearbox had over-drive on top gear. (*Randolph Brandt collection*)

Henry Leland built the Lincoln cars before Henry Ford purchased the marque. The 1921 model was the last made by Leland; the 136-inch-wheelbase chassis mounted an advanced 36-horsepower, V-8 engine. Not overly large by present standards, the length overall was 200 inches. (*Henry Ford Museum*)

The 1923 Lincoln, built by Henry Ford, was larger than the Leland-made cars: wheelbase and length 136 and 209 inches respectively. Thomas A. Edison once owned this tourer. (*Henry Ford Museum*)

A 6-cylinder, overhead-valve Rochester engine was used in its latter years by the mighty Mercer. Thus powered, this 1922 Raceabout's 5.5-litre engine pushed it to the 80-mph mark with ease. Though production was by this date greatly decreased under Locomobile management, the car still had sporting flavor. Note the golf bag. Owner: Lindley Bothwell. (*Photo by Author*)

The Wills St. Clair is regarded by many enthusiasts as one of the technically finest cars ever made in this country. Harold Wills was a perfectionist.

The overhead-camshaft, V-8 engine developed 65 horsepower in this 1922 Model A-68. (*Harrah's Automobile Collection*)

The Stutz Speedway roadster of 1923 had a dual-valve six giving 75 horsepower and was a genuine 80 mph car. This restored example is owned by Kenneth Valentine of Birmingham, Michigan, shown here being awarded a silver cup by Harriet

Stoner for the grand championship in the 1917–25 division at the Old Car Festival at Greenfield Village in Dearborn in a recent year. (*Henry Ford Museum*)

Harry C. Stutz originated the H.C.S. as a low-priced version of his famous namesake marque in 1914 and it lasted until 1926. This is the 1923 four-seater with 3.5 x 5-inch, overhead-valve, 6-cylinder, 80-BHP engine on a 126-inch wheelbase, once used by the San Francisco Fire Department. (*Randolph Brandt collection*)

The 1927 boat-tailed, four-seater Stutz "Speedster" with hydraulic brakes, single overhead-camshaft, 4.8-litre, straight-8 engine. On a 131-inch wheelbase, with quick steering, handling was superior and 100 mph was possible. The related 5.2-litre supercharged "Blackhawk" placed fifth at Le Mans in 1929. (*Randolph Brandt collection*)

The famed Cannonball Baker drove a 1930 short-wheelbase Stutz DV-32 (double valves operated by dual overhead-camshafts, 6.25 litres) from New York City to Los Angeles in a record 60 hours.

Produced until 1933, the DV-32 was guaranteed for 100 mph despite its considerable weight. Wheelbases were 134.5 and 145 inches. (*Randolph Brandt collection*)

By 1922, the Oldsmobile had graduated into the semi-fine car class. This sedan, owned by Fenton

Creith of Dearborn was a competitor in the 1959 Glidden Tour. (*Photo by Glenn Kopp*)

Produced irregularly in Ohio during 1900–14, the Cleveland blossomed again during 1919–26 as a dependable, 3-litre six. Note drum-type head- lights, abbreviated fenders and stylish step boards on this 1923 sports tourer; 112-inch wheelbase. (*Randolph Brandt collection*)

Made in Indianapolis (1909–25), the Cole was a fairly large car of quality in its later years. The 40- HP "Eight" of 1922; wheelbase, 127 inches. (*Randolph Brandt collection*)

The 1922 Cole "Eight" (8-cylinder) tourer was one of the better looking open cars of the American vintage era. The extra cost road and parking light design is interesting. Prices started at $2,000 plus. (*Randolph Brandt collection*)

The 1923 Chevrolet Model "M" had a 4-cylinder engine with the block completely surrounded by copper fins; called the "Copper Cooled" model, the object was to eliminate the water radiator. An air scoop in the place of the conventional radiator was fitted with movable louvres to control the air flow. Fairly luxurious with mohair upholstery, yet rather small with a 103-inch wheelbase, the "Copper Cooled" sold new for $680. (*Harrah's Automobile collection*)

From 1922 to '27 the Hat-in-the-Ring of Captain Eddie Rickenbacker's 94th Aero Squadron of the A.E.F. was the emblem of the Rickenbacker cars which were built in Detroit. Exclusive among American cars of the time, the Rickenbacker had four-wheel hydraulic brakes. (*Automobile Manufacturers Association*)

Small boys watch a 1923 Rickenbacker proving its four-wheel hydraulic brakes on a rocky San Fran- cisco hill. (*Randolph Brandt collection*)

"The Car Worth Its Name" was the Rickenbacker, shown here with the famous Captain
Eddie in front of a West Coast showroom. The
1923 club coupe. (*Randolph Brandt collection*)

After initial success with steam cars, the Locomobiles of 1902–29 were gasoline-powered and were
originally designed by Andrew Riker of electric
car frame. In 1908, "Old 16" won the Vanderbilt
Cup Race after a 100-mph duel with an Isotta-
Fraschini. Model 48 of 1910–29 was the line's
finest. Shown is the elegant town car of 1917.
(*Randolph Brandt collection*)

A terminal model of the splendid Locomobile 48. Other than in bodies, changes were minor in two decades of production. The 8-litre (475 cu. in.), 6-cylinder engine's output was 90 BHP; there were seven main bearings. A vast variety of coach work was mounted on the well-designed 142-inch-wheelbase chassis. (*Randolph Brandt collection*)

In an effort to stave off the ultimate disaster that was to overtake so many car manufacturers, Locomobile brought out the Flint in 1923. A good quality car in the lower priced field, it succeeded moderately for a time, then sales dwindled. This is the 1927 model, the last of the marque to be made. It was built in Bridgeport, Conn. (*Automobile Manufacturers Association*)

High performance from a big in-line eight with a nautical touch to the cowl forward of the folding tonneau seat on the 1927 Jordan "Line Eight," one of Ned Jordan's fine cars that inspired him to wax poetic in the famous advertisement about the girl "somewhere west of Laramie" and the sort of car she would demand. (*Randolph Brandt collection*)

Jordan was built in Cleveland from 1916 to 1931. The 6-litre, 6-cylinder luxury sedan of 1923 had plate glass windows in splendid coachwork and cost well over $2,000. (*Randolph Brandt collection*)

In 1923, the Ajax Auto Parts Company of Racine, Wisconsin, brought out a limited production line of phaeton and sedan models in conformity with what others were making. This 1925 phaeton was brought out about the time that Nash Motors absorbed the struggling organization. (*Automobile Manufacturers Association*)

The 1924 Chandler was advertised as the car "with the traffic transmission—no shifting of gears"; the device was semi-automatic. In those days, children's pedal cars looked like the real thing. (*Randolph Brandt collection*)

Hesperia is a small city on the high Mojave Desert in Southern California with a lively community newspaper. The press car is this attractively restored, fringed-top Dodge of vintage '26. (*Photo by Author*)

A feature of the 1926 Chandler was one-shot chassis lubrication; engine was a 4.7-litre six rated at 30 HP. Made in Cleveland, Ohio, 1913–29, a large 6.3-litre, 8-cylinder model was introduced in 1928. Note large, four-wheel brakes. Wheelbase was 123 inches on this dual-cowl phaeton. (*Randolph Brandt collection*)

One of the most forward looking experiments in American automotive history was that of the Aluminum Corporation of America in cooperation with Pierce Arrow which culminated in the ten Aluminum cars of 1925. The overall length was 194.5 inches; width and height were 70 and 74 inches respectively. A 6-cylinder, 75-horsepower Pierce engine was used. (*Henry Ford Museum*)

A naval flying officer and his 3.6-litre, 114-inch wheelbase Hupmobile sports sedan of about 1925. Sixes and eights were built until 1941, the latter with streamlined bodies. The marque began in Detroit in 1908. Hupmobile claimed to be "the largest user of aluminum—without regard to class or price—in the world" before World War One. (*Randolph Brandt collection*)

The popular, 2.8-litre, 6-cylinder Oldsmobile of 1926 was quite compact on a wheelbase of 110.5 inches. Though seldom realized there were Oldsmobile V-eights in 1916. (*Randolph Brandt collection*)

The 1927 Kissel Speedster had a 124-inch wheelbase, track of 56 inches, and a 310-cubic-inch, straight-8 engine developing 65 horsepower at 3,200 rpm; this gave the car a top speed of 80 mph. A sporting type, the single seat had a bench type back, not buckets. (*Henry Ford Museum*)

After more than 15 million were built in the United States alone—plus thousands in foreign assembly plants—the last of the wonderful Model "T" Fords left the assembly lines late in 1927. (*Ford Motor Co.*)

The lines of the '27 Kissel Speedster were excellent. Jack Dempsey once owned this example now preserved in the Henry Ford Museum. (*Photo by Author*)

The pride of Hartford, Wisconsin, where it was built during 1906–30, the Kissel was also made as stylish sedans on 126-inch wheelbase with either 65 HP 6 or the higher-torque, straight-8 engine. This sedan of around 1925 could reach about 70 mph. (*Randolph Brandt collection*)

When Roy D. Chapin and Howard Coffin founded the Hudson (1909–57), a Detroit financier and department store magnate gave the car his name. Respected for its stamina and quality, the car enjoyed a following throughout the world.

This 1928, right-hand-drive, 4.7-litre "Super Six" export model's wheelbase was 127 inches. A Hudson hallmark was its chrome steel engine block. (*Randolph Brandt collection*)

The Whippet, successor to the Overland, was built in Toledo during 1926–31; convertible tops with landau irons, and a virtually indestructible, 4-cylinder, L-head engine at a low price. The 1926 model similar to the optimistic entry in the Le Mans race the same year where its 2.2-litre L-head engine was hopelessly out of its element. (*Randolph Brandt collection*)

The Falson-Knight used a 6-cylinder, 2.5-litre, double-sleeve-valve engine in a better than average 109.5-inch wheelbase chassis with four-wheel brakes. Built in Detroit 1926 through 1928, this is the last and sportiest model with a unique arrangement of separate roadster tops over normal front and the optional rumble seat. (*Randolph Brandt collection*)

The "Lanchester Balancer" meant a smooth running engine and was a selling point on the 1926 Willys-Knight made in Toledo by Overland. The 1926 Model 66 with 3.9-litre, double-sleeve-valve, 6-cylinder engine on 126-inch-wheelbase chassis ran with valor sans victory in the Le Mans 24-hour race the same year. (*Randolph Brandt collection*)

The 4.7-litre Willys-Knight of 1930–31 was also available on a long, 135-inch-wheelbase chassis. Quality, elegance, silence with moderately high performance. Seldom seen today, the W-K was built in Toledo from 1914–33. (*Randolph Brandt collection*)

A quality phaeton with unusual color pattern, the finest Willys-Knight for 1930 with 4.7-litre, sleeve-valve six. Note stylish luggage rack and triple-bar bumpers. (*Randolph Brandt collection*)

Finest, most luxurious sleeve-valve American car was the Stearns-Knight built in Cleveland. This 1930 model was the last: straight-8 engine of 6.3-litres capacity, 145-inch wheelbase, impressive performance. The marque originated at the beginning of the century. In the $2,500-up price class at the end, the Knight-type engine was used from 1913. (*Randolph Brandt collection*)

A Judkins coach-built body graces this 1927 Lincoln Model L-134B. Technically the body style was known as the Coaching Brougham. (*Harrah's Automobile collection*)

The Oakland was built from 1907 to the final V-8-powered models of 1932 right where its successor, the Pontiac, is made today. The original caption from the General Motors press offices said: *"Plenty New's Zis! The new Oakland All-American Six landau sedan had come to Hollywood,* *along with a new radiator emblem, exemplifying an American eagle in flight. That's what Sally Blaine, Paramount screen player, is pointing out."* The year was 1928. (*Automobile Manufacturers Association*)

Before World War One the Oakland had a German silver radiator shell with other trim nickel-plated. The engines ran anti-clockwise. During the '20s all models had long-stroke, 3-litre, 6-cylin-der engines on 113-inch wheelbases. Here we have a model of about 1926 with a vintage era pair of litterbugs. (*Randolph Brandt collection*)

Model "A" Fords came in all varieties including the pick-up illustrated between 1928 and late 1931. Syd Holloway (left) and Kenneth Schwartz of the Henry Ford Museum staff restored this '29 model for the museum's collection. (*Henry Ford Museum*)

The Moon Motor Car Company of St. Louis, Missouri, built the remarkable Ruxton to the order of the New Era Motor Co. of New York City from 1929 to 1931. A Continental straight-8 engine was used in conjunction with front-wheel drive. Underslung and beautifully topped off with a custom built body by the Budd works. Height overall with the top raised was a mere 58 inches. The owner of this cream and green trimmed phaeton is J. LeRoy Forsythe of Millheim, Pennsylvania. (*Photo by Author*)

The stylish 1930 Oakland; the ladies were extras. The marque was discontinued in favor of the Pontiac (first, 1926) in 1932. In the late twenties, an Oakland six averaged 67.88 mph for 500 miles. (*Randolph Brandt collection*)

Chrysler Corporation's new, low-priced six, the DeSoto of 1929—a typical promotional photo of the era. This car survived the depression only to succumb during post-war prosperity. (*Randolph Brandt collection*)

Only some 300 Ruxtons were built during 1929–31. The sleek sedan was nearly a foot lower than its competitors. Ruxton styling and front-wheel drive was more than thirty years ahead of its time. (*Drawing by Author*)

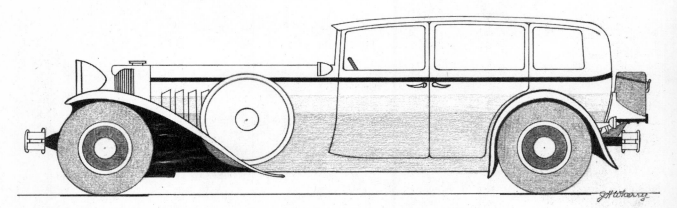

RUXTON 1929

Packards were much favored by coach builders in the late twenties and early thirties. The 1930 Speedster Model 7-34 had boat-tail body on a 134½-inch wheelbase and weighed over 4,500 pounds. Despite weight, the 6.3-litre, straight-8 engine, which put out 145 horsepower at around 3,400 rpm, drove Speedster at top of 95–100 mph. (*Harrah's Automobile collection*)

From 1900 until '32, the magnificent Peerless was produced in Cleveland. The 1923, boat-tailed, straight-8 sports coupé on 128-inch wheelbase. This marque was competitive in every way with Pierce Arrow and Packard. (*Randolph Brandt collection*)

Harry Miller believed in simplicity and, thereby, achieved high efficiency. The frame of his '32 Miller Special cradled the lightweight body with extreme rigidity. (*Photo by Author*)

From 1915 to the early thirties, Harry A. Miller built racing specials in Los Angeles. While most of them were front-wheel-drive cars, the '32 model shown, owned by Tony Luther of Westport, Connecticut, had conventional rear-wheel drive; engine was a 4-cylinder, 3-litre developing some 50 BHP at 4,000 rpm. Top speed was in excess of 110 mph. Miller's engines evolved into the famous Offenhauser. (*Photo by Author*)

The suspension of the '32 Miller Special. (*Photo by Author*)

The 1930 Peerless straight-8 just two years before the marque faded away; quality and luxury at a price few could afford. Evidently the Boston bulldog approved his mistress's choice of car. (*Randolph Brandt collection*)

The de Vaux-Hall Motor Corp. of Grand Rapids, Michigan was a short lived concern which built a Continental-engined quality car in the lower priced range from late 1930 through '32. The styling was in conformity with others in the same price range. Four-point, live rubber engine mounts and fully synchronized transmission with freewheeling were features. (*Automobile Manufacturers Association*)

In 1930–31, the Graham had 6 or 8 cylinders on a near sporting 113-inch wheelbase chassis or more luxurious 129-inch models. Originating in 1908 as the Paige-Detroit, car became Graham-Paige in 1927. Superchargers were introduced in '30s and a blown Graham special won the last race on the Brooklands track in England. One of America's better, forgotten cars. (*Randolph Brandt collection*)

A limited production luxury model was this 1932 Ford V-8 landau. Few were built; fewer exist to-day. (*Ford Motor Co.*)

Auburn cars, built from 1900 to 1937 in the Indiana city of the same name, came into fame during their later years. The 1931 Speedster with boat-tail styling was available with either of two engines: the 5-litre L-head Lycoming with which it won the Pike's Peak mountain climb in '29, first year of Speedster production, or the delectable 6.3-litre, Lycoming V-12 engine. With the V-12, the Speedster sold for the amazingly low price of just $1,850. (*Photo by Author*)

There are those who contend that the '31 boat-tailed Auburn Speedster would be a smashing suc- cess if it were revived today. (*Photo by Author*)

For 1934 the top of the Auburn line was this cab- riolet sedan with the 165-horsepower, V-12 engine. Optionally, the supercharged model was guaran- teed for 100 mph-plus with five passengers aboard. (*Chrysler Corp. photo*)

The supercharged, Auburn straight-8 of 1935 developed 150 horsepower and was also guaranteed for more than 100 miles an hour. The exhaust headers outboard of the hood were genuine. (*Automobile Manufacturers Association*)

In 1936, the engine of the Auburn Speedster was commonly a straight-8 supercharged to deliver 150 BHP from just under 5-litres displacement. This was one of the last production cars in the United States to retain a solid front axle, a feature that impaired the handling of this 3,500 pound and up car not at all. The Model 851 Speedster shown has coachwork by Central. (*Harrah's Automobile collection*)

An all-time favorite is the Cord L-29 of 1929–32, powered by a 5-litre, Lycoming straight-8 developing 125 BHP at 3,500 rpm. The first mass-produced American car with front-wheel drive. (*Randolph Brandt collection*)

Mrs. LeMunyon. Several months after departing from the Mongolian capital, LeMunyon heard that the Model T was in fine fettle. All this happened about five years after the first cars—competitors in the 1907 Peking-to-Paris race—had braved bandits, wild dogs, and the fierce Gobi storms. LeMunyon's trip, though, was the first such for a Ford Model T, the first car of any make to be exported from anywhere to Mongolia.

In 1913, there appeared on the market in the U.S.A. the first comparatively successful car using the sliding valve engine. The Knight sleeve-valve engine had actually been around since about 1900: Daimler in Germany, Daimler in England, Minerva in Belgium, and other Continental firms had produced Knight-type engines. The inventor had brought out the Knight Junior in

1902 and, although it lasted until '14, it had served mainly as a portable proving ground, a demonstration and licensing sales device.

In place of poppet valves either in block or head, the Knight engines had a sleeve inside the cylinder which was ported, for intake of fuel on the piston's down-stroke, and for exhaust after compression and firing. Thus, there were fewer moving parts, a virtual impossibility of a carbon buildup, and a much lower noise level because there was no usual valve gear and train with myriad lubrication needs.

In 1906, the Knight & Kilbourne car had been the unsuccessful attempt of the inventor to "get the show on the road."

Finally, due largely, it is suspected, to the Knight engine's success in Europe, Willys-Overland of Toledo brought out the Willys-Knight. As an effort in the quality car field,

680

A quality not since achieved in the U.S.A. was built into the Duesenberg. Cost was no object. This 1932 type "J" was restored by owner Donald Turkletop of Oakland, California; quite naturally this one is a frequent awards winner at concours events. (*Photo by Author*)

the W-K survived until 1932 and was every inch a splendid if unspectacular vehicle.

The Lyons-Atlas Company in Indianapolis followed in 1914 mating both 4 and 6-cylinder engines to a worm drive rear axle. This latter not-so-common approach to the noise problem made the Lyons-Knight a very silent car. However, one year later, Lyons-Atlas, the builders, were making no noise at all.

Still a fifth Knight-engined car in the U.S.A., the Stearns-Knight, had been on the market ever since 1900 without causing any stampedes. Willys-Knight executives, though, were able to capitalize for several years on several creditable features: no valve grinding, no need to de-carbonize the engine—a bother at least every 20,000 miles in most cars of the time—and the most genuinely silent operation of any gasoline engine before or since. The Knight engine even though quiet and durable was, however, not what the public wanted. Sensational stunts rather than honest value seem to have been preferred.

Priced in the upper-medium range, the W-K like a hundred other fine cars went the sad route because the average buyer equated quantity then—as now—with quality. The worst that could be said about the Knight engines was that, while they used a bit more oil than others, they rarely wore out, and in an economy geared to engineering obsolescence, this was a mortal shortcoming. Today, the Knights are forgotten cars.

Maxwell brought out the first adjustable front seat on the 1914 model, and Dodge Brothers came out with the first all-steel body in the U.S.A. Two years later, Dodge

681

The coachwork on this 1933 Duesenberg "J" chassis is by Bowman & Schwartz. The unblown, straight-8 engine displaces 420 cubic inches and develops 265 horsepower. (*Harrah's Automobile collection*)

A few boat-tailed Speedsters were built in 1933 by Schwartz on the Duesenberg chassis. The external headers here disclose the presence of the "SJ" supercharged engine which developed 320 horsepower. (*Harrah's Automobile collection*)

introduced what we now call hardtops. Packard became the first car in the quality field to standardize left-hand drive, and the Owens Magnetic came out in 1913 without a clutch pedal, the clutch being actuated by solenoids.

The Owens Magnetic was a most interesting car with a 6-cylinder engine of 45 HP, a camshaft driven by helical gears, semi-pressure lubrication system, and all six cylinders cast en bloc instead of in pairs as was normal practice then.

Studebaker marketed the first 6-cylinder car in 1913 to sell for less than $2,000 and the South Bend firm that built "Conestogas" for pioneers in the 1850s moved into the semi-prestige field.

Chalmers, built from 1908 to 1923, introduced a new starter-generator combination in a single unit. With Maxwell, Chalmers merged under the presidency of Walter P. Chrysler.

The wise motorist of 1915–25 carried spare spark plugs, gaskets, a mending kit for

Extremely rare is this Continental straight-8-engined Brewster Town car built in 1935 for Charlie Chaplin. The shell surrounding the unusual finned radiator is of burnished aluminum alloy. The exquisite machine is now owned and shown frequently by John Ritchie of San Francisco. (*Photo by Author*)

The dual-ignition, straight-8 Nash phaeton of 1932; comfort on 130-inch wheelbase for parades and fast touring. (*Randolph Brandt collection*)

the fragile inner tubes, and tools to supplement those with which most cars were equipped.

Both Hupmobile and Oakland also had steel bodies in 1913 leading to frequent controversy with the Dodge claim. The Hupmobile body was made by the Pullman Company. Hupmobile, built in Detroit, also advertised that they were *"the largest users of aluminum*—without regard to class or price—in the world."* Oakland's body was more interesting because the firm was importing German silver for the V-shaped radiator shell. Oaklands were big, 130-inch-wheelbase cars made in 4 to 7 passenger touring models and as a raceabout. The latter was a limited production car and would be a valuable find for a person starting his search for a distinctive antique. The Hupmobile averaged about $1,200 new; the Oakland about twice as much, with a V-8 engine in its later years.

Made in Jackson, Michigan, from 1910 until '14, the Cutting was a 120-inch-wheelbase, 4-cylinder, 40-HP car that had a forced pressure lubrication system—most unusual in 1913. The Cutting also had other innovations: the rear main bearing was 4 inches long while the other two mains were also outsize at 2.75 inches. The three main bearings were of white bronze. Longitudinal cooling fins covered the exhaust manifold and the two-wheel brakes were mechanically equalized. The seats were 10 inches thick, probably the most comfortable seats on any car costing less than $1,500.

In Muncie, Indiana, the Interstate (1908–19) had a device in 1914 causing the promotion department to belittle the electric cars still favored by most women drivers—ignition key starting like that in modern cars. Interstate engines had 4 cylinders, ranging from 40 to 50-HP and the price was a maximum of $3,400.

About this time, an auto show sponsored by importers of foreign cars had an unusual

684

The 1934 Nash Ambassador had an excellent straight-8 engine with dual ignition and a record of dependability and comfort; its quality was seldom appreciated. (*American Motors Corp.*)

Hupmobile weathered the depression better than many of its contemporaries and continued in active production until the outbreak of World War Two. The 1935 model reflected advanced design concepts and was powered by a 3.5-litre six (3¼ x 4¼ inches bore and stroke). (*Automobile Manufacturers Association*)

The Marmon achieved lasting fame when the 4.8-litre "Wasp" won the first Indianapolis 500-mile race in 1911. Driver Ray Harroun introduced the rear view mirror in that race. Production models in 1916 had aluminum engine blocks. Shown is tourer of about 1920 with "all-weather" Gould top, a 5.5-litre six on 136-inch wheelbase. The related Model 34 "Speedster" exceeded 80 mph. (*Randolph Brandt collection*)

Remember this famous actress of the silent screen? A 1927–28 Marmon sedan, the 125-BHP, L-head eight. (*Randolph Brandt collection*)

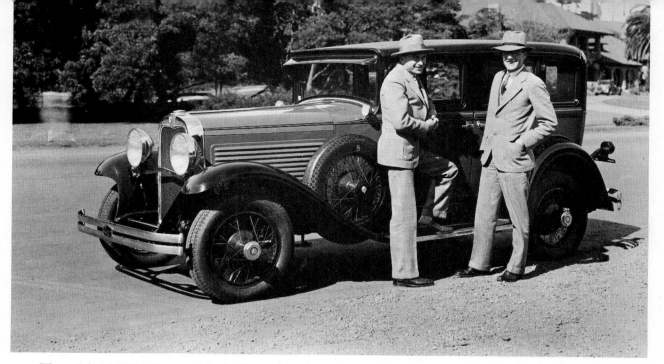

The ads said "The first straight Eight to be offered at less than $1,000" when Marmon introduced the Roosevelt in 1929 to counter falling sales. The crest bore an excellent likeness of Theodore R. Displacement, 3.5 litres. Wheelbase, 115 inches. (*Randolph Brandt collection*)

exhibit—an American built car, the $2,250 to $3,000 Keeton Six that was made in Detroit from 1908 to '14. The Keeton Six looked very much like the Arrol-Johnston of Scotland. Some clever advertising writers bought newspaper space and printed a thought-provoking proclamation that sounds familiar in these times: "The best of *foreign* practice adapted to American road and touring conditions." Still another pearl from Keeton's "think people" was, "The only true *French* type car built in America." The Scottish Arrol-Johnston of the period looked French, too, as was discussed in Part IV.

The *foreign* and *French* claims were obviously influenced by Renault which enjoyed popularity over here. From the side view, the Keeton could easily have been mistaken for the French car that was soon to have a dramatic part in preventing the capture of Paris by the advancing Germans.

The sloping hood was nearly identical and the radiator was placed behind the engine, each side extending outward from the body. The color scheme, dark on the hood, and light shades for the body—which was a good job of custom coachwork—carried the "French" or Renault flavor even further. Wire wheels, chrome vanadium gears and shafts, *imported* ball bearings (Chadwick was right, the bearing business was good and with the coming war would get better), an engine with all six cylinders cast en bloc and a slightly angled spare wheel mount completed the appeal to those persons still under the influence of European cars. Keeton made their home-built "foreign car" even more desirable with a long 136-inch wheelbase, an 8-day clock, a silk-mohair top with side curtain pockets, a built-in emergency lamp that could be extended outside for tire changing, huge 12½-inch-diameter headlights, a toned electric horn that could

687

Called the "All-Weather Phaeton," the finest Cadillac for 1933 was the Model 452-C with body by Fleetwood. The big V-16 engine delivered 165 horsepower for smooth, high speed cruising. (*Harrah's Automobile collection*)

be heard a half mile away, a splendid set of tools, and *no* advertised horsepower rating à la Rolls-Royce.

There are few sales approaches today that were not well worn by 1920.

Other events of interest in the second decade of the 1900s were the introduction by Cadillac of the first production V-8 engine in this country in 1914. Pierce-Arrow put the headlights in the fenders of all models except the fabulous Raceabout in 1914.

Packard, the prestige leader of the time, countered with their big Twin Six. In 1916, Packard amazed the industry by selling more than 10,000 cars. Following Packard's lead were the Pathfinder (1911–17) and the National (1900–24) with their V-12 engines later in 1915. Packard's V-12, however, also had the first aluminum pistons and the angle of the cylinder banks in relation to each other was 60 degrees, rather than the conventional 90-degree angle. The new pis-

tons weighed only one-fourth as much as those in the contemporary Packard Six, and the new engine ran with virtually no vibration at rpm so low that the car would creep along in top gear under 5 MPH, yet spring to life with no noise other than that of the air rushing into the carburetor. Displacing 414 cubic inches, only slightly larger than the Six because of the smaller 3.00-inch bore, the Twin Six was the most outstanding engine of the decade. Ralph De Palma had a specially tuned Twin Six that set a flying mile American record in 1919 of 149.9 MPH!

In 1916, most of the high-priced cars had hand-operated windshield wipers, stoplights, and rear-view mirrors without extra cost, and in 1917, Chevrolet's Model 490 sedan had removable door posts while Nash had a special sedan with folding posts.

World War One gave great impetus to the automotive industry. Nash produced

688

The 1930–31 Marmon V-12 was more successful if slightly less magnificent than the elegant V-16 which hastened the marque's end in 1933. Ahead of their time, Marmon had aluminum engine blocks and gearbox cases. Many rate Marmon as America's finest car. (*Randolph Brandt collection*)

America's first four-wheel drive trucks for the Army and many of them served with the A.E.F. overseas.

Chevrolet celebrated its adoption by General Motors with a new $1,400 car with an overhead-valve, V-8 engine in 1918. With a 120-inch wheelbase beneath a 170-inch body, a luxurious, mahogany-trimmed interior, side curtains that stowed away in pockets sewn into the black leather top, an up-to-date water pump and a cellular radiator, and a ventilating windshield, that V-8 Chevy was potent sales material. Marketed, however, when a lot of veterans were arriving home from the wars and when the nation had matters more critical than new cars to consider, the new V-8 did not sell well and was discontinued after about one year.

In 1919, Studebaker, which had built cars since 1902, finally stopped building horse carriages. In 1920, 9 million cars were on the roads of the U.S.A., and Europe had lost its initial lead in car production, never again to regain it in numbers, although retaining the edge in quality.

With a racing background that included 10th place driving a Duesenberg 4-cylinder car with horizontal valves and vertical rockers in the 1914 Indianapolis 500, Captain Eddie Rickenbacker brought out his famed "Hat-in-the-Ring" car in 1922. The second car on the market with four-wheel hydraulic brakes, the Rickenbacker, a splendid car, lasted only until 1927.

Between 1921 and '26, Harold Wills, a metallurgical specialist and inventor who was disillusioned after years of working for large firms, manufactured the Wills-Sainte Clair in Marysville, Michigan. His own chief engineer, Wills would often stop the production line while his latest improvement was incorporated. The fine 6-cylinder engine was rated at 25 HP. The car was a

The 1938 Cadillac V-16 continued the powerful 450 cubic inch (7.4 litres) engine. Seen at the most recent Peacock Gap Concours d'Elegance is this example owned by Allan Jones of Byron, California. (*Photo by Author*)

sporty roadster 192 inches long. In 1926, a strictly stock '25 model with 23,000 miles service set a new speed record over the 3,368 miles between San Francisco and New York City in 83 hours, 12 minutes. "The Gray Goose," as the car was known, had an overhead-camshaft, a cooling fan which automatically free-wheeled at highway speeds, and other features now characterized, erroneously, as advanced.

In 1922, the Essex was America's first fully-closed, low-priced car and the race was on to emulate the mass-production success of the Model T Ford. In 1923, Chevrolet brought the famous "copper cooled" coupe out at $680. The cylinders were encircled by copper fins for air cooling. The public, however, stuck with thermo-syphon cooling despite the seasonal troubles; in 1925 thermostatically controlled cooling systems were introduced and they're still with us in all but air-cooled cars.

Engine vibration had never been successfully eliminated until three major developments helped the entire industry. These were: the development of Ethyl, or antiknock gasoline, in which "Boss" Kettering of General Motors played an important role; the rubber-cushioned engine mounts pioneered by Nash; and Plymouth's "Fleeting Power" or 3-point engine suspension. By 1930, all three developments had been adopted by the motoring industry.

In 1925, Pierce-Arrow nearly foundered and was rescued by Studebaker, a firm that has introduced more "firsts" than the public

A very desirable classic is the Lincoln model KB. This touring sedan, a 1932 model, is owned by James Weston of San Francisco. (*Photo by Author*)

is generally aware of: the soundproofed direct-flow muffler in 1927, the modern fuel pump in 1928, overdrive, the hill-holder, and others.

As with Wills-Sainte Clair, cross-country records impressed only the enthusiasts who knew cars—not the public. Thus many superior cars gradually lost sales to inferior cars backed by eye-catching slogans. For instance, a '27 Studebaker Commander Six lowered the San Francisco-New York City record to less than 78 hours; and "Cannon Ball" Baker ramrodded a '28 air-cooled Franklin Airman model from Los Angeles to New York City in 74 hours and 23 minutes. And yet, neither of these performances were matched by increased sales.

The American car had matured by 1930. Some enthusiasts are inclined to believe that in recent years the automobile has regressed —gone into its second childhood. It's true that "they don't make 'em like they used to" and, consequently, the faithful search for the "fine ones." Not all of the old ones, though many were excellent, could be truly termed classics.

The Golden Age of the American automobile produced a few exclusive cars of elegance which are loosely called "classics." In England, "thoroughbred" is the word employed to designate the infinitely small percentage of total production which truly represents the ultimate in cars.

Almost without exception these cars were built to the personal order of discriminating persons of highly individualistic taste, and with the bank account to match the desire.

Large, powerful, tastefully appointed

691

A very limited production characterized the huge 1934 Lincoln V-12. Despite great weight, the low speed torque of the 150-horsepower engine made this limousine exceptionally quiet with top gear useful down to less than 10 mph. Alex Holcombe of San Francisco owns this model with coachwork by Judkins, last shown publicly at Peacock Gap. (*Photo by Author*)

—and this does *not* mean chromed ostentation—possessing the refinement of invisible and visible details that only meticulous attention can accomplish—these are the attributes that distinguished the better cars.

The demands of purchasers of cars now called "classics" made obvious several structural and technical requirements.

One: a *soft ride* necessitated a long wheelbase and this meant a long and generally heavy frame.

Two: operational *quietness* and *high performance* required large engines with (in America) a usual minimum of eight cylinders for the smoothness that permits these two qualities.

Three: a *usefulness* over a period of years with *styling integrity* and *distinction* dictated accommodations and fittings that could scarcely come from an assembly line like doughnuts.

These requirements make obvious a fourth factor which was production in very limited numbers. Almost all of the American "classics" and European "thoroughbreds" (discussed in Part IV) were built largely by hand and with artistic devotion. The chassis—which included the engine and usually the radiator shell, the hood and dashboard cowling, but *not* the dashboard—was built in the factory of the manufacturer.

Once the chassis was completed and tested, it was then taken to a firm of custom coachbuilders like Brewster, Central, Derham, Hibbard & Darrin, Judkins, LeBaron, Murphy, Rollston, Schwartz, Teague or Willoughby. There were a few other coachwork firms in the U.S.A. during the classic period but these represented the cream of designers and artisans who worked with fine woods, leathers, aluminum and steel.

Occasionally, American makes were graced with European coachwork, and this

692

The "Sunshine Special" was built in 1939 for President Franklin D. Roosevelt. Casablanca, Teheran, and Yalta roads were travelled by this armor-plated monster which also has thick, bullet-proof windows and a special compartment for weapons used by the Secret Service. The chassis is a lengthened Lincoln Continental unit; engine is a 150-BHP V-12 with bore and stroke of $3\frac{1}{8}$ x $4\frac{1}{2}$ inches. The wheelbase is 161 inches and weight exceeds 7,000 pounds. (*Henry Ford Museum*)

brings us to a brief discussion of the Ruxton built by the Moon Motor Company of St. Louis. One often hears that Ruxton bodies were coach-built in England by Wolseley. Not so; they were, however, custom-built by The Budd Company.

Back in 1911, the Moon, introduced in 1905, was one of the comparatively few makes which could advertise "electric cranking and lighting." By 1929, the Moon was in its final phase and, as a last gasp effort to remain afloat, the firm brought out the Ruxton in a bid for the prestige market.

Each Ruxton was custom crafted from the ground up, then marketed through New Era Motors in New York City. The largest investor in New Era was a man named Ruxton, hence the name of the car. Expensive—prices started at $4,500 for the roadster and skyrocketed to well over $8,000 for the sedans—these cars were worth it. With front-wheel drive, ahead of the Cord L-29 by several months, Ruxton was the first such American car since the ill-fated FWD of 1911. The engine was the 100-HP, straight-8 Continental 18S driving a transmission bisected in the middle by the axle shafts which, quite unusually, were driven by a worm gear. Classically long, the Ruxton was a full 10 inches lower than any other American car of the time. Running boards were simply not needed. With a wheelbase of 130 inches, the car looks even longer; weight is about 4,000 pounds. Introduced just before the Wall Street crash, only about 375 were built. Today, a good one is worth as much as when it was new.

Though Lincoln built some fine cars, rarely are they accorded classic rank. This is not precisely correct. In the late '20s, several Model L-134B chassis, powered with well tuned versions of the big 90-HP, V-8

693

When King George VI and his Queen visited the United States and Canada in 1939, this specially constructed 1939 Lincoln V-12 phaeton was placed at their disposal. Note the royal crest at peak of windshield. (*Henry Ford Museum*)

engine, were fitted with some splendid coach work by Judkins. One of these, a "Coaching Brougham," is shown here.

In 1939, the long, 150-HP, V-12-powered chassis became somewhat of a favored car for dignitaries. When King George VI and his Queen visited the U.S.A. and Canada, they rode in an especially regal appearing Phaeton. An extremely long sedan convertible was built for the White House; called the "Sunshine Special," this machine had bullet-proof glass, hidden compartments for weapons, and was used for many years by Presidents Roosevelt and Truman. When retired, this presidential carriage had been driven more than 37,000 miles. Both of these fine cars are now on public display in the Henry Ford Museum at Greenfield Village in Dearborn. To the enthusiast, however, neither would rate as high as the '27 built by Judkins.

Those who have said there were no genuinely fine cars built in the U.S.A. are mistaken. Late in the '20s, there was a sudden effort to compete with the ultra-expensive European cars for the carriage trade. Cadillac introduced a V-16 in 1930 as did Marmon. Pierce-Arrow and Auburn soon introduced large V-12 engines. All of these were powerful—for a time the Pierce-Arrow led with a 200-HP rating. The straight 8s, however, led the classic field.

For the most part these were long stroke engines designed to produce exceptionally high torque in a smooth power flow at low speeds.

A good example of these superb American fine cars was the Packard "Speedster"—

One of the last of the great line of Pierce Arrow cars is this elegant 1933 model now on display in Harrah's Automobile collection, Reno. (*Photo by Author*)

a fast, boat-tailed vehicle introduced in 1929 on a 126.5-inch wheelbase. In 1930, the "Speedster" was lengthened to a wheelbase of 134 inches and designated the Type-734. Factory bodies were available but for those demanding the ultimate, the chassis were sent out for coachwork. The "Speedsters" used the "Big Eight" engine which had bore and stroke of 3.5 and 5.0 inches respectively. With the displacement at 384.8 cubic inches, the torque was terrific but the rated output of 145 HP seems ludicrous compared to advertised claims today. Yet with the heavier than factory coachwork bodies making a curb weight well over 4,500 pounds, these cars would run up through the gears to 60 MPH in about 17 seconds. Maximum speeds were on the order of 90-100 MPH. Post-World War Two cars were

unable to achieve any better performance with less weight until the compression ratios and carburetion went well over the Speedster Packard's 6.3 to 1 and a relatively simple two-barrel carburetor. What's more, the 734 sedan with the same engine would accelerate in top gear from 5–6 MPH without vibration or lugging.

No, they certainly don't make them the way they used to—nor do they rate the actual output as modestly, either.

Take the last Stutz, for instance. The 1930–35, DV-32 Bearcat (the DV meant double valves, or 4, in each cylinder running off dual overhead-camshafts) with a coachbuilt coupe body weighed in at around 5,000 pounds ready to go. The big, straight-8 engine teamed with either a 3 or 4-speed transmission was *guaranteed* to give

695

Peanut wagons were as popular in the early days of the automobile as they were when Dobbin was king. Built on all sorts of truck chassis, few remain. C. Cretors & Son of Chicago made a number of these colorful carriers of goodies. The hard rubber tires mark this example as of around 1920 or earlier. (*Photo by Author*)

this $6,000-up Bearcat an honest 100 MPH. The rated output sounds silly in these days of status horsepower—just 160 HP at 3,900 RPM, obviously a conservative rating.

There was the Auburn, also a pleasant memory, a wonderful, straight-8, Lycoming-powered Model 125 of circa '30–'32. At 3,400 RPM, the modest factory brochures claimed only 120 HP. With heavy custom bodies, that mark was actually attainable and the supercharged Model 851 would bet-

ter that mark. The same engine powered the Cord L-29 of 1929–32.

When E. L. Cord bravely decided to determine whether the public would buy a really advanced car for from $2,000 to $3,-500—a veritable steal even in those days—he turned the front-wheel-drive project over to one C. Van Raust. When the L-29 came out, it was a winner by any standards, yet in three years fewer than 5,000 were sold. Later when the Auburn-Cord-Duesenberg combine decided to give the public a chance at a car of the future at less than $3,000 in the form of the Cord 810 and 812, the results were even sadder—an indictment actually of the average motorist's inability to know a genuinely good car when he saw one.

The Cord 810 was powered by the Lycoming V-8 engine developing an advertised 125 HP at 3,500 RPM. The 812 had an identical engine with a centrifugal supercharger as a topping; power was then 170 HP at 4,250 RPM. There was a single simple carburetor, the transmission was a vacuum operated pre-selector, the wheelbase was 125 inches, the weight was 3,300 pounds up, the styling was terrific and is inspiring a particular special car builder as this is written, and the car was a dream to drive. Roadability was the equal to anything Detroit builds today—and superior to most.

But guess how many were sold in three years ending in 1938? About 2,800!

The day of the genuinely fine car in the U.S.A. may not be past—really fine cars, not just a walnut veneer inset on a glovecase door and cattlebrand designs printed on sheets of plastic upholstery covers.

The Duesenberg may return, a new release by the sons of the late Fred D.

No finer car was ever built in America than this great car. The Duesenberg brothers, August and Frederick, learned engineering the hard way—they were self-taught. Bicycle makers in 1900, the brothers turned to gasoline engines and produced racing cars named Mason for their financial angel. About 1910, management disagreements caused the Duesenbergs to depart and in 1913 they founded their own firm. During the First World War, they secured contracts to build the massive 16-cylinder Bugatti aircraft engine, the genesis, the story goes, of Fred's interest in high performance, fully

balanced, straight-8 engines. (More than one fine automobile engine, incidentally, has been based on a single bank of a V-type airplane engine—the post-war Hispano-Suiza among them.)

From 1916, Duesenberg's engines were used in several quality cars including the Revere (1917–27) and Roamer (1916–30). But the Bugatti-inspired straight-8, a curious mill with only three main bearings, is what started the brothers to thinking about building America's best car regardless of cost. In 1921, a Duesenberg Special won the French Grand Prix.

Having brought out their own brand-name passenger car in 1920, the brothers called it the Model A. With an overhead-camshaft, straight-8 developing slightly more than 80 HP at 3,000 RPM, with the first 4-wheel hydraulic brakes on a production car, and with a host of other technical innovations, by 1926 this excellent car had found only about 90 buyers. Instead of oblivion for the marque, however, E. L. Cord bought out the Duesenbergs.

Fred Duesenberg, who stayed with Cord in the new Auburn-Cord-Duesenberg combine, set to work developing the car that still intrigues the enthusiast.

In 1928, the first Duesenberg Model J was ready. Magnificent, the new car's frame was more than 8 inches deep, the 3-inch-wide brake drums were 15 inches in diameter, and the power train was, from front to rear, a 3-speed sliding pinion transmission, a torque tube, and a hypoid differential. Two wheelbases, 153.5 and 142.5 inches, were offered. On this chassis was mounted a magnificent 420-cubic-inch, straight-8 engine with dual overhead-camshafts, double valving (four per cylinder), and a massive crankshaft with five main bearings. The shaft was both dynamically and statically balanced and, to assure absolute absence of vibration, a vibration damper filled with mercury was built in as a final exclusive feature. The combustion chambers were almost exactly hemispherical in contours.

Wherever practicable, Fred Duesenberg used lightweight alloys in engine and frame. These chassis, the finest ever built in America before or since, alone weighed upwards of 4,500 pounds and ready for coachwork seldom cost less than $11,000. Once the custom coach builders practiced their superb arts, a Model J Duesenberg cost, on the average some $20,000.

Ready to roll, the J weighed a minimum of 6,000 pounds, yet would move away, accelerating rapidly to clocked speeds of 115 MPH in around 25 seconds. When called upon, the mighty car would creep through town at 5 MPH in top gear and accelerate smoothly without a gear change. The advertised output was 265 HP at 4,200 RPM with either one or two carburetors.

In 1931, the SJ engine was virtually identical but with the necessary manifold changes to accommodate a centrifugal supercharger. So equipped, the car developed a rated 320 HP at 4,750 RPM. Prices for a complete SJ often topped $25,000.

When E. L. Cord called a halt to automobile production in the Auburn-Cord-Duesenberg factories in 1937, about 500 of the J and SJ models had found buyers. Happily, most of the Duesenbergs built since 1928 are still either in private collections or closely guarded by owners who refuse to part with their Duesenberg.

The custom coachwork included the finest leathers, woods, ivory inlaid with silver, and carpeting, imaginable. Many with phaeton coachwork had instrumented panels on the rear side of the front seats duplicating the driver's dashboard equipment. Duesenberg left nothing to be desired.

America's most magnificent car certainly deserves rank with the finest of Europe—those equally interesting, durable, and marvelous cars of a more appreciative and gracious age.

Appendix

FIRSTS IN AUTOMOBILES

Musty records often differ as to who or which car was first with a certain innovation. The following are known firsts; however, there have been others and some may be somewhat controversial.

1878   *Anton Løvstad*, Norway
Transverse torsion bar suspension system patented for horse wagons; similar system applied by Porsche in '30s.

1888   *John Boyd Dunlop*, a Scottish veterinarian patented a pneumatic tire.

1891   *Panhard & Levassor*, France
First to install engines in front and to develop chassis frame specifically designed for motor vehicles.

1893   *Daimler*, Germany
Maybach invented first float-feed-spray carburetor. Daimler used it, and soon other manufacturers followed.

        Duryea, U.S.A.
Charles Duryea built first gasoline car in U.S.A.

1894   *Haynes*, U.S.A.
Generally considered first successful gasoline car in U.S.A. Elmer Apperson built car to Haynes' design.

        France
First automotive competition anywhere —Paris-Rouen Race.

        De Dion, France
Axle half-shafts and transverse tube to position rear wheels patented by De Dion-Bouton; still known today as De Dion axle.

1895   France
First pneumatic tire made for motor vehicles by André and Edouard Michelin.

1896   *Panhard & Levassor*, France
First vertical 4-cylinder engine.

        Panhard & Levassor, France
Sliding gears with cone clutch.

        Winton, U.S.A.
Electric starter, but was not standardized until some years later.

c. 1896   *Andrew L. Riker*, U.S.A.
Slotted core generator armature by designer of *Riker* electric cars and of the first *Locomobile* gasoline cars.

1897   *Gräf & Stift*, Austria
Front-wheel drive said to have inspired Ferdinand Porsche; however, there is possibility that the *Stoewer*, Germany, may have been first with front-wheel drive in 1896.

1898   *Mors*, France
First V-4 engine.

        Renault, France
Shaft drive (rather than chain) with direct drive on top gear. (In 1901, Auto-

699

car in U.S.A. was first to adopt shaft drive.)

Entz, U.S.A.
Electric-magnet type automatic gearbox, used later on Owen Magnetic.

1899   *Packard*, U.S.A.
Automatic spark advance.

Lohner, Austria
World's first electric motors in wheel hubs (designed by Ferdinand Porsche).

1900   *Packard*, U.S.A.
Steering wheel rather than tiller (first in U.S.A. only; in Europe most cars were already using wheel steering).

James Gordon Bennett, U.S.A.
Started international racing with races that bore his name and was responsible for start of racing at Le Mans.

Darracq, France
Was possibly first with tubular steel frame.

1900   *Renault*, France
Renault coupé first completely glass-enclosed car.

Lohner-Porsche, Austria
"Rekordauto" probably world's first four-wheel-drive car; electric motor in each wheel hub.

1901   *Mercedes*, Germany
First modern car in twentieth century designed by Maybach—used steel frame when others used hardwood.

Honeycomb radiator core when others used massive lengths of space consuming metal tubes for water circulation.

Gate gear change (to get away from tricky quadrants) and mechanically operated inlet valves.

Lanchester, England
Aluminum bodies.

c. 1901   *Scania*, Sweden
Ball-bearing wheels.

1902   *Locomobile*, U.S.A.
First American car to use heat-treated steel alloys, and front-mounted, vertical, 4-cylinder, water-cooled engines.

Humber, England
First known adjustable steering wheel.

Mors, France
Friction shock absorbers. First magneto electric ignition system.

Spyker, The Netherlands
Six-cylinder automobile (only a few were built—not series produced); also first known 4-wheel drive petrol car.

Daimler, Germany and *Peugeot*, France
Experimenting with superchargers.

1903   *Lozier* and/or *Chadwick*, U.S.A.
Ball-bearing crankshaft.

Lanchester, England
Disc-brakes on rear wheels (2-cylinder car).

Napier, England
Series produced 6-cylinder cars.

1903   England
First organized speed traps (20 mph limit).

1904   *Rover*, England
Revolutionary "backbone" chassis frame —tubular "backbone" enclosing propeller shaft—cast in aluminum for the very popular 1-cylinder, 8-HP model.

1904   *Christie*, U.S.A.
Patented 4-wheel-drive car, first only in U.S.A.

Fischer, Switzerland
"Quick release" detachable wheels, an idea later perfected for mass production by Michelin of France, usually credited with this device.

Winton, U.S.A.
Steering column shift lever, first only in U.S.A.

Hutton, United Kingdom
Hydraulic brakes; however, they were not overly successful and this marque regressed to mechanical brakes.

Darracq, France
Pushrod-operated valves.

c. 1904   *Wilson-Pilcher*, England
This car was built in small numbers from 1901–07 by Armstrong-Whit-

worth, introduced the "pre-selector" gearbox.

1905 *Locomobile*, U.S.A.
First American car to use 4-speed gearbox.

Fiat, Italy
Full pressure lubrication by high efficiency pump.

Panhard & Levassor, France
Limousine with removable hardtop; when top was detached, car became a phaeton.

Dufaux, Switzerland
Probably first to produce a small series of cars with 8-cylinder, in-line engines.

American Underslung, U.S.A.
Underslung frame (frame rails slung beneath axles to lower center of gravity) designed by Harry C. Stutz.

Mors, France
First efficient self-starter, a compressed air device.

De Dion, France
Single-plate dry clutch.

Darracq, France
Probably first V-8-engined racing car.

c. 1905 *Hotchkiss*, France
Enclosed propeller shaft called "torque tube"-drive; even today such device is called "Hotchkiss drive."

1906 *Marmon*, U.S.A.
Publicly displayed this country's first automobile V-8 engine in New York. Aluminum block, air-cooled, 60 BHP; the engine was not produced. But Marmon went on to pioneer extensive use of aluminum alloys in engines.

1906 *Fiat*, Italy
Detachable-rim wheels, first such to achieve relatively high production.

1907 *Hutton*, England
Hydraulic type gearbox with semi-automatic operation.

Oakland and *Brush*, U.S.A.
Introduced coil springs and friction shock absorbers in U.S.A.

Brush, U.S.A.
Fully balanced crankshaft, first only in U.S.A.

Chadwick, U.S.A.
Superchargers on passenger cars.

Chrome-nickel steel gears and frames; first only in U.S.A.

Reo, U.S.A.
First car to carry a President of the United States (during a visit by Theodore Roosevelt to Lansing, Michigan); manufacturer Ransom E. Olds was the driver.

Northern, U.S.A.
Compressed air brakes and integral tire-inflation mechanism.

Sizaire-Naudin, France
Independent front suspension with lateral members.

c. 1907 *De Dion-Bouton*, France
Marketed V-8 engines in production passenger cars.

1908 *Ford*, U.S.A.
Standardized left hand drive on newly introduced Model T.

Fritchie, U.S.A.
Electric auto able to go 100 miles per charge; little is known of this car, however, and it did not long survive.

1908 *F.W.D.*, U.S.A.
First four-wheel drive car produced in America; firm still makes trucks.

1909 *Marion*, U.S.A.
V-12 engine with dual ignition, but very few were produced.

Hudson 20 Runabout, U.S.A.
First quality car under $1,000 with sliding gear transmission.

Mors, France
Introduced hydraulic shock absorbers.

1910 *Isotta-Fraschini*, Italy and
Arrol Johnston, Scotland
Four-wheel brakes (mechanical) on passenger cars.

Chenard-Walcker, France

Forced lubrication through drilled crankshaft.

1911 *Locomobile*, U.S.A.
First passenger car to mount spare tires on the rear in U.S.A.

Chenard-Walcker, France
Aluminum pistons in production models.

Lorraine-Dietrich, France
First mass production side valve (L-head) engines.

Delahaye, France
Possibly first with V-6 engine, but possibly a conflict with an Isotta-Fraschini (Italy) prototype.

Electric starter listed as optional on Porsche-designed Austro-Daimler (Austria). Usually credited with this "first" is Charles F. Kettering who, in 1912, designed such a device for the Cadillac (U.S.A.) which was manufactured by Henry M. Leyland (later builder of Lincoln). Note that there were predecessors: compressed air, acetylene gas (the famed "Presto-Lite" system).

1911 *Marmon*, U.S.A.
Rear-view mirror first used on "Wasp." Whether Marmon engineers or driver Ray Harroun conceived this device is not known.

1912 *Peugeot*, France
Dual overhead-camshaft engine—inclined valves in hemispherical combustion chambers—designed by Ernest Henry, a Swiss.

Packard, U.S.A.
First mass-produced, 12-cylinder car, the famous "Twin-Six."

Marion, U.S.A.
Cast aluminum transmission housing.

1913 *Peugeot*, France
Dry sump engine lubrication by forced pump feed to bearings in the Henry-designed 3-litre, double overhead-camshaft engine.

Hudson, U.S.A.
Introduced modern four-door sedan in this country on "Super Six" model.

Ford, U.S.A.
Established first moving assembly line.

Maxwell, U.S.A.
Adjustable driver's seat (in 1928, Buick became second American car to offer same).

1914 *Mercedes*, Germany
First fully automatic gearbox on special limited production cars for high officials.

Interstate, U.S.A.
Ignition key starting.

Delage, Peugeot, France
Fiat, Italy
Pic-Pic, Switzerland
First four-wheel brakes on Grand Prix cars.

1915 *Dodge*, U.S.A.
All-steel body, first car to dispense with hardwood framing.

1916 *Dodge* and *Hudson*, U.S.A.
Removable door posts; modern "hardtop" appearance. (In 1917 Chevrolet followed this lead on the popular Model 490.)

c. 1917 *Franklin*, U.S.A.
Push-button door lock on top of window sill.

1919 *Guy V-8*, England
Fully automatic chassis lubrication.

Premier, U.S.A.
Push-button, solenoid-operated semi-automatic transmission.

Hispano-Suiza, Spain and France
First genuinely successful 4-wheel mechanical brakes with servo assistance on production cars.

1920 *Duesenberg*, U.S.A.
Four-wheel hydraulic brakes with oil-based fluid; experimental only.

Alvis, England
Synchromesh transmission; in 1933 included first gear in synchromesh.

Studebaker, U.S.A.
Engine vacuum operated fuel tank warning mechanism—when down to one gallon, device blew a whistle.

1921 *Duesenberg*, U.S.A.
Hydraulic brakes actuated by water; an experiment on a racing car.

1921 *Leland Lincoln*, U.S.A.
Turn signals standardized; this marque later came under Ford Motor Company. The maker, Henry M. Leland, was the originator of the Cadillac.

1922 *Hotchkiss*, France
Finned brake drums standardized.

Lancia, Italy
Integral or unit-type chassis frame and body on the "Lambda" model.

Lancia, Italy
V-6 engines in mass production cars; 4-wheel independent suspension.

Essex, U.S.A.
Fully enclosed low-priced car, first in this country.

Cadillac, U.S.A.
Ventilated crankcase; chrome plating on grilles, bumpers, etc.

1925 *Villard*, France
Disc brakes with chain drive; a low production car.

Citroën, France
One-piece, all-steel body on 9 CV-type B-12.

Star, U.S.A. and Canada
First production car in America with full pressure lubrication; manufactured by W. C. Durant. This feature was not general in American cars until after World War Two.

Pierce-Arrow, U.S.A.
All-aluminum car, first in U.S.A., built in cooperation with Aluminum Corporation of America as an experiment.

1927 *Bugatti*, France
Aluminum alloy wheels with integral cast-in brake drums; latter had steel liners.

Studebaker, U.S.A.
Direct flow muffler, acoustic control by steel wool.

1928 *Studebaker*, U.S.A.
Modern fuel pump, basically like those used today.

1928 *Alvis*, England
Mass-produced front-wheel-drive passenger car, the Model 12/75; the system was originally introduced in 1925 on a limited production competition sports car.

1929 *Cord*, U.S.A.
First series-produced car in America with front-wheel drive.

1930 *Buick*, U.S.A.
Vacuum-controlled clutch.

Reo, U.S.A.
Semi-automatic transmission with selector lever on dash.

1930 *Daimler*, England
Fluid flywheel in combination with "pre-selector" semi-automatic gearbox. This device was soon applied to the Lanchester cars, then built by Daimler.

1932 *Graham-Paige*, U.S.A.
Valanced or "skirted" fenders.

Wanderer, Germany
All torsion-bar suspension system; designed by Ferdinand Porsche.

1936 *Peugeot*, France
All-steel convertible top; when not erected, top was concealed beneath rear deck cover.

Impéria, Belgium
Fully automatic transmission combined with a V-8 engine and front-wheel drive.

703

Index

JOSEPH H. WHERRY was born in Everett, Washington, and now lives with his wife Bettye, and their four children in Santa Rosa, California. He is the author of many general and special interest magazine articles and twelve books, and when "time permits, which it seldom does," likes to build airplane and railroad models to scale. A photographer as well as a writer, Mr. Wherry illustrates many of his own works. He has been contributor to *Motor Trend* and *Road and Track* magazines, and from 1956 to 1958 was the Detroit editor of *Motor Trend*. With his interest in things automotive, it was natural for him to turn his skills to books on the subject. Among his published titles in this field are *Economy Car Blitz, Antique and Classic Cars, The MG Story, The Jaguar Story* and *The Alfa Romeo Story.*